The Cloaking of Power

The Cloaking of Power

Montesquieu, Blackstone, and the Rise of Judicial Activism

Paul O. Carrese

The University of Chicago Press
Chicago and London

Paul O. Carrese is associate professor of political science at the U.S. Air Force Academy. He is the coeditor of John Marshall's *The Life of George Washington.*

The University of Chicago Press, Chicago 60637
The University of Chicago Press, Ltd., London
© 2003 by The University of Chicago
All rights reserved. Published 2003
Printed in the United States of America

12 11 10 09 08 07 06 05 04 03   1 2 3 4 5

ISBN: 0-226-09482-0 (cloth)

Library of Congress Cataloging-in-Publication Data

Carrese, Paul.
    The cloaking of power : Montesquieu, Blackstone, and the rise of judicial activism /
Paul O. Carrese.
    p. cm.
Includes bibliographical references and index.
    ISBN 0-226-09482-0 (cloth : alk. paper)
    1. Judicial process—Political aspects—History.   2. Political questions and judicial
power—History.   3. Judicial power—History.   4. Montesquieu, Charles de Secondat,
baron de, 1689–1755.   5. Blackstone, William, Sir, 1723–1780.   I. Title.

K2146 .C375 2003
340'.11—dc21
                                                                    2002152313

⊗The paper used in this publication meets the minimum requirements of the American
National Standard for Information Sciences—Permanence of Paper for Printed Library
Materials, ANSI Z39.48–1992.

For my parents, Arnold and Kathleen Carrese

Contents

Acknowledgments

In the spirit of a work that traces a complex tale of political ideas, institutions, and traditions, I should acknowledge the variety of people who planted the seeds of this book, nurtured the project over several years, and sustained its author. My first teachers of political philosophy, Paul Nelson, Murray Dry, and Eve Adler, now are mentors and colleagues in liberal education. Along with several other teachers and mentors at Middlebury College and in Middlebury, they introduced me to liberal inquiry and serious study, doing for me what their teachers had done for them. At Oxford University the Rhodes Trust, Zbigniew Pelcyzsnki, and the Dominican Friars, among other influences and friends there, permitted me to broaden and deepen my conceptions of philosophy, politics, and liberal education. Robert Faulkner supervised the dissertation from which this book grew. He has proved a steadfast, encouraging, and discerning guide to issues large and small, both in my work on this book and in our work on Marshall's *Life of George Washington*. David Lowenthal first plowed the furrow in which several fine Montesquieu studies have taken root, and I am grateful that my work could benefit from such fertile soil. In subsequent years I have consulted his teaching more than he knows. Robert Scigliano taught me much about the American framers, Blackstone, judicial power, and constitutional law. These teachers and other faculty at Boston College, including Father Ernest Fortin, Susan Shell, Christopher Bruell, Dennis Hale, and Marc Landy, sent me into the world of thinking, teaching, and writing with a fund of moral and intellectual resources.

I have taught politics, philosophy, and letters at two institutions during this long project, Middlebury College and the U.S. Air Force Academy, and I owe many thanks to colleagues, staff, and students at both institutions. I have learned much about politics and thinking from conversation with more colleagues than could be named here, but I should mention Steve Knott, John Hittinger, Ken Masugi, Jeff Anderson, and Lt. Col. Lance Robinson, my former and current colleagues at the Academy. Todd Breyfogle and Tim Fuller introduced me to Liberty Fund colloquia, through which I have learned much about the Western intellectual tradition, and I am especially grateful for seminars on the common-law tradition conducted by Ellis Sandoz, Jim Stoner, and Steve Sheppard. Harvey Mansfield and Delba Winthrop provided support through a fellowship in the Program on Constitutional Government at Harvard University, funded by the Olin Foundation and the Bradley Foundation. That leisure, and my exposure to a wider circle of conversation and ideas, proved crucial for turning an unwieldy manuscript into a coherent book.

I am grateful for conversation with and advice from many scholars and colleagues, representing a variety of views about politics and philosophy, about the conference papers and ideas that, over time, have formed the book. I should particularly thank, beyond those already mentioned, Paul Ludwig, Sharon Krause, Robert Eden, Dan Mahoney, Chris Wolfe, Patrick Deneen, Stuart Warner, Diana Schaub, David Carrithers, Michael Mosher, Paul Rahe, Sue Collins, and William Allen. Parts of the manuscript were read at different stages by Lorna Knott, Peter Lawler, Sharon Krause, and Jim Stoner. I am grateful to Stuart Warner for suggesting that I send the manuscript to the University of Chicago Press and for his encouragement regarding my work on Montesquieu. John Tryneski has been a patient, encouraging, and wise editor, guiding many steps of revision. He secured two excellent and demanding readers, Paul Rahe and Michael Zuckert, whose suggestions and criticisms helped to substantially improve the final argument and presentation of the book. Since I make a case for rediscovering traditions of thought and practice that can improve our human lot, I should affirm the standard caveat that none of these colleagues, friends, or critics can be held responsible for the good advice I have not taken, or the good ideas I did not comprehend.

A separate note of thanks is owed to Jim Stoner, who has been a mentor both for this project and, more broadly, in my liberal education for a decade. His intellectual guidance and practical judgment about the book have proven indispensable from beginning to end.

I could not have availed myself of so many helpful colleagues, institutions, and critics without a foundation of support in my family and personal friends. My parents, Arnold and Kathleen, have supported my studies and career as an outgrowth of their ever-enduring care for me. My brothers, sisters, and other family and friends have offered encouragement and support for many years. My late uncle, Fr. Donald Mooney, O.F.M., has long been an example in matters of scholarship and life, embodying for me the virtues of tradition, inquiry, perseverance, and service.

My wife, Susan, has endured this project from start to finish, during which time she completed her own dissertation and then subordinated her academic career to the duties of wife and mother. For her love, conversation, support, and patience, and for rearing Hannah and Dominic with such love and skill, I am eternally grateful. I hope that the book will in some small way prove itself worthy of such a long, varied, complex chain of support, across many years, institutions, mentors, colleagues, friends, and family.

Material in chapters 9 and 10 was published previously in "Judicial Statesmanship, the Jurisprudence of Individualism, and Tocqueville's Common Law Spirit," *Review of Politics* 60 (1998): 465–96, and I am grateful to the editors for permitting me to develop those ideas here. The professionalism of the University of Chicago Press staff and the editing of Nick Murray further improved the book in its final stages. Finally, all opinions in this book are those of the author and do not represent the views of the United States Air Force Academy, the United States Air Force, or the United States government.

Note on Texts

All references to Montesquieu's works, unless otherwise noted, are to the Pléiade edition, *Œuvres complètes de Montesquieu*, ed. Caillois, 2 vols. (Paris: Gallimard, 1949–51), by volume and page number. The Société Montesquieu critical variorum edition of the complete works, in twenty-two volumes (Oxford: Voltaire Foundation; Napoli: Instituto italiano per gli studi filosofici, 1998–), has published only a portion of Montesquieu's masterpiece, *De l'esprit des lois* [Of the spirit of laws] as yet. References to *The Spirit of the Laws* cite book, chapter, and page (and short title where appropriate) of volume 2 of the Pléiade edition (e.g., 11.6, 398).

For translations of *De l'esprit des lois* I have consulted *The Spirit of the Laws*, ed. Cohler, Miller, and Stone (Cambridge: Cambridge University Press, 1989), revising it for a more literal or precise rendering. I also have consulted the first English translation of Thomas Nugent (New York: Hafner, 1949 [1750]), with which Montesquieu and his friends were pleased. From 1750 to 1900 all editions of Nugent's translation used the more compact title, *The Spirit of Laws,* which properly suggests a broad, philosophic scope for the work; however, for a century now it has been conventional to use *The Spirit of the Laws,* and I employ that convention here for the sake of clarity and consistency. For *Lettres persanes*, I have consulted George Healy, *The Persian Letters* (Indianapolis: Hackett, 1999 [1964]), revising it as needed. David Lowenthal's translation, the *Considerations on the Causes of the Greatness of the Romans and Their Decline* (New York: Free Press, 1965; Ithaca, NY: Cornell University Press, 1968), largely has been followed without revision. Translations of other writings of Montesquieu, and from secondary sources in French, are mine unless otherwise noted.

Montesquieu published *The Spirit of the Laws* anonymously in 1748 in Geneva and corrected it twice (1749, 1750) before his death in 1755. Notes for revision left with his son yielded the 1757 edition, reprinted in a complete works of 1758. There is no critical edition as yet, since even Brethe de la Gressaye's edition (1950) does not include all variant readings and changes. The Pléiade text is based upon the 1757 text, with some editorial changes reflecting Montesquieu's intentions (see 2:1496–97; see also the Cohler translation, xxv–xxvi). The *Œuvres complètes* edited by André Masson, 3 vols. (Paris: Nagel, 1950–55) is more comprehensive than the Pléiade edition, but the differences were not relevant here, and the latter is more widely available.

References to Blackstone's *Commentaries on the Laws of England* are to the edition by W. C. Jones (Baton Rouge, LA: Claitor's, 1976 [San Francisco: Bancroft-Whitney, 1915]), a revision of William G. Hammond's edition (Bancroft-Whitney, 1890), long out of print. Hammond uses the eighth edition of 1778, the last in Blackstone's lifetime. I cite the reprinted 1915 Jones edition since it is more widely available. A widely used paperback edition of the *Commentaries* (Chicago: University of Chicago Press, 1979) reprints the first edition of 1765–79, with the sound intent of removing the accretions of later editors. The Hammond and Jones editions generally are preferable for scholars, however, since Blackstone supervised changes to eight editions; notes in chapter 5 discuss these issues in more detail.

Notes in the relevant chapters address issues regarding *The Federalist*, Tocqueville's *Democracy in America*, and other works examined.

Introduction

The Subtle Judge and Moderate Liberalism

The presidential election of 2000 should have reminded the broader American citizenry of the stakes involved in a century of contentious debates about the role of the judiciary in liberal democracy, debates that had become tiresome or were of interest only to an initiated few. The highest courts of Florida and the United States, by insisting that one or the other would effectively select the president of the United States, demonstrated the presumption among judges and lawyers that practically any political or social question is within their purview. This phenomenon raises important questions not only about modern judicial power and law, but also about modern constitutionalism and liberal democracy. Just as striking is the partisan reaction to these rulings from many legal and academic voices, who presumed that the judges with whom they disagreed, on whichever court, made political rulings only thinly disguised with legal reasoning. This agreement beneath the rancor exposed a view long prevalent among American lawyers and political scientists that judging is political or "ideological" and should be discussed as such. In the heat of debate few commentators reflected upon what this means for the rule of law, judicial independence, and constitutional self-government in the long term, or in a deeper sense.

What links these pressing questions with the seemingly arcane topics of Montesquieu's conception of judging and consti-

[1]

tutional liberalism, and its legacy in Blackstone, Hamilton, Tocqueville, and Holmes? Montesquieu's constitutionalism and its American legacy are a primary source of the powerful judiciary now central to liberal theory and practice, and this judicialized politics directly shapes our fundamental notions of liberty, law, and rights. The twentieth-century debate about judicial power in America largely concerned legal interpretation, the original intent of particular constitutional clauses, and the comparison of evolving notions of law and judging to the views of the American framers. The continued growth of judicial power confronts all the liberal democracies, and especially America, with a distinct if related set of questions. Do we understand the philosophical sources from which this powerful judiciary sprang? Why has a constitutional politics that has eschewed the republican, complex design of its founders for a more democratic spirit simultaneously granted greater power to a few unelected, life-tenured judges? What happens to a liberal democratic politics and constitutional order, and to the character of the citizenry, when politics increasingly is defined by a judicial emphasis on individual rights and claims? What are the consequences for international affairs, and for national security, of the effort to judicialize all matters of politics?

This book addresses these questions by arguing that the eighteenth-century French philosopher Montesquieu was the first to propose a potent but discrete judicial power for liberal government, and that important issues about modern judicial power and its broader consequences require an understanding of his thought and legacy. Montesquieu (1689–1755) was the most cited European author in America at the time of the Constitution's framing, but his complicated style and the criticism that his republicanism was aristocratic led to a gradual decline in his status for leading American thinkers and statesmen.[1] Nonetheless, his political philosophy, especially as expressed in *The Spirit of the Laws* (1748), is indispensable for understanding modern liberalism in its true complexity. A few devoted political theorists still decipher and debate his masterwork, convinced of his profound influence on a range of political ideas, from law, rights, political culture, and history to climate, commerce, and toleration. His importance for a constitutionalism of separated powers is more widely, if casually, noted. For most political scientists and jurists, however, Montesquieu's text is a bygone classic, more mentioned than studied. It is encouraging that the enduring insights of *The Spirit of the Laws* have recently been reaffirmed by studies about the importance of political institutions and constitutions for shaping political life, especially regarding democratization in the post–Cold War era.[2] Students of political theory, jurisprudence, judicial power, and law would do well to pursue this reaffirmation.

Given the prominence today of judicial power in America and beyond, we should take seriously a dimension of Montesquieu's philosophy rarely noted even by Montesquieu scholars: the idea that "the central and continuous theme of *The Spirit of the Laws* is that the independence of the courts of law more than any other institution separates moderate from despotic regimes."[3] Careful study of the entire work, as Montesquieu specifically requests in the Preface, reveals a persistent teaching that elevating the judicial power within liberal politics, or any political order, moderates partisanship and ensures individual security. He recommends a "cloaking of power" in two senses: placing the robed power at the center of politics but concealing the subtle judge behind juries, and a quiet inculcation of the teaching itself. This effort to carefully judicialize politics also shines through in his legacy, especially in the English jurist William Blackstone and his *Commentaries on the Laws of England* (1765–69). Blackstone's constitutionalism distills for England and its dominions Montesquieu's conception of judges who subtly transform law, politics, and mores. Alexander Hamilton's exposition of federal judicial power in *The Federalist* captures this dimension of modern judicial power, while citing Montesquieu to argue that independent judges pose no threat to liberal politics. Hamilton's judges are invisible, null, and the least dangerous branch, but they also enjoy judicial review, a largely novel power to judge the constitutionality of statutes and other acts. Little noticed, however, is his subsequent argument that such judges will imperceptibly moderate the laws, even if found constitutional, by "mitigating the severity and confining the operation" of "unjust and partial laws." Such "benefits of the integrity and moderation of the judiciary" are both crucial and overlooked, "a circumstance calculated to have more influence upon the character of our governments, than but few may imagine."[4] These arguments suggest that in Montesquieu's own work, and in the legacy he deliberately sought among thinkers and statesmen, a moderating reform of both classical political philosophy and earlier modern liberalism is cloaked in the robes of a subtly powerful judiciary.

Tocqueville, in *Democracy in America* (1835–40), marvels at the power of judicial review that was generally assumed in America's founding debates and secured by Chief Justice John Marshall. Our French visitor remarked that "a more immense judicial power has never been constituted in any people," and that "there is almost no political question in the United States that is not resolved sooner or later into a judicial question."[5] The great prominence of American judges is, then, no recent event, but what astounded Tocqueville is now commonplace, suggesting the degree to which judicial power has grown and been transformed since the Marshall era. The judiciary has been crucial at many moments in American politics, but judges, courts, and the lawyers who propel the legal system now permeate our politics. While the U.S. Supreme Court ruling in *Bush v. Gore* (2000) is not as defining for American constitutionalism as some rulings by the Marshall, Taney, New Deal, and Warren courts, it confirms the pervasiveness of judges, both state and federal, in American life. This twentieth-century phenomenon has prompted debates about a judicialized politics, with regard not only to America but also to the rise of judicial power around the globe.[6] A range of political theorists now warns that litigation and courts increasingly have supplanted a politics of self-governance. The jurist Alexander Bickel was one of the first such critics, in the name of both participatory politics and the legal, institutional integrity of the judiciary, and his arguments have been elaborated by a diverse group of legal scholars.[7]

Despite such concerns, the dominant view in Anglo-American political theory and jurisprudence today embraces a judicialized politics. The liberal theory of John Rawls and Ronald Dworkin endorses a central political role for legislatively inclined judges, who set the tone for the liberal political order and its commitment to fairness and equal respect. This brand of liberalism elevates judicial reasoning, of the right sort, to the status of public philosophy: "In a constitutional regime with judicial review, public reason is the reason of its supreme court." Such judges must shape law and public opinion to protect individuals in their decisions about themselves and other consenting adults, so as to leave all individuals free to be the persons they choose.[8] Michael Sandel criticizes the twentieth-century Supreme Court for enacting these novel notions of individual rights and judicial power, preferring a civic republican philosophy to a "procedural liberalism" that undermines both citizenship and communal moral understandings.[9] A fuller understanding of these debates about a judicialized liberalism requires, however, a reconsideration of the origins in modern political philosophy of our current politics and jurisprudence. To begin with, Locke's philosophy is important for liberal constitutionalism and America; nonetheless, modern judging and jurisprudence actually owe more to Montesquieu and his legacy as a distinct philosophical tradition that is not simply reducible to Locke.[10] Montesquieu's more complex liberalism, emphasizing political moderation and tranquillity, better explains how an independent judiciary could judicialize modern liberal democracy itself. Rediscovering him also restores to us issues and thinkers that can help in redressing the legalism we now suffer and in repairing the battered legitimacy of the very concepts of law and judging that are at once wielded and squandered by many jurists today.

Calling Montesquieu to the Stand

While not as prominent a part of recent American life as judicial power, it is noteworthy that the two hundredth anniversary of *The Spirit of the Laws* at mid-century sparked a gradual renewal of Montesquieu studies in France and

America.[11] This is good news for philosophy, since his place in the first rank of political philosophers was well established in his lifetime. His stature was eclipsed by the French Revolution and by democrats elsewhere—including Jefferson, who found him conservative—and by schools of Anglo-American philosophy defined by skeptical epistemology, analytical precision, and theorizing from contemporary "intuitions." Such novelties provoked criticism in turn from the even more skeptical school of postmodernism, which aspired to broaden the horizons of philosophical and political understanding but more often than not has narrowed them. If we are reluctant to abandon reasonable debate yet resist a narrowly rational study of politics and fundamental human questions, then the patience needed to penetrate Montesquieu's complexity can return substantial rewards. Those accustomed to modern treatises must adjust to the range of topics and genres in which he composed his political philosophy, from humane letters (*Persian Letters*, 1721) to history (*Considerations on the Romans*, 1734) and a kind of political theory more complex and comprehensive than that of his predecessors Hobbes and Locke. This philosophic seriousness, free of analytical doctrine and mixed with observations on history and political practice, made him the leading philosophic figure for the American founders and should make his work attractive again today.[12] More leading politicians studied and cited Montesquieu in America's founding era than read Rawls today, which says something about both our politics and our philosophical inclinations. Those who nonetheless wince at the thought of tackling a tome like *The Spirit of the Laws* can take heart from the defense of its complicated style given by the encyclopedist d'Alembert: that one "must distinguish apparent disorder from real disorder" and that "voluntary obscurity is not obscurity."[13]

D'Alembert's apology echoes Montesquieu's own explanation of his subtle, complex philosophy, and these characteristics certainly mark his conception of judging. Discovering the full import of his project for judicial power involves an intricate, hardly obvious reading of his works and legacy. Studies of *The Spirit of the Laws* rarely discuss judicial power beyond noting that its independent status is Montesquieu's contribution to separation of powers doctrine, distinguishing his constitutionalism from Locke's.[14] His influential study of the English constitution seems to suggest only that judging should be left to popular juries, and that because such rotating judges are "not continually in view," the judging power is, "so to speak, invisible and null."[15] There are clues here and elsewhere, however, that judicial power plays a more central role in Montesquieu's moderate liberal constitutionalism than first meets the eye. He eventually finds more robust judging in the English constitution, since the upper house of the legislature has a "supreme authority to moderate the law" through its exceptional judicial functions (11.6, 404). Montesquieu then declares, in this work brimming with advice for constitutional founders and legislators, that among a free people "the masterwork of legislation is to know how to place well the power of judging" (11.11, 411). His examination of civil liberty confirms this prominence, declaring that individual "security," defined as the essence of liberty, "is never more attacked than in public or private prosecutions." Indeed, knowledge of "the surest rules one can observe in criminal judgments, concerns mankind more than anything else in the world," and it is "only on the practice of this knowledge that liberty can be founded" (12.2, 432–33). Never in the work does Montesquieu declare legislative or executive power so singularly essential to a liberal constitution, nor so important for individual security or liberty.

The prominence of judges, courts, and lawyers is Montesquieu's foremost legacy in liberal constitutionalism, as is evident in such theorists of liberal democracy as Blackstone, Hamilton, and Tocqueville, and in our everyday politics. While his advocacy of judicial power was cloaked or opaque, however, today's judges and lawyers often are anything but, especially in America. The question immediately arises as to whether his reforming of judicial power is the seed of the recent American and now global phenomenon termed judicial activism. The evidence suggests, in fact, that the "imperial judiciary" criticized in the twentieth century stems much more from the jurisprudential revolution led by Oliver Wendell Holmes Jr. than from the constitutional understanding of Montesquieu, Blackstone, and Hamilton.[16] In the most obvious link between Montesquieu and the American judiciary, Hamilton quotes the "celebrated Montesquieu" to insist that, relative to the executive and legislative powers, "the judiciary is next to nothing."[17] Hamilton does protest a bit much, since he, like Tocqueville, hoped that a quiet judicial statesmanship would moderate the democratic excesses to which republics are prone. Still, the subtle, distinctly legal influence sought by these Montesquieuan jurists involves neither legislating nor a rejection of the separation of powers, both of which characterize Holmesean skepticism and pragmatism. Study of Montesquieu and his legacy nevertheless helps to explain how the judicial activism ushered in by Holmes ever could have arisen. In one sense Montesquieu's notion of subtle judges is alien to the branch of Holmesean legal realism that views constitution and law as essentially malleable, to be shaped by judges in accord with the times. His emphasis upon natural rights and separation of powers sanctions only gradual reform within stable parameters, not the historicist, legislative spirit informing the twentieth-century jurisprudential imagination. The paradox is that Montesquieu and Blackstone liberalized law and judging in ways that permitted unintended consequences, certainly beyond the discrete role for judges they proposed.

Part 1 of this book traces this complicated history of modern judicial power by examining judging as the linchpin in Montesquieu's constitutionalism of liberty, which in turn points to his development of a new jurisprudence and constitutionalism throughout *The Spirit of the Laws*. His new ideas for political and legal reform percolate in the refrain that judging is a crucial means to gradually tempering laws about morals, politics, and religion. Indeed, he closes the work with a new historical jurisprudence aimed at judges, lawyers, and statesmen sympathetic to a legalizing of politics, teaching that from the medieval era a Gothic, common-law judicial power had fostered the growth and reform of European liberty itself. Montesquieu's new judicial power and jurisprudence synthesizes elements from the classic common law and earlier liberal theory, including a view of human nature oriented to both moderate sociability and individual tranquillity. As if to signal his independence from the Cartesian rationalism of earlier liberal philosophy, he transcends his abstract generalizations about law and the state of nature in book 1 to develop his principles through analysis of particular, historical phenomena. His experience as a senior judge in the province of Bordeaux from 1716 to 1724 thus informs his initial remarks on judging in the work, which use a discussion of France's traditional courts to raise fundamental themes about liberty and separation of powers (2.4). The jurists who perpetuated Montesquieu's conception of prudence, in later writings on constitutionalism and judicial power, similarly kept one foot grounded in the philosophic life and the other in the field of political practice.

Montesquieu's Complex Legacy and the Dilemmas of Jurisprudence

Montesquieu courts readers who will apply his cloaking of power and other reforms to achieve a properly moderate liberalism, making it natural to examine how figures such as Blackstone, Hamilton, and Tocqueville adapt his teaching to Britain, America, and liberal constitutionalism generally. Part 2 of this book examines the Montesquieuan conception of judicial power in the founding text of modern Anglo-American jurisprudence, Blackstone's *Commentaries on the Laws of England*. Part 3 turns to the Montesquieuan judicial legacy in America, sketching the more complicated relationship that Montesquieu and Blackstone have with Hamilton, Tocqueville, Holmes, and twentieth-century constitutional law. These investigations, which conclude by discussing the Supreme Court's controversial right-of-privacy and abortion jurisprudence, permit some critical evaluation of the Montesquieuan project. I make no claim to comprehensively examine such a range of authors and issues, only to demonstrate the need to account for Montesquieu's teaching and its subsequent influence in our debates about judging, constitutionalism, and a healthy liberalism.

Since Montesquieu speaks quietly about his notion of judging, it is helpful to study what was made of his teaching by jurists and statesmen closer to him than we are, in both time and understanding. If one properly understands Blackstone's *Commentaries* as a comprehensive work of constitutionalism informed by a serious political philosophy, then it becomes evident that he modeled both the manner and substance of his work largely upon *The Spirit of the Laws.* Blackstone adapts to England Montesquieu's project for a cloaking of power—the principle of political and moral moderation; the complex constitution of separated powers; the education of lawyers, judges, and leading citizens in gradual, liberal reform; and a subtle presentation of these ideas themselves. Brief encounters with Hamilton, Tocqueville, and Holmesean jurisprudence then permit reflection upon the virtues and dangers of the project to judicialize politics. Blackstone and Hamilton both place constitutionalism above judicial power, in contrast to later modes of legal interpretation and judicial activism. Each seeks the greatest role for judging and its moderating, liberalizing effects consistent with a complex constitution, the rule of law, and natural rights. Tocqueville's analysis of modern, and particularly American, democracy indirectly criticizes Montesquieu's liberalism, and this brings to light subtle but important differences between Hamilton's constitutionalism and the versions espoused by Montesquieu and Blackstone. Hamilton and Tocqueville certainly adopt the Montesquieuan line by emphasizing a professional judiciary, and Tocqueville even describes Supreme Court Justices as "statesmen," and lawyers and judges generally as an "aristocracy." He does so, however, because judges trained in a tradition of common-law reasoning counteract the isolated, skeptical "individualism" and rootless pragmatism that endanger modern democracy.[18] This challenges Montesquieu's liberalism, which had raised civil law—the criminal and civil law directly affecting individuals—to parity with political law by emphasizing a judicial power attuned to individual tranquillity.

The question raised by Tocqueville, and even by Hamilton, is whether this atomistic rationale for a prominent judiciary ultimately undermines law, judging, and constitutionalism itself. Their jurisprudence, informed as much by the classic common law as by liberalism, provides us with resources to question whether judges should be partisans in a progressive effort to emancipate law and mores from traditional moral and political teachings. Beyond illuminating how such progress in fact undermines the rationale for an independent judiciary and judicial review, Tocqueville reminds us that judges at one time elevated the citizenry above "individualism" and pragmatism by instructing in principles of law and right. He also warns against the corrosion of the very capacity for self-government and liberty, since a corrupted spirit of law corrupts the souls of citizens. It is telling that two prominent American lawyers, the dean of Yale Law School and the Learned Hand Professor of Law at Harvard Law School, recently have lamented that America's judiciary and legal profession no longer ennoble our constitutional democracy as Tocqueville had hoped.[19] The question arises as to whether Montesquieu's project for a cloaking of power ultimately causes harm to both the judicial power and his own cherished separation of powers. Both consequences in turn raise questions about the perpetuation of, or prospects for, a juridical constitutionalism itself. These issues sharpen upon encountering Holmes, the self-proclaimed epitome of the neither subtle nor moderate judge. Law, for Holmes, is ever evolving, since it is irrational to believe in enduring principles of right or justice. The best judges will help to chart the future path of law and society, either by deferring to dominant majorities or by themselves prophesying where the law will go. Montesquieu might reply that such legal realism or pragmatism supports neither the moderating prudence he sought from judges nor the political equilibrium he sought from distinctive constitutional powers. Still, in a largely forgotten essay on Montesquieu, Holmes displays considerable familiarity with the *Persian Letters* and with the larger import of *The Spirit of the Laws*.[20] He saw confirmation for his own legal positivism in Montesquieu's depiction of a jurisprudence that separates procedure from content and emphasizes evolution as much as enduring essence.

Looking back after a study of Montesquieu and Blackstone, it seems harder to explain how Holmesean legal realism could have repudiated so successfully classic common-law jurisprudence if the groundwork had not been laid, within the judge's chambers, for such a revolution. These Enlightenment jurists may not have intended this rupture, but their innovations in jurisprudence and judicial power made it possible. Nevertheless, studying these founders of our constitutionalism reveals how profitable it is to rediscover them. The paradox of law in our time is that judges and lawyers have never been so powerful in human history, yet the foundations for and legitimacy of judging and the law have never been so contested. We put at risk this great achievement of Western civilization, the rule of law enforced and perpetuated by independent courts and a legal profession, as one pillar of a free but stable constitutional order. As Americans grow accustomed to a steady diet of charges about "ideological" judging, those who study the courts should offer a long-term approach for restoring principle and legal integrity to the theory and practice of judicial power. The eighteenth- and nineteenth-century jurists who drew upon a millennium or more of thought and practice to establish the modern judiciary and modern constitutionalism did not have the leisure of our sophisticated skepticism about fundamental principles and institutions. Their belief in natural right, separation of powers, and liberty is a tonic amid our narrow debates between contending versions of Holmesean skepticism and pragmatism, whether progressive or conserva-tive. Especially if studied alongside the classic common-law tradition that both Montesquieu and Blackstone admired but tried to reform, the ingredients are at hand for a much-needed reconsideration of the foundations of America's moderate constitutionalism and jurisprudence.[21] Such a reconsideration would have benefits beyond the courts and, given our influence upon law and politics across the globe, even beyond America.

PART ONE

Montesquieu's Jurisprudence
and New Judicial Power

After four decades as a lawyer and judge, poet and historian, scientist and philosopher, Charles de Montesquieu produced a work of political philosophy that would leave its mark on modern thought and civilization. *The Spirit of the Laws* (1748) reflects the complexity of Montesquieu's life and thought, his balanced portrait of the myriad phenomena of human life and the varied perspectives from which we judge politics and morals. Unlike the rationalist works of his Enlightenment predecessors, and more in the spirit of Montaigne, Montesquieu insisted on accounting for the numerous complexities in human thoughts and deeds. Unlike the more fatigued and skeptical of his late-modern and postmodern successors, he resisted the temptation of moral and political relativism. This moderate philosophy helped to make his masterwork an immediate success among both thinkers and statesmen. Later modernity has separated theory and practice, so that relatively few academics today appreciate his effort at a mutually instructive dialectic between the perspective of the jurist and that of the philosopher and political theorist. Similarly, few lawyers or jurists today appreciate Montesquieu's achievement as a political philosopher and constitutionalist, or how his thought undergirds the independent courts and powerful legal professions of the past two centuries.

This larger spirit of moderation and complexity guides the gradual development of a new theory of judicial power throughout the early books of *The Spirit of the Laws*, which is eventually presented more clearly in the liberal constitutionalism of books 11 and 12. A distinctive jurisprudence and constitutionalism inform this conception of judging, and a brief comparison with both earlier liberal theory and English common-law jurisprudence confirms that Montesquieu sought a novel synthesis of elements from these earlier schools. This first call in liberal political philosophy for an independent judicial power stems from the fundamental principles of his science of politics, especially the "spirit" and "moderation" he found in the complex interrelations among political phenomena. He links judging with political moderation early in the work, when praising a "depository of the laws" within European monarchies as a source of political and civil liberty (2.4). Such a judicial power provides both political balance and true individual security, features he finds lacking in earlier liberalism and republicanism, as well as in classical political philosophy. Montesquieu thus argues that a blending of monarchy and republic is the best liberal regime, since he advocates a revitalized, "open" nobility as the institutional home of this judicial depository of laws. The basis for this new liberalism is his new conception of natural right, in terms of the tranquillity individuals seek and the sympathy they share with their close fellows. A cloaking of power can reorient the political order toward a humane natural justice, moderating political law to accord with the private affairs addressed by the judiciary and civil law.

Montesquieu's new judicial power, and his slowly unfolding presentation of it, characteristically depart from the cleaner, more deductive rationalism of Descartes, Hobbes, Spinoza, and Locke. The texture of particularity in his thought echoes the classic common-law mind of the English jurist Sir Edward Coke, but Montesquieu employs complexity and concreteness for more liberal, individualistic aims than the common-law mind could endorse. His praise in the early books for juridical due process, common-law complexity, and a role for courts in moderating political disputes and criminal penalties prepares for his more explicit treatment of a modern liberal politics in books 11 and 12. Throughout, he advises constitutional and ordinary legislators about properly structuring laws, institutions, and processes, especially with regard to the peculiar spirit—the prudence—of judging, properly conceived. After defining the proper judicial power for liberal constitutionalism Montesquieu turns, in book 12 and beyond, to more openly instructing statesmen, judges, and lawyers on how to achieve this moderate regime. If the spirit of law is the spirit of moderation, as he states only in the final part of the work, one dimension of moderation is a prudential capacity to apply what philosophy discovers (29.1). *Esprit* con-

notes not only spirit but also mind or wit, and the
founding legislators and ordinary—if reforming—
and lawyers, with a prudence that can translate pri
Preface he speaks of the political effects he hopes
the first authority cited in book 1 is the great He
of statesmanship, Plutarch; the second is a fellow
jurist Gravina (1.1, 1.3). The bulk of *The Spirit of th*
to bring forth and educate a new spirit of reform i
depository of such a spirit being a new order of the robe. He advises about due
process and moderation in criminal laws and penalties (book 12), and about
how to moderate laws on commerce, morals, and religion (books 19 to 26).
He permeates the closing study of Roman and Franco-German laws, which he
considers a neglected chapter in the history of human liberty, with suggestions
about the institutional structure and practice of judging (books 27 to 31).

For the reader of Montesquieu today, dulled by the sophisticated legal
skepticism that has been dominant in Anglo-American jurisprudence for nearly
a century, such delicacy in suggesting a reforming political role for judges must
seem naive or quaint. We are confident that judges are political actors as much
as legislators or administrators are, always activist in promoting their moral
and social views, albeit using conventional modes of adjudication to hide this
from the uninitiated and to temper their most blatant policy making. Montesquieu, however, knew what we either ignore or confidently dismiss: that
the function of judging must be truly distinct if it is to be accepted by other
governing powers and by the citizenry as a legitimate, independent agent in
human affairs. Moreover, to get only more of the same, except now in robes,
would neither temper political conflict nor secure individual tranquillity. Thus,
throughout the work Montesquieu recommends to the statesmanlike judge the
quiet, juridical method of seeking the humane spirit of the law. When law in-
jures humanity or works against individual and political tranquillity, the humane statesman must try to follow the spirit of the law over, and even against,
its letter (6.13; 11.6; 28.9). The liberal education in law and prudence which
The Spirit of the Laws provides, especially in its final parts, inculcates through repeated examples that "[i]t is moderation which governs men, and not excesses,"
whether these are extremes of wickedness or severe moralism (22.22). He increasingly defines philosophy in terms of this humane, moderate prudence,
even declaring "the sublimity of human reasoning" to be an understanding of
the "different orders of laws" and how they relate to the human things they
would govern (26.1). It is fitting that Montesquieu makes the reader wait until
the sixth and final part of the work (books 27 to 31) for a fuller understanding
of fundamental aspects of his political philosophy and jurisprudence—why

y praises "moderation," why he frequently cites poetry and history, distrusts abstract "systems" of reasoning (see chapter 4, below). Montuieu offers such teachings slowly, by indirection, and with great attention to particulars and practical ends, a model for the statesman and statesmanlike judge who undertake liberal reforms. It is no surprise that *The Spirit of the Laws* was most influential in America just when its founders sought prudential advice about how to construct a constitutional order. Its only real rival was the *Commentaries* of his disciple William Blackstone, which further delineated the complex constitutional forms necessary to achieve liberty and political stability and was itself sprinkled with prudential advice about legal reform undertaken by judges.

one

Moderating Liberalism and Common Law: Spirit and Juridical Liberty

Montesquieu introduces *The Spirit of the Laws* as propounding "new ideas" of man and politics, and as "the work of twenty years" of reflection upon an "infinite number of things" ("Notice," 227; "Preface," 229). His bold ideas about politics, jurisprudence, and judging are in the service, paradoxically, of moderation and tranquillity, and throughout he strives to balance practice and theory, experience and reflection. It is widely noted that he restored to political philosophy a concern with prudence and an attention to the diverse particulars of political history and practice not yet seen in modernity, nor even attempted since Aristotle, although Machiavelli is a precursor.[1] This concern with both the realities and potentialities of political life partly explains why Montesquieu does not openly declare the importance of judicial power for his constitutionalism, since both the aims and the novelty of his conception provide reasons for cloaking such a proposal for reform.

This reading of Montesquieu is not shared, however, by most historical studies, which treat his views on judging and French constitutional history as largely representative of eighteenth-century juridical and political debates.[2] A recent elaboration of this view argues that *The Spirit of the Laws* in fact propounds a political philosophy of historical particularity, rooted in Montesquieu's experience as a provincial judge.[3] The paradox here is that, for all the rich details provided about his career as a senior judge in the *Parlement* of Bordeaux and its influence upon his writings, this approach undervalues the importance of judicial power in his constitutionalism. A more serious study of this dimension of his political philosophy has argued that judicial independence is the key to his constitutionalism, but its Marxist reading traces this to the class bias of a nobleman judge.[4] A comparative jurist has detected contradictions in Montesquieu's account of judging which suggest his endorsement of something more than a jury-centered power, but then finds such signals incoherent or sporadic.[5] The French scholar Simone Goyard-Fabre is one of the few to find a genuinely bold teaching about judicial power in Montesquieu's philosophy, arguing that his judicial and constitutional reforms together emphasize "the same *equilibrium* of elements among themselves and on the whole: the just measure, that which is called moderation in politics or justice in a court, expresses the same *right ratio*" or "*juste milieu* [golden mean]."[6] James Stoner also has discovered "intimations in *The Spirit of the Laws* of a judiciary quietly instructed in reform." Montesquieu's larger aim is a juridical liberalism; books 6 and 12 teach that the "best protection for the individual is a series of judicial procedures, not devised abstractly, but developed through historical change from the manner of judging practiced by the Germanic tribes 'in the woods.' The telling of this tale occupies, on and off, no small part of the remainder of the work." In the spirit of Montesquieu's emphasis on commerce, Stoner finds a teaching that the "security of persons depends upon a kind of commerce in sound judicial practices—with philosophers as merchants and their writings as bills of exchange."[7]

Still, most readers of *The Spirit of the Laws* have not found this distinctive conception of subtle judges and a judicialized liberalism. This intentional cloaking by Montesquieu is less perplexing in light of d'Alembert's defense of the work's confusing style, which reiterates the jurist's own remarks on the complexity of his writings and the careful reading they require. In the Preface to *The Spirit of the Laws,* Montesquieu insists that his tome does have a design, asking that "one not judge, by a moment's reading, a labor of twenty years; that one approve or condemn the whole book, and not some few phrases" (229).[8] He further encourages reading between his lines by stating that "one must not always so exhaust a subject, that one leaves nothing for a reader to do," since he wants people not only to read his work but to "think" (11.20). Montesquieu's conception of judicial power is one beneficiary of this complicated approach to philosophy, since there are sound reasons for cloaking this proposed transformation of political power. Such a project redefines moderation in order to soften the moral character and standards of political life, through judicial attention to the interests and desires of particular individuals. Such aims would be considered morally doubtful in Montesquieu's own time and in the light of Western philosophy and Biblical religion—although, given his success and that of liberalism generally, they are less so today. Openly questionable reforms invite controversies that can hinder their reception and their ultimate efficacy. Even with Montesquieu's prudent cloaking of his intentions and teachings, *The Spirit of the Laws* was placed on the Catholic Church's Index of prohibited books in 1751.

Using judicial power to shelter private concerns, even vices, from public authority also involves a shift in political power. The executive and legislative powers and their traditional supporters lose some ground as professional lawyers and judges rise. Montesquieu's indirect presentation of this new teaching seems aimed at fellow jurists, judges, and lawyers, and at those who generally shared his concern to temper political life with the reasonable, measured spirit of courts of law. Blackstone, Hamilton, and Tocqueville indicate their grasp of this larger message in Montesquieu's detailed analyses of judicial procedure, legal forms, and jurisprudential principle. None of this suggests that the complex constitutional government he promotes is anything but genuinely representative, as is evident in the clash of partisan views in his pluralist, liberal, best regime (see 11.6; 19.27). He is less confident, however, than are Machiavelli, Hobbes, and Locke about completely novel founding and artifice, or rational planning by the sovereign, or the adequacy of popular consent alone to justify legislative or executive projects. Such a shift of power, then, must occur imperceptibly. A main advantage of having a judicial, lawyerly body moderate the factional conflict between classes and institutions is that it is less partisan and passionate than the other powers, at least having different kinds of passions and concerns. It certainly is weaker than its rivals, as Hamilton argues by citing Montesquieu in *Federalist* no. 78, and this further entails a quiet, careful growth of influence. Moreover, this approach accords with the larger aim of moderation by judicialization, namely, the security of individuals, defined as lack of fear about their liberty and security. If this requires a learned, quasi-noble judging power, then the latter should keep free of the fray of politics and focus strictly upon judging. A humane natural right, attuned to natural sentiments, points to a discrete judging power and not an omni-competent, fearsome arm of public administration. The moral compromise inherent in such moderation indicates that judges defined by their humanity, tolerance, and mildness are hardly meant to invoke the Biblical notion of Judgment Day.

Montesquieu's general preference for quiet and steady reform over revolution, announced at length in the Preface to *The Spirit of the Laws*, also recommends an intricate presentation of this new conception of judicial power. He views with anxiety the doctrinaire republicanism of a Cromwell or a Locke, and at moments he seems to see a Robespierre ahead.[9] Knowledge of judicial procedures and attention to the interests and fears of individuals will not foster rationalist theories about the costly but necessary gains of a Hegelian slaughter-bench of history. True, Montesquieu is concerned to show that political communities change and reform over time. For Rousseau, Kant, Hegel, and later moderns, however, these seeds of historical thinking grew into the sort of rationalist, universalistic praise for revolution and progress that the French jurist feared. His attachment to the natural rights inhering in individuals prevented his own adoption of historicism, and Montesquieu instead recommends gradual, imperceptible reform of laws and constitutions. The judging power is eminently more suited to such a strategy than are the powers more animated by passion and more inclined toward grand plans.

A Humane Natural Right and New Jurisprudence

It is only in book 29 of *The Spirit of the Laws* that Montesquieu explains the principle by which the abstract, Enlightenment pronouncements that open the work—on the "invariable laws" that govern all beings in the world (1.1)—fit with his general emphasis on the particularities of politics and law: "I say it, and it seems to me that I have brought forth this work only to prove it: the spirit of moderation ought to be that of the legislator; the political good, like the moral good, is always found between two extremes" (29.1, 865). Throughout the work Montesquieu's concept of moderation guides both his philosophizing and his political advice, continually seeking to avoid the extremism of adopting any single, rigid dogma. His political philosophy thus blends elements of a Newtonian science of the equilibrium achieved among forces and ideas, a Machiavellian realism about lowered moral aims for politics, and the humane sensibilities of his predecessor as a counselor in the *Parlement* of Bordeaux, Montaigne.[10] The ultimate goal of his new science of politics is liberty, but a modern conception of moderation is for him the prerequisite for liberty. He argues in particular that liberty perishes under any structural imbalance of forces or any stagnation of dynamic activity—that is, under despotism. He will not have man patiently suffer despotism, whether physical, political, or moral, as a good citizen of the city of God. He seeks means for realistically reforming the city of man to make it a more tranquil, hospitable abode, especially through inculcating a proper political and legal prudence. To be sure, his analysis of these fundamental issues in book 1, and later in the work, is indebted in some respects to the modern rationalism of Machiavelli, Hobbes, and Locke.[11] Still, the debt generally wanes as one moves farther into the thirty-one books, which emphasize complexity, particularity, and moderation. Upon considering the whole work, as the Preface directs, one finds it tempering earlier modern attempts to establish an abstract foundation for politics—whether Machiavellian acquisition of glory and rule by one alone, or a Hobbesian, Lockean liberalism of a state of nature and natural rights.[12] Even in book 1, in the passages that bear the strongest imprint of Enlightenment theorizing, Montesquieu suggests his independence even when stating his most general, abstract conception of law, that law governs all dimensions of reality (1.1, 232). He cites Plutarch for the maxim that "law is the king of all, mortal and immortal," taken from an essay advising a prince about a natural law that stands above human power and directs rulers to be just. Montesquieu refers to a classical moralist and biographer, not a modern Cartesian philosopher, for this fundamental ontological and jurisprudential premise; moreover, Plutarch himself is quoting the poet Pindar.[13] Unlike Hobbes, Spinoza, and Locke, Montesquieu is more concerned to educate statesmen than to indulge in abstract analysis. Unlike Machiavelli's education of princes, his own will teach that all rulers are governed by a higher law.

Montesquieu nonetheless is very much a modern, since his ateleological conception of divine law and the law of nature yields only the most minimal of natural laws (1.1–2). In contrast to Aristotle and Thomas Aquinas, who found principles of natural right or natural law in the fabric of the world, placed there by a divine mind that draws us toward itself as our ultimate goal, Montesquieu finds in nature only a general set of physical and psychological laws. His typically moderate stance on these fundamental issues, neither entirely subjective nor universalistic, is evident in the ambiguous character of the natural laws or "relations of equity" which, he argues, pre-date any political order. These indicate, for example, that "supposing that there were societies of men, it would be just to conform to their laws"; or that "if there were intelligent beings that had received some benefit from another being, they ought to have gratitude" (1.1, 233). This conception of natural law anticipates the more explicit discussion of man's prepolitical nature in the sequel on "the laws of nature" (1.2). When read in light of the whole work, the treatment of human nature in book 1 is not so much a version of earlier state-of-nature theories as an effort to moderate their claims. Montesquieu adopts those elements that accord with his more phenomenological, political analysis of politics while exposing the excesses and difficulties of this favorite method of early liberalism. Especially because the very next usage of *droit naturel* in the work is so distinctly non-Hobbesian (3.10), defining it as the natural affections we hold for family and loved ones, the complicated presentation in book 1 suggests a redefinition of natural right in terms of such humane sentiments. These new ideas inform his new conception of judging as distinct from—indeed, as tempering—any Biblical or Aristotelian notions of moral judgment at the bar of a higher or transcendent truth. Montesquieu's jurisprudence and new judicial power accord with a basic natural right to individual security and tranquillity even as they moderate the Hobbesian and Lockean conceptions of natural right, with their emphasis upon force and necessity.

Montesquieu's four "laws of nature" elaborate these principles by defining man as a sentimental animal with a capacity for reason. Peace is "the first natural law"—in terms of historical appearance, it seems—since by nature each man in his timidity "feels himself inferior" and would hardly attack his fellows. Hobbes is explicitly criticized for projecting such a "complex" idea as desire for power and domination upon natural, prepolitical man (1.2, 235). The second law is "nourishment," and the third is man's natural sociability, understood as the "natural entreaty" which people "always make to [one] another" through a blend of our capacities for fear, pleasure, and sexual charm. Montesquieu then shifts from our defining capacity for sentiment to our eventual drive for "knowledge," conceived of not as an end in itself but as another "bond" that other animals lack, making "the desire to live in society" the fourth natural law (236). This complex view of human nature informs his conceptions of politics and judging, since our natural passions or sentiments, which orient us toward peaceful, tranquil sociability, define us more fundamentally than our reason or any higher ambitions.[14] We are neither as naturally sociable nor as naturally selfish as either Aristotle or Hobbes would have it, nor are we as radically historical or malleable as Rousseau later suggests. The genius of a moderate politics—of the spirit of laws properly conceived—is to grasp our nature in all its complexity and constitute laws and institutions that will preserve all its dimensions.

Montesquieu develops these numerous themes throughout the early books of *The Spirit of the Laws*, and in doing so turns from an initial concern with the structures and motivating principles of different forms of government to a more fundamental concern with the distinction between moderate and immoderate governments (see 3.10; 8.8).[15] Only in book 5, after exposing the harshness of despotism but also proposing measures to moderate it, does he explicitly frame the essential problem of politics. Book 1 indicates that the human condition lies between divinity and brute matter, caught between the liberty of intelligence and the necessity of material existence. This middling condition is nowhere more evident than in the fact of despotism, for "despite men's love of liberty, despite their hatred of violence, most peoples are subjected to this type of government" (5.14, 297). This widespread problem and its underlying causes perpetually confront the political philosopher, the political founder, and the prudent reformer. He advises all three, or anyone with the genius to fuse these capacities, to work toward a quasi-Newtonian, moderate solution that is possible but difficult: "In order to form a moderate government, one must combine powers, regulate them, temper them, make them act; one must give one power a ballast, so to speak, to put it in a position to resist another; this is a masterwork of legislation that chance rarely produces and prudence is rarely allowed to produce" (5.14).

Early in the work, long before the core treatment of constitutionalism in books 11 and 12, Montesquieu provides this fundamental rationale for his new conceptions of the separation of powers and of judicial power. His political science argues that liberty can of itself achieve security only if our activities and passions are structured according to the dynamics prescribed by the laws of nature. Since our natural condition is not so low and desperate as Hobbes thinks, there is no *need* for the foundational contract and the absolute Leviathan. However, our natural condition is not so favored as either the Bible or Aristotle indicate, so there is no *warrant* for a moral orientation to politics and laws that would substantially restrict individual liberty. Man need face neither the fearsome judgment of an all-powerful Leviathan nor the troubling prospect of divine judgment or ethical censure. Nature indicates that politics must be structured in terms of multiple powers and perspectives that at once check and facilitate the free movement of political passions and energies. Montesquieu gradually develops his view of the separation of powers on this basis in *The Spirit of the Laws*, culminating in the liberal constitutionalism promulgated in book 11 and the judicialized politics recommended there and in book 12. Nature and human nature indicate the need for independent, nonpartisan judging that secures the tranquillity of each individual's interior motions. The fundamental principles of Montesquieu's new science of politics require, therefore, a new jurisprudence. The outlines of that jurisprudence become clearer when compared with the liberal theory and traditional common-law reasoning of his predecessors, and upon examining even the earliest treatments of law and judging in *The Spirit of the Laws*.

Liberalism, Common Law, and Juridical Tranquillity

The Spirit of the Laws refers to numerous Western jurists and legal texts, ancient, medieval, and modern, and Montesquieu's political science has a distinctly juridical cast. Although he cites Hobbes only once, and Locke and the common-law jurist Coke not at all, Montesquieu's peculiar relation to both England and earlier liberalism raises the question of his relationship to such predecessors. Hobbes and Locke are the leading liberal philosophers against whom Montesquieu either measured himself or now must be measured, and Coke embodies the classic common-law jurisprudence these theorists attacked.[16] His conception of judging borrows much from classic common law, even though he shares some of the liberal criticisms of common-law prudence, and his published work never mentions such great expositors as Fortescue, Saint Germain, or Coke. This ambiguous relationship to earlier jurisprudence accords with the very character of Montesquieu's judicial power. A consideration of his originality in relation to his predecessors further reveals why the content of his new jurisprudence and judicial power requires such a subtle, complicated presentation.

A safe point of departure for sketching the liberal jurisprudential landscape Montesquieu inhabited is to note that Hobbes and Locke seek to construct a rationally sound, politically stable legal order on a new foundation, man's pre-political state of nature.[17] For Hobbes, the necessities that define man's natural state are premises from which one derives further principles of civil society and governance. Locke's method is essentially identical, though more deftly presented. Their new foundation for a science of politics requires a sovereign power to constitute and govern civil society, but they disagree as to whether that foundation warrants, or requires, a separation within the sovereign. More to the point, judging is independent in neither of their accounts of the only rational, just political order. Locke follows Machiavelli's republican theory in separating and balancing forces so as to achieve security and prosperity in politics. He agrees with Hobbes, however, that judging must be under the sovereign, even if Locke would divide sovereignty into law-making and law-enforcing powers. The paradoxical explanation of this subordination of judging in both of these early liberal theorists is that judging, once conceived in light of man's prepolitical state of nature, somehow lies behind both legislating and executing. War is the natural human condition precisely because there is no effective judge to settle disputes. This is more evident in Locke than in Hobbes, for Locke makes judging the central metaphor of the state of nature: "[T]hose who have no such common Appeal, I mean on Earth, are still in the state of Nature, each being, where there is no other, Judge for himself, and Executioner." Hobbes, in contrast, simply subsumes judging under the establishment of that "common Power" which is the source of making and executing law.[18]

It is Locke's definition of "Political Society" that precipitates his break with Hobbes on the separation of powers, even as it transforms judging from a natural to a strictly positive power: "[T]here only is *Political Society*, where . . . all private judgment of every particular Member being excluded, the Community comes to be Umpire, by settled standing Rules, indifferent, and the same to all Parties."[19] These teachings reflect and reinforce the liberal theory that there is no natural law in the ancient or medieval sense, no natural reason that discerns a morally substantive natural right.[20] Hobbes concludes *The Elements of Law* by declaring that "right reason is not existent," since there is no "such thing to be found or known *in rerum natura*." Locke, too, rejects premodern natural law, if more subtly, suggesting that we are "ignorant for want of study of it" and that it is "unwritten, and so nowhere to be found but in the minds of Men." He is more candid when stating that nature in itself provides no practically meaningful guide for resolving conflict. Regardless of what natural justice means in the state of nature, men, once in society, "through Passion or Interest" will "miscite, or misapply it." Moreover, they "cannot so easily be convinced of their mistake where there is no established Judge."[21] Locke's modern law of reason requires elaboration and, more definitively, enforcement. For liberal philosophy, it is man who posits all genuine law, and any particular positive law can appeal only to the posited legal order as a whole or to individually inhering natural rights. This constructed order, built on the solid ground of necessity, is amenable neither to premodern natural law nor to a traditional common-law understanding of custom and precedent.[22] Only the natural rights of individuals are real and distinct, since their bases are the passions of an individual afraid to lose life, liberty, or property. The difficulty with this view of human nature and politics is that naturally apolitical people might not easily forfeit their rights in order to construct a positively binding contract on so shifting a ground as their own interests.

The lesson Hobbes draws from the problematic authority or legitimacy of positive law is that sovereignty must not be divided, and the sovereign must be the final judge of all subjects. Of course, subordinate magistrates are necessary, but the sovereign stands over them as appellate judge, able to revise or reverse as needed.[23] Locke's disagreement with Hobbes regarding the judging power stems not, then, from any influence of the common-law tradition but from the different conclusion he draws from his premises about the state of nature. Locke's doctrine of the separation of powers in effect turns the positivist conception of law and judging in Hobbes against the very idea of super-sovereignty. Hobbes addresses the problematic authority of posited law by setting up a person beyond judgment; for Locke, however, this is to think that "Men are so foolish that they care to avoid what Mischiefs may be done them by *Pole-Cats*, or *Foxes*, but are content, nay think it Safety, to be devoured by *Lions*."[24] Locke prefers the polecats of the factional conflict entailed by a separation of powers, in which the legislature judges the executive and stands judged by it, while both powers and all the citizens supposedly can appeal to a neutral judge on earth. That is, the legislative power is "Supream," but one can appeal over it to the posited legal order as a whole, and Locke's rules for appeal are delineated in a strikingly tripartite form: political society is "bound to govern by establish'd *standing Laws*, promulgated and known to the people," by "*indifferent* and upright *Judges*, who are to decide Controversies by those Laws," and by an executive power which can be used only "*in the Execution of such Laws.*"[25]

Polecats and foxes, however, remain. Locke later formulates in the *Second Treatise* both an executive prerogative that occasionally transcends law to cope with necessity, and a right of revolution. As to prerogative, the people and legislature might agree with such action after the fact, but there is "no *Judge on Earth*" who can declare an instance of it right or wrong by a natural, reasonable standard. This by itself raises the prospect of revolution, in which "[*t*]*he People shall be Judge*" after all, but this puts everyone back in the state of nature.[26] His criticism of Hobbes thus turns back upon his own account, since political stability and individual security rest on grounds potentially turbulent or less-than-civil. Hobbes and Locke never mention a separate judiciary because of the challenge such an independent source of judgment would pose to sovereignty. While Locke occasionally employs the language of tripartite powers, his judges could be independent of the sovereign only if they could appeal to something above the sovereign, if they could check the sovereign in an ultra-political way.[27] These early liberal theorists deny that there is any such appeal, seeing only the dangers to peace and security of appeals to divine law or divinely supported natural law. They deny that judging at law is ultimately based on nature or right reason, or that there is reasonableness in legal custom understood in a traditional, Scholastic sense. This is evident not only from their rejection of natural law but from their retention of only three of the four elements of Thomas Aquinas's definition of law. To Hobbes and Locke, law is for the common weal; it is promulgated; and it issues from the authorized power. Both philosophers drop precisely the fourth element, reason, which Aquinas lists first.[28] The instrumental reason of modern natural right cannot appeal to an ultimate, natural reason—to something other than self-interested force or will—for even if such a thing exists, its primary manifestation is in the claimed rights of individuals. Such rights are what is being contested in political disputes, not what settles them. Locke implicitly admits that his laws of reason and self-preservation, which govern legislators and by which they are judged, are as prone to being miscited and misapplied as all the other laws of nature. Judges, just like legislators, would do so when gripped by their passions, and Locke clearly authorizes revolution against legislators. Independent judges, then, would be just other predators running around, and for Locke, two are enough for keeping each other in line with the posited legal order. One is plenty for Hobbes.

Montesquieu departs in important ways from Hobbes and Locke, and these divergences are crucial both for his new constitutionalism and for the distinctive role that judging plays within it. *The Spirit of the Laws* suggests that the geometrically sound structures that Hobbes and Locke have built on their state-of-nature foundation in fact yield little tranquillity for individuals. Montesquieu thus applies Locke's criticism of Hobbes to Locke himself. If citizens fear their government and view politics with anxiety, who cares about the precise number or size of the predators? His own liberal solution appeals only weakly to natural reason or natural law, even though the opening book of *The Spirit of the Laws* seems to emphasize such an approach. Alternately, Montesquieu's conception of judging and constitutionalism does rest upon the low necessities of fear and tranquillity, although less exclusively and starkly than did the liberalism of his predecessors.[29] Locke had begun the moderating trend, tempering the stark sovereignty of Hobbes with reasonable customs for the many and reasonable thinking for the few. Montesquieu further argues that the very structure of politics can determine affairs safely, if constituted so that decisions are made both as necessity requires and in accord with a moderate, humane conception of natural right. His analysis of the separation of powers in the English constitution observes that the "three powers ought to form a repose," but since "by the necessary motion of things, they are constrained to move, they will be forced to move in concert" (11.6, 405). The crucial innovation is adding a third power, of a distinctly nonpredatory and more reasonable character, to provide the individual security that his liberal predecessors seek, without their constant worry about regression into war. A judicialized constitution builds the safety valve into the everyday system, in accord with the actual judicial practices and legal customs developed in many European countries through a "Gothic" common law and court system (see books 6, 12, and 28). This secures the liberal advantages of positivist legal theory more effectively than either super-sovereignty or an unstable cocktail of consent, revolution, faction, and prerogative. A crucial dimension of this innovative constitutionalism is that judges focus not upon "political law" or public law but "civil law," the criminal and civil law that directly affects individuals (1.3). Montesquieu's judges, even in his most developed account of constitutionalism in books 11 and 12, therefore lack a power of judicial review. His judicial power, informed by a moderate natural right, employs the advantages of premodern conceptions of judging without claiming the traditional foundation in natural law or right reason.

Montesquieu's disagreement with Hobbes and Locke on judging does not cancel his debt regarding the orientation and structure of modern constitutionalism. His dissent from these predecessors as well as the monarchical or aristocratic character of his independent judging power together raise the question of the English common law that Hobbes so severely criticized for its Scholastic and Aristotelian provenance. Montesquieu's relationship to the classic common law is as ambiguous as his relation to these liberal philosophers, and for a similar reason. He takes from the common law what seems reasonable according to man's natural right to liberty and humane tranquillity, and excludes those elements deemed extreme for their threat to individual security and a moderate constitution. In this Montesquieu follows Bacon, who advanced a reformulated common law that would protect man's real interests and thereby complement— and moderate—the realistic sovereign or state. In doing so, Bacon implied the deficiencies of the great expositor of traditional English common-law reasoning in his own era, Sir Edward Coke.

Classic common-law jurists such as Coke claimed that reason can refine immemorial custom and that judgments at law can reconcile the requirements of positive law with natural law or right reason. For Aristotle, justice requires both law and equitable judgment to interpret and apply the law in difficult cases, and laws based upon custom are more authoritative than written laws.[30] The English common-law jurist and Lord Chancellor Sir John Fortescue (d. 1476) cites mainly the authority of Aristotle, as well as St. Thomas Aquinas, in his *De laudibus legum Anglie* (*In Praise of the Laws of England*, c. 1471). Fortescue instructs young Prince Edward, in exile in France, on the superiority of England's common law and mixed constitution to France's civil law and absolute monarchy.[31] J. G. A. Pocock's widely noted study of "the common law mind" and "the ancient constitution" in seventeenth-century England emphasizes the deeply historical, insular quality of Coke's thought, but Coke often blends Scholastic principle with historical particularity in his jurisprudence, both implicitly and explicitly.[32] Even though the classic common law is not fond of abstractions or theories, its Aristotelian provenance helps in formulating the theory behind its reasoning. The common-law judge works from precedent cases and maxims to exercise a judgment informed by both particulars and generalities. Coke defined this judgment as an "artificial perfection of reason gotten by long studie, observation and experience," a reason "fined and refined by an infinite number of grave and learned men."[33] Hobbes's *Dialogue between a Philosopher and a Student of the Common Laws of England* seeks to supplant the traditional explication of common law provided in Christopher Saint Germain's *The Doctor and Student, or Dialogues between a Doctor of Divinity and a Student in the Laws of England*. As such, it is the most thematic development of the Baconian strain permeating Hobbes's major works. Only a more rational, and less Christian and customary, conception of law and sovereignty, more scientific than the vague concepts of legal judgment or prudence, could achieve a more enlightened politics.[34] Locke's critique of the common law is subtler, in part because it works largely by giving Coke the silent treatment, but the implications for common-law courts are evident in his theorizing and his constitutionalism.[35]

Montesquieu's silence about the English common law is puzzling, given that he is a jurist who presents his liberal constitutionalism through an analysis of the English constitution, and that he places judging at the center of his political science of moderation. He never mentions the common law or its great jurists Bracton, Fortescue, Saint Germain, or Coke in *The Spirit of the Laws*, a work otherwise brimming with citations. Professional common-law judges all but disappear in the analyses of England in books 11 and 19. These omissions are curious, since he practically paraphrases Coke's description of common-law reasoning when praising juridical complexity in monarchies—which have "so many rules, restrictions, extensions, which multiply particular cases, and seem to make an art of reasoning itself" (6.1, 307).[36] More curious still is the fact that Coke's life and jurisprudence combined to oppose absolute monarchy. This makes him a splendid example of the moderating force available in judges and "intermediate bodies," the embodiment of the complex, balanced constitutionalism Montesquieu propounds.[37] Finally, while it is not clear what knowledge of English courts and jurisprudence he gained during his stay in England from 1729 to 1731—his travel journal was lost or destroyed—it is known that he later met and regularly corresponded with Charles Yorke, son of the then Lord Chancellor and later Chancellor himself. Montesquieu's notebooks contain important remarks on what he discussed with this "very celebrated barrister" about courts, law, and lawyers, apparently during a visit by Yorke after publication of *The Spirit of the Laws*:

> M. Yorke tells me that a foreigner could not understand a single word in milord Cook and in Littleton; I tell him that I have observed that, with regard to the feudal laws and ancient laws of England, they do not seem to me very difficult to understand, no more than those of all the other nations, because, all the laws of Europe are gothic, they all have the same origin and are of the same nature; that on the contrary modern laws and jurisprudence are difficult to understand, because the times and circumstances of things have changed the gothic law in each country, and because that law everywhere takes the measure of one country and has changed like the political laws. He agrees with this.[38]

Montesquieu's extensive examination of the origins and evolutions of Franco-German law in the final books of *The Spirit of the Laws* confirms this private notation on the Gothic root shared by English common law and French law. Nonetheless, his published references to the feudal laws and ancient laws of England are rare. He does cite Coke's predecessor Littleton (d. 1481) in the penultimate chapter of *The Spirit of the Laws* (31.33, 993 n. *b*). However, the reference is to a lesser-known work, not to Littleton's treatise on feudal tenures, the basic work of the English common law of property, known as the *Tenures nouelli*; Coke's commentary on this, known even to the American founders as "Coke-Littleton," begins Coke's own classic work, the *Institutes*. In two other unpublished notations, Montesquieu records his intention to purchase classic common-law treatises by Bracton (d. 1268) and Fortescue, including *In Praise of the Laws of England*.[39] A fuller understanding of why Montesquieu's jurisprudence seemingly approximates but largely ignores the common law requires examination of his treatment of Franco-Germanic laws and of a juridical prudence in the closing books of *The Spirit of the Laws*, but a brief comparison with Hobbes and Locke prompts some conjectures by itself. In his conversation with Yorke, he characteristically suggests that Gothic law transforms itself in each particular country, taking on a new, ever-developing spirit and bewildering variety among each people. This hardly seems justification for overlooking English common law, since Montesquieu seems to makes good on his announcement in the Preface of the work's "infinite" scope, given his citations to peoples and laws spanning the available literature on diverse continents and centuries. The suitability of common-law judging to Montesquieu's purposes, his private recognition of a shared Gothic root, and his earlier travels to England and friendship with a future Lord Chancellor suggest a silence more deliberate than accidental. The provenance of the common law is, after all, partly Scholastic and Aristotelian. Beyond Fortescue's *In Praise of the Laws of England*, this is evident in the text targeted by Hobbes, Saint Germain's *Doctor and Student*, which opens by paraphrasing Aquinas's fourfold classification of divine, eternal, natural, and positive law.[40] The "artificial reason," the developed prudence or judgment, exercised by the common-law mind ultimately understands itself both as customary and as rooted in natural truth or justice, even though English common law distinguishes itself from Scholastic natural law.[41] Common law seeks right reason and natural justice through the common-law mode of refining customs and precedents and by discerning right in particular cases. Its attention to particulars and precedents, so different from the code of Roman or civil law, suits Montesquieu. However, neither a root in natural law nor a prudence understood as the legal perfection of nature's right reason fits the spirit of his modern, liberal science.

Montesquieu departs from the classic common law because of his moderately liberal notions of nature and human nature, which in turn inform his distinctive jurisprudence and constitutionalism. His humane, softer conceptions of moderation and natural right directly guide his new versions of constitutionalism, jurisprudence, and judging. Nonetheless, his serious investigation of nature as the basis for understanding people and politics distinguishes him from later liberal political philosophers, certainly from the recent liberal theory of Rawls and Dworkin. This orientation by nature explains the fundamental importance of constitutionalism and the separation of powers in his liberalism, and it precludes the possibility that his project to elevate judicial power sought to have it replace the others. For Montesquieu, the idea that any power, even judging, could rule absolutely does not square with our nature.

Similarly, his new conception of moderation marries institutional with moral aims. The moderating of moral and political expectations in this new jurisprudence is evident in his advice for reform about suicide, which English common law flatly condemned. In climates that dispose men toward such remedies for their personal ills, the laws should stop moralizing and simply leave people alone (14.12–13). While Coke and his predecessors employ an Aristotelian practical science, Montesquieu originates the efforts by modern social science to achieve a neutral, objective understanding of any particular phenomena, even if only of its contextual meaning and social import.[42] On the basis of his liberal conception of human nature, Montesquieu would use the moderating influences of independent judging and juridical complexity to secure both individual tranquillity and a peaceful sociability. The natural desire, and right, to tranquillity requires a judging power attuned to our sentiments and attachments, paring from the law any frightful implications of a legal prudence informed by classical and medieval moral philosophy. Montesquieu's distinctive conception of the judging power is both a standard for and quiet engine of his transition from the theory and practice of both ancient and early modern politics to his more complex, moderate liberalism.

The Moderation of Monarchy and a Judicial Depository of the Laws

A fundamental concern of *The Spirit of the Laws* is that political extremes had often dominated the great European powers during the seventeenth and eighteenth centuries—from the republican absolutism of Cromwell that Montesquieu saw just beneath the surface in England to the monarchical absolutism of the French Bourbons. One of Montesquieu's favored models for restoring a moderate constitutional politics in Europe was France's *parlements*, the regional bodies of nobles who exercised judicial and administrative functions even after feudalism ended. He knew their strengths and weaknesses intimately, and thought their independence and legal prudence could check either the populist extreme within republicanism or the autocratic extreme within monarchy. To Montesquieu, these extremes tended to reinforce each other, swinging the scale of authority from one lopsided position to the other, while the independent, moderating role of courts and a legal profession were mostly overlooked.

Republican voices in France associated the *parlements* with the monarchy and unjust privilege, temporarily replacing them just prior to the French Revolution and abolishing them after 1789. Monarchical voices in both France and England, on the other hand, suspected independent courts of weakening a central administrative authority. Montesquieu's own view is closer to that of the noble, parliamentary revolt against monarchical absolutism in seventeenth-century France known as the Fronde, and to the judicial independence from both crown and parliament asserted by Coke in seventeenth-century England. His failure to associate himself explicitly with either the Fronde or Coke thus seems deliberate. He seeks the advantages of independent courts without a moralizing jurisprudence, and a check upon the monarchy without defending other, less defensible noble privileges. The liberal spirit of Montesquieu's political science uses these traditional judicial institutions both to analyze and to moderate despotic rule of all kinds, whether classical political philosophy or a pure republicanism, Biblical judgment or Bourbon absolutism.

The first significant discussion of judging comes early in *The Spirit of the Laws*, in the first treatment of monarchy, and Montesquieu uses the occasion to plant essential themes for the work. Monarchy is constituted not by royal power but by "[i]ntermediate, subordinate, and dependent powers," a government in which "one alone governs by fundamental laws" (2.4, 247). If it were governed by "the momentary and capricious will of one alone," it would be a despotism, for in such a case "nothing can be fixed and consequently there is no fundamental law" (2.4, 247; 2.1, 239). The "most natural intermediate, subordinate power" in a monarchy is, therefore, the nobility, the power or order that is "the essence of a monarchy" by ensuring royal obedience to law (2.4, 247). In this early discussion of separation of powers, the only function ascribed to the nobles is their judicial power, "the *justices* of the lords," understood as both the feudal right and the institution whereby nobles judged certain crimes and disputes apart from royal power (see 30.20, 919). He observes that, if England has abolished such noble privileges, as well as ecclesiastical and local ones, then it is essentially a republic. When a monarchy abolishes such privileges, "you will soon have a popular state or else a despotic state." The English have "removed all the intermediate powers that formed their monarchy" so as to "favor liberty," and they are "quite right to preserve that liberty," or "they would be one of the most enslaved peoples of the earth" (2.4, 247–48). Only later in the work does he indicate the extremism of such changes. England is "a nation where the republic hides under the form of a monarchy," and there one "would often see the form of an absolute government over the foundation of a free government." It is, indeed, the "one nation in the world whose constitution has political liberty for its direct purpose" (5.19, 304; 19.27, 580; 11.5, 396). His initial remark, however, is only that they are right to preserve that liberty, not that abolition of noble judging is the correct means. When later discussing the legal simplicity that defines despotism, he lists Cromwell's England alongside Caesar's Rome (6.2, 310). This distinction between England and traditional monarchies is part of Montesquieu's persistent effort to bring moderation to politics, given his concern with the revolutionary bent of doctrinaire republicanism. Monarchic absolutism thus is bad both in its own right and because of the violent reaction it provokes. He also warns, about an unnamed monarchy, that for "several centuries" royal magistrates have been unjustly attacking the traditional noble and ecclesiastical courts, and he wonders "to what extent the constitution can be changed in this way" (2.4, 247–48). This foreshadows the closing argument of the work—that complex, moderate government arose naturally, so to speak, over many centuries in France, making Bourbon absolutism the historical novelty (books 28, 30, 31). A separation and balancing of powers in a constitutional equilibrium is, given the right conditions or necessities, the most natural or historically prevalent form of government for certain peoples, especially in Europe. Throughout the work Montesquieu suggests that the judicial power is, over time, an important agent in this process of separating and balancing, and that it is the crucial institution for maintaining such a constitutionalism.

The early parts of *The Spirit of the Laws* establish a pattern for the work that links the themes of moderation, judging, separated powers, and prevention of despotism. Montesquieu anticipates the doctrine of the separation of powers famously discussed in book 11 in his early discussions of monarchies, and in a series of warnings about the need for intermediate orders or bodies to keep monarchy from sliding toward despotism (8.6–9). This makes separation of powers, not republicanism, the essential corollary of moderate government, which in turn is the key to liberty. His first discussion of judging establishes these themes by defending the *parlements* (2.4). The *Parlement de Paris*, the greatest of these French assemblies of nobles, began in the twelfth and thirteenth centuries as a royal court and particularly as a court of appeal. Until 1790 it remained the central law court of the monarchy.[43] Montesquieu emphasizes both its negative, oppositional nature and its long historical development by initially referring to "intermediate, *subordinate*, and dependent powers," and then eventually calling them "intermediate ranks" and "political bodies." The thrust of his discussion clearly becomes the role of independent judging, and he declares that "[i]t is not enough to have intermediate ranks in a monarchy; there must also be a depository of laws" (2.4, 247, 249; emphasis added). He develops this theme of judges as a *dépôt de lois* in books 3, 5, 6, 20, and 28, making this a defining aspect of his judicial power and of *The Spirit of the Laws* itself. His analysis of the judging functions given to the upper legislative house in England's constitution also indicates that he does not confine this judicial role to monarchies strictly or traditionally understood (see 11.6, 404). William Blackstone later paraphrases Montesquieu by terming an independent judiciary a "depositary of the laws" and a bulwark of individual rights, and Blackstone's importance for American jurisprudence suggests that Montesquieu plants a seed of judicial review. Still, it is telling that the French jurist never explicitly contemplates such a power for judges. The initial account of judging in the work never questions the political limitations on its power, defining it as a legal depository in those "political bodies" independent of the king that "announce the laws when they are made" and "recall them when they are forgotten" (2.4, 249). In light of his historical inquiries into these matters later in the work, this clearly refers to *parlements* and to their rights of *enregistrement* and *remonstrance* (see 28.39, 855; 28.45, 864). *Parlements* could refuse to register a royal edict, and they could petition the king in objection to an edict.[44] Montesquieu provides numerous justifications for this institution, specifically for why it must be independent of the monarchy and why a distinct legal corps is needed within the nobility. He eventually defines this body and function as the depository of the *fundamental* laws. The stakes are high, since in "despotic states, where there are no fundamental laws, neither is there a depository of the laws," and his list of justifications grows lengthy:

> The ignorance natural to the nobility, its laxity, and its scorn for civil
> government require a body that without ceasing brings the laws
> out of the dust in which they would be buried. The prince's council
> is not a suitable depository. By its nature it is the depository of the
> momentary will of the prince who executes, and not the depository
> of the fundamental laws. Moreover, the monarch's council constantly
> changes; it is not permanent; it cannot be large; it does not sufficiently
> have the people's trust: therefore, it is not in a position to enlighten
> them in difficult times or to return them to obedience. (2.4, 249)[45]

These are properly judicial and not legislative duties, since they are passive and reactive limitations on sovereign power. While the depository function has some of the characteristics of the later American development of judicial review, it is not as institutionalized, regular, and bold as that power has become. Montesquieu further implies that a written constitution in itself is no panacea, for it is crucial to have the right qualities in those jurists who can and must interpret the law. This fundamental principle of a separation of distinct types of powers in constitutionalism distinguishes his jurisprudence from later conceptions of law, such as that of Oliver Wendell Holmes Jr., which fuse judging and legislating, law and raw politics.

In the early books of *The Spirit of the Laws*, leading up to the constitutionalism fully presented in books 11 and 12, Montesquieu continues this praise for the moderating power of monarchical judging. It becomes clear that this pillar of his constitutionalism also is a weapon in his critique not only of autocratic despotism but of the moral despotism in classical republican virtue and classical political philosophy. A judicial depository of laws, in tempering monarchical executive power, embodies the balance and complexity that are "the excellence" of monarchy (5.10). Monarchies can avoid the cycle of despotism and popular revolution only through such "intermediate dependent powers," and he cites Cicero's comparison of them to Tribunes of the people who, in revolutionary moments, possess the "prudence and authority" to propose compromises and restore the rule of law (5.11, 290–91). Such moderate government has a good civil order or *police*, milder than the republicanism of Plato or Lycurgus, because it respects the everyday passions and ambitions characteristic of commercial monarchies (4.5–8).[46] Montesquieu describes a despotism not only of fear but also of virtue, which paves the way for his moderate alternative, a constitutional, commercial monarchy that mixes aristocratic and republican elements. A judicial depository of laws in such a regime can best protect each individual's natural feelings for security and tranquil sociability, a theme he develops early in the work through his liberal redefinition of honor, the principle or motivating passion of monarchy. For Montesquieu honor actually is "ambition," a demand for "preferences and distinctions," and therefore, "[s]peaking philosophically," it is a "false honor."[47] It animates politics by freeing all the passions, but "like the system of the universe," the action and reaction of competing passions keeps the whole order in balance. This argument, that "each person works for the common good, believing he works for his individual interest," anticipates Adam Smith's theories of a spontaneous moral order (3.7, 257).[48] Montesquieu tempers the brutal moral realism of Machiavelli with the milder, more scientific views of Bernard de Mandeville on mutually beneficial selfishness, in order to teach that such private vices can become public virtues.[49] A politics of enlightened self-interest cloaked as honor accords best with nature, since the opposing despotisms of fear and virtue exact too great a toll upon human nature and individual security.

Shortly after these remarks Montesquieu affirms his new conception of natural right, thereby tempering the Hobbesian and Lockean emphasis on self-preservation and natural liberty. These are legitimate in themselves, but they should also be means for securing "natural feelings" such as "respect for a father, tenderness for one's children and women, laws of honor, or the state of one's

health" (3.10, 260). Such a natural right is neither as base and harsh as that
of Hobbes, nor as high and rational as that of classical and medieval political
philosophy. It concerns the propriety of providing for our basic passions and
interests—neither our lowest nor highest, but rather our humane, middling
ones—in as mutually beneficial a manner as possible. A political philosophy of
moderation points to a cloaking of power, since the institution discussed above
all others as a moderating influence is the judicial depository of laws. Holmes
noted that these themes from *The Spirit of the Laws* already characterized the
Persian Letters, and he cites the definition there of the "government most conformed to reason" and "most perfect" as one that "attains its goal with the least
friction," thereby "lead[ing] men along paths most agreeable to their interests
and inclinations."[50] It is fitting that Montesquieu closes the subsequent discussion of how all the laws "should be" and prepares for his extended analysis of
judging in book 6 by arguing that even such seemingly corrupt practices in
monarchies as selling of offices can promote individual tranquillity and liberty
(5.19). A hereditary nobility is not suited for a judicial role if it is not artifi-
cially invigorated by the fresh talent made available through advancement of
the ambitious *nouveaux riches*. These arguments effectively defend the French
parlements and their mixed hereditary lordships, some anciently held and some
recently purchased. Later in the work he heaps praise upon just such a *noblesse
de robe* in his first book on commerce, since the pattern in which merchants
come to wealth and purchase these offices is among the best consequences of
a mercantile civilization (20.22). As the argument of *The Spirit of the Laws* ad-
vances, Montesquieu develops his constitutionalism of separated powers more
through such praise of juridical complexity than through any other theme in
his analysis of humankind and politics.

two

Moderate and Juridical Government:
The Spirit of Constitutional Liberty

Montesquieu's efforts early in *The Spirit of the Laws* to redefine honor and natural right and to quietly elevate judicial power point to a complex constitutionalism that elevates civil law in relation to political law. In properly moderate regimes, the civil and criminal laws affecting individuals should have equal status with the public law of governmental powers and interests. A complex judging power becomes the crux of his moderate constitutionalism because its rules and procedures stymie excesses of raw power, or of high idealism, that could damage individual interests and tranquillity. The first extended analysis of judicial power in the work, in book 6, argues that the power most attuned to individual interests helps to keep all power operating along the lines of mutual self-interest and self-restraint. The full exposition of his constitutionalism, presented in and around his analysis of the English constitution in book 11, develops these seeds. For Montesquieu, judging is not so much a potent mechanism in itself as a safety valve, the key to avoiding political extremes. This invisible power and the moderation it helps to achieve lie at the heart of his constitutionalism and new spirit of laws.

Due Process, Complexity, and Juridical Liberty

Montesquieu's exhaustive analysis in book 6 of the relative complexity of civil and criminal laws in various governments contrasts with the Benthamite argument, predominant since the nineteenth century, for revising laws to achieve a uniform legal code. He traces the essential moderation of monarchy to the complexity of its laws and judicial procedures, known in Anglo-American law as due process, or civil and criminal procedure. The analysis here summarizes themes from earlier books, encapsulating a jurisprudence in a few lines. Monarchies, unlike despotism, must have courts, which give decisions, and "these decisions should be preserved; they should be learned, so that one judges there today as one judged yesterday and so that the property and life of the citizens are as secure and fixed as the very constitution of the State." This is because in monarchies such courts decide "not only about life and goods, but also about honor," and this "requires scrupulous inquiries," such that the "fastidiousness of the judge grows in proportion as he is a greater depository, and as he pronounces upon greater interests." Such states contain, therefore, "so many rules, restrictions, extensions, which multiply particular cases, and seem to make an art of reasoning itself" (6.1, 307). Montesquieu specifies this beneficial complexity of civil laws and adjudication in a properly complex way—by enumerating the different kinds of property, the various laws and customs permitted in different provinces, the occasional need for legislators to correct or make uniform the decisions of different courts, and the numerous issues that arise from the differing privileges and honors of individuals in a monarchy (6.1, 307–9). Such complexities in monarchical judging embody an art of legal reasoning, a description that echoes Coke's definition of English common law and its reasoning. An Aristotelian tradition that refines prudential and moral judgment differs, however, from a social science that views discrete acts and cases as part of a "spirit" of law, a spirit that well may need humane reform. Montesquieu's candid remarks on litigation develop these themes. In despotisms shorn of judicial protections for individual security, the lawyerly sophisms of "disputes and proceedings" are of no use, and "pleaders are mistreated" because "the injustice of their petition appears baldly, being neither hidden, mitigated, nor protected by an infinity of laws" (6.1, 309; see 28.35). Montesquieu harbors no illusions about the character of such litigants or the injustices they perpetrate. These "formalities of justice" pose "difficulties" to the just cause and often deny the victim "satisfaction," and as a matter of justice one would "doubtless find the formalities too many." However, with regard to "the liberty and security of the citizens," one would "often find them too few." In reality, "the penalties, expenses, delays, and even the dangers of justice are the price each citizen pays for liberty" (6.2, 310).

This line of argument redefines justice, perhaps the central concept of politics and political philosophy, just as his 1757 "Notice" to the work indicates his intention to redefine virtue. Justice as right primarily should mean administration of proper procedures, since these forms and formalities protect the security and tranquillity of individuals.[1] Such criticisms early in the work indicate that, while Montesquieu endorses complex conceptions of judging and law, he does so with open eyes. Such thoughts call to mind recent complaints in America about excessive litigation as "the death of common sense," for impeding commerce and efficiency, but Montesquieu's warnings point to deeper themes in his constitutionalism. They anticipate his praise in books 11 and 12 for a balance between monarchical and republican judging, or complex and simple modes of jurisprudence. A call for balance does not weaken his fundamental praise for a monarchical spirit of judging, but it does suggest doubts about the kind of judge-centered constitutionalism propounded by Oliver Wendell Holmes Jr., and more recently by John Rawls and Ronald Dworkin. For Montesquieu, separation of powers is crucial to avoiding political extremes, and no power can go unchecked if the aim is to preserve moderation and liberty. In this spirit of balance or moderation, he praises the protections for property, honor, and commerce typical of monarchies as a friendly soil for the growth of modern liberal constitutions, while bluntly warning republicanism about juridical simplicity and despotism:

> [W]hen a man makes himself more absolute,* his first thought is to simplify the laws. In these States he begins by being struck more by the particular inconveniences than by the liberty of the subjects, with which he is not concerned.
>
> One can see that there must be at least as many formalities in republics as in monarchies. In both governments, formalities increase in proportion to the importance given to the honor, fortune, life, and liberty of the citizens. (6.2, 310–11)
>
> * Caesar, Cromwell, and so many others.

Montesquieu amplifies these themes by turning from the simplicity of civil and criminal laws to the form of judgments and then, in the bulk of the book, to the establishment and character of penalties. The complex judging typical of a moderate monarchy, attuned to the false honor of individual interests and claims, is a depository of those formalities of justice that are "the thing in the world most important for men to know" (6.2, 310). Such complexity and moderation in the laws requires an effectively independent judicial power, yet one not so powerful as to pose its own threat to balance and liberty. The rule of law, the bulwark for liberty against despotism, will only exist if judging is separated from the passions of the sovereign and is guided by judgment under law (6.3–8). His first argument in this vein distinguishes judging according to the letter of the law from judging according to its spirit (6.3). In criminal cases republicanism lies at the extreme of no judicial discretion, and despotism lies at the other of total discretion for the despot; it is monarchy that holds the middle. Monarchies embody a complex relationship with law, for "when it is precise, the judge follows it; when it is not, he seeks its spirit" (6.3, 311). Montesquieu must address, however, the apparent juridical protections for liberty in republics, such as those of ancient Rome and modern England:

> In republican government, it is in the nature of the constitution for judges to follow the letter of the law. There is no citizen against whom one can interpret a law, when it is a question of his goods, of his honor, or of his life.
>
> In Rome, judges pronounced only that the accused was guilty of a certain crime, and the penalty was found in the law, as can be seen from various laws that were made. Likewise, in England, the jury decides whether the accused is guilty or not of the deed brought before it; and, if he is declared guilty, the judge pronounces the penalty that the law imposes for this deed: and, for that, he needs only his eyes. (6.3, 311)

By removing the discretion of judges and making them equally subordinate to law, republics maintain the spirit of equality and, by preventing arbitrary judgments, protect security and liberty. By comparing the juridical simplicity in republics and despotisms, however, Montesquieu suggests that, while there is no interpretation *against* citizens in republics, there can be no interpretation *for* them either—no moderating of the law's requirements. Our jurist observes that, in monarchies, "judges assume the manner of arbiters; they deliberate together, they share their thoughts, they come to an agreement; one modifies his opinion to make it like another's; opinions with the least support are incorporated into the two most widely held" (6.4, 312). Such judicial reasoning and discussion "is not in the nature of a republic," for "the people is no jurist [*jurisconsulte,* person learned in the law]"; thus, "the modifications and temperings of arbiters are not for them." In the Roman republic, "the state of the question had to be fixed in order for the people to keep it before their eyes," for otherwise, "in the course of a great lawsuit, the state of the question would continually change, and be no longer recognizable" (312). Genuine judging, which seems "to make an art of reasoning itself," occurs in governments where judges have some independence and discretion—some distinctive learning and status apart from both king and people (6.1). Montesquieu emphasizes this by linking the collegial deliberation and reasoning of monarchical judges with their capacity to moderate the law, to judge according to the spirit of its letter. Roman judges originally accepted "only the precise suit," but the more learned judges, the praetors, "imagined other maxims or rules for lawsuits, which were called *in good faith*" and in which "the manner of pronouncing was more at the disposition of the judge." This mode was "more in agreement with the spirit of monarchy," and learned French jurists still say, "*In France, all actions are in good faith*" (6.4, 312; emphasis in original, notes omitted).

Montesquieu connects these themes to his fundamental constitutional teaching on the separation of powers by examining the relationship between sovereignty and judging (6.5). He cites Socrates, Plato, Cicero, Tacitus, and Machiavelli in the course of arguing that the sovereign power in any government, whether the people or the king, should never judge if it aims to avoid despotism and secure the liberty and tranquillity of each citizen. This marks his only explicit reference in *The Spirit of the Laws* or even the *Considerations on the Romans* to Machiavelli's *Discourses on Livy,* although both of Montesquieu's works are indebted to Machiavelli's treatment of the Romans and, in particular, Roman republican faction.[2] Montesquieu carefully adopts and, for the most part, quietly moderates Machiavelli's bold new teachings, and he also moderates their legacy in earlier liberalism. *The Spirit of the Laws* cautiously accepts what the *Considerations* openly embraced: that factional dispute between the many and the few is both essential to and good for republicanism. The occasion for finally citing the *Discourses* is, however, a dispute with Machiavelli's populist conception of republican judicial power:

> Machiavelli* attributes the loss of liberty in Florence to the fact that the people did not judge as a body, as in Rome, the crimes of high treason committed against them. . . . I would gladly adopt the maxim of this great man; but as in these cases political interest forces, so to speak, civil interest (for it is always a drawback if the people judge themselves their offenses), it is necessary, in order to remedy this, that the laws provide, as much as they can, for the security of individuals. (6.5, 313)

> * *Discourses on the First Decade of Titus-Livy,* bk. 1, ch. 7.

Machiavelli had noted the ill consequences for Florence of the fact that "the multitude was not able to vent its animus in an ordered way against one of its citizens." He defends popular accusations, particularly the accusation and exile of the nobleman Coriolanus, when endorsing republican faction as a means to Rome's imperial expansion.[3] Montesquieu does not reject all of Machiavelli's teachings on faction, but he does moderate them so as to provide greater protection for individual security and tranquillity. The point is so important that, after disputing Machiavelli, he calls upon a famous cast of ancients for support. He then dramatically invokes "the constitution," a term rarely used before book 11, to underscore his own view:

> In despotic States, the prince himself can judge. He cannot judge in monarchies: the constitution would be destroyed, the intermediate dependent powers, annihilated: one would see all the formalities of judgments cease; fear would invade all spirits; one would see pallor on every face; no more trust, no more honor, no more love, no more security, no more monarchy. (6.5, 314)

To inculcate the proper prudence about these themes Montesquieu offers "reflections" on particular practices, and these anticipate further concerns about the need for moderation in the judicial power, especially in books 11, 12, and 29. He echoes his early discussion of the depository of laws by recounting a remonstrance by the Comte de Montrésor, president of a French *parlement,* against a decision by King Louis XIII to personally judge a nobleman. The judgment eventually was changed, and the moral of the story is that "[j]udgments rendered by the prince would be an inexhaustible source of injustices and abuses" (6.5, 315). Another reflection revives a theme from the *Considerations,* that "[s]ome of the Roman emperors had a passion for judging" and that "no reigns stunned the universe more by their injustices" (6.5, 315).[4] He again notes, however, abuses of power and threats to individual security arising from republican judging. The decemvir Appius Claudius effectively ruled the Roman republic as a "single magistrate," making it a "despotic government" (6.7, 316–17; see 11.15). Montesquieu then recommends the "admirable" monarchical institution of public prosecutor as a corrective to accusation by citizens. Whether populist judging is motivated by Machiavellian faction and ambition or by Platonic virtue, he declares it despotic (6.8, 317; see 11.18–20).

Having endorsed the judicial moderation achieved by legal complexity and the separation of judging and sovereignty, Montesquieu turns to reform of penalties and punishments, a subject so close to his spirit that he treats it again in book 12. He contrasts the severity of penalties characteristic in despotisms with the "mildness" that "reigns in moderate governments," the latter being "monarchies and republics" (6.9, 318–19). He also links these moderate states, their mild penalties, and liberty: "[I]n all or nearly all the States of Europe, penalties have decreased or increased in proportion as one has approached or departed from liberty" (318–19). Mild penalties also are just as effective in addressing crime. In "moderate states, love of homeland, shame, and fear of blame are motives that serve as restraints and so can check many crimes"; their "civil laws will make corrections more easily and will not need as much force." The "good legislator," therefore, "will insist less on punishing crimes than on preventing them; he will apply himself more to giving mores than to inflicting punishments" (318–19). While republics and monarchies share "moderate" penal codes, there is a zealotry in republics that in fact makes them more akin to despotisms. Mediocrity in morals and manners, leading to mild expectations for human conduct and the passions, yields mildness in punishments. He declares such moderation to be most in accord with "human nature," with "moderate government," and with "liberty"—a coincidence of fundamental concepts that drives home his point.

When he suggests that a virtuous people needs few penalties, the implicit premise is his redefinition of virtue as a middling state between the severity of classical virtue and the violence of despotism (6.11, 320; see 11.18). On this basis he formulates a principle of moderate punishment: "Men must not be led by extreme blows; one should manage the means that nature gives us to guide them. . . . Let us follow nature, which has given men shame for their scourge, and let the greatest part of the penalty be the infamy of suffering it" (6.12, 321). Aristotle's more demanding ethics explicitly excluded shame from the moral virtues, since those who have formed proper character would avoid shameful acts.[5] Montesquieu dilutes the meaning of "shame," just as he has "honor," to make it a useful tool for his humane reformation of criminal law. These references to mores once again give new meanings to old and important words, so as to reshape man and politics. He exploits the ambiguity of *moeurs*, which denotes either morals in the sense of morality or manners in the sense of customs, to emphasize not virtue but the middling customs of various peoples. People of proper mores do not need severe punishments because they are not wicked, and—given Montesquieu's readjustment of moral expectations—few people are wicked.[6] This effort to reform not just criminal punishments but also the mores of peoples and their governments extends even to despotisms (see 12.29, "Putting a Little Liberty in Despotic Government"). From the beginning of the work, Montesquieu has indicated his intention to be a modern Solon or Plato, since seeking to "instruct" even despotic rulers is to "practice the general virtue that comprehends love of all" ("Preface," 230). The impotence of Japan's despotic punishments stems from the fact that "almost all crimes are punished by death." Even lying to a magistrate earns this, a penalty "contrary to natural defense" (6.13, 322; see 12.14; 26.3–4). These "opinionated, capricious, determined, eccentric people" are accustomed to, not deterred by, such "atrocious laws." He turns from admonition to remarkable advice about the stealth through which rulers of such a government should work to moderate both laws and mores:

> A wise legislator would have sought to lead men's spirits back by a
> just tempering of penalties and rewards; by maxims of philosophy,
> of morality, and of religion, matched to this character; by the just
> application of the rules of honor; by the torment of shame; by the
> enjoyment of a constant happiness and a mild tranquillity; and, if he
> had feared that these spirits, accustomed to being checked only by a
> cruel penalty, could no longer be checked by a mild one, he would
> have acted* in a secret and imperceptible manner; he would have, in
> the most pardonable particular cases, moderated the penalty for the
> crime, until he could come to modify it in every case. (6.13, 323)

> * Observe this well as a practical maxim in cases where spirits have been
> corrupted by overly rigorous penalties.

This advice to the wise legislator embodies Montesquieu's fusion of moderation and prudence in *The Spirit of the Laws*. Rarely in the work is he so blunt in teaching about subtle reform. In the immediate sequel, though, he remarks that "despotism does not know these means (*ressorts*); it does not lead in these ways." This advice might be aimed, then, not so much at reformers in despotisms but at those in moderate states who quietly work to improve criminal justice. While the audience appears to be legislators, in fact this is one of Montesquieu's first indications that subtle judges should work to reform criminal justice and thereby the very character of government. In criticizing ignorance of such moderate *ressorts,* he employs a term he usually reserves for the "springs" or activity of a government, but in this context the phrasing alludes to judging and jurisdiction, as in the phrase *en dernier ressort,* a court of last appeal or last resort.[7] A still clearer allusion to judging arises when considering the reforms to be undertaken so imperceptibly. An executive or kingly power might pardon a crime, or equitably moderate an assigned punishment. Such clemency can be scandalous, but if an act of clemency was genuine, then why wouldn't an executive seek some credit for it? A judge better fits this description of imperceptibly determining which cases are most pardonable and then imperceptibly moderating the penalty. Montesquieu never identifies himself in *The Spirit of the Laws* as having been a senior judge who mostly presided in the Chambre de la Tournelle, the criminal court, of the Bordeaux Parlement. Still, the work reveals an authority or command on juridical topics unavailable to someone not a jurist, while nonetheless giving no indication that its philosophical teachings aim at anything less than universal truth.

Montesquieu's analysis in book 6 closes as it began, recommending moderation, but now in the form of a just proportion between penalties and crimes, mildness and severity (6.16). He cannot even bring himself to speak of the

cruelty and torture to which "slaves among the Greeks and Romans" were subjected in criminal cases, for he hears "the voice of nature crying out against
me" (6.17, 329). In discussing torture in cases of high treason, he explicitly
contrasts classical republicanism with "the English nation," a "nation very well
policed," which does not use torture in prosecuting any crimes (6.17, 329 and
nn. a–b; see 12.18–19; 29.11). A modern republic or constitution that arises
out of a moderate monarchy is superior in this crucial respect to Athens and
Rome. Similarly, Europe's medieval barbarians are a better model than classical
republicans, since "[o]ur fathers the Germans" almost always used mild and
monetary penalties, praise that anticipates his arguments about the Gothic origins of European constitutional liberty (6.17, 329 n. b; 6.18, 329–30; see 11.6;
11.8). To better inculcate moderation, he formulates a maxim: "A good legislator takes a golden mean (un juste milieu); he does not always order pecuniary
penalties; he does not always inflict corporal penalties" (6.18, 330). He then
phrases the sequel broadly enough to include executive and judicial roles in
reforming both laws and the administration of criminal justice: "But, one will
ask, when is one to punish? when to pardon? This is something which is better
sensed than prescribed" (6.21, 332). Here and throughout *The Spirit of the Laws*
Montesquieu counsels gradual, evolutionary reform of particular political systems to achieve moderation and greater individual security, not revolutionary
imposition of a universal blueprint. If he wrote this work "only to prove" that
"the spirit of moderation should be that of the legislator," then wise legislators
should increase the prominence of judging in politics (29.1). They also should
encourage judges to imperceptibly reform the administration of justice, which
in turn can reform the whole spirit of politics.

Constitutionalism and Separation of Powers

Montesquieu presents his liberal constitutionalism in books 11 and 12 of *The
Spirit of the Laws*, with the fundamental theme being the liberty and security
of individuals. This is more explicitly so in book 12 than it is in the preceding
analysis of institutional structures to secure political liberty, but an independent
judging power is crucial in both books. This novel institutional teaching arises
because of Montesquieu's new definition of liberty. Earlier books praised a depository of the laws for being attentive to individual interests and liberty. The
definition of liberty as tranquillity early in his widely read study of England's
constitution reaffirms the call for just such a power: "Political liberty in a citizen
is that tranquillity of spirit which comes from the opinion each one has of his
security; and in order for him to have this liberty, the government must be
such that one citizen cannot fear another citizen" (11.6, 397). Montesquieu's

doctrine of separation or distribution of powers aims to secure this individual tranquillity, and early remarks in book 11 also imply that independent judging is the *sine qua non* of moderate constitutions.[8] He initially offers a terse statement on the separation of powers, one that presupposes the political science elaborated in the preceding ten books (11.4). To prepare for his examination of the only constitution devoted to political liberty, he suggests replacing the classical constitutionalism of virtue, as well as classical political philosophy, with a constitutionalism of liberty, moderation, and separation of powers. Neither democracy nor aristocracy inherently secure freedom; rather, "[p]olitical liberty is found only in moderate governments." Such moderation occurs "only when power is not abused; but it has eternally been observed that any man who has power is led to abuse it." The classical quest for the philosopher king is gravely mistaken: "Who would say it! even virtue has need of limits." These premises yield Montesquieu's classic argument for a distribution of powers: "So that one cannot abuse power, power must check power by the disposition of things. A constitution can be such that no one will be constrained to do things the law does not oblige him to do, or be kept from doing things the law permits him to do" (11.4, 395).

Moderation is the key to political liberty, with the key to moderation being the separation and balancing of political powers by an explicit constitution thereof. Virtue is displaced by security as the guide to politics, leaving the way open for a kind of Newtonian equilibrium among competing forces, passions, and reasonable views in politics. Book 11 therefore begins by assessing the various meanings of liberty: "No word has received more different significations and has struck minds in so many ways as has liberty" (11.2, 394).[9] Montesquieu seeks to correct the republican view that "ordinarily places liberty in republics and excludes it from monarchies," as well as the related prejudice for democracy in which "the power of the people has been confused with the liberty of the people" (11.2, 394).[10] He does not state that monarchy is by its nature free, but it alone naturally enjoys the moderation of a complex constitutional order, the essential precondition for liberty. From the first discussion of monarchical moderation in book 2, Montesquieu emphasizes the intermediate political bodies that check the monarch's power, especially the *parlement*, the judicial depository of political and civil laws. A complex constitutionalism thus provides liberty and moderation by mixing features of monarchy and republicanism—specifically, by blending the modern liberal doctrine of separation of powers with the classical notion of a balance of orders. Montesquieu further emphasizes the necessity of law and structure for liberty, and asserts that the natural home of such complex structures is not republicanism but monarchy. Genuine liberty secured by a balanced governmental structure is the aim: "It is true that in democracies the people seem to do what they want, but political liberty in no way consists in doing what one wants" (11.3, 395). A democratic people's "independence" from the constraint of law, either by sheer strength of numbers or by the passage of new laws to reflect the majority view, does not provide security and tranquillity for individuals: "Liberty is the right to do everything the laws permit; and if one citizen could do what they forbid, he would no longer have liberty because the others would likewise have the same power" (395). Earlier, when Montesquieu diagnosed the kinds of corruption likely in the traditional forms of government, he began his survey of self-inflicted modes of destruction with democracy. Of particular note was the corruption of a professional judicial power through populism. Democracy self-destructs "not only when the spirit of equality is lost but also when the spirit of extreme equality is taken up," when the people "want to do everything themselves: to deliberate for the senate, to execute for the magistrates, and to throw off (*dépouiller*) all the judges" (8.2, 349–50). *Dépouiller* also means "to disrobe," suggesting that extreme equality particularly rejects the nobility of the robe. Such judges, defined by their distinct learning and professional status, characterize monarchy more than republicanism, and Montesquieu again suggests the need to blend elements of the traditional regimes to attain a proper constitutional balance (see 8.3; 8.6). Still, even in his most thematic discussion of judicial power, in book 11, Montesquieu's characteristic moderation avoids the opposite extreme. He never mentions a formal power of constitutional review of the laws, a significant difference from the power of judicial review propounded by Alexander Hamilton and John Marshall. Although Montesquieu's is the most potent judicial power advocated in liberal political philosophy to that point, both in presentation and substance it adheres to the notion that stealth can enhance power.

When Montesquieu turns to study the English constitution, he begins not with England but with a further development of the theory of separation of powers (11.6). He defines the "three sorts of powers" that constitute "every state," and does so with characteristic complexity, offering three versions. The "three powers" initially are "legislative power, executive power about the things depending on the right of nations, and executive power about the things depending on civil right" (11.6, 396). He further defines the latter two and renames them: with the second the prince or magistrate "makes peace or war, sends or receives embassies, establishes security, and prevents invasions," while with the third "he punishes crimes or judges disputes between individuals. The last will be called the power of judging, and the former simply the executive power of the State" (396–97). The sequel defines liberty as tranquillity of spirit about one's security, and stipulates that "there is no liberty" if the legislative and executive powers are joined, since "one can fear" that "the same monarch or senate" that would make tyrannical rules would "execute them tyrannically." He further stipulates, "Nor is there liberty if the power of judging is not separate" from the legislative and executive powers. If judging were joined to legislating, "the power over the life and liberty of the citizens would be arbitrary, for the judge would be the legislator," and if it were joined to executing, "the judge could have the force of an oppressor" (397). Montesquieu then refines his formulation a final time, defining the powers as "that of making laws, that of executing public resolutions, and that of judging the crimes or the disputes of individuals." Executive power now covers both foreign and domestic "public resolutions," entailing a narrowed definition of judging. Judicial power is now only "judging" crimes or other disputes and not, as in the second definition, "punishing" them.

In this curious unfolding of a separation of powers doctrine, Montesquieu begins with Locke's formulation—legislative, domestic executive, foreign executive—but then reverses the order of the latter two and develops a distinct judging power. Since Locke effectively fuses his executive and federative powers, the only genuine difference between the theories is that Montesquieu separates "judging the crimes or disputes of individuals" from executive power.[11] This emphasizes a role for reason in the constitution and softens the Newtonian quality of the political dynamic. Montesquieu reinforces this prominence for judging in England's constitution when he shifts from general principles to specific examples. His analysis is oddly abstract at first, referring not to England but to "every state," and employing neither proper names nor examples until he mentions "the kingdoms of Europe," "the Turks," and "the Italian republics." These first examples in this important chapter concern the independence of judging from the other two powers, as the key to separation of powers, moderate government, and liberty. He declares that in most European monarchies, "the government is moderate because the prince, who has the first two powers, leaves the exercise of the third to his subjects." The Turks unite all three powers in their sultan, yielding "an atrocious despotism," while in the Italian republics, which also unite the powers, "there is less liberty than in our monarchies." He cites the Venetian use of state informers to prosecute those suspected of sedition, a "means as violent as in the government of the Turks" (11.6, 397). Only monarchies are moderate, for only there is the judging power independent. This qualifies the earlier statements about liberty and separation of powers, weakening the warning about fusing executive and legislative power while strengthening the declaration that there is no liberty without separate judging. Montesquieu fully endorses these qualifications at the chapter's close and in the sequel, stating that he does not want to "disparage other governments" or say that "this extreme political liberty should mortify those who have only a moderate one" (11.6, 407). He then addresses anew the topic of moderate liberty, arguing that the "monarchies we know" each have a "distribution" of the three powers which, while not identical to England's, nonetheless "more or less approach political liberty"—for "if these did not approach it, the monarchy would degenerate into despotism" (11.7, 408). For Montesquieu, the greatest concern is whether a government is moderate, not whether it has the traditional form of republic or monarchy.

Judging in the Constitution of Liberal Tranquillity

When Montesquieu finally addresses England itself, the tone of abstraction lingers as he discusses not how the English constitution is but how it "ought to" or "must" be (*devoir, falloir*). He addresses this tone only at the chapter's close: "It is not for me to examine whether at present the English enjoy this liberty or not. It suffices for me to say that it is established by their laws, and I seek no further" (11.6, 407). Still, his work will not emulate James Harrington's utopian *Commonwealth of Oceana* (1656), which Montesquieu criticizes as taking too much "trouble" to find liberty in the English constitution: "If it can be seen where it is, if it has been found, why seek it?" (11.6, 407; see 11.5, 396). This is not his first criticism of the abstractness of earlier liberal philosophy, and his efforts here seek to distinguish his philosophy from modern rationalism. He seeks the nature and "springs" of an actual constitution and their necessary consequences, and he frames this approach by initially examining the purpose of various states. There is "one nation in the world whose constitution has political liberty for its direct purpose" and he will "examine the principles on which this nation founds political liberty" (11.5, 396). For Montesquieu, an analysis of principles grasps the deeper reality of the English constitution, discerning how the constitution ought to be or is likely to be even if current practice diverges from this essence. This is especially relevant in the case of English judging, since he indicates the populist extreme it is capable of reaching.

The first topic of Montesquieu's analysis of England is, oddly, judging: "The power of judging (*la puissance de juger*) ought not to be given to a permanent senate" (11.6, 398). In all the preceding remarks he describes judging as the third power, and this shift compounds the further oddity that throughout the chapter he adopts a distinctive lexicon for this power. Much later he uses an adjectival form, as he always does with "legislative" and "executive" powers, referring to "the judicial order" (*l'ordre judiciaire*) and "judicial forms" (e.g., 28.23; 28.39). In book 11 and earlier, however, it is "the power of judging."[12] The reason for this becomes evident as the initial analysis of English judging unfolds:

The power of judging ought not to be given to a permanent senate, but ought to be exercised by persons drawn from the body of the people,* at certain times of the year, in the manner prescribed by law, to form a tribunal which lasts only as long as necessity requires.

In this fashion, the power of judging, so terrible among men, being attached neither to a certain estate, nor to a certain profession, becomes, so to speak, invisible and null. People do not continually have judges present to their view; and they fear the magistracy, not the magistrates. (11.6, 398)

* As in Athens.

If the distinctive aspect of Montesquieu's separation of powers and constitutionalism is the independence of the judging power, then that power's distinctive aspect, initially, is that it should be invisible and null. The terrible aspect of being judged might connote the Judgment Day or moral censure, although the context suggests the trauma of being hauled into court and losing life, liberty, or property. Either way, judgment can entail loss of the defining aspect of liberty for Montesquieu's political science—the tranquillity arising from a sense of one's security (11.6, 397). In a constitution devoted to liberty, only an independent yet invisible and null judging power ensures tranquillity by first ensuring moderation, rule of law, and separation of powers. Each individual must *feel* that he is being judged by law and offices, not by men and officers, since a particular estate or profession may be thought to have particular prejudices or biases. The second distinctive aspect of these initial remarks on English judging thus is its quite democratic mode. Judging ought to be performed by juries of citizens, "[a]s in Athens," not by a professional or noble judiciary.[13] Given Montesquieu's earlier discussions of judging, this suggests an English judging power more republican than monarchical. He avoids the words "judiciary" and "court," since both imply professional bodies and monarchical forms of judging, which in turn raise the terrifying possibility of abusive power. By selecting terminology that fits the supposed diffuseness of this third power, Montesquieu avoids the connotations so evident in Blackstone's description of the same constitution only two decades later. The paradox is that the *Commentaries on the Laws of England* is deeply indebted to Montesquieu, even while its account of English judging is more factually accurate than this emphatic portrayal of a juror-based power.

Montesquieu's putative justification for this democratic account is England's concern for individual security. His final analysis, however, is unflattering: "[T]his extreme political liberty should not mortify those who have only a moderate one. How could I say that, I who believe that the excess even of reason is not always desirable; and that men almost always accommodate themselves better to middles than to extremities?" (11.6, 407). His complete analysis of judging here and throughout book 11 in fact endorses a much less popular conception of judging, in accord with his critical remarks on popular judging in earlier books. In light of such passages, and his repeated pronouncements on moderation, Montesquieu appears to use juries not only to cloak the judging power but also to cloak professional judges. He prefers that subtle judges quietly persist in and shape liberal constitutions, just as Blackstone depicts them as doing in his less obscure, though hardly stentorian, treatment. Juries are, for Montesquieu, a kind of cloaking device.[14] Invisibility long has been understood as enhancing power, as is evident from Glaucon's tale of the ring of Gyges in Plato's *Republic*, and from its precursor in the *Persian Wars* of Herodotus. For Plato and Herodotus, these episodes bespeak the injustices that men will attempt when no one is looking.[15] Montesquieu, however, seeks to use the freedom of invisibility to achieve a justice defined by humane and tranquil ends, since such judges will imperceptibly mitigate the severity of the law. A cloaking of power quietly reforms the severe moral standards of either classical or Biblical justice.

After equating judging and juries, Montesquieu states that "in great accusations" the accused must pick the "judges" or at least have recourse to what Anglo-American jurisprudence terms a jury strike (11.6, 398). This example of due process confirms the necessity of juries: "The two other powers may rather be given to magistrates or to permanent bodies, because they are not exercised upon any one individual; the one being only the general will of the State, and the other, the execution of that general will" (399). These references to the general will while insisting upon trial by popular juries suggest a more complicated issue than first meets the eye. In his dispute with Machiavelli, Montesquieu criticizes partisan judging that is a tool of faction (6.5). The proper equilibrium of the passions in politics and the quasi-Newtonian balancing of governmental powers will not occur if people continually fear such a prospect. His analysis of the constitution of liberty initially stipulates rotating jurors, because the powers that form the general will and execute it should not be directed at individuals. An intermediate power, the judicial power that lies between arresting and punishing, can protect the individual will from the general will. The difficulty is that the people themselves represent a willful faction, as Machiavelli knew, and when judging an individual some animus can motivate them, as Machiavelli both knew and praised. Immediately after remarking that politics and governance are matters of will, Montesquieu indicates the first limits that should be placed on popular judging. If "the tribunals ought not to be fixed," the judgments certainly should be, so that "they are never anything but a precise text of the law." Judgments cannot be "the individual opinion of a judge," for then one would not know "precisely what engagements one has contracted." Similarly, judges must be "peers" of the accused, "so that it cannot get into his mind (*esprit*) that he has fallen into the hands of people inclined to do him violence" (11.6, 399).

This concern with mind or spirit reminds us that Montesquieu's political science speaks not of the classical or Biblical "soul," nor of spirit as divine inspiration, but of mind or spirit understood through scientific analysis of motions and relations.[16] In his constitutionalism the desire for tranquillity leads to the new notion of "self," which accords with a judicializing of politics that more adequately protects tranquillity. In his second analysis of England he reiterates that a constitutionalism of liberty entails the free motion and conflict of individuals, given the freedom of the passions there (19.27). In such a politics it is essential that these interactions be moderate, so that each can achieve as much security and tranquillity as possible. This requires a judging power equal to and independent of the visible powers, one diffusely, invisibly exercised in juries. It also requires, however, that the people as a faction not be able to burst the bounds of law.

When discussing legislative power, he again declares judging invisible but simultaneously provides it with a second, more institutional depository for its moderating functions. In a constitution of liberty there "ought to be" and "will be" a bifurcation of legislative power into a body for the people and a body for the nobles, since in any state "there are always some people who are distinguished by birth, *wealth*, or honors." This quietly echoes earlier remarks that favor a more republican, commercial aristocracy through the selling of noble offices, a practice Montesquieu himself undertook (11.6, 400–401; emphasis added; see also 5.19; 20.22). While justifying an upper house, he seems to replace the judging power with the nobles' legislative power as the third power in the system. This is the first clear sign of Montesquieu's shift from a modern view of the separation of powers to that of the classical mixed regime or balanced constitution: "Among the three powers of which we have spoken, that of judging is in some fashion null. There remain only two; and, as they need a power whose regulations temper them, that part of the legislative body composed of the nobles is quite appropriate for producing this effect" (11.6, 401). He reiterates this movement between modern and ancient versions of the "three powers" when summarizing "the fundamental constitution" of England: "As its legislative body is composed of two parts, the one will be chained to the other by their reciprocal faculty of vetoing. The two will be bound by the executive power, which will itself be bound by the legislative power." Such opposing structures might yield only gridlock, but since "by the necessary motion of things, they are constrained to move, they will be forced to move in concert" (11.6, 405). This necessary motion, which draws in part upon Newtonian law and Machiavellian necessity, dictates a constitutionalism of moderate faction. His subsequent remarks on the "concert" or "harmony" among the three powers therefore blend the ancient and modern definitions of these powers, denoting both functions and rival claims to rule (e.g., 11.8, 409; 11.12, 412–13; 11.19, 428). The apparent eclipse of the judging power by the legislature's upper house is one part of this complex treatment of constitutionally balanced powers.

After describing an executive power that contains several exceptions to the separation of legislative and executive powers, Montesquieu describes "three exceptions" to the separation of judging from legislative power, each founded on "the particular interests of" the accused (11.6, 404). There is no talk of judicial review, but these passages clearly endorse a skilled, prudent judging power. The putatively noble house of the legislature should judge in order to protect against popular faction and to exercise a greater discretion than is possible with juries. This strongly qualifies the republican conception of English judging he initially presented, blending republican with monarchical modes. This blending occurs in part through the implicit openness of a "noble" house whose members sell their offices and titles, thereby republicanizing a decrepit, hereditary body and injecting the energy and ideas of a new commercial class.[17] These three exceptions are striking, not least because the opening statement about judging in this constitution declared that it should not be given to a permanent senate (11.6, 398). The first exception develops the stipulation about judgment by peers, here called "the privilege of the least citizens of a free state" (399, 404). Nobles must be judged by the upper house of the legislature because "[g]reat men are always exposed to envy; and if they were judged by the people, they could be endangered" (404). The third exception also ensures such protection, since in popular accusations the people are an "interested party" represented by the lower house of the legislature, who will feel that someone has violated "the rights of the people" and committed "crimes" (404). These two restrictions on popular judging are Montesquieu's constitutional response to the Machiavellism of making the people prosecutor, judge, and jury. Posing these points in a series of rhetorical questions, Montesquieu's verdict brings to bear the power of his style: "No: it is necessary, in order to preserve the dignity of the people and the security of the individual" that the popular house prosecute before the jury of the upper house, since the latter "have neither the same interests nor the same passions" (404).

Montesquieu's full analysis of judicial power in England recommends, then, a mixture of the popular with the professional or "noble." Rotating juries make it both less terrible to the people and seemingly prevent its domination

by any one faction in this active, partisan constitution. Still, if liberty requires
such popular judging, it must be limited so as not to endanger that very liberty.
Having begun this analysis by citing Athens as a model of rotating juries, his
final words on judging here sound the opposite note. The third exceptional
exercise of judging by the upper house marks "the advantage of this government over most of the ancient republics," for it avoids the "abuse" that "the
people were at the same time both judge and accuser" (11.6, 398 n. *a*, 404).
The second, or middle, exception confirms that republican judging must be
modified in the direction of medieval and modern monarchy to secure liberty
and peace of mind for all: the upper house must have a broad, largely undefined
power of equity. The law, by definition both "clairvoyant and blind," might be
"too rigorous" in certain cases. Since citizen jurors are "but the mouth which
pronounces the words of the law," able to "moderate neither its force nor its
rigor," the upper house is "a necessary tribunal" once again: "it is for its supreme
authority to moderate the law in favor of the law itself, by pronouncing less
rigorously than the law" (11.6, 404). Montesquieu prescribes few bounds for
this "supreme authority," and even these vague limits imply judicial discretion
as to compliance itself. They do suggest a passive power confined to particular
cases, and his other discussions of criminal law and judicial procedure imply
further constraints on this equity power, such as the legislature's power to
pass a bill of attainder overriding a judgment. Even so, this second exception
establishes an appellate judging power for discretionary interpretation of the
law, to be exercised largely at the discretion of the upper house whenever a case
is appealed to it. This is a further crucial exception to the republican mode of
judging initially presented in the chapter, for it establishes a characteristically
monarchical capacity to judge according to the "spirit" of the law. The equity
power termed "necessary" in the English constitution seems greater, in fact,
than what Montesquieu earlier ascribed to monarchical judges, who follow the
law "when it is precise" and seek its spirit only when it is not. Here, he accords
the upper house supreme authority to judge in a way that moderates all laws,
precise or not, by finding the law's moderate spirit (6.3, 311; 11.6, 404).

The monarchical character imparted to judging in the constitution of liberty by these three exceptional grants, especially the central one, does not fit
easily with Montesquieu's initial treatment of English judging. This difficulty
calls to mind the very first discussion of judging in *The Spirit of the Laws*, which
remarks that England has transformed itself from a monarchy to a republic
by abolishing "the prerogatives of the lords, clergy, nobility, and towns," thus
removing "all the intermediate powers that formed their monarchy" (2.4, 247–
48). Because the later discussion of a judicial power in the upper house restores
what England was said to have removed, and given the many discussions of the

advantages for individual security of a complex, moderating, judicial depository of laws, Montesquieu's earliest discussion of judging seems to constitute a warning. The loss of monarchical judging in England could make it "a popular state or else a despotic state," and subsequent remarks on Caesar, Cromwell, and Machiavelli—and about "throwing off" independent judges—indicate that, for Montesquieu, purely popular governments are at least potentially despotic. The early analysis of judicial power is the first of many warnings about the danger of despotism stemming from those efforts to "favor liberty" that strip away all non-egalitarian powers or privileges (2.4, 248). Montesquieu uses the phrase "to favor liberty" (*pour favoriser la liberté*) again when discussing Roman judging (11.18). In both cases it warns against abolition of a distinct, noble judicial order. Without the exceptional grants of judicial power to England's upper house—the most important of which the English had supposedly abolished—its constitutionalism might be even more "extreme" than Montesquieu ultimately declares it to be (11.6, 407).

The only preparation in this analysis of the English constitution for the equity power granted to such quasi-noble judges is the initial praise for monarchies in contrast to despotisms and republics, which affirms that most European kingdoms are moderate because the prince leaves the judging power to his subjects (11.6, 397). These subjects, it turns out, are not only the jurors but also the professional judges in these monarchies, such as those in the *parlements*. One lesson of this analysis is that Montesquieu's support for the selling of noble offices would make a monarchical judiciary more republican. Conversely, security for liberty requires that judging in republics, especially those hiding under the form of monarchy, should become more monarchical—though in the properly moderated mode of an only quasi-aristocratic judicial class. Such a power must be cloaked so as to secure the tranquillity of the accused and to protect judges from those jealous of, or opposed to, their moderating power. This does not mean that judging is to dominate, plainly or imperceptibly, the legislative or executive powers. To allow it to do so, or to attempt to, would violate Montesquieu's principle of distribution of powers and squander the distinctively moderating capacity of judging. In the remainder of his study of constitutional liberty in book 11, Montesquieu examines the historical antecedents of such a judicial power, the disadvantages of its absence, and the prudent measures a humane spirit might take to judicialize politics.

Gothic Jurisprudence, the Decline of Rome, and Liberty

Montesquieu's political philosophy is not Anglophilia writ large, for in the bulk of this book on constitutionalism, he develops his conceptions of the separation of powers and of judicial power by examining the medieval Germans and the ancient Greeks and Romans. His political science differs from its liberal predecessors by observing the particular phenomena of diverse governments and peoples, and by favoring prudent adaptation of principles to circumstances rather than the imposition of a theoretical blueprint. Certain principles and practices nonetheless are better, and even best, either for all people or in given circumstances, and by making the reader sort through these matters Montesquieu hopes to inculcate a prudence true to the realities of politics. In the sequels to his analysis of English constitutionalism, he explores how moderate constitutions are achieved or lost among various peoples and circumstances, from medieval and modern Europeans in monarchies or mixed regimes to ancient Greeks and Romans in republics or despotisms. Amid this messy discussion of examples ancient, medieval, and modern—and not in the analysis of England—Montesquieu defines the best form of government. He continues with the themes of moderate government, separation of powers, and a judicial depository of laws after the long analysis of England, defending the moderate approximations of liberty that are suited to moderate monarchies (11.7). Such monarchies aim not at liberty but at "the glory of the citizens, the state, the prince," fostering a "spirit of liberty that can, in these states, produce equally great things and can perhaps contribute as much to happiness as liberty itself" (11.7, 408). His humane liberalism avoids not only the extreme of overt despotism but also its opposite, the morally perfect happiness of Aristotle or the Bible. This plea for moderation sets the stage for the usually neglected analysis of constitutionalism in the remainder of book 11. Montesquieu consolidates his earlier teachings about balanced and complex constitutions into clear statements of philosophic judgment, with judicial power at the heart of the discussion. These remarks also prepare for his prudential advice on judging and due process in the sequel, his book on individual liberty.

Montesquieu turns to criticizing the classical conception of monarchy so as to drive home his argument that a complex political order that gradually evolves toward liberty is the best-tempered government (11.8). England's Cromwellian tendencies are problematic, but the ancient republics are no better, since they had "no clear idea" of the mixed, moderate government that constitutes a proper monarchy. This analysis of the origins of Europe's moderate monarchies echoes earlier themes, including the claim that if one "reads the admirable work by Tacitus, *On the Mores of the Germans*, one will see that the English have taken their ideas of political government from the Germans. This fine system was found in the forests" (11.8, 408–9; 11.6, 407). This "Gothic government" stems from a spirit of freedom among the early Germans that established certain laws or institutions and then informed their gradual evolution. Montesquieu announces his discovery of the seed of the separation of powers and moderate government, and foreshadows the "historical" jurisprudence about the evolution of laws in the closing books of the work:

> Here is the origin of Gothic government among us. . . . it was a good government that had within itself the capacity to become better . . . soon the civil liberty of the people, the prerogatives of the nobility and of the clergy, and the power of the kings found themselves in such concert, that I believe there has never been a government on earth as well tempered as that of each part of Europe during the time that this government continued to exist; and it is remarkable that the corruption of the government of a conquering people should have formed the best kind of government men have been able to imagine. (11.8, 409)

The best government is not the child of philosophy, ancient or modern, but of rustic Germans gradually corrupting their government to moderate it. This declaration swiftly leads to verdicts on other failed candidates, theoretical and practical. Classical Western philosophers, such as Aristotle, have fundamentally misunderstood monarchy. The Germans achieved a government better than any imagined one, no matter the efforts of Plato or More, Machiavelli or Locke (11.9–10; see 29.19).

Having defined the best government, Montesquieu returns to the theme of judging through a discussion of kingship in heroic Greece (11.11). If the medieval Germans had read old books, they might have learned from Greek errors about judging, thereby improving their Gothic constitution and their liberty—although, as the closing books indicate, the Germans stumbled upon the right organization over several centuries. He cites Aristotle three times in discussing early Greek monarchy, along with Thucydides and Plutarch, though none of these ancients grasped that the crucial flaw of the heroic constitution was its misplaced judging power. Of "the three powers," the people had the legislative, while the king had both executive and judging, whereas in the superior, modern "monarchies we know," the "prince has the executive and the legislative power" but "does not judge" (11.11, 410–11; see 11.7; 11.6). The heroic Greek monarchy self-destructed because it "badly distributed" the three powers, for when an executive with the judging power "became terrible," he was attacked by the people and their legislative power. "It had not yet been discovered that the prince's true function was to establish judges and not to judge," and neither statesmen nor philosophers among the Greeks "imagine[d] the true distribution of the three powers in the government of one alone" (11.11, 411). Throughout *The Spirit of the Laws* Montesquieu suggests that while the Romans enjoyed this intermittently, it is the medieval Germans who slowly developed this best form of government and enjoyed such moderating benefits as due process and mild penalties. If Montesquieu considers the Germans to be "our fathers" on this point (6.18), his political philosophy obviously amounts to more than Gothic romanticism. It is Montesquieu who defines this complexity and independent judging as the key to a humane constitutionalism and who discerns that its principle can and should be communicated to all peoples, places, and times: "Among a free people who have legislative power . . . the masterwork of legislation is to know how to place well the power of judging" (11.11, 411). The elided phrase suggests that this maxim concerns only peoples "enclosed within a town," but its broader significance becomes clearer when we recognize that this is one of three places in the work where Montesquieu designates a *chef d'œuvre de la législation*. He first employed such praise, in this work devoted to educating legislators, when adumbrating the sort of moderate constitutional order he formulates in book 11: "In order to form a moderate government, one must combine powers, regulate them, temper them . . . this is a masterwork of legislation that chance rarely produces and prudence is rarely allowed to produce" (5.14, 297). The one subsequent use of the phrase praises the constitutional reform of judicial power in thirteenth-century France by King Louis IX as "a masterwork of legislation" (28.39, 855). Two of the three references to masterworks of constitutional founding or reform in *The Spirit of the Laws* concern judging, and only the proper placement of this power is termed "the" masterstroke.

After this climactic teaching, his final analyses of judging and constitutional liberty concern Rome. His task in the remainder of the book is to examine how the principles discerned in studying England, modern Europe, medieval Germany, and ancient Greece might be clarified by this most famous of governments, since "[o]ne can never leave the Romans" (11.13, 414). Judging plays no small part in this examination of liberty and constitution, and not only because the second longest chapter in the book concerns judging in Rome. Montesquieu turned to Rome early in his philosophical career and never left it, from his earliest extant work, "The Policy of the Romans in Religion" (1716), to the *Considerations on the Romans* (1734), to his masterwork. He grappled not only with republican and imperial Rome but also with St. Augustine's criticism of Roman pride, since his own humane philosophy seeks a new City of Man and not a City of God. The *Considerations* clearly shows a debt to Machiavelli, although *The Spirit of the Laws* shows less of an agreement with the *Discourses*. Even the *Considerations*, though, rejects Machiavelli's endorsement of Roman populism and his animus toward the nobles, and that disagreement informs this last section of book 11.[18] The theme here is the downfall of Roman government, both its imperfect but moderate monarchy and its republic, due to imbalances of power. A weakening of the Roman senate and other intermediate powers was always the price paid for strengthening the power of the people, and this populism ultimately brought tyranny. Montesquieu employs "the three powers" in dual senses here, as in the analysis of England. The most moderate and stable yet dynamic constitution is one that separates the three political powers—legislative, executive, judging—while blending this with recognition of three claims to rule—those of the one, the few, and the many. In describing the tragedy of this decline into Roman populism and the reactionary lurch to tyranny, he terms the people's decimation of the middling, senatorial power "a frenzy of liberty" (11.16, 419). Throughout the account, he links the senate and judging, suggesting that the latter power must always be kept away from the dominant or extreme powers, whatever they may be. He includes England in some early "general reflections" on Roman government, when describing the straining of its "springs" (11.13). Montesquieu hopes that England will maintain the kind of balanced constitution, with a preponderant middling power, that Rome failed to keep. Modern liberal constitutionalism should comprise a perpetual struggle of factions and powers, the constitution always in search of itself, always moderately moving within a certain balance of action and reaction. States "often are more flourishing during the imperceptible shift from one constitution to another than they are under either constitution." In such a moment "all the springs of the government are stretched," and there arises "a noble rivalry between those who defend the declining constitution and those who put forward the one that prevails" (11.13, 415; see 5.1, 273; 19.27, 576).

Montesquieu closes the book on constitutional liberty by describing how the Romans could not hold this middle way, oscillating instead between populism and tyranny (11.14–19). Judging is at the center of this tale, either as a football contested by rival factions or an instrument of popular tyranny. He concludes with separate chapters on each of the three powers in Rome, understood in modern, separation-of-powers terms, and a final chapter on the provinces. His examination of legislative and executive powers reinforces his theme that a popular "frenzy of liberty" caused a decline to despotism (11.16–17). Rome's nadir, however, concerns its judicial power, and his extensive examination of it provides the occasion for announcing fundamental lessons (11.18). This remarkable discussion compares Roman, English, and French judicial practices, and in doing so clarifies the relationship between the topics of books 11 and 12, constitutional liberty and individual liberty. Montesquieu analyzes several stages in the history of both civil and criminal judging in Rome, noting how each jurisdiction was distributed among the competing orders, and the specific rules shaping administration of justice. He commends the professional judges of the patrician, senatorial class known as praetors, who established a temporary pool of jurors each year and formed a jury for each suit, remarking that the "English practice is quite similar." Indeed, praetors selected jurors "with the consent of both parties," a practice "very favorable to liberty" and similar to jury strikes in civil suits "in England today" (11.18, 422). Of five historical stages of criminal judging the third, which established the tribunes of the plebs, brought the long process of reducing patrician judging power to a populist extreme. The "affair of Coriolanus," a constitutional crisis as serious as any other clash between patricians and plebs, saw the tribunes judging him in the archetype of "public accusation" that Machiavelli praised in the *Discourses* and which Montesquieu criticized (see 6.5).[19] He declares that the tribunes' judging could be "odious," which anticipates his later judgment that their very establishment pulled Rome toward popular despotism. He praises the balance later achieved between the senatorial class of judges and temporary juries, recalling that "[o]ne has seen, in chapter six of this Book," that such juries are "favorable to liberty in certain governments" (11.18, 425). He then reinforces the link between liberty and complex, professional judging by lamenting the populist judicial reforms of the brothers Gracchi, tribunes of the people in the second century B.C. This episode prompts the only thematic statement in this book on the crucial relationship between constitutional liberty and citizen liberty. He observes that "the three powers may be well distributed in relation to the liberty of the constitution, though they are not so well distributed in their relation with the liberty of the citizen." In Rome, the only way that the senate could balance the people, who held by then some or most of all three powers, was to retain its traditional part of the judicial power, and "it had a part when judges were chosen from among the senators." A spirit of extreme democracy upset this balance: "When the Gracchi deprived the senators of the power of judging, the senate could no longer resist the people. Therefore, they struck at the liberty of the constitution, in order to favor the liberty of the citizen; but the latter was lost along with the former. Infinite ills resulted . . . and the chain of the constitution was broken" (11.18, 425–26).

Montesquieu's political science of moderation counsels that constitutional changes which theoretically advance individual liberty in fact can cause its decline. The liberty embodied by a complex constitution is indispensable to the liberty of the individual, a lesson that holds true especially for judicial power. From book 2 to the end of book 11, Montesquieu steadily warns that constitutional changes that directly or quickly seek individual liberty often backfire, a warning usually made in reference to judging. The error of the Gracchi prompts him to praise "the ancient French laws" about judging, since their practices were informed by "distrust" about "men of [public] affairs" (11.18, 426). The Gothic separation of powers achieves moderation and liberty, especially by separating judging from factional politics through a judicial depository of the laws. The sequel reinforces the idea that the worst imbalance of power is misplaced judging by highlighting the judicial abuses in provincial governments where a single magistrate was neither legally learned nor balanced by juries (11.19, 428–30).

Montesquieu closes his book on constitutional liberty by reinforcing the link between moderation, separation of powers, and degrees of possible liberty (11.20). He explains that he has not studied this link "in all the moderate governments we know," so that there will be "thinking" left for the reader to do (11.20, 430). For the philosopher, thinking is a kind of doing in itself. For this philosopher, thinking is meant also to instruct political doing. A crucial if imperceptible purpose in the remainder of *The Spirit of the Laws* is to educate judges and constitutional legislators about the cloaking of power, both its benefits and the means to achieve it. By instructing, and instructing about, the subtle judge, Montesquieu seeks to place into circulation the coin of a universal commerce in the rules and formalities of judging, toward the end of achieving humane, moderate government.

three

Projects for Reform: Due Process, National Spirit, and Liberal Toleration

After thematically presenting his new constitutionalism in book 11 of *The Spirit of the Laws*, Montesquieu seeks to inculcate practical wisdom through a steady stream of examples and advice. Prudence is a great theme of the work, and a characteristic of Montesquieu's philosophy, blending description with prescription and theory with practice. His new conception of philosophy and prudence supports the cloaking of political power by instructing statesmen and judges to gradually, imperceptibly temper the laws to accord with moderation and a humane natural right. He employs the term *prudence* sparingly in the work, but it is fitting that he uses it twice early in book 29, after stating that the main point of the work is that "the spirit of moderation ought to be that of the legislator," since the political and moral good always are "found between two limits" (29.1, 865). This book of advice on how to compose laws ends by criticizing five "legislators," all political philosophers or theorists, for the "passions and prejudices" that deny them the spirit of moderation (29.19, 882–83).[1] Early in the book he refers to an ancient Greek law as not "prudent" and another as being made without "prudence" (29.5; 29.7). In this last theoretical book, amid extraordinary efforts at a new historical jurisprudence in books 27–28 and 30–31, Montesquieu claims to understand the spirit of moderation, the spirit of law, and prudence better than any predecessor has done so. The importance of practical wisdom in his analyses of moderation and constitutionalism confirm this view, especially regarding a cloaking of power. Thus, an early analysis of judicial power admonishes potential reformers to observe well his "practical maxim" about how a wise "legislator" would secretly temper a harsh penalty in particular cases until he could reform the law entirely (6.13, 323). Having linked spirit, moderation, law, and prudence, his aim is to nurture a spirit that combines the statesman and the philosopher.[2] It is this spirit that animates the whole work, and this is particularly true of parts 3 to 6, spanning books 14–31.[3]

Montesquieu declares three times in the Preface that he would be "the happiest of mortals" if mankind were to benefit from his work. This marks a profession of faith about prudential reform of politics by philosophers, a pledge reiterated in his praise for the Stoics as "watching over mankind" and working for the good of society (24.10, 721–22). He knows human nature well enough to offer general principles to guide reformers, but the teacher of prudence must exercise it himself. He "lets an ill remain if [he] fears something worse" and "lets a good remain if [he] is in doubt about a better"; he examines parts and whole, and tests both causes and results ("Preface," 230). The prudent philosopher must overcome widespread ignorance about fundamental principles more than ignorance about external things; thus, his philosophical prudence seeks to help man with "knowing his own nature" ("Preface," 230; see 1.2). The calls for reform throughout the work indicate how laws have violated natural feelings or sympathies, or how a prudential moderation could revive an oppressed humanity (see 3.10; 6.13; 26.3–7; 26.14; 26.25). This conception of prudence informs the liberal education in law that Montesquieu provides for those who might constitute a new order of the robe and a cloaking of power. Such a jurisprudence lies midway between Coke's Aristotelian legal prudence and the pragmatic, amoral legal realism embodied by Oliver Wendell Holmes. Nature indicates that our ultimate aims in politics and law are definite yet moving targets, since political moderation and individual tranquillity can be secured in an "infinite" number of ways ("Preface").[4] A humane prudence can enjoy a "natural empire" if, little by little, it perceives how to effect moderation and tranquillity in the laws (28.38). The substantial moral flexibility in this modern notion of prudence is essential to the liberal, humane education provided in *The Spirit of the Laws*.[5]

A spirit of prudence, of seeking to better achieve the moderation that nature suggests for the laws, directly informs the analysis in book 12 of laws affecting individual liberty. The final three parts of the work then provide suggestions for gradual reforms of politics, morals, and religion that only occasionally mention the judging power; after book 12, this power is more often than not invisible until book 28. Within the intervening books, however, there are subtle, occasionally striking reminders of the important role the invisible power plays in moderating constitutions and laws.

Individual Security, "The Surest Rules" in Judgments, and Moderation

Montesquieu opens the book on individual liberty with his most explicit statement on constitutionalism as a means to individual security. He emphatically relates the actual liberty of a citizen and the constitutional structure of a government: "It can happen that the constitution is free, and that the citizen is not. The citizen can be free, and the constitution not. In these cases, the constitution will be free by right, and not in fact; the citizen will be free in fact, and not by right" (12.1, 430–31). In a putatively illiberal constitution, the individual can be free, as in the European kind of monarchy regularly mentioned in book 11; such freedom can even occur, albeit more sporadically, under despotic government. Conversely, in constitutions putatively devoted to freedom, such as Cromwell's England, the individual can be threatened with or actually suffer harm; either condition entails a loss of the tranquillity or opinion of security by which Montesquieu measures liberty. The core books of *The Spirit of the Laws* always pair the fundamental priority of individual liberty with an insistence upon prerequisite constitutional or legal structures. After indicating these dual senses of political liberty, his final definition of liberty emphasizes the juridical protection for individuals thematically examined in book 12. In the book on constitutional liberty he stated that political liberty is a tranquillity felt about one's own security, and this requires that "the government must be such that one citizen cannot fear another citizen" (11.6, 397). Montesquieu then refines his conception of liberty so as to emphasize the implicit legalism of a moderate constitutional order. While "[p]hilosophical liberty consists in the exercise of one's will," political liberty "consists in security, or at least in the opinion one has of one's security." This in turn entails the definition of the greatest threat to, and support for, political liberty: "This security is never more attacked than by public and private prosecutions (*accusations*). It is therefore on the goodness of the criminal laws that the liberty of the citizen principally depends" (12.2, 431).

The liberty of the constitution concerns "the government" and separation of powers, while the liberty of the citizen concerns the particular laws and judicial procedures treated in books 6 and 12, and throughout the work. This bifurcation in liberty is more analytical than real, however, and Montesquieu argues that judging is the crucial link between constitutionalism and individual liberty. He draws out this implication of his constitutionalism of liberty and sounds the keynote of these core books: that a moderate, constitutional politics must elevate judicial power so that a legalistic cast to politics and governance will yield greater protection for individual tranquillity. Montesquieu opens his analysis by suggesting that he will leave behind broad institutional questions, relating citizen liberty only to the "mores, manners, and received examples" that can give rise to it and to "certain civil laws [that] can favor it" (12.1, 431). The exception to this shift away from institutional issues is judicial power, because if liberty means individual tranquillity, then, he declares, civil and criminal prosecutions pose the greatest threat to it. Laws about civil and criminal procedure therefore represent the greatest area of potential good to be achieved by humane reform. The power most directly implicated is judging, the placement of which he deems the masterwork of constitutional legislating (11.11). To amplify this, Montesquieu lists several criminal laws in need of reform, concerning not punishments but due process, the rules and formalities for conducting legal investigations and court proceedings. After ranging from Aristotle's *Politics* and the early Roman kings to the medieval Franks and back to Aristotle, he draws the conclusion that "[w]hen the innocence of the citizens is not secure, liberty is not either" (12.2, 432). He raises this juridical conception of liberty to its highest pitch by connecting it to his theme of prudence:

> The knowledge already acquired in some countries, and yet to be acquired in others, respecting the surest rules one can observe in criminal judgments, concerns (*intéressent*) mankind more than anything else in the world.
>
> It is only on the practice of this knowledge that liberty can be founded; and in a state which had the best possible laws in regard to it, a man against whom proceedings had been brought, and who was about to be hung the next day, would be much freer than is a pasha in Turkey. (432)

The *sine qua non* of liberty is an independent judging power, and a legal profession practicing in its courts, which together embody the knowledge of these proper rules. Montesquieu's declarations about this legal prudence also address his paradoxical statement about a citizen being free when a constitution is not. The emphasis here on proper juridical knowledge develops the constitutionalism of book 11, praising most European kingdoms as moderate because the prince leaves judicial power to his subjects (11.6, 397). Fusing of the two visible powers may mean less constitutional liberty while still providing liberty for individuals, since each person can be tranquil in the knowledge that even a powerful government must allow him his day in court.

Montesquieu underscores this continuity between books 11 and 12 by re-calling the name of Coriolanus, and with it his criticism of Machiavelli's doctrine of public accusations (12.3; 6.5). He does so while proclaiming that the French procedure requiring a majority of two votes among judges or jury to condemn in capital cases was "established by the gods" (12.3, 432). Assured that French jurisprudence is more divine than ancient Roman or Greek due process—both of which required only a majority of one in such cases—Montesquieu now can tackle a complete revision of the categories and subjects of criminal law (12.4). This discussion reveals the real topic of book 12. Montesquieu initially refers to "certain civil laws" that can favor liberty, and notes that "public or private accusations" are the chief threat to such liberty. This importance for juridical procedures elevates civil law in relation to political law, since legal prudence moderates not only civil or private suits between citizens but criminal prosecu-tions by governments against citizens. Montesquieu thus undertakes a subtle but wholesale revision of the spirit and letter of all criminal codes, including that of eighteenth-century France, arguing that "liberty is favored by the na-ture of penalties and by their proportion." The bulk of book 6 discusses such penalties, but the treatment here is more thematic. This emphatic attention to the political importance of civil law led the leading liberal reformer of criminal law in eighteenth-century Europe, Cesare Beccaria (1738–1794), to cite "the immortal President Montesquieu" as a "great man" in whose steps he followed. Indeed, Beccaria cites Montesquieu not only in the introduction to his *Essay on Crimes and Punishments* (1764) but throughout.[6]

Montesquieu opens his discussion of penal reform with the same emphatic tone used earlier in this book: "It is the triumph of liberty when criminal laws draw each penalty from the particular nature of the crime. All arbitrariness ends; the penalty does not issue from the caprice of the legislator, but from the nature of the thing; and man does not do violence to man" (12.4, 433). This Stoic defense of humanity, coupled with instruction in what such a defense requires, leads to a further appeal to nature: "All that I say is drawn from nature, and is quite favorable to the citizen's liberty" (435). Montesquieu's instruction in the nature of things, specifically in the juridical prudence needed by reforming legislators and statesmanlike judges, redefines criminal law. A humane code will delineate four kinds of crimes—against religion, mores, tranquillity, and the security of citizens. On the premise that the "penalties inflicted ought to derive from the nature of each of these kinds," his main point is that only the fourth category, regarding the security of citizens, is properly a subject of criminal law at all (433).

According to Montesquieu all "crimes" regarding religion that do not di-rectly affect the security of citizens are falsely categorized, since "there is no criminal matter: it is all between man and god" (433). He instructs about moderation in religious penalties with his characteristic blend of boldness and subtlety, recounting how a thirteenth-century Pope reminded a saint about the importance of religious toleration. King Louis IX of France (1226–1270)—always "Saint Louis" for Montesquieu—serves later in the work as a model of prudence and enlightened judicial reform, but here he provides a different lesson: "Saint Louis made such exaggerated laws against those who swore that the Pope felt obliged to caution him about it. This prince moderated his zeal and softened his laws" (12.4, 433 n. *a*). The knowledge required to punish crimes about faith is held only by the "infinite being," for it is not suited to "the weakness, ignorance, and caprice of human nature" (434). A starker case of disproportionate religious laws recounts the story of some "weak spirits" in Provence who took the law into their own hands when a Jew accused of blaspheming the Virgin Mary was to be flayed alive. Montesquieu dramatically breaks off his narrative, recalling his interrupted recounting of a case of torture, which he cannot complete because he hears "the voice of nature crying out against" him (12.4, 434; 6.17, 329). He strikes this pose again regarding Japanese punishments which violate "modesty," not only by exposing women's bodies in public but even, he cryptically suggests, by humiliating family members: "when [the magistracy] wanted to compel a mother, . . . when it wanted to compel a son, . . . I cannot go on, it made even nature tremble" (12.14, 445).

Montesquieu continues to inculcate prudence and moderation in analyzing the second and third categories of "crimes," those against mores and tranquillity. Montesquieu decriminalizes these, too, in a manner that brings to mind John Stuart Mill's bolder statement of "one very simple principle" in these matters, that "the sole end for which mankind are warranted . . . in interfering with the liberty of action of any of their number, is self-protection." Mill, writing a century later and in considerably safer conditions for liberal reform, could speak more bluntly on such topics, and he is inclined to do so. Mill's formulation, however, abstracts from the realities of political communities, given its bold confidence about progressive reform—characteristics absent from *The Spirit of the Laws*. Mill's strong individualism declares that an agent can be prevented "against his will" from acting only in order to "prevent harm to others"; that agent's "own good, either physical or moral, is not a sufficient warrant" for using public "power" against him.[7] Montesquieu is less idealistic and strident while more convinced of the importance of proper manners and mores for the perpetuation of liberty, a reflection of the fact that his concern is the liberty of individuals who also are citizens (12.1). He discusses the last category of crimes, against security, with a severity that may have reassured contemporaries who suspected him of not just reforming the criminal code but reforming it away.

Here he explicitly affirms use of "corporal punishments" (*supplices*), not just the softer "penalties" (*peines*) appropriate for the first three categories. Such punishments are "a kind of retaliation" against the security of one who has deprived, or sought to deprive, another of it. Indeed, such a mode is "derived from the nature of the thing," from "reason," and from "the sources of good and evil" (12.4, 435). The rare use of such absolute philosophic terms amid a discussion of due process emphasizes the priority of individual security for Montesquieu; this marks, in fact, his second usage of "the nature of the thing" in this discussion. The bluntness of his remarks further underscores his emphasis: a citizen "deserves death" either for taking or attempting to take a life, and the "death penalty is, as it were, the remedy for a sick society." The mention of society in this context implies that a correction of mores or manners is needed, and Montesquieu later argues that mores should be reformed, for the most part, by mores (19.14). By remarking that society, and not just the alleged or convicted criminal, is sick, he also suggests that moderation must govern considerations about the use of capital sentences. The prudential voice of proportionality arises even more clearly when distinguishing punishments for crimes against life from those for crimes against property: "When one violates security with respect to goods there can be reasons for the penalty to be capital; but it would perhaps be preferable, and it would be more natural, if the penalty for crimes committed against the security of goods were punished by loss of goods" (12.4, 435). Still, with characteristic sobriety, he admits that "the corporal penalty has had to replace the pecuniary penalty" since most thieves are poor. The nature of things, and a focal concern for liberty, does not go to the extreme of liberation from criminal laws, or of judicial reforms that nullify such laws. Rather, these principles instruct reformers to pursue moderation only to the degree compatible with security for all.

The remainder of his analysis of citizen liberty takes the course set by this discussion of penal reform, as is evident in the title to the sequel, that criminal accusations or prosecutions are in "need of moderation and prudence" (12.5, 435). Some accusations require greater prudence, or liberal reform, than others, and Montesquieu speaks as directly to statesmen here as he had in his earlier analysis of judging. He employs a didactic tone to serve moderate ends: "Important maxim: one must be very circumspect in the pursuit of magic and of heresy. Prosecution of these two crimes can offend liberty in the extreme and be the source of infinite tyrannies if the legislator does not know how to limit it" (12.5, 435; see 6.13). The examples he provides seek to "cast doubt on all accusations founded on public hatred" (12.5, 435–36). This is one of many implicit criticisms in the book of Machiavelli's praise for the populist accusation against, then exiling of, Coriolanus—which range from a note on "the judgment of Coriolanus," to recalling that he has "already spoken of that Athenian law that permitted one to go into exile before the judgment" and praise for a Persian custom permitting anyone to leave the kingdom, including those accused of crimes (12.3; 12.20; 12.30). Regarding the "hidden" crime of homosexuality, "the crime against nature," he advises that nature can defend itself with the help of a mild *police* (12.6, 437–38). Throughout the work, he subtly redefines this term for civilized mores or social order to submerge any connotations of Aristotelian or Biblical morality. A proper, mild police power should seek individual security and tranquillity—the kind of social and political life that reflects and reinforces the importance of a moderating judicial power (see 4.6; 11.11; 12.13; 26.24). Montesquieu's discussion of homosexuality implies that there are other more serious crimes against nature, such as a child testifying against his parents. He concludes that homosexuality should be decriminalized and considered a violation of "mores"—which can mean morals rooted in natural right or merely customary manners. Even so, he forestalls the likely objections from Christian theologians or moral philosophers by continuing to call it a crime. This puts a moderate, reasonable face on this mild forerunner to Mill's argument that all activities among consenting adults, if not physically harmful to another person against their will, lie beyond the reach of criminal law.

Having argued against prosecuting heresy—but in such a way as to avoid the charge himself—Montesquieu's particular lessons to legislators and judges continue with chapters on criminal laws against high treason (12.7–10; 12.18) and on laws that criminalize thoughts, speech, and writings (12.11–13). In this latter discussion he expresses a thought relevant to reading his own works, one rooted either in fear of controversy or in a prudent reserve that would prevent misunderstandings: "Silence sometimes expresses more than any speech" (12.12, 442). His extraordinary remarks on toleration regarding thoughts, speech, and writings echo Locke's *Letter Concerning Toleration* (1689), and Montesquieu later will apply them to religion (books 24–26). Laws that criminalize words exemplify a kind of "despotism" that can afflict any kind of government through the extreme, inhumane aspects of its criminal code (12.7, 438). An essential lesson about moderation and prudence is, therefore, that it is a "great tyranny" if criminal laws seek to punish anything other than "external actions" (12.11, 441). Only when thoughts, speech, or writing pass over into action, only if they "prepare the way for" some crime, are they "material to the crime" (12.13, 443). Satirical writings can be "prohibited," but they should be made "an object of *police* rather than of crime" (444). He largely agrees with Locke that law and politics should be confined to bodies and their interactions—that the coercive power of laws should not reach to higher moral concerns or a citizen's soul. This privatizing of political life, elevating the importance of civil law and private life over political law and the traditional claims of either "the police power" or the criminal code, reinforces his elevation of the judiciary and of individual tranquillity in liberalism. He suggests further reforms by examining self-defeating criminal laws that actually promote slander (12.15; 12.16). Laws that violate modesty or natural, familial sympathy violate the very security they should protect (12.15–19).

Montesquieu's analysis also provides lessons not so much for legislators who might repeal or revise such laws but for judges, who can reform through adjudicating cases. He quotes instructions from several Roman emperors to a praetorian prefect regarding his judicial powers, advising that when accusations of seditious speech arise, a policy of toleration and moderation should avoid punishment, if possible (12.12, 443). He also offers some of his periodic warnings about extremism in the very power he hopes will yield the most moderation. Magistrates in aristocracies—some of whom may well exercise judicial functions, as did the Roman decemvirs whom he cites—can be "little sovereigns" who tolerate no satirical criticism, an echo of his warning against judging by a single magistrate (12.13, 444; see 6.7). He reiterates his criticism of Rome's tribunes by recounting the despotic tendencies of populist judging (12.21; see 6.5; 11.18). He emphasizes moderation in forming and applying the rules for criminal judgments by concluding with a topic mentioned at the opening of the book, the "mores, manners, and received examples" favorable to liberty. The ambitious scope of his instruction in juridical prudence and humane reform extends to despotism, from the "civil laws appropriate for putting a little liberty in despotic government" to the role that "judges" can play to achieve as much moderation as possible. He articulates the hope that, through advice to judges, he can foster some small presence of separation of powers, of a moderating equilibrium among distinct powers. Having advised judges in despotisms to consult religious ministers "in cases that are unclear," so as to make their judging less "arbitrary," Montesquieu seeks another toehold: "[I]f the case merits death, the particular judge, if there is one, may also suitably seek the advice of the governor, so that the civil power and the ecclesiastic power are further tempered by the political authority" (12.29, 456–57). This is a pale shadow of the complex formalities of judging and due process enjoyed by more moderate constitutions and therefore by citizens more secure in their liberty. Indeed, he signals his doubt that despotisms will even have independent judges. Still, such formalities concern humankind more than anything else— humankind everywhere and at all times. Particular arrangements and laws may vary greatly, so judges will need prudence to know how best to secure moderate government, liberty, and a humane conception of natural rights in those circumstances. Montesquieu's spirit of benevolent cosmopolitanism suggests that a new coin of judicial prudence and due process might bring some liberty to places that know little of it.

Nature, Prudence, and a National Spirit of Liberty

With part 3 of *The Spirit of the Laws,* Montesquieu breaks the implicit ascent in parts 1 and 2 of the work, which move toward a new constitution of liberty that can escape the despotism variously embodied by classical and modern republicanism, earlier political philosophy, and Christianity. He turns in books 14–19 to examine the natural, historical, and cultural obstacles to a humane constitutionalism.[8] He analyzes several ways in which people must temper hopes for the security and comfort of liberal constitutionalism with recognition of nature's unsympathetic power. Throughout this sobering journey, however, he sprinkles advice to those interested in prudent reform. The book on climate suggests a deterministic view of suicide in England's gloomy climate, and then strikes a note of penal reform for judicial and legislative ears: "[I]n England one can no more punish [suicide] than one can punish the effects of madness" (14.12, 486). When discussing civil slavery, Montesquieu encourages enlightened reformers by pronouncing that "[k]nowledge makes men gentle, and reason inclines toward humanity: only prejudices cause these to be renounced" (15.3, 493). He declares that the "laws of modesty are a part of natural right and ought to be felt by all the nations in the world," and that a "prudent legislator avoids the misfortune of becoming a terrifying legislator" (15.12, 499; 15.16, 502–3). He offers "reflections" on laws to emancipate slaves in republics, but just what laws are needed "depends too much on circumstances" for him to formulate universal rules (15.18, 506; also 16.12, 517–8). He takes up the Machiavellian and Baconian theme of conquering nature by damming or channeling rivers and reclaiming land from the sea, and then prepares for the discussion of the general spirit of a nation in book 19 by analyzing the steps one might take to change either laws or mores and thereby change a nation's spirit (book 18). A brief analysis of medieval, Germanic inheritance law also foreshadows the final books of the work, on gradual evolutions and reforms within a law or system of law (18.22; 18.27; 18.30). These brief remarks on Gothic legal reform include judicial overtones developed in book 28, but with book 19 Montesquieu returns to the topic of judicial power in a somewhat more thematic way.

After the dreary topics that occupy most of part 3, Montesquieu examines how laws relate to the general spirit, mores, and manners of a nation, and he begins by discussing how "spirits" must be "prepared for the best laws." All the examples concern courts and due process, including the complaints by Asians and Germans under the Roman empire about Roman judging (19.2, 556–57).

The discussion links a people's spirit, the laws, and judging in a way that echoes his maxim from book 1, that laws "ought to be so appropriate to the people for whom they are made that it is a very great chance if the laws of one nation can suit another" (1.3, 237). The only other explicit reference to judging in book 19 similarly suggests that simple mores correspond to simple judicial procedures, another of Montesquieu's many warnings against simplistic juridical rules (19.22). He cites Plato's *Laws* in observing that "an extremely religious people" could dispatch "all trials speedily by having only an oath sworn on each count," while a less religious people can rely on an oath "only on occasions when those who swear it, such as the judge and witnesses, are without interest" (19.22, 571–72). The early Germans who rebelled against Roman lawyers, and the Asians under Mithridates who complained of "the formal procedures of [Roman] justice," were simpler in their mores or general spirit than the medieval Germans who developed the complex constitution that Montesquieu favors. Unlike the Asians or early Germans, a more complex, historically developed people might be able to breathe the "pure air" of these laws, having arisen from their "swampy countries" so as to both appreciate and benefit from a more complex jurisprudence and due process (19.2, 557).

This is Montesquieu's introduction to the central theme of book 19, the general spirit of a nation or people. This is a less comprehensive but essential counterpart to his concept of a spirit of laws, since perception of this general spirit permits the prudent legislator or statesmen to conform to the spirit of law manifested in a given country or people. Montesquieu lists seven things that "govern men," which together produce a general spirit: "climate, religion, laws, the maxims of the government, examples of past things, mores, and manners" (19.4, 558). He analyzes the spirit of an unnamed country, obviously his own France, under the headings "how careful one must be not to change the general spirit of a nation," and, "that one must not correct everything." At certain points his instruction in a liberal prudence is even more direct, as when he pleads, twice, "May we be left as we are" (19.6, 559; 19.5). He follows these injunctions of *laissez faire* with the second of two citations in the work to Mandeville's *Fable of the Bees*, in both cases omitting the subtitle—*Private Vices, Public Benefits* (19.8; see 7.1). Like Mandeville, Montesquieu endorses commerce while acknowledging its controversial consequences. Commerce promotes changes in manners, which he defines as codes of external conduct, and promotes the spoiling of mores, defined as internalized rules and beliefs but also as the formation of "taste" (see 19.16). These bold thoughts lead him to depart from his advice to leave mores alone, for he now explores "the natural means of changing the mores and manners of a nation" (19.14, 563–64). This new counsel for the prudent legislator qualifies the earlier admonition: a general spirit conducive to humane mores and laws deserves benign neglect, while nations which are morally, spiritually, or politically despotic can and should be gradually, imperceptibly changed (19.10; 19.12–13). He advises that "when a prince wants to make great changes in his nation, he must reform by laws what is established by laws and change by manners what is established by manners" (19.14, 564). This advice also contains a judicial note: "Every penalty that does not derive from necessity is tyrannical. The law is not a pure act of power; things indifferent by their nature are not within its jurisdiction (*ressort*)" (565). This subtle call for judicial reform prepares for his equating of a people's "fundamental constitution" with their "general spirit," thereby giving a broad connotation to *constitution,* an important word rarely used outside the context of books 11 and 12 (19.19, 570). The subsequent remarks on judging and Plato's *Laws* also imply reform, confirming the importance of a complex judicial power (19.22).

The last section of the book addresses the relation between constitution as general spirit and as institution, the relation that sets the theme for Montesquieu's return to the English in the widely read analysis that concludes both this book and part 3 of the work (19.27). This second study of England influenced Madison's tenth *Federalist* essay and Tocqueville's account of enlightened self-interest in *Democracy in America*. Its premise explicitly reverses the causal relation of mores and laws, of spirit and institutions, that dominates both this book and part 3. He examines not the effects produced on laws by climate and by the spirit of a people, but how "laws can contribute to forming the mores, manner, and character of a nation" (19.27, 575). The new term *general spirit* is synonymous with the new term *character,* and Montesquieu argues that the liberal constitutionalism of England he examined in book 11 (and, more broadly, in part 2) has had certain "effects" upon English character and mores. He immediately mentions "the two visible powers" and the factional conflict between two parties that poses no danger to the liberty of either the constitution or individuals (575). After he refers implicitly to the invisible power so prominent in books 11 and 12, judging seems to disappear from his crucial discussion of English character. The main theme is the dynamic equilibrium of English politics, which moderates the passions by promoting private enterprise and commercial opportunity for its secure individuals. He commends the liberty given to "all the passions" in such a political order, since this yields a beneficial conflict between partisans of the "two visible powers," legislative and executive (19.27, 574). Hatred, envy, jealousy, greed, and pride all flourish, fueling the "hatred between the two parties" (19.27, 575). Montesquieu anticipates Adam Smith's notions of emulation and the invisible hand by arguing that a principle of action and reaction prevents any one agent or power from doing more than unintentionally benefiting others through the increased productivity of the whole system. He endorses passion, faction, and injustice because they maintain liberty for each and all: "[T]hey would even have the good effect of straining all the springs of the government, and rendering all the citizens attentive" (576; see 5.1).

It slowly comes to light in this analysis that while judging and its effects are out of sight, they are not out of mind, for Montesquieu paints a rather mixed portrait of the English. For all the benefits its constitution produces in the character of its people, the "extreme liberty" diagnosed in book 11 produces an extreme individualism.[9] He surveys a host of ills produced by the excessive English devotion to individual liberty. Their "repressive" laws against Catholics are not bloody but "do all the evil that can be done in cold blood"; a "frenzy of liberty" prevents even Protestant clergy from deciding doctrine and reserves this for Parliament, to prevent backsliding against religious tolerance; the English have wit (*esprit*) but not "taste," and while polite in a businesslike way, they lack a mannered *politesse*, since each is always "busy with one's own interests"; the men ignore the women and, "lacking gallantry," they "throw themselves into a debauchery that would leave them their liberty as well as their leisure"— apparently prostitution and homosexuality, among other practices. The closing refrain is that this witty people would be "tormented by that very wit" and would live "mostly alone with themselves." The "very character of the nation" would appear above all in "their works of the mind (*ouvrages d'esprit*)," which reveal "a withdrawn people, each of whom thought alone" (19.27, 580–83). The English "frenzy of liberty" affects scholarship, too: "[I]n extremely free states [historians] betray the truth because of their very liberty," since "every one becomes as much the slave of the prejudices of his faction as he would be of a despot" (19.27, 583).

The English conflict between the "two visible powers" produces such problems that Montesquieu's analysis contains, in the end, allusions to judging and his core argument about constitutionalism and judicial moderation. A significant theme of the historical researches in *The Spirit of the Laws* is the role of judging in the evolution of laws and constitutions, especially the examination in book 28 of both legislation about judging and the practice of it. The initial remarks in this analysis of English political faction, including a reference to visible powers that reminds us of the invisible one, prepare for a portrait that praises English individuality and forcefulness while warning of an extremism, of an inhumanity born of immoderation. These threats to liberty from extreme liberty point to the importance of the invisible power for moderating constitutionalism and thereby genuinely securing liberty, as argued previously, and as subsequent books, especially book 28, will reinforce. Just before his return to the English, Montesquieu hints that a politically well developed people, in terms of both laws and mores, would balance juries with more professional judging and thereby better moderate its politics (19.22; see 2.4; 6.1; 6.3; 11.6; 11.18). He cites Plato's *Laws* for the lesson that the good mores of an extremely religious people brought forth a jurisprudence of minimal due process under the ancient Cretan ruler Rhadamanthus. Rhadamanthus relied simply on oaths by the parties to a case, although Plato suggests that, for a nonreligious people, oaths are sufficient only if the parties and judge have no conflicting interests (19.22, 571–72). Plato himself notes that "now" most people are not so religious; thus, they require a more complex judicial procedure. When read in light of the opening remarks of book 19 on complaints by Asians and Germans about Roman judging, Montesquieu suggests that a not-so-religious people is more politically mature and humane, at least regarding justice and due process, since they assume everyone is interested and cannot be trusted. A mature people knows that human justice cannot rely on divine oaths, that each testimony and each person's will—including the judge's—must be checked or moderated if politics is to be humane and tranquil.

The larger lesson of book 19 and thus part 3 is that, despite natural or traditional obstacles, and with some prudence, laws can shape the general spirit or character of a people. The second half of *The Spirit of the Laws*, parts 4 to 6, continues this emphasis upon the actual and potential achievements of prudent legislators and reformers, albeit sobered as to both ends and means by the many obstacles facing prudence and humanity. This discussion of general spirit and character thus prepares the way for the topics that complete the work—commerce and economics; population and the "general welfare" of a people; religion; and analyses of ancient Rome and medieval France that synthesize historical evolution and prudential legal reform. The subtle presence of judicial power throughout book 19 reinforces Montesquieu's conception that judging is a model for prudent reform, since it proceeds gradually, imperceptibly, case by case (see chapters 2, 14, 22, and 27). It can achieve better reforms than either legislating or executing, at least in certain cases, because both its nature and its effects are more stable and lasting but also less sweeping, ambitious, and potentially harsh than those of the visible powers. This independent brake on faction and ambition moderates first the execution of the laws and eventually their making—indeed their very aims. Representative powers look forward and with a general gaze to secure some common aim, perhaps sacrificing the security of individuals for the collective security promised by some law or venture. Judging, in contrast, looks inward and backward: inward in its attentiveness to individuals and their claims to security under the law, and backward to existing laws and principles that ostensibly aim to protect and pacify.

Judicial Moderation of Politics, Morals, and Religion

Montesquieu opens book 20, the first of three books on commerce and economics, with an epigraph from Virgil's *Aeneid* that suggests an Epicurean tone
for all of part 4 (books 20–23). The analysis of population policies in this part
begins, in fact, with a long quotation from the *De rerum natura* by the Roman
Epicurean poet Lucretius (23.1). After quoting Virgil in book 20, he offers his
own "Invocation to the Muses," a poem that employs the Lucretian technique of
the honeyed cup to mask bitter medicine with sweet verses. He hopes to move
from the realm of "pain, fatigue, and worry" just traversed in part 3 to the possibilities of achieving "wisdom and truth through pleasure" (20, "Invocation,"
584). This launches an epic narrative on commerce, in which Montesquieu
compares a poem on Portuguese explorers and navigators with "the charms of
the *Odyssey* and the magnificence of the *Aeneid*" (21.21, 642).[10] These modern
deeds are not guided by the Homeric or Virgilian virtues of martial courage,
crafty wit, or devotion to a humane mission ordained by the gods. The new
heroes open up new vistas for productivity, commerce, comfort, and the exchange of moral and political views; the two "new worlds" they discover are
not only the Far East and West Indies, but the achievements of technology
and navigation, and the benefits of commerce and a gentler civilization. The
wisdom and truth wished for in the "Invocation" are to be found in the work of
prudent statesmen, who found new lands of technological progress and moral
moderation. These analyses of commerce and population thus continue the
fundamental work of the book, to equip reform-minded rulers with a humane
prudence. The lode star of this new moral and political compass is the prosperity already achieved through scientific invention and commerce, and the
greater potential lying ever ahead: "Europe has reached such a high degree
of power that nothing in history is comparable to it" (21.21, 641–45).[11] The
twenty-first century in fact finds the European spirit of science, invention, and
commerce having ushered in still another "globalizing" era in liberal economics
and politics. It also finds American might, which both protects and enjoys this
worldly spirit, unrivalled across the globe, despite enemies whose efforts to
circumvent that superiority implicitly recognize it. Montesquieu's counsel to
be as concerned with economic and technological development as with military might prepared the way for statesmen who advocated a balance between
"hard" and "soft" power in international affairs, blending force with fairness and
buttressing both with a dynamic, attractive prosperity. From Washington and
Hamilton to Lincoln and George Marshall, this blend of realism and idealism,
of interests and humane principles, has particularly defined American policies
in the world, seeking to counter the militarism and brutality of old-fashioned

powers while keeping America safe from those same passions.[12] Montesquieu was among the first to argue that the domestic principle of enlightened self-interest also could safely guide relations among nations, confident that this kind of high-minded hedonism could be simultaneously humane and successful. The project for a cloaking of power is, albeit in a predominantly domestic mode, a similar effort to use soft power to moderate the harsher aspects of politics and human affairs.

In these books on commerce, Montesquieu argues that, while commerce corrupts pure mores, which was a concern for both classical political philosophy and Biblical religion, it also softens harsh mores in both private and public life (20.1).[13] This characteristically modern moderation partly stems from commerce having "spread knowledge of the mores of all nations everywhere: they have been compared to each other, and good things have resulted from this" (20.1, 585). Montesquieu's emphasis on comparative empirical study breaks from the rationalist liberalism of Hobbes and Locke, prompting the birth of several comparative disciplines in the social sciences. More practically, this principle of comparative study informs America's policy of engagement with regard to many illiberal regimes, which hopes that increased commercial and cultural contacts gradually will liberalize mores and laws among illiberal regimes. Since the "knowledge already acquired in some countries, and yet to be acquired in others, concerning the surest rules one can observe in criminal judgments, interests mankind more than anything else in the world," and since it is "only on the practice of this knowledge that liberty can be founded," it is fitting that Montesquieu promotes a commerce not only of humane prudence but particularly of due process and judicial formalities (12.2). Montesquieu clearly joins these concerns with comparative enlightenment and judging in a discussion of "judges for commerce" that cites both Plato's *Laws* and an economic work ascribed to Xenophon, the *Ways and Means* (20.18). Xenophon is prudent to call for special judges to expedite commercial disputes, anticipating the rise of "consular jurisdiction" in late medieval and early modern Europe; Plato rightly noted that when a city has no maritime commerce, only "half the number of civil laws are needed" (596). Montesquieu elaborates by arguing that commercial dealings are "only slightly susceptible to formalities" or strict formulas in judging, since in these dealings—unlike the one-time events of marriages, wills, or trusts—new matters arise that "must be decided every day." Moreover, commerce "brings into a country different sorts of peoples, a great number of contracts, of kinds of goods and of manners of acquisition." Thus, "in a commercial town there are fewer judges and more laws" (20.18, 596). This implies a need for a small number of trained, professional judges who can master complex volumes of laws and exercise prudence on a day-to-day basis. Such a prudential depository of the laws, capable of mastering the "art of reasoning itself" entailed by numerous laws and precedent rulings, is preferable to a popular or strictly republican mode of judgment by bodies of juries (see 6.1).[14] As will be noted, in the decades just after *The Spirit of the Laws* appeared Blackstone praises the judicial art of Lord Mansfield to develop a new "law merchant" for England, on the basis not of statutes but of judicial rulings and precedents.

Montesquieu drives home the importance of judging for liberal civilization by praising France's nobility of the robe. A "particular reflection" about the "greatness of the kingdom" and how it "has endlessly increased its power" traces both phenomena to "the goodness of its laws" (20.22, 599). However, a new commercial class can buy the offices of this hereditary nobility, thereby giving "the prize of virtue to wealth." He protests that he is not endorsing the morality of the practice, only suggesting that "there are governments in which this can be quite useful." Because the new class invigorates the *parlements,* this benefits both the entire French legal system and, in turn, national greatness. This is how Montesquieu's ancestors gained, and how he passed along, a presidency in the *parlement* of Bordeaux, and this rationale informs his preference for moderate, modernized monarchies over pure republics as arenas for progress toward liberal constitutions (see 5.19). While he praises the "warlike nobility" of the sword, he raves about the nobility of the robe, so as to emphasize its moderate, middling character. Such judges also might know more about, and be able to promote, both economic commerce and the exchange of ideas that promotes more tolerant mores. This "honorable profession" and estate of the robe "lies between the great nobility and the people," and while it lacks "the brilliance of the former," it enjoys similar privileges; each member has only a "moderate fortune," but "the depositary body of the laws is left with glory"; and, each has "no way to distinguish [him]self but by sufficiency and virtue" (20.22, 599). France's greatness especially is due to "the goodness of its laws and not to fortune, which does not have this sort of constancy." These several references to virtue in relation to a nobility partly marked by purchased offices also recall Montesquieu's notice to readers regarding virtue—that he has "had new ideas; new words have had to be found or new meanings given to old ones" ("Notice," 227). Judging again prompts comprehensive reflections, and it is characteristic of Montesquieu's philosophy of "spirit" to discern the relations between these larger issues and the question whether nobles can engage in commerce or sell offices.

Montesquieu elaborates upon the spirit linking commerce, moderation, and judging when contrasting Visigoth and Roman law, since the former, while often more severe, was friendlier to commerce in at least one case. Under Gothic law foreign merchants were "judged by the laws and the judges of their own nation," an instance of a general principle he will "discuss later at length," that "each man should live under his own law" (21.18, 638; see 28.2). Montesquieu's prudent eye finds moderation in unlikely places, while the Cartesian, liberal eye needs help in seeing that the medieval Germans are in some ways a better model for a humane politics than the ancient Romans. This observation leads to a striking discussion that cites Aristotle, the Gospels, and Machiavellianism to examine "how commerce in Europe penetrated barbarism" and ushered in the modern age (21.20). Commerce softens and moderates politics because both rulers and ruled in a commercial regime become more concerned with interest, profit, and success than with pride, mastery, or greatness. When Europe's rulers imposed great tyrannies on the Jews, the latter resorted to inventing credit or "letters of exchange." The consequent prosperity was so great that Scholastic theologians dropped their objections, and princes "had to govern themselves more wisely," since "great strokes of authority were so clumsy that experience itself has made known that only goodness of government brings prosperity" (640–41). Montesquieu's prudence seeks a middle way between the unrealistic moral perfection of classical philosophy and Biblical religion on the one hand, and the brutality of Machiavelli's realistic provision for necessity on the other. Europe "has begun to be cured of Machiavellism" and has learned that "there must be more moderation in councils." So-called acts of state now would be, "apart from their horror," only "imprudences" (21.20, 641; see 23.13). The subsequent books reinforce this middle way with further discussions of usury and calls for legal prudence and reform, declaring that "[l]aws extreme in the good give rise to extreme evil" (22.21, 677; see 22.22, 682; and 22.19).

The book on population reiterates the need for moderate law and judging, one grounded in a humane conception of natural right. Montesquieu begins with a quite amorous rendering by a French poet of the opening of the *De rerum natura*, in which Lucretius praises the passions and sexuality (23.1). This sets the tone for the book, encouraging the "prudent" legislator to discern a middle state between the worldliness of the Romans and the otherworldliness of Christianity. Both extremes overlook "the pleasures of innocence," such as sexuality, marriage, and children, the same natural sentiments by which Montesquieu redefines natural right (23.1; 23.7; 23.20; 23.21; see also 1.2; 3.10; 6.13). These books on commerce and population, which occasionally discuss judging and regularly extol a moderating prudence, thus prepare for part 5, where Montesquieu seeks to temper Christian perfectionism. The spirit of prudential, liberalizing reform that links parts 4 and 5 is evident not only in this last book of part 4 but also in his remark that the English are "the people in the world who have best known how to take advantage of each of these three great things at the same time: religion, commerce, and liberty" (20.7, 590).

The two books on religion examine moral perfection broadly conceived, whether demanded by Biblical religion, classical philosophy, or their mixture in medieval Scholasticism (24.1; 24.6; 24.7). He even invokes the title phrase of the work in discussing "the rights of natural defense" as grounds for moderation. Montesquieu casts himself as an apologist for Christianity against the atheistic arguments of Pierre Bayle (1647–1706), stipulating that one must understand "the spirit" of Christianity as itself distinguishing between its "precepts," or commands, and its "counsels" of perfection. The prudent lawmaker, whether of a civil state or of the Christian religion—presumably a church hierarchy, but perhaps Christ himself—knows that if counsels are made into laws, then such a high expectation or demand would be "contrary to the spirit of laws" (24.6, 719).[15] This conception of Christianity prepares for his remarkable praise of the Stoics, a confession of faith in a this-worldly, active benevolence. Perhaps with the censors in mind, he prudently qualifies his esteem: "if I could for a moment cease to think that I am a Christian, I would not be able to keep myself from numbering the destruction of Zeno's sect among the misfortunes of human kind" (24.10, 721). The sequel echoes his state-of-nature analysis from book 1 by warning against otherworldliness: since men are "made to preserve, feed, and clothe themselves, and to do all the things done in society," religion "should not give them an overly contemplative life" (24.11, 722; see 1.2). He recalls the Christian connotations of judgment, with its moral severity and inculcation of fear, then warns that such an absolute religion can eclipse the civil laws by consuming the citizen with either hope or fear for the next life and its judgment (24.12). Still, unlike Machiavelli, he suggests that religious sentiment should be not mocked but moderated or reformed, since it is "the greatest spring there is among men" (24.13–14). The crucial lesson in prudence embodied by these books is that "it is less the truth or falsity of a dogma that makes it useful or pernicious to men in the civil state than the use or abuse made of it" (24.19, title). Here Montesquieu makes a rare reference to the soul (âme), suggesting the need for its salvation in this world from the extremes to which religion can drive politics (24.19; see also 12.18). Book 25 thus discusses toleration and advocates penal reform regarding religious crimes. Part 5 continues this line of argument with a general discussion in book 26 about how all the laws "should" relate to the things regulated. Montesquieu revises Locke's liberalism by insisting that toleration concerns more than the individual, since a balance between individual conscience and communal mores is best for achieving individual and political liberty.[16] The complexity and moderation of Montesquieu's advice on religion, appreciating the private and public importance of faith while warning of the extremism possible when religion and politics intertwine, informs the American constitutional principles that balance non-establishment, free exercise, and a cautious accommodation of religion in the public sphere.

Montesquieu further counsels moderation by noting that "the pious man" who loves religion is the counterpart to "the atheist" who hates it, and that men generally "are exceedingly drawn to hope and to fear" (25.1, 735; 25.2, 737). His most specific advice on moderation in religion and politics follows, in an extended treatment of "toleration in religious matters" (25.9–15). Religions driven only by hope or fear ultimately adopt intolerance toward each other so as to "propagate" themselves. Toleration, understood as political moderation and tranquillity, requires, paradoxically, that if the civil law already favors one religion, another should not be allowed—except, he immediately notes, if the new religion would be Christianity. The "fundamental principle" for "political laws" about religion is to avoid conflict by permitting only one religion, but if more than one already exists, then each must be tolerated by the laws and by the other religions (25.10, 744). After the call in part 4 to spread knowledge of diverse customs, the further advice here is to reform the penal laws so as to decriminalize religion. Montesquieu offers a remarkable remonstrance by a Jew addressed to the Catholic inquisitors of Spain and Portugal, protesting the execution of a young Jewish woman (25.12–13). Penal reform, the Inquisition, and a remonstrance all call to mind the judicial power and reinforce the connection between the cloaking of power and prudential instruction in humane reform.

Montesquieu closes part 5 with a book on how the laws in general "should" be. Earlier he had more narrowly addressed how laws should relate to the "principle" of each government, but book 26 examines how laws should relate to the entire "order of things upon which they are to enact" (cf. book 5). Montesquieu lists nine "sorts" of law, from natural right and divine right down to civil and domestic right. Curiously, he uses *droit naturel* and *loi naturel* interchangeably here, perhaps suggesting that the true spirit of laws transcends any Scholastic or esoteric distinction between classical natural right, medieval natural law, and modern natural rights. Moreover, his categories of law move from the most universal to the most specific right, but he lists natural right before divine right. This confirms the arguments of parts 4 and 5 about subordinating the claims of religion and divine law to human needs, and redefining natural law. A further indication of some metamorphosis afoot is that, after this curious ordering, the sequel turns first not to natural but to divine right. Indeed, among the categories listed, natural right is the only one left undefined (26.1, 750–51; 26.2). It is no surprise that this subtly unconventional book for reformers and legislators inculcates a legal prudence and addresses judging specifically. His raises both specific questions and fundamental issues, and he declares that "knowing well" these orders of law, and how various human phenomena relate to each, is "the sublimity of human reason" (751). The central theme becomes clearer as the book progresses—a redefinition of natural right in terms of the rights of "natural defense" and "natural modesty" that the accused should retain in a legal proceeding or court of law. Montesquieu criticizes laws proposed by Plato, by the English monarchy, and by ancient Rome that violate this humane natural right and the due process that should protect it (26.3, 752–53; see 3.10; 6.13). To force family members to testify against one another in prosecuting a crime is "against nature," and such laws have "overturned nature," in which "mores have their origin" (26.4, 754). When a civil law violates natural law, then "natural defense" becomes a political issue, and Montesquieu teaches that self-preservation trumps even religious teachings: "Who can fail to see that natural defense is of a higher order than all [religious] precepts" (26.7, 757–58). These maxims set the tone for the remainder of the book, which turns first to confusions about whether a law is in the order of natural law or of either civil or political law (chapters 3–6). He recapitulates the principle of both books on religion, that civil or political law must seek communal equilibrium and security for individuals above religious perfection (chapters 7–14). His final topics include confusions regarding political laws and civil laws (chapters 15–18), and conflicts between the order of civil laws and domestic laws, or *police* (chapters 19, 24, 25), and then the distinction of the claims of the law of nations from those of political or civil law (chapters 20–23).

Montesquieu's attention to judging in this book on how the laws should be includes a discussion of deciding "cases" by "reason." His analysis of a Roman inheritance law that forbade women to be heirs foreshadows book 27 on Roman law, and he quotes St. Augustine as saying, "[T]here was never a more unjust law" (26.6, 755). Montesquieu then criticizes the "human tribunals" of the Inquisition for judging not by reason but by "the maxims of the tribunals which regard the next life," and thus in a manner "contrary to all good *police*" and "unbearable." The principle throughout is that "human justice" can see only acts, since the standard of "divine justice" sees too much to be safe for individual security (26.11–12, 761–62; see 26.7–13). He instructs, as he did in confronting Machiavelli over populist judging, that political right should not trump civil right, and that the public good is the aggregate of individual goods. Individual security, therefore, must never be violated except in cases of absolute necessity. Here Montesquieu mentions "the remarkable work by Beaumanoir," discussed extensively in book 28. This thirteenth-century jurist shows that the Goths who sacked and plundered Rome initially did violate the civil rights of the vanquished, but that "the spirit of liberty called them back to that of equity." Subsequently they "exercised with moderation" the barbaric rights of conquerors, and in general, spirit, liberty, and equity were central to the "jurisprudence [of] the twelfth century" (26.15, 767–68). He reiterates the negative definition of liberty from books 11 and 12, that it "consists principally in not being forced to do a thing that the law does not order." He reinforces this jurisprudence by appeals here and in the sequel to "the nature of things" and to "reason, drawn from the nature of things" (26.20–21, 772–73).

Montesquieu concludes this book, and part 5, with two further teachings on prudence. The need to preserve a state threatened with destruction by its own political law justifies abrogation of such a law, given the fundamental political law of preservation. Like his predecessors Bacon, Hobbes, and Locke, he recommends a basic precept of modern liberalism: "THE WELL-BEING OF THE PEOPLE IS THE SUPREME LAW" (26.23, 774; emphasis in original).[17] He again addresses judging to reiterate that, according to "the nature of things," matters of *police* are the everyday things of little moment that should not be confused with "the judgments of crimes" (26.24, 775–76). The *salus populi* may require elevating the political law above the civil law, or political right above civil right, but the closing theme of this book of prudent instruction about laws is that these should be rare exceptions. By the nature of things, the end of politics and governance is to provide for the security and tranquillity of individuals. A judging power can provide that security if it has the independence to conduct complex proceedings that give every person his day in court. The spirit of laws and of legal judgments should make the law as much like a moderate *police* as is consistent with a humane natural right. Legislators and judges also must have the prudence, however, to know when law and judging can only provide security through their own restraint, that is, by leaving certain matters to the less formal, less severe arena of police and local custom. *The Spirit of the Laws* teaches that the threat of rationalism, of trying to do too much, is ever-present in politics and legislating, and in judging as well.

four

The New Aristocracy of the Robe:
History, Reason, and Judicial Prudence

It is fitting that the final part of *The Spirit of the Laws* develops a new historical jurisprudence in two books (27–28), then punctuates historical reasoning with one last theoretical book (29), and finally develops a new, historical "theory of the laws" (30–31). With this dialectical structure for part 6 Montesquieu teaches that the particular, practical, and historical dimension of his new prudence must balance its theoretical aspect. This blending of general principles and particulars, of theoretical reasoning and attention to precedents, corresponds to the quasi-monarchical, complex judicial power he advocates. He recommends to statesmen and reformers the legal prudence of judges who regularly balance principles and circumstance, old precedents and new cases. He would teach legislative and executive statesman, and reaffirm for judges, that liberty and moderation are best achieved by gradual, moderate means. This liberal education in law restores judicial power as a prominent theme after its relative obscurity in parts 3 to 5, concluding the work by reiterating his arguments for a cloaking of power. The jurist-philosopher emphasizes that the natural authority of reason and the true spirit of law are achieved when legislating becomes a bit more like judging and when judging blunts the sharp edges of legislating. This longest, and usually neglected, part of *The Spirit of the Laws* reveals both crucial and exasperating aspects of Montesquieu's political philosophy, as befits a work that would moderate philosophy and human affairs by elevating the importance of the more obscure, complex dimensions to political life. Four of the books provide histories of Roman and then French laws in terms of their origins and evolutions, interrupted by a book of general remarks on how to compose laws. The topics thus range from a crucial statement of what Montesquieu has "brought forth this work only to prove," to an apology for the "deadly boredom" that his antiquarian researches in law "must produce" (29.1; 30.15). Lest the reader's hair turn as white as Montesquieu reports his own did in writing on medieval French laws, only a glance can be cast at his historical jurisprudence. Montesquieu himself provides a defense for such a survey, concluding the long book on French jurisprudence by confessing "I am like the antiquarian who left his country, arrived in Egypt, cast an eye on the pyramids, and returned home" (28.45, 865).

Scholars often treat part 6 of *The Spirit of the Laws* as an appendix, with the exception of book 29.[1] Such demotion is due partly to a subtitle used in the early editions, and partly to the reader's fatigue upon reaching book 27 and finding book-length versions of the historical inquiries already sprinkled throughout—a weariness to which Montesquieu himself admitted in the poem launching book 20.[2] The reader who would understand the work neglects these closing books at his peril, however, for there are gems here of a kind not found elsewhere in the work, indicating Montesquieu's philosophic ambition to instruct mankind in liberal reform and a juridical prudence. It is no accident that another ambitious jurist, Oliver Wendell Holmes, complained to the author of a major text in comparative law that it erred by omitting a discussion of Montesquieu.[3] The historical jurisprudence developed in the closing books implicitly criticizes the abstract liberalism of Hobbes and Locke for either attacking or neglecting the liberty and security already embodied in the traditional law of Europe.[4] Montesquieu's blend of liberal principles and tradition legal prudence prepares the way for Blackstone's similar blending of common law and liberalism, of historical inquiry and theoretical clarity, in his *Commentaries*, which in turn is a fundamental source for American constitutionalism and jurisprudence.

Historical Jurisprudence and Judicial Reform of Laws

In book 29 the reader learns that Montesquieu wrote the work "only" to prove that the spirit of moderation is the spirit of the true legislator, but learns this only after two lengthy books propounding a new approach to law. This historical jurisprudence teaches about the juxtaposition of letter and spirit in Roman law; about the medieval French jurists who "followed the spirit of the law without following the law itself"; about the roots of English due process in medieval French judging; about the gradual reforms of King Louis IX that reveal a "natural empire" for reason; and about the "misfortune attached to the human condition" that "great men who are moderate are rare," since it is easier to find virtuous than prudent men (27; 28, chs. 9, 13, 27, 38, 41). After the advice in book 29 on the prudence needed to properly compose laws, the final two books develop this jurisprudence by emphasizing the particularity of laws and their gradual evolutions. The structure of part 6 indicates that Montesquieu sought to envelop his general advice to legislators in antidotes to any rationalist, utopian plans for sweeping acts of legislative founding. The final two books thus instruct that "it is impossible to inquire further into our political right if one does not know perfectly the laws and mores of the German peoples"; that in a nation with a spirit of "independence" statesmen must learn to "invite rather than to constrain" through the laws; and that Charlemagne's "genius" consisted not only in "so temper[ing] the orders of the state that they were counter-balanced and that he remained the master," but also in "a spirit of foresight that includes everything" (30.19; 31.5; 31.18).

Such pronouncements, sounding essential themes of the work in new keys, suggest that these books on a historical jurisprudence and legislative prudence are hardly appendices. Indeed, Montesquieu's list of the "relations" or categories of law outlined in book 1 indicates that the historical books clearly correspond to topics he thought essential to grasping the spirit of laws (see 1.3). Books 27 and 28 treat the relations laws have "to their origin"; 29 treats the relations laws have with "the purpose of the legislator"; 30 and 31 then return to the relation with origin. Montesquieu concludes this listing of fifteen or so relations that form "THE SPIRIT OF THE LAWS" by stating that laws "must be considered from *all* these points of view" and that his work "shall examine *all* these relations" (1.3, 238; emphasis added). Several scholars now accept this fundamental consistency between the historical jurisprudence and the whole work, arguing that it is characteristic of Montesquieu to use Roman and French history to illustrate the seeds of the moderate constitution he propounds throughout the work.[5] The publication history and surrounding correspondence confirm what a careful study of the work itself suggests, that the books on Roman and French legal history illustrate theories of constitutional complexity, historical development, and political and juridical prudence at the core of his political philosophy. Montesquieu's political science shares an affinity with Aristotle's attention to particular contexts, political history, comparative analysis, and prudence. However, the book on the manner of composing laws closes by arguing that Aristotle, as a "legislator," was too consumed either by "his jealousy of Plato" or "his passion for Alexander" to discern a true political philosophy or constitutionalism (29.19). Throughout the work Montesquieu criticizes Aristotle's classical moralism, since this prevents his prudential, empirical method from yielding the more tolerant, pluralistic conclusions natural to it. The French jurist adapts or revises the comparative prudential spirit of the *Politics* so as to avoid either Plato's rule by the intellectually virtuous and philosophic few or Alexander's rule by the morally virtuous and practically wise one alone. This new political science thus is even more attentive to historical contexts and the particularity required for prudence, a concern with diversity that yields a slimmer set of universal principles in nature and human nature. This permits Montesquieu to redefine the virtuous aspirations of Aristotle's regime toward the milder, security-conscious *police* of a modern France, with its false honor and humane individualism. The elevation of judging is a fitting focus for this new political science and politics, since judging is the power best attuned to the security and tranquillity of each individual.

The wealth of topics and teachings in part 6 features steady attention to judging and jurisprudence, especially in the books on French jurisprudence (28) and proper legislating (29). Montesquieu begins his analysis of historical jurisprudence and legislative prudence by discussing the seeds of medieval legal complexity in ancient Rome (book 27). This is not surprising for a philosopher whose earliest extant work concerns Roman policy regarding religion (1716), who authored the *Considerations on the Romans*, and who states in a substantial discussion of Rome earlier in this work that "[o]ne can never leave the Romans" (11.13, 414).[6] What is surprising about his study of Roman inheritance law is that it is the only book in the work with one chapter, which Montesquieu emphasizes by listing "ONLY CHAPTER" with its title. His treatment of the origins of and revolutions within Roman civil law is somehow both a book and a chapter, suggesting that things are not always what they seem, nor easy to discern. Book 28, with forty-five chapters, has far more than any other, so that Montesquieu seems deliberately to contrast the books that have the most uniquely simple and most complex structures.[7] The epigraph for book 28, quoting the *Metamorphoses* of the Roman poet Ovid on the theme of changing forms and bodies, further suggests a shift from simplicity to complexity. Montesquieu begins part 6 by juxtaposing the simplicity and stability of Roman law—and, implicitly, its legacy in continental civil law and the ecclesiastical law of the Roman Catholic Church—with the complexity, evolutions, and gradual reforms of Gothic law. Blackstone regularly cites the books in part 6, and the *Commentaries* as a whole adopts Montesquieu's blend of investigating the origins and development of laws with a quest for universal principles of right in those same laws. Blackstone also takes from *The Spirit of the Laws* a fundamental concern with property and its security, especially in the form of laws of inheritance, the subject of book 27. Montesquieu is confident that he sees in these Roman laws of "a very remote antiquity" something of theoretical importance that "no one has seen there before" (27, 778; see 5.5; 5.14; 28.22; 31).

One lesson Montesquieu discovers in these laws is that no matter their particular origins, all laws change because of particular circumstances and rulers, or in order to moderate the original laws. The "spirit of the Voconian law" on wills and testaments contradicted "natural feelings" of "filial piety" and other "sentiments of nature," and the Romans eventually abandoned it because of its severity toward family attachments and women. The larger lesson of book 27 is that it was professional judges, the praetors, who effectively changed the law, preempting legislative or executive reform:

> The old Roman law had begun to appear harsh. The praetors were no longer affected except by reasonings of equity, moderation, and decency. . . .
> The same cause which had restrained the law keeping women from inheriting had little by little overthrown the one which had hampered inheritance through relatives on the woman's side. These laws were very much in conformity with the spirit of a good republic, where one should make it so that this sex cannot avail itself, for the sake of luxury, either of its wealth or of the expectation of wealth. (27, 787–89)

Montesquieu instructs legislators, but more especially judges, in the spirit of gradual, case-by-case reform. When observing that "the whole system of inheritances was changed," he again mentions praetors, a select and predominantly patrician office, as the primary agents. The book closes by reporting that the emperor Justinian considered the reforms embodied in his code as "follow[ing] nature itself," since they set aside "the embarrassments of the old jurisprudence" (27, 789). It was the judges, however, who took the first step in that reform and many little steps thereafter. For Montesquieu, the "reasonings" of judges who, little by little, reform the law to accord with "equity, moderation, and decency" are the best mechanism for bringing the law up to nature's standard. This muted teaching on judicial reform of the laws prepares for book 28, which contains not only explicit analyses of judicial power but perhaps the most extraordinary remarks on judging in the work. In pairing these books Montesquieu suggests that if gradual judicial efforts could reform the singular, severe spirit of Roman inheritance law, then the complex jurisprudential history of France is all the better suited to maintaining—or, in the eighteenth century, restoring—France's complex, moderate constitution. Perhaps one can never leave the Romans, but Montesquieu's study of Franco-German civil law is the culmination of many remarks in *The Spirit of the Laws* suggesting that a humane constitutionalism taps a predominantly Gothic, not Roman, root.

Judicial Prudence and the "Natural Empire" of Reason

Montesquieu's analysis of the origins and evolutions of French civil law constitutes the first and most important of his three books on Franco-German law. After the relative invisibility of judging in parts 3 to 5 of the work, his analysis of French medieval law teaches that reform toward a humane natural right and a complex, moderate politics is achieved best by a quietly prominent judiciary, a cloaking of power. The titles of the four historical books in part 6, which refer to either "origins" or "revolutions" of laws, indicate the theme of gradual, step-by-step reform, a mode more characteristic of judges than of ambitious executives or overactive legislators. Montesquieu further indicates change, and perhaps reform, by choosing the first lines of Ovid's *Metamorphoses* as an epigraph for book 28: "My soul brings me to speak of forms changing into new bodies." This is only the third epigraph in the work, and after the motto to the whole work from the *Metamorphoses*, the only other book so graced employs an Epicurean line from Virgil's *Aeneid* to launch an epic about commerce, communication, and enlightenment (book 20). This subsequent book on metamorphoses in medieval French law seeks to launch a new jurisprudence of historical evolution toward humane enlightenment, with judging as a crucial component and means. Book 28 thus contains striking remarks about judging, restoring the theme of a cloaking of power to the prominence it quietly if persistently established in part 2 of *The Spirit of the Laws*. One sign of this shift is that the historical jurisprudence and "new theory of the laws" in these closing books replaces the peculiar term "power of judging," used in book 11 and earlier, with the more institutional and powerful terms "judicial power" and "judicial."

Montesquieu's specific topic in book 28 is French civil law, by which he means, in light of book 1, both civil and criminal law effecting individuals as distinct from political or constitutional law (1.3). He begins with the Germans, specifically the "character" of their laws. He reveals his inclination toward the Gothic roots of the French constitution in several remarks in parts 1 through 5, including three invocations of "our fathers the Germans" (6.18; 10.3; 14.14).[8] A book on French law that looks largely to Germanic origins, not to the Roman law just examined in book 27, reinforces the point. Here and throughout the work, he notes that Roman or civil law, especially the Justinian code or *Corpus iuris civilis*, is no small influence on the French laws and constitution. Rome is slighted in book 28, however, because of the important lesson that moderate European government has a Germanic origin and character. Montesquieu's emphatic references to the Germans in book 11 confirm the relevance of book 28 for the core themes of the work. In the midst of his first thematic exposition of a modern constitutionalism, he checks modern rationalism by citing Tacitus, *On the Mores of the Germans*, to argue that the English government actually stems from the Germans, who stumbled across it in the forests. He again cites that source in proclaiming the Gothic form of government the best men have ever devised (11.6, 406; 11.8, 409). He continues this theme by noting how medieval Germanic rulers moderated their criminal codes and due process (12.2; 12.4). Montesquieu is not suggesting the perfection of the German spirit, nor should one overlook the great praise for and prominence of England in the work. In Montesquieu's dialectical, quasi-Newtonian view of humankind and the universe, every idea or power stands in need of development or refinement—even his own political philosophy, about which he remarks there is further work "for the reader to do" (11.20). He criticizes the Germans several times, in one case noting the "extreme" and "excessive" laws of the Visigoths, although he traces this development to their move into the steamier climate of Spain (14.14).[9] Generally, however, *The Spirit of the Laws* encourages prudent legislators, reformers, and judges to build upon the spirit of medieval Gothic law rather than Roman civil law because of the severity of Roman republicanism and imperialism, and the close ties between ecclesiastical law and the civil law tradition. In an earlier discussion of "natural right" and "modesty" in laws on civil slavery, he cites "a law of the Lombards" that is "good for all governments," for, by giving freedom to both a slave and his wife if a master rapes the wife, it tempers a master's passions "without too much severity" (15.12, 499).[10]

The thematic treatment in book 28 of the Gothic spirit of French law is important both for Montesquieu's essential teaching on moderation and for his payment on a note repeatedly promised in earlier parts. He explicitly cites or directs the reader to book 28 three times—when contrasting Germanic mildness and Roman severity; when contrasting the despotic and slavish "spirit" of Asia with the milder "spirit of Europe" informed by "the manner of thinking of the German peoples"; and, when praising a Visigoth law protecting foreign merchants, which thus embodied a principle he will "discuss later at length," that "each man should live under his own law" (10.3; 17.5, 528 n. *b*; 21.18, 638). Moreover, he substantially previews book 28 when discussing laws and the nature of a given terrain (book 18). There he examines the Salic inheritance law first established by the Frankish king Clovis (fifth century A.D.) and finds that its provisions, which limited inheritance by women, later were moderated by customs or formulae developed on a case-by-case basis. These judicial usages were then collected in the *Marculfi formulae, Formulae Sirmondi*, or *Formulae Salicae*:

> when the Franks had acquired extensive lands after the conquest, it was found harsh that the daughters and their children could not have a share. A usage was introduced, which permitted a father to restore (*rappeller*) his daughter and his daughter's children [to his will]. . . . Among all the formulas, I find a singular one. A grandfather restores his grandchildren to inherit with his sons and daughters. What had the Salic Law become? It must have been no longer observed, even at that time, or the continual usage of restoring daughters must have qualified them to inherit in the most ordinary case (18.22, 544–45).[11]

This analysis foreshadows the theme of book 28, that legal reform is practiced best in the case-by-case mode of the judge or through a cloaking of power. The investigations of a historical-legal prudence which follow book 26 and precede book 29 thus temper any rationalist ambitions that might be stirred by the calls for legal reform in those more theoretical books. Book 28 teaches the prudent reformer, whether legislator or judge, to adopt both the mode and the aim of judging. Such a gradual method will best attain the goals of the reformer—the moderation of politics, the elevation of civil concerns in relation to political ones, and the tranquillity of individuals. Montesquieu opens the book by deeming the "spirit" of the German penal laws "quite judicious" for their mildness. By its close, he explains how this Germanic spirit of law further embodies the "natural empire of reason," the proper role for reason in politics. Laws found in the woods, over time, and by a people devoted to liberty contain a juridical due process laudable both for its historical development and the substantive aims it secures.

Montesquieu's narrative first recounts the tensions between the various Germanic laws and Roman law after the empire fell in the West and then the fate of these different kinds of law in ancient France during ensuing centuries. He denies that this is merely antiquarian research, for these matters will "shed light" on others that have "been obscure until now," and he is "saying new things." He even declares that "[e]verything bows before my principles," while citing Machiavelli on the history of Florence (28.4, 796, 799; 28.6, 799–800). This portrait of flux, complexity, and tension shows the aptness of the epigraph from Ovid on metamorphosis and foreshadows the criticism in book 30 of the monarchist historian Dubos, who claims a tidy harmony between imperial Rome and the Franks. Recent scholarship considers the historical understanding in all three books on French law sound, and at times path-breaking.

Moreover, Montesquieu's approach to these issues raised the sights and the stakes of such historical inquiry. He put forth a position that transcended the Romanist versus Germanic feud among seventeenth- and eighteenth-century French historians about the origins of their laws and constitution by comprehending these issues in a new political philosophy.[12] The importance of these historical books for his larger project is evident even from a few of his most thematic remarks in part 6.

Having set a fluid historical scene, Montesquieu explains how, due to judicial initiative, the barbaric laws "little by little" ceased to be used among the early French. This announces a crucial theme: over time the Franks "followed the spirit of the law without following the law itself" (28.9, 802). One theme in this narrative is the threat to Germanic freedom from the Roman or civil law and its kin, ecclesiastical law (e.g., 28.1; 28.13; 28.14). This concern about oppression of the Germanic spirit by the spirits of Roman and Christian law reinforces his judicial or procedural lesson. In discussions with peculiar titles—"Reflection," "The way of thinking of our fathers"—Montesquieu argues that "the general spirit of the German laws" brought a basic reasonableness even to the barbaric practice of trial by combat and ordeal. These practices "had a certain reason founded in experience" since they punished cowardice and sloth and rewarded valor and industry (28.15, 810; 28.17, 811–12). His praise for metamorphosis develops by recounting the actions and interactions of these various kinds of laws and customs. The genius of the ancient French was their ability to develop this *mélange* in such a way that each element had its worst edges taken off by the others (28.8, 802; 28.38, 854; 28.41).

The apex of the book is the greatness of the thirteenth-century King, Saint Louis, in using the reintroduced Roman civil law as a means to restore reasonableness and moderation to customary law. Louis IX does so, however, by drawing upon the native Germanic moderation that is, for Montesquieu, the source of moderate constitutionalism and law throughout modern Europe. The Salic law that was said to have completely rejected negative proofs or trial by oath in fact did use this in some form, but only in conjunction with "concurrent positive proofs" in testimony from both plaintiff and accused. Montesquieu comments that "the judge sought the truth in both sets of testimony" and then adds that this is "[a]s it is still practiced today in England" (28.13, 808 n. *f*). By suggesting that medieval due process is the source of the English civil and criminal procedure that he praises throughout the work, he quietly endorses a Germanic prudence regarding not only "the circumstances of the times" but also the "agreement between these laws and the mores" of these peoples (see also 28.17, 812–13). The natural reasonableness and moderation of the Germans did what it could: "One thought only of giving form to the law of judicial combat and of making a good jurisprudence come from it" (28.19, 818). For Montesquieu this is nothing less than a "jurisprudence" of judicial combat, a mode of reasonableness that prepared for the great reforms of St. Louis, "who made such great changes in the judicial order":

> One will perhaps be curious to see the monstrous usage of judicial combat reduced to principles, and to find the body of so singular a jurisprudence. Men, at bottom reasonable, place even their prejudices under rules. Nothing was more contrary to good sense than judicial combat; but once this point was posited, the execution was done with a certain prudence. (28.23, 823–24)

On this basis Montesquieu turns to a work on customary law he earlier termed "remarkable," the *Coutumes de Beuvaisis* by Beaumanoir, a thirteenth-century jurist whom he considers "the luminary of that time, and a great luminary" (28.45, 863; see 26.15). He points to Beaumanoir's observation that, little by little, judges placed limits on trial by combat in the name of reason. Indeed, Montesquieu's account reminds us of the English common-law principle of *stare decisis*: "When, in the lord's court, one had often judged in the same manner, and the usage thus was known, the lord refused to let the parties combat, so that customs would not be changed by the differing outcomes of combats" (28.25, 826). He defends judicial combat, given the circumstances, as a way to "return force to the tribunals" and thus "restore to the civil state" those who had reduced themselves to "the right of nations." This mixed state of affairs elicits a judgment on the importance of prudence in law and politics: "As an infinity of wise things are managed in a very foolish manner, so there are many foolish things conducted in a very wise manner" (28.25, 827). Using Beaumanoir and another thirteenth-century work that compiled and commented upon customary law, Montesquieu discusses numerous legal developments or evolutions. These include the rise of a jury of peers to balance the lord-judge; the slow transition from the *appel* as a combative mode of challenging a judgment to an "appeal" as a further round of testimony and reasoning in the higher court of an overlord; and the way in which the king developed a central, appellate jurisdiction (28.26–28). When noting that all in the jury of peers over whom the lord presided had to be present when their judgment was challenged or appealed, he recalls the core themes of his work: "I believe that it is this manner of thinking which gave rise to the usage still followed today in England, that all the jurors must be of one opinion in order to condemn to death" (28.27, 833). He further suggests that the concern with "point of honor," "courtesy," and "loyalty" at the root of much medieval judicial procedure is the source of the attention to individual security in modern due process—just as the "false honor" of monarchy is a better basis for a moderate politics of individual tranquillity than the zealous concern for pure liberty in republics (28.19, 818; 28.20; 28.27, 833; see 3.7).

These observations bring Montesquieu to a stage in the history of French civil and criminal procedure at once produced by earlier forces, accidents, and decisions and itself a crucial cause of later developments, the "age of the reign of Saint Louis" (28.29). The thirteenth-century reforms of judging and due process initiated, but not imposed, by Louis IX are more than another link, however, in an evolutionary chain. The mode and the aim of this king's reforms are for Montesquieu the model for a prudent legislator who would restore or elevate both reason and moderation in the laws. His remarks here are among the most theoretical and general of the work; some of them sound like Montesquieu's descriptions of his own philosophy of prudence and prudential philosophy.[13] Saint Louis achieved the "revolution" of abolishing judicial combat within his own domains but not, crucially, in those of his barons. The exception to the king's respect for such baronial autonomy was the challenge for false judgment, so as to fully change the "appeal" from the mode of combat to that of judicial reason. Appeals were to be decided "by witnesses, following a form of procedure for which he [Louis IX] gave rules." Judgment in this new mode of appeal was given not according to "the ancient jurisprudence" of combat but "according to right" (28.29, 839–41). Montesquieu suggests that "the reason" for this partial reform lay in the king's prudent understanding that he had to "manage carefully" the procedure for removing cases from the courts of his lords to his own, or another, appellate court without the appellant having to fight the lord. He thus permitted combat in the local or trial courts and retained the terminology by which an appeal was a "declaration of falseness," while removing combat from the substance of the appeal. Montesquieu's lesson about the prudent subtlety of Saint Louis is surprisingly candid: "[T]hat is to say, so that the change would be felt less, he removed the thing, and let the terms continue to exist" (28.29, 841). He also notes the outrageous abuses and injustices of lawyers when "the new opportunities for appealing increased" and "the new art of proceedings multiplied," with the remedy being to award costs to the winner of an appeal and assess them against the loser (28.35, 847). His awareness of corrupt lawyers rivals anything uttered by twenty-first-century Americans about the litigiousness of our life and politics (see also 6.1–2). This confirms his clarity about the potential for injustice in judges and lawyers, his own first profession. Ever balanced, he then credits the establishment of a public prosecutor to gradual judicial practice and not to any royal act, since the latter only confirmed that "the judicial form had changed" (28.34–36).

True to his project for the cloaking of power, Montesquieu instructs in judicial prudence and its importance through several such particular, obscure discussions. His historical examination next argues that the work called *Les Etablissements de Saint Louis* is not an exact compilation of the laws of Saint Louis but a mélange of the actual *Etablissements* with Roman law. He regularly refers to the new "judicial order" established by Saint Louis, using the more forceful, institutional term for this power (28.37). More important, he emphasizes the prudent genius of these reforms. The king "saw the abuses" of the old jurisprudence and handled the thorny issue of how to reform a power controlled by his lords by seeking to "make the peoples disgusted with it." He "accomplished his purpose" by instituting his new judicial procedures not as "a general law for the kingdom, but as an example that each one could follow and would even have an interest in following." Montesquieu declares this the epitome of prudence and moderation:

> He took away the worse, by making the better felt. When one saw in his tribunals, when one saw in those of the lords, a manner of proceeding more natural, more reasonable, more in conformity to morality, to religion, to public tranquillity, to the security of the person and of goods, the one was taken up, and the other was abandoned.
>
> To invite, when one must not constrain; to lead, when one must not command, is the supreme ability. Reason has a natural empire; it has even a tyrannical empire: one resists it, but this resistance is its triumph; yet a little time, and one is forced to come back to it. (28.38, 852–53)[14]

The very spirit of Montesquieu's political philosophy animates these extraordinary pronouncements.[15] From an examination of the judicial reforms of Saint Louis comes the judgment that this medieval monarch grasped the same constitutional principles promulgated in books 11 and 12 of *The Spirit of the Laws*— that tranquillity and security for individuals, and thus for the political order, are of the greatest importance and touch upon the greatest of political questions. Montesquieu and Saint Louis agree that better provision for these ends is worth the risks involved in significant, delicate reform of a power held either by semi-autonomous lords in their fiefs, or kings, or bodies of quasi-noble judges such as *parlements*, or popular juries. Married to the substance or strategic aims of this prudence is a tactical judgment regarding the best means and maneuvers for achieving such ends. Rather than censor or ban an abuse, prudence suggests that one should trust to revealing the better alternative, for nature and reason eventually will have their sway ("Preface," 229–30). Perhaps he cites

Plato and Socrates in the Preface because they occasion reflection on how a more prudent philosopher or statesman should act when one cannot constrain or command but finds oneself, to the contrary, commanded by those in need of reform.

Book 28 reveals the spirit of Montesquieu's prudential philosophy and philosophic prudence not only because the occasion for these extraordinary remarks is the judicial power or because of its echoes of the work's Preface; a further import lies in the understanding of reason embodied by these declarations. He only infrequently addresses an abstract conception of reason in The *Spirit of the Laws*, but a revealing progression arises in those few remarks. Book 1 refers to "a primitive [or primary] reason" that establishes the necessary relations between all things; then his core treatment of modern constitutionalism states that "the excess even of reason is not always desirable" (1.1, 232; 11.6, 407). In discussing polygamy he declares, amid a bleak recounting of the burdens facing most women in the world, that "[k]nowledge makes men gentle, and reason inclines toward humanity: only prejudices cause these to be renounced" (15.3, 493). His "Invocation" then suggests that the Muses want to "make reason speak" and portrays reason as "the most perfect, the most noble, and the most exquisite of our senses" (20, "Invocation," 585). The reformer and legislator learn that "knowing well" the distinct orders of law is "the sublimity of human reason," and the culminating conception, buried in a historical exegesis of medieval French law, is that reason can have a natural, tyrannical empire in human affairs (26.1, 751). The general portrait is that the primitive reason of a universal law of necessary relations might be analogous to a human reason so acute and powerful that nothing human, in the end, escapes its empire. However, Montesquieu also emphasizes that reason promotes moderation, and here the most authoritative reason appears in a subtle legislator who transforms the judicial power, ultimately suggesting that ruling in accord with natural reason requires gradual means and indirection. A remark made in examining the spirit produced by the English laws elucidates this paradoxical conception. He states that England, "always heated, could more easily be led by its passions than by reason, which never produces great effects on the spirit of men" (19.27, 577). This marks a shift from a primitive reason that rules the whole universe toward the limitations and frailties of human reason. He reinforces this through the poetic characterization of reason as a "sense" of the body, not a faculty of the mind akin to the soul (20, "Invocation," 585). Perhaps reason is most powerful when it is most natural, most in accord with man's passions and the inclinations of his senses. Conversely, reason might be justifiably tyrannical when the spirit of the laws outlasts the work of two rival extremes—the actions of those who neglect reason for their passions, and the best-laid plans of the abstract reasoner who lacks a prudence attentive to particulars, realities, and passions. Similarly, he instructs that political science should temper Aristotle's moralistic prudence with that of Saint Louis, concerned more with public tranquillity and with the security of persons and their goods.

Montesquieu's prudential view of reason, or redefinition of it, accords not only with the shifting meanings of reason throughout his work but with his one other metaphorical use of the term *empire*. If reason has an empire that is natural and tyrannical, he also has observed that the "empire of climate is the first of all empires" (19.14, 565). This indirectly confirms that a prudential reason that accounts for man's passions and inclinations in the manner of Saint Louis, or of Montesquieu himself, can rule imperially but gently. Such a reason accounts for the primitive empire of climate that influences the passions and inclinations, but which a legislator still can temper or guide. Indeed, he mentions an empire of climate when discussing "the natural means of changing the mores and manners of a nation," in which he criticizes Peter the Great for his "tyrannical" and "violent means" in changing Russian ways. Since the older Russian mores were a product of Asian invasions and Christian despotism, they were actually "foreign to the climate," and they did not need to be changed by laws or coercion. If Peter had possessed the prudence of Saint Louis, he would have led by "examples," for "it would have been sufficient for him to inspire" other mores and manners (19.14, 564–65).

Montesquieu elaborates upon the reforms of Saint Louis when reflecting that his new mode of appeal paved the way for a "general authority" and "general decisions" in the form of the *parlement* of Paris, which "judged in the last resort on almost all the business of the kingdom" (28.39, 855). This in turn led to its establishment as a permanent, sitting body that compiled its decisions and precedents, and then to the institution of regional *parlements*. This discussion of Saint Louis further echoes the core themes of the work not only by emphasizing the *parlements* but by using the rare encomium "masterwork of legislation." Montesquieu reserved such praise for achievement of the equilibrium of powers that defines moderate government and for placing well the judging power in the constitution of a free people (5.14; 11.11). There the phrase characterized relatively abstract phenomena, but here he attributes such a masterwork to a particular statesman. Moreover, an avoidance of both rationalism and coercion led this medieval statesman to greater success than one could ever plan to achieve, revealing the normally untapped power of one who perceives and acts according to the flexible, balanced spirit of the laws: "Thus the laws made by Saint Louis had effects that could never have been expected of a masterwork of legislation. Sometimes many centuries must pass to prepare for changes; events ripen, and there are revolutions" (28.39, 855).

Montesquieu's narrative continues by reinforcing the enduring relevance of the Germanic spirit embodied by Saint Louis. A discussion of the "ebb and flow of ecclesiastical and lay jurisdiction" reads like a case study in the constitutionalism of books 11 and 12, describing the imbalances, then checks, and eventual equilibrium achieved in the fourteenth and fifteenth centuries between clerical courts, royal courts, and the *parlements*. He describes the role of the *parlements* in correcting "abuses" of "royal jurisdiction" concerning various particular wills, inheritances, and even conjugal relations following a wedding. The subject of judging once again occasions provocative remarks that encapsulate the complexity of his political science and treatment of judging:

> When in a century, or a government, one sees the various bodies of the state seek to increase their authority, and to get certain advantages over each other, one would often be mistaken if their enterprises were considered a sure mark of their corruption. By a misfortune attached to the human condition, great men who are moderate are rare; and, as it is always easier to follow one's force than to check it, perhaps, in the class of superior people, it is easier to find extremely virtuous people, than extremely prudent (*sages*) men.
>
> The soul takes such delight in dominating other souls; even those who love the good love themselves so much, that no one is so unfortunate as to distrust his good intentions: and, in truth, our actions depend on so many things, that it is a thousand times easier to do good than to do it well. (28.41, 858)

Montesquieu addresses some of the central themes of Western political philosophy by discussing the flux and balance among governing bodies. His characteristic instruction to the reforming legislator or judge is that sagacity is more valuable than, and must be understood in contrast to, virtue. Moderation is more important than greatness, for each person's force needs to be checked due to the human soul's delight in domination: even virtue has need of limits (11.4). Here as throughout the work he emphasizes the *parlements*, the historical precursors to an independent judging power in modern constitutionalism, since they moderate the conflict between not only rival institutions but rival orders or classes.

Montesquieu closes his discussion of the metamorphoses of French laws and the prudence that best coped with them by examining even further consequences of Louis IX's subtle statesmanship. These include not only the rise of "works of jurisprudence" and of "a certain art of jurisprudence," but also the required balancing of a competent judge by a jury of peers. This evolutionary treatment suggests that the harmony with the natural empire of reason achieved by this thirteenth-century statesman yields consequences in geometric proportions: "All this happened little by little, and by the force of things"; "All this was quite reasonable" (28.42–44, 860–62). Montesquieu repeatedly states that "it was not a law" that brought about these changes, which included the rise of a legal class neither noble nor plebeian that could record and master, study and adjudicate, according to the precedent decisions of local courts, *parlements*, and the *parlement* of Paris (28.43). He implicitly identifies the natural "force of things" and that which is "quite reasonable" with this new, partly bourgeois body of professional lawyers and judges, who are the embodiment of the cloaking of power—a conception that Tocqueville will employ in the introduction to *Democracy in America*. Indeed, he sings the praises of the "great luminary" Beaumanoir as well as Fontaines and other medieval jurists who, by recounting "everything" and capturing "the truth," have beyond doubt "served well in the rebirth of our French right" (28.43–45, 861–65).

As noted, Montesquieu excuses himself at the close of this extraordinary book for not further examining the history of French laws, comparing himself to an archaeologist who only glances at his far-flung destination in Egypt. The honor, however, of being the last pyramid at which he glances is given to the rise of *parlements* as the depository of laws, and he at last provides a precise description of this crucial judicial power first mentioned in book 2 (28.45). He praises "the great body of our French jurisprudence," and the fifteenth-century *parlements* of the "great epoch" of Charles VII for their role as legal depository. In tones that Blackstone will adopt in the closing narrative of the *Commentaries*, Montesquieu depicts a time "not so distant from our own," but remarkably better,

> when [Roman] right was the object of knowledge of all those who were
> destined for civil employment; in the times when one did not glory
> in being ignorant of what one ought to know, and of knowing that
> which one ought to ignore; when quickness of spirit served better to
> learn one's profession than to engage in it; and when being continually
> amused was not even the attribute of women. (28.45, 864–65)

Montesquieu the philosopher of prudence instructs mankind through examples of how the proper spirit of the laws can beneficially inform jurisprudence, the legal profession, and politics, in hopes that it can do so in future times and other places. It is not surprising that this blend of principles and particulars would deeply influence such diverse jurists as Beccaria, Blackstone, Hamilton, Tocqueville, and Holmes, over many generations.

A New "Theory of the Laws"

Book 29 sustains this high attention paid to judging even as it shifts beyond any particular historical context to provide the work's last general treatment of the spirit of laws and of prudence. It is as complicated a book, and as important for Montesquieu's philosophic and political project, as book 19, and it is noteworthy that both books open their instructions to the prudent legislator by discussing spirit and judging. Book 29 is, in a sense, Montesquieu's summation to the jury, especially to minds at all interested in practice. He reiterates that moderation is the spirit of law in part because no human power can go unchecked if it and other powers are to flourish. In the opening lines of this later book he confirms the maxim from book 11 on the importance of placing the judicial power, just after declaring that his sole purpose in writing the work was to prove that "the spirit of moderation ought to be that of the legislator" (29.1). The persistent if muted theme of *The Spirit of the Laws* is that a founder only abides by the true spirit of a legislator when he has undertaken the masterpiece of legislating, namely, properly structuring and orienting the judicial power. Since Montesquieu steadily if subtly emphasizes the reforming power of judging throughout the work, and especially in book 28, the warnings about judicial immoderation in book 29 check the imbalanced view that judging is the only element needed in constitutionalism (29.1; see 6.5; 6.7). Far from canceling the earlier emphasis, the examples of Roman abuse of judicial power warn that judging should never lose its character by aiming to dominate the other powers. It must keep its own house in order by maintaining moderation in its due process, even as it works to moderate other political powers. This emphasis on moderation even regarding judging also serves Montesquieu's general warning about rationalism in politics. Book 28 explains in detail that a judicial system "found in the woods" in tandem with the development a people's mores can produce the very due process that a prudent philosopher finds the most protective of individual security and tranquillity.

Judging and due process are important themes again later in book 29, especially when Montesquieu compares civil and criminal procedure in modern France and England to clearly suggest the superiority of England's moderate, complex due process. He cites the *Etablissements* of Saint Louis to note that procedures similar to those of modern England were integral to "the ancient French jurisprudence" but were subsequently forgotten by modern French monarchs, judges, and lawyers (29.9–12; 29.11, 872). The final section of the book discusses first the "genius" required to be a legislator and then judicial discretion and judging, before taking parting shots at the prejudiced philosophic legislating of Plato, Aristotle, Machiavelli, More, and Harrington (29.16–19). Once again Montesquieu seeks to instruct those legislators who, in an echo of the Preface, "have a genius comprehensive enough to be able to give laws to their nation or to another" (29.16, 876). Amid this very broad discussion, judging arises repeatedly. He criticizes Plato's *Laws* for asking a judge to discern whether a man committed suicide because of desire to avoid ignominy or due to weakness, as an example of kinds of laws that unwisely ask judges to seek motives or to presume something about a defendant's action. Montesquieu warns that it would be better to have a principle of law, rather than motives that are so difficult to discern, at issue in a court: "When the judge presumes, judgments become arbitrary; when the law presumes, it gives a fixed rule to the judge" (29.16, 879–80). The sequel, tucked in among parting advice for legislators in this last book on how to compose all laws, thematically discusses judicial power. Questions of judging and a humane natural right arise from a discussion of a "bad way of giving laws" in Rome by which judges surrendered independent jurisdiction and petitioned the emperor to directly judge particular cases. The resulting "rescripts," or imperial edicts, are both bad judging and bad law, just as Montesquieu has repeatedly warned about any such usurpation of judging by other powers. All the proper Roman laws, those that are "founded on the nature of things, on the frailty of women, the weakness of minors, and the public utility," must be distinguished from such corrupt modes (29.17, 881–82). He criticizes this Roman practice of surrendering judicial functions to one ruler, while the previous chapter criticized the opposite extreme of unchecked judicial discretion. Not just virtue, but also judging, has need of limits, as Montesquieu regularly notes (6.5; 6.7; 6.15; 11.6; 11.18). The penultimate chapter of the book then reiterates that uniformity and simplicity are the hobgoblins usually of "small" but sometimes even of "great spirits," such as Charlemagne— indeed, as the sequel indicates, of spirits both philosophic and statesmanlike (29.18, 882; see "Preface," 230). American criminal law at the close of the twentieth century sought to reduce judicial discretion and achieve greater uniformity and simplicity through sentencing guidelines or "three strikes and out" provisions, not without criticisms from judges and defense attorneys. This obscure discussion at the close of *The Spirit of the Laws* suggests that a general principle of moderation or balance, one avoiding small-minded extremes, should be used to formulate not strict juridical policies but judicial maxims or rules of thumb.

This praise for an imaginative, flexible prudence within the bounds of law is the prelude to Montesquieu's declaration of independence from his philosophic predecessors at the close of book 29. His remarkable criticisms here are a late and bold complement to his introductory announcement that he believes his work has not "totally lacked genius" ("Preface," 231). In opening the work Montesquieu strikes the theme of poetic innovations through references

to Virgil and the Renaissance painter Correggio, while the theme now is prudence. Just before listing five political philosophers and theorists who failed
as legislators, Montesquieu asks, "[D]oes not the greatness of genius consist
rather in knowing in which cases there must be uniformity, and in which cases
there must be differences?" (29.18, 882). Book 29 mentions Plato several times
before accusing him of legislating according to "passions and prejudices," yet
Aristotle rates only one prior mention in the book. Moreover, Aristotle comes
first in this list of philosophers, making Plato and Aristotle the only two out
of historical order. Montesquieu mentions Aristotle only twice, in fact, in all of
part 6 of The Spirit of the Laws—in this final chapter of book 29 and just earlier,
in chapter 7. There Montesquieu argues that the Syracusan law of ostracism, for
which he cites Aristotle as a source, was made "without prudence" (29.7, 869).
His citation about such laws, however, is to "Aristotle, Republic, Bk. 5, ch. 3."
In fact, this discussion occurs in the corresponding book and chapter of the
Politics, and this is the only time that Montesquieu misnames Aristotle's main
work of political science. This may signal his attempt to replace Aristotle as the
teacher of a true prudence, based on his judgment that Aristotle drifts toward
Platonic utopianism on certain points. Aristotle's famed attention to prudence is
so far from being accurate regarding the realities and character of humankind,
Montesquieu suggests, that his political science is as abstract and moralistic
as Plato's Republic.[16] Having distanced himself not only from these classical
philosophers but also from such modern thinkers as Machiavelli, More, and
Harrington, Montesquieu indicates the striking originality proclaimed, however cryptically, in the epigraph to the work—"A child born without a mother,"
from Ovid's Metamorphoses (title page, 227). His philosophic work is so novel,
and therefore such an improvement on the incomplete, partial reflections of
his predecessors, that he can claim it cannot be traced to any one influence or
cause outside his own spirit.

The final two books of the work, on the medieval French constitution and
laws, depart from this overt commentary on philosophy and prudence but
nonetheless offer fundamentally important teachings about political philosophy and constitutionalism. Having just castigated his predecessors for failing
to be objective and comprehensive, Montesquieu states that there would have
been "an imperfection in my work if I had passed over in silence" the feudal laws
(30.1). These books begin and end with quotations from Virgil's Aeneid, calling
to mind the philosophic originality and humane attention to the passions which
Montesquieu signals in his many citations to poets throughout the work (30.1;
31.34). Moreover, he indicates that the task of these books is nothing less than
"the progress of knowledge," and that he is "instructing" and "correcting" both
prior philosophers and prior statesmen (30.15). Indeed, these historical books

contain a reflection on prudence that is as thematic and important as any in the work. Montesquieu joins a simmering if somewhat subterranean constitutional debate in eighteenth-century France about the historical origins of the French constitution—submerged because its real concern is the legitimacy of the near-absolutist conception of the monarchy held by the Bourbons.[17] He provides in painstaking detail his own "theory" of the historical development of the French constitution during the feudal era, largely through examining the work of two historians, the Comte de Boulainvilliers (1658–1722) and the Abbé Dubos (1670–1742). The issue of prudence arises from the argument that each author has made a "system" that abstracts from reality and the facts, an error that explains how they have arrived at such opposite and false extremes. Neither Boulainvilliers's portrait of an almost exclusively noble origin of the French constitution nor Dubos's portrait of an almost exclusively monarchical one captures the truth. It is fitting that Montesquieu uses Ovid to convey this message, through the Roman poet's version of the story of Apollo and Phaeton:

> The Count of Boulainvilliers and the Abbé Dubos have each made a system, the one seeming to be a conspiracy against the third estate, and the other a conspiracy against the nobility. When the Sun gave his chariot to Phaeton to drive, he said to him: "If you climb too high, you will burn the celestial residence; if you drop too low, you will reduce the earth to ashes. Do not go too far to the right, or you will fall in to the constellation of the Serpent; do not go too far to the left, or you will go into that of the Altar: stay between the two." (30.10, 891–92; citing *Metamorphoses* 2.134–39)

Montesquieu links prudence with moderation and law by insisting, against either extreme, that the French constitution is balanced both regarding powers and the classes that exercise them. He later hails the "greatness" and "genius" of King Charlemagne for seeking to check "the power of the nobility" and thereby "curtail the oppression of the clergy and freemen." Charlemagne's constitutional prudence grasped that equilibrium or moderation was the essential spirit of law: he "so tempered the orders of the state that they were counter-balanced and that he remained the master. Everything was united by the force of his genius" (31.18, 968). More profoundly, this reference to Ovid instructs not only in a political moderation and prudence but also in an epistemological or methodological aversion to extremes, a dimension addressed by criticizing the erroneous "system" constructed by each author. He is particularly severe with Dubos's *Critical History of the Establishment of the French Monarchy* (1742), which is made throughout book 30 to epitomize the folly of constructing systems: "If the system of the Abbé Dubos had had a good foundation, he would not have been obliged to make three deadening volumes to prove it; . . . reason itself would have taken up the charge of placing this truth in the chain of other truths" (30.23, 926). This verdict about a long, complicated work may raise thoughts about rocks thrown by authors living in glass castles. Still, these remarks are consistent with Montesquieu's earlier dismissal of James Harrington and his *Commonwealth of Oceana* at the close of the famous chapter on England, which asserts that Harrington misunderstood liberty because "he built Chalcedon with the coast of Byzantium before his eyes" (11.6, 407; see 11.5, 396). [18]

This critique of systems or of Cartesian foundationalism, with its distinction between simply finding and elaborately seeking, has bigger targets in mind than Harrington and Dubos. In Montesquieu's judgment Hobbes and Locke, too, sought to build elaborate systems upon foundations that are abstractions. His more empirical, prudential approach seeks a middle way between such modern foundationalisms and the ancient Greek political philosophy that sought to clarify the most respectable opinions of political actors themselves. [19] Such attention to particulars and the judgments of statesmen is more alert to historical change and context than the political philosophies of Hobbes or Locke. Indeed, Montesquieu employs a telling phrase in criticizing Dubos, lumping him with other "modern authors with particular systems," all of whom ignore the flux and particularities in human politics that they could discover through observation (30.14, 901). His own attention to metamorphoses in nature, human nature, and politics leads to his novel emphasis upon historical changes in political and legal meaning—although a cue also may have been taken from Machiavelli's *Discourses*. Montesquieu's spirit is neither abstract nor doctrinaire but prudential, attending to the actual plights and possibilities of the humanity over which his philosophic spirit watches. This suggests that the complex jurisprudence of a Blackstone, Hamilton, or Tocqueville, not the simpler rationalisms of either Kantian moralism or Holmesean legal realism, better accords with the constitutionalism and conception of judicial power elaborated by Montesquieu, which so deeply influenced the American founders.

The final two historical books of *The Spirit of the Laws* combine such general reflections on prudence and jurisprudence with particular reminders about the importance of judicial power. Several examples reiterate that the roots of eighteenth-century English due process lie in the medieval Franks, and Montesquieu concludes that "it is impossible to inquire further into our political right if one does not know perfectly the laws and mores of the German peoples" (30.17; 30.19, 912). He later examines Charlemagne to teach once again that the true legislator must learn to invite rather than to constrain, and that Charlemagne's "greatness" was to combine in his laws "a spirit of foresight that includes everything" with "a certain force that carries everything along" (31.5; 31.18). Finally, Montesquieu argues that a crucial element of the mixed constitution achieved in medieval France was the independent judging power of the nobility, a power that on such crucial questions as inheritance "little by little" extended and modified the laws (31.21; 31.28; 31.30). The penultimate chapter of the entire work surprisingly cites Sir Edward Coke's predecessor as master of the English common law of tenures or property, Sir Thomas Littleton. This raises again the ambiguous relationship between Montesquieu's jurisprudence and the obvious English precedent for the kind of judicial depository of laws advocated throughout the work. Here at the very close lies the only reference to a common-law text or author in the work, and it can hardly be accidental that Montesquieu utterly overlooks the prominence of this tradition of judging and jurisprudence in the modern constitution that he most highly, if qualifiedly, praises. Moreover, this neglect occurs just a century after theoretical and practical disputes between Coke, Bacon, and the Crown over matters central to Montesquieu's political science.

These closing books provide further evidence that this silent treatment of the common law is deliberate. Montesquieu's aim is to promote a distinct, non-Aristotelian mode of Gothic or customary law in France and other countries. One sign of this comes in his use of the phrase "theory of the laws" in the titles to books 30 and 31. He uses that phrase here for the first time in the work, and the new theory seems to be Montesquieu's modern blending of theory with historical particularity. It is as if he were a scientist examining samples of medieval constitutions and laws under a microscope, seeking to develop a theory of their evolution.[20] This is alien to the professional, distinctly practical mode of reasoning of a classic common-law jurist such as Coke, a mode contentedly practical in part because of its ultimately teleological conception of reason, human nature, and law. Montesquieu redefines the concept of "theory" in accord with the political science of spirit and complex relations propounded in the preceding 29 books. The result is a theory less abstract or rationalist than that of some predecessors, but even more practically oriented than that of classical philosophy. A world comprising relations between bodies and powers in flux both requires and supports a prudence that embodies a poetic flexibility and imaginativeness. Because it is less sure about the higher aims of human conduct, a modern prudence must be attuned to the particular circumstances and passions of human politics. Montesquieu thus surveys the drama of human history and politics like a judge with much testimony at hand. His judgment is guided by no more substantive natural laws than the preservation and tranquillity of each person, an equilibrium of relations among all, and rudimentary inclinations toward sociability, knowledge, and pride.

In the end, watching over humankind requires the same blend of minimalist principles of right and attention to particulars that defines judging and a just due process. Montesquieu's liberal education in law seeks to instruct at once philosophers, legislators, and judges in this spirit. To understand such a philosophy it may be crucial to understand, then, the legacy among statesmen and thinkers that it sought and achieved, perhaps especially in the realm of modern conceptions of jurisprudence and judicial power.

PART TWO

Blackstone and the Montesquieuan Constitution

Because Montesquieu's philosophy emphasizes enlightenment for mankind and practical wisdom for reforming statesmen, one can better understand the subtle jurist himself by examining the influence he achieved among important figures in both the theory and practice of modern constitutionalism. Moreover, this approach is helpful because of the quiet character of his project to judicialize politics, which could be expected to meet as much resistance as any program for political reform. Montesquieu thought his aims required an indirect presentation of his teaching, and the reader can better penetrate such a presentation with the help of character witnesses among his immediate successors in jurisprudence. Blackstone, Hamilton, and Tocqueville, who are closer to Montesquieu than we are not only in time but also in frame of mind, provide important testimony about his intentions. His indirection partly took the form of speaking more clearly to fellow jurists, judges, and lawyers than to other readers, and the mark he left upon leading European and American jurists is evident. The philosophers, writers, and statesmen whom Montesquieu deeply influenced span a remarkable range, from Blackstone, Hume, Burke, Gibbon, and Smith, to Rousseau, Hegel, Constant, Guizot, and Tocqueville; and among the American framers, John Adams, Madison, and Hamilton. Recent scholarship ranks him among the most influential figures in Western law, and another assessment of "great jurists of the world" identifies him as founding the comparative school of jurisprudence.[1] More relevant to his constitutionalism and conception of judging is his influence upon such eighteenth-century jurists as the penal reformer Cesare Beccaria, the liberal constitutionalist Jean-Louis Delolme, and, most especially, the English jurist and judge Sir William Blackstone (1723–1780). This range of jurisprudential theories itself confirms the complexity and capaciousness of Montesquieu's teaching. Beccaria was the leading liberal reformer of criminal codes and opponent of capital punishment in eighteenth-century Europe.[2] On the other hand, Bentham, Jefferson, and other advocates of a more democratic, Lockean liberalism criticize Blackstone as a conservative who put forth a muddled account of law so as to protect the status quo. However diverse his legacy may be, Montesquieu's distinct achievement within modern liberal constitutionalism, one even more important than his novel advocacy of federalism, is to place judging at the center of his constitutional theory. His program to reform liberalism and even illiberal regimes features a judicial power that looks to the spirit of the law, not solely its letter. Some consequences and characteristics of this philosophy readily appear through examining Blackstone, Hamilton, Tocqueville, and the American jurist Oliver Wendell Holmes Jr. These are Montesquieu's most prominent heirs regarding judicial power—however odd such a designation seems for such a diverse set of thinkers and statesmen.

The first step in tracing Montesquieu's legacy in modern judicial power is to rediscover the serious constitutional project in Blackstone's *Commentaries on the Laws of England* (1765–69). Blackstone understood Montesquieu to be quietly elevating judicial power and redefining liberalism in juridical terms, and he carried this project into the English-speaking world. Both jurists formulate a constitutionalism of liberty, and propose a cloaking of power and moderation of political liberty for the sake of both political and civil liberty. Both deeply influenced statesmen in England, and eventually America, while they eventually were criticized by more progressive minds as confused and confusing, and as insufficiently liberal. Further similarities arise upon serious comparison of *The Spirit of the Laws* and the *Commentaries*, and these features suggest that the powerful judiciary of twentieth-century liberalism is the fruit of a deliberate project. The central constitutional principle for each jurist is separation of powers, which in part means rival institutions or parties checking each other, and both emphasize an independent status for a judicial power that uniquely moderates the other powers. A stable, enduring constitutionalism will protect liberty, and because their view of law and liberty is rooted in a doctrine of natural right, the legal prudence of the judiciary best understands how to protect natural right for individuals in specific cases. These principles—liberty, a complex constitutionalism, and natural right—have been steadily discredited since the eighteenth century in the jurisprudence and political theory of liberal democracy. It was these principles, however, that distinguished judging from legislating for both Montesquieu and Blackstone, and that guided a subtle judicial statesmanship to avoid the political immoderation of legislating from the bench. Our disregard for these principles of modern judicial power fosters the sophisticated, revisionist claim that there never was a real distinction between judging and legislating in English common law, or elsewhere in the Western tradition. Part 3 of this book argues that Holmes's skepticism about natural right and any enduring meaning in the law prompted him to take direct aim at Montesquieu and the Blackstonean common-law tradition that had come down to him. If he could transform or discredit their teachings, especially their conceptions of separation of powers and constitutionalism, then he could erase the notion of judges as stewards of a legal inheritance rooted in fundamental principles and natural right. Most jurists and political scientists today cannot recognize the principled difference, affirmed by Montesquieu and the jurists he deeply influenced, between liberty and short-term utility, nor the distinction they drew between separation of powers and a formless policy-making or administrative power in a government. What eludes us is how and why Montesquieu and Blackstone link the means of complex constitutional forms and enduring natural right to the ends of liberty and natural rights. While they advise judges to exercise a distinctly legal discretion in discerning the moderate spirit of laws, so as to promote political and individual tranquillity, they also warn that if judges boldly legislate and radically transform the law, they sacrifice not only the forms but the ends of a decent legal order. Blackstone thought that Lord Mansfield was a model of judicial statesmanship, but he also thought that Mansfield was not always careful to distinguish between reform within the spirit of law and legislating a wholly new spirit for law. For Blackstone, blurring this distinction threatened the separation of powers and the rule of law in a way that ultimately would threaten judicial independence, all of which put at risk these necessary bulwarks of individual rights and liberty.

Legal realism in twentieth-century America entails the sacrifice of both traditional forms and traditional legal ends to the formless, pragmatic judging which serves utility and enforces agnosticism about whatever ends each individual seeks to promote. Holmes and other progressives effectively persuaded twentieth-century American law not so much to criticize the Montesquieuan and common-law traditions as to mock them as a "legal formalism" that hid the real activity of judging. Holmes and his colleagues did so through advancing a circular proposition: that because there is no enduring essence to the law, all judges are really administrators and policy makers, and because all judges are lawmakers, there really is no enduring essence to the law. We tend not to ask whether this understanding of law is feasible in the long term, and whether an ever-progressive, legislative conception of judging in fact undermines the legitimacy and stability of judging and of the law. After a century of Holmesean realism gradually corroding the stability, distinctness, and legitimacy of law and the legal profession, we should be more pragmatic, in a larger sense, about our narrow, dogmatic pragmatism. It is enough to justify the rediscovery of Blackstone undertaken here to note that, even today, the Holmesean acid of realism has not completely removed our conceptions of separation of powers, natural right, and the importance of liberty and natural rights. We also can ponder the fact that Blackstone and Montesquieuan constitutionalism produced so much liberty, security, prosperity, and power during the eighteenth and nineteenth centuries that later jurists and political scientists have had the leisure to ignore or scorn their supposedly formalistic, inegalitarian, dated principles.[3] There are now sufficient difficulties evident in the theory and practice of legal realism, and of post-Enlightenment thought generally, that we have cause to reexamine the founders of modern liberal jurisprudence beyond the narrow legal positivism of Hobbes, Locke, and Austin, and beyond the spell of Holmes.

five

Blackstone's Liberal Education for Law and Politics

If lawyers in the British Commonwealth and America today must acquire a degree from a university, no longer rising to the bar through apprenticeship, then Sir William Blackstone is the founding architect of the modern Anglo-American legal profession.[1] With enduring form, however, comes enduring substance, and Blackstone intended not only to influence the training of lawyers and judges in liberal constitutions, but to make them a subtle but important influence on liberal politics. He understood the *Commentaries* as embodying a reform project in English law, contrary to the portrait of him painted by Jeremy Bentham and others impatient for progress toward more radical reforms of liberal constitutionalism. The opening words of the work profess the "novelty" of lecturing on English common law in an English university and, more broadly, of promoting "knowledge of our laws and constitution" as "a liberal science."[2] Prior to his lectures on English common law at Oxford University in 1753, both Oxford and Cambridge had taught only the civil law, rooted in the Roman Empire and partnered with the Roman Catholic and then Anglican Church and the ecclesiastical courts. The study of English common law still was the sole province of the Inns of Court in London, governed by senior barristers and judges. Unlike the rest of Europe, then, in England a university faculty did not supervise professional training in law. Blackstone boasts of his innovation in legal education, but, like his teacher Montesquieu, he only quietly indicates in the *Commentaries* that he has in mind a more extensive enterprise, both legal and political. A fresh look at this often mentioned yet rarely studied work reveals Blackstone as a direct source for the American founders' novel idea to establish an independent judicial power in the 1787 Constitution. This in turn laid the foundation for the political influence of the legal and judicial professions in America, and, subsequently, for the American export of a juridical conception of liberalism around the globe.

The derision of Blackstone's critics is proportional, paradoxically, to this striking achievement in the history of Anglo-American and modern law. Much scholarship on Blackstone, whether purporting to be hostile or not, is a variation upon Jeremy Bentham's *A Fragment on Government* (1776), published in Blackstone's lifetime in an effort to puncture the great reputation that the *Commentaries* immediately gained in the English legal profession. Bentham rushed out his fragment before his larger commentary was completed, confident that his limited study showed that Blackstone never saw a part of the established legal order he didn't like or a reform of English law he did like.[3] The possibility that Bentham's indictment is more polemical than jurisprudential arises not least from the fact that he never examines Blackstone's announcement of a project for reform at the very opening of the work, a program neither expeditious nor radical enough for a revolutionary spirit.[4] Blackstone's conventional yet graceful approach to reform, however, made the four books of the *Commentaries* an immediate and lasting success and spurred a reform of English law that subsequently took a more Benthamite, legislative turn. The *Commentaries*, like *The Spirit of the Laws*, is more congenial to the statesman than to the abstract thinker. It has been influential precisely among those of a practical yet thoughtful bent who do not grasp complicated human and political problems in the neat categories of analytic discourse.

Blackstone's preface to the work describes his search for "the elements of the law, and the grounds of our civil polity" as being unique because it was "so new, so extensive, and so laborious." This recalls Machiavelli's comparison of his *Discourses* to Columbus's discovery of new continents, or Montesquieu's references to explorers and to inventions like the compass.[5] The poetic style particularly reminds us of *The Spirit of the Laws*, with Blackstone employing the arts of his own verse compositions and Shakespeare criticism to make the law more attractive to thoughtful statesmen of the law and beyond. This mirrors Montesquieu's versifying and comparison of himself to a painter in a work whose motto bespeaks the transformations of an Ovid.[6] Even Bentham admitted that it was Blackstone who "first of all institutional writers, has taught Jurisprudence to speak the language of the Scholar and the Gentleman," for he had "enlivened her with metaphors and allusions."[7] Montesquieuan phrases and purposes shine forth from the very opening of the *Commentaries*. Particularly evident are ambitions to reeducate lawyers and judges in order to remake law and judging, and a tone suited to achieving such practical aims:

> [A]ll, who of late years have attended the public administration of justice, must be sensible that a masterly acquaintance with the general spirit of laws and the principles of universal jurisprudence, combined with an accurate knowledge of our municipal constitutions, their original, reason, and history, hath given a beauty and energy to many modern judicial decisions, with which our ancestors were wholly unacquainted. (1, "Preface," xxxviii)

Blackstone drank deeply from *The Spirit of the Laws*, more deeply than most Blackstone or Montesquieu scholars have recognized, and then wrote a work of similarly impressive influence. The *Commentaries* became a fundamental text for American law and constitutionalism almost immediately. It was a source for the colonists about English law and for the revolutionaries about the rights of men and Englishmen, and then it served as a guide to the framers about the principles of a moderate constitutionalism. The standard list of testimonials and evidence is worth rehearsing in order to counteract the complacency or contempt bred by our vague familiarity today. Burke, in his 1775 speech to Parliament on conciliation with the Americans, explained the Americans' insistence upon their rights by noting that "they have sold nearly as many copies of Blackstone's *Commentaries* in America as in England"; indeed, one thousand copies had been sold before the first American edition of fourteen hundred sets appeared in 1772. *The Federalist* cites Montesquieu and Blackstone numerous times but never cites Hobbes or Locke; John Marshall cites Blackstone in some of his most important rulings, including *Marbury v. Madison, Fletcher v. Peck,* and *Dartmouth College*; Chancellor Kent and Justice Story each modeled their treatises on American private and public law upon Blackstone; and, in the 1850s Lincoln recommended that a lawyer still should begin, as he had, by reading the *Commentaries*.[8] Had Montesquieu lived to see the *Commentaries* and their influence, one can imagine his satisfaction that the politically ambitious men of such great and future world powers were being educated in Montesquieuan prudence, through an attractive if complex blend of generalities and particulars. As does no other work but Montesquieu's, the *Commentaries* describes the spirit of a nation's laws and suggests a new constitutional equilibrium of power. Blackstone translates the project for a cloaking of power to English circumstances: common-law judges are to temper the King-in-Parliament, and the political class is instructed in incremental reform—mainly by judges—toward a moderate liberalism.

The claims about Blackstone's importance for American law reach a zenith with Daniel Boorstin, who proclaimed that in "the history of American institutions, no other book—except the Bible—has played so great a role." In fact, he declares the *Commentaries* "the bible of American legal institutions" for the colonists, founders, and nineteenth-century lawyers.[9] Boorstin concludes that Blackstone's commonsense reason is preferable to the "rationalist" and "hyper-scientific approach" of Bentham, but he often damns Sir William with faint praise, thereby furthering the work of Bentham and Jefferson to demote him from established authority to a historical and politically wrong-headed curiosity. Boorstin's judgment that he perpetrated a "mysterious science" of law upon the British and Americans adopts, wittingly or not, the reigning view among critics since Bentham's attack in 1776. As I will discuss, the *Commentaries* is said to cunningly coat the law in something or other—honeyed commercialism and conservatism according to Jefferson and other progressives, deliberate perplexity in the defense of the status quo according to Bentham and later analytical critics.[10] The fortunes of the *Commentaries* did revive somewhat early in the twentiethth century, as is most evident in the sympathetic treatment by William Holdsworth in his encyclopedic *A History of English Law*.[11] In the latter half of the century more studies in British and American legal academia have taken seriously the *Commentaries* than have dismissed them, perhaps due to the search for principles and guidance amid the uncertainty produced by legal realism and judicial activism.[12] Before dismissing Blackstone as a clever but dated magician, it would behoove students of modern law and constitutionalism to take seriously the phenomenon of the *Commentaries*, to understand why it was so deeply influential, and for so long, in English-speaking lands devoted to law, liberty, tranquillity, commerce, and a moderate politics.

Because of the complexity not only of the entire *Commentaries* but in particular of its view of judging, one must grasp the structure of the work to understand its concept of judicial power. Blackstone seeks to describe and praise, but also to reform, a constitutionalism of liberty and complexity. The difficulties of deciphering his jurisprudence, including how its principles relate to those of Hobbes, Locke, and Montesquieu, demand a careful examination of general issues before the question of judging in his constitutionalism properly can arise. One must first consider that Blackstone's work reflects a coherent intention and design, and that his work endorses neither parliamentary supremacy nor conservative monarchism, if one is to further consider that he sought to quietly elevate the judicial power within a liberal constitutionalism that is Gothic, complex, and balanced.

The Spirit of the *Commentaries'* Structure

Blackstone nowhere explains the meaning of the title to his work, nor does he indicate that "commentaries" marks a largely novel choice within the history of works on English law, and scholars mostly have met silence with silence.[13] An obvious model is the alternate title of Coke's *First Part of the Institutes of the Lawes of England*, which he termed *Commentaries upon Littleton's Tenures* (often simply known as "Coke-Littleton"). Still, this was only an alternate, and the main title adopted a traditional term, "institutes," rooted in Justinian and the civil law. "Commentaries" suggests something of a nontitle, subordinating the commentator and indicating no comprehensive theme that represents the author's stamp on the topic. Blackstone might be casting his work in the tradition of commentaries on the Bible or Aristotle, which would suggest a Scholastic genre. He might wish it to be understood as a more comprehensive successor to Coke's classic common-law commentaries on English property law. In either case, such a title does not immediately reflect the spirit of novelty and ambition in the work. Part of its ambition is further concealed by the later elements in the title, which identify the topic as "the laws of England." The dedication to the Queen alone reveals that Blackstone considered the topic to be broader; there he describes his work as a "view of the laws and constitution of England."[14] The preface and introduction to the whole work further confirm that the topic is not only England's laws but its constitution, and this in the broad sense of the English "polity"—the term Blackstone used when first announcing his lectures in 1753.[15] Moreover, Blackstone analyzes law, constitution, and polity through comparative jurisprudence and law, to include political philosophy, and with reference to both ancient and modern sources. He deems himself competent to examine all the laws of England, not just one area of law, and beyond that to examine the constitution and political regime of England in comparison to the theory and practice of constitutionalism in other times and places. Part of what the narrow title obscures, then, is some similarity to the scope and character of Montesquieu's *The Spirit of the Laws*.

As noted, the preface announces an ambition to propound a novel and liberal science of "our laws and constitution" and "the grounds of our civil polity," although one that opens up to knowledge of "the general spirit of laws" and "the principles of a universal jurisprudence" (1, "Preface," xxxvii). The introduction then begins with Blackstone's 1753 inaugural lecture as Vinerian Professor, "On the Study of the Law." This is the first section of an introduction to the whole work that provides the philosophy or spirit lying behind all four books, for not until the beginning of book 1, more than one hundred pages hence, does Blackstone explain his fourfold division into books. The introduction does not even mention that explicit structure—the rights of persons, constitutional as well as individual (book 1); the rights of things, or property law (book 2); private wrongs, or civil injuries (book 3), and public wrongs, or criminal law (book 4).[16] Much Benthamite criticism has been aimed at this structure as incoherent and merely a device of political conservatism, or as an unsuccessful attempt to analyze English law using the ancient Roman classifications of Justinian.[17] Bentham himself, on the other hand, correctly realized that the main target of his criticism had to be the introduction, not the structure explained in book 1, although his *Fragment* attacks only the analysis of laws in general in the second section of the introduction.[18]

Bentham would have been more correct had he had taken seriously all four sections of the introduction. He was right to think that some more fundamental principle or idea informs the division into four books, although his Hobbesian, analytical inclinations led him to focus solely on Blackstone's theoretical discussion of natural law, positive law, and sovereignty. Blackstone implies the subordinate status of the fourfold structure of books by extensively discoursing upon four separate topics in the introduction before even mentioning that structure. Moreover, he provides the rationale for the later sections of the introduction—"On the Nature of Laws in General," "Of the Laws of England," and "Of the Countries Subject to the Laws of England"—in his initial account of the ends and means of the study of law. Bentham dismisses this opening lecture as "rhetorical," but this only proves the narrowness of his own rationalism. Bentham's search for the first principles of a mathematical proof about sovereign will and a rational system of law could not take seriously Blackstone's argument about the fundamental rationale or end of the British constitution. That rationale, Blackstone's principle or end, is liberty, and it is this that directs his reform of both the study of law and the laws themselves. The authority cited for this fundamental orientation toward the law and constitution of England, and the first modern authority cited in the work—before even Coke or Locke— is Montesquieu. Blackstone's immediate point, early in his lecture, is that the first reason why students should see the "utility" of studying English law is its singular devotion to liberty. England is a "land, perhaps the only one in the universe, in which political or civil liberty is the very end and scope of the constitution." He cites Montesquieu not only to adduce international testimony, but for the essential teaching that liberty is *the* principle by which to interpret, and improve, England's laws and constitution (1, "Intro.," sec. 1, *6).[19]

Bentham's contrasting aim is reform in the name of the abstract principle of utility, which for him is the only rational postulate that can justify sovereign authority. This disposition leads him to declare Blackstone an "enemy" for discouraging reform. The contrast sharpens when Bentham treats liberty as subordinate to utilitarian reform—as merely "Reformation's harbinger."[20] If, however, one tries to understand Blackstone's work rather than pronounce sentence, then one can grasp that the opening lecture reveals the seminal themes of the *Commentaries*, understood as an examination of and a program for the quiet reform of the law of liberty. Blackstone begins by inviting all to join him at the very "infancy" of "academical" study of law and closes by declaring that what follows will give students "a general map of the law"—to include more than English common law (1, "Intro.," sec. 1, *3, *35). This introductory discourse is replete with references to his efforts to bring order, a plan, and science to the law. One cannot understand the *Commentaries*, either to praise or pan, unless one grasps Blackstone's plan and the understanding of legal science that informs it.

The first paradox of Blackstone's plan and science arises from his dual position as doctor of laws (Oxford, 1750) and member of the bar (Inns of Court, 1746). He insists to his colleagues "within these philosophical walls" that English law is at once a "most useful and most rational branch of learning" but is in so backward a state that it is a "novelty" to call it a "science" (1, "Intro.," *30, *3, *4). Not only must he reform the law and the study of it to improve what is done at the Inns, but he must reform liberal education both for gentlemen and the nobility in the universities. While study of English common law is "neglected, and even unknown" to all but professionals graduated from the Inns, England must now attain the general level of legal learning long enjoyed by the Continent and Scotland. Blackstone seeks to ensure that "a competent knowledge of the laws of that society, in which we live, is the proper accomplishment of every gentlemen and scholar; an highly useful, I had almost said essential, part of liberal and polite education" (*4–6). By the end of his apologia he presents a second paradox: that while he seeks a modern science of the common law, it is nonetheless essential to understand its origins in the Gothic past. The "method" of the *Commentaries* will be that of his *Analysis of the Laws of England* (1756), and he forms his general map of the law in the manner Sir John Fortescue recommended in the fifteenth century, by "tracing out the originals and . . . the elements of the law" (*34–35). Since Fortescue's time, Hobbes had published his own *Elements of the Law*, but Blackstone's explicit references here are to Fortescue, Justinian, and his own *Analysis*, which in turn acknowledges Sir Matthew Hale's *Analysis of the Law* (1713). This new science seems indebted to the great English common-law writers and in a lesser way to Justinian, but not to Hobbes, an avowed critic of the common law, who is cited not once in the four books.[21] Still, if the traditional common-law expositions of Fortescue and Coke truly were adequate, then Blackstone's account would not be a novel science. He cannot consider recourse to the Roman civil law his great advance, for while the introductory lecture cites Justinian and declares it profitable for common-law lawyers to know the civil law, the common law is "its equal at least, and perhaps an improvement on the other" (1, "Intro.," sec. 1, *21).

Indeed, Blackstone explicitly reminds those who would raise the civil law above the common law, or "sacrifice our Alfred and Edward" for "Theodosius and Justinian," that they are choosing "the despotic monarchy of Rome and Byzantium" over "the free constitution of Britain" (1, "Intro.," sec. 1, *5). Roman law forms one part of his analysis, but in his "general map of the law" the first element listed is Gothic custom, and the most important source is the feudal law. Moreover, as his favorable references to Bacon and Montesquieu indicate, Blackstone's project presumes that mere practice or art—thus the "artificial" legal reason about which Coke boasts—is inadequate for both the theory and practice of a law of liberty. He complements, and at times supplants, Coke's artificial wisdom with the natural scientific reason of liberal philosophy. All of these dimensions to this analysis of the origins or elements of English law recall Montesquieu's first definition of the many relations that compose the "spirit" of the laws. Indeed, Blackstone lays out his task in Montesquieuan terms:

> These originals should be traced to their fountains, as well as
> our distance will permit; to the customs of the Britons and Ger-
> mans, as recorded by Caesar and Tacitus; to the codes of the north-
> ern nations . . . to the rules of the Roman law . . . but, above all,
> to that inexhaustible reservoir of legal antiquities and learning, the
> foedal law . . . the law of nations in our western orb. These primary
> rules and fundamental principles should be weighed and compared
> with the precepts of the law of nature, and the practice of other
> countries; should be explained by reasons, illustrated by examples,
> and confirmed by undoubted authorities; their history should be
> deduced, their changes and revolutions observed, and it should be
> shewn how far they are connected with, or have at any time been
> affected by, the civil transactions of the kingdom. (1, "Intro.," sec. 1,
> *35–36; cf. *The Spirit of the Laws*, 1.3; 30.1)

How can the study of the common law be a science if that study now is in such disarray, and how can common-law reasoning be a mode of liberal science if its essential spirit lies in the feudal past? The answer to Blackstone's initial paradoxes lies in the influence not of Hobbes or Locke but of that liberal and scientific lawyer-judge who moderated liberal, positivist jurisprudence. Like Montesquieu, Blackstone would reap the benefits of modern philosophy but temper the excesses of its rationalism, as is evident in the *Commentaries*' subsequent discussion of the state of nature, or of Locke on revolution, or of Beccaria on a precise scale of punishments. Like his French predecessor, he finds the law of liberty not in some new Enlightenment rationalism but in the woods, with the medieval Goths. The French jurist and his English disciple recommend a moderate spirit of liberal reform because the only path to effect quicker, deeper reform would be to push aside the nobles and all other customs and start anew on the basis of a principle entirely abstracted from the experience of each country. Just as Montesquieu cautions against revolutionary reform in the Preface to *The Spirit of the Laws*, so Blackstone can see a Bentham on the horizon—advising the legislature to address all injustices by striking off a new code, as if to fix all the contradictions and injustices of English law in one sweep. Indeed, like Montesquieu, Blackstone is critical of the English figure who represents the tumult of such utopian reform, referring to "the subversion of our ancient constitution under Cromwell," and to "Cromwell's government" as "the worst of times" (3.21, *322; 4.14, *178; see also 1.2, *160; 1.3, *212; 4.33, *438).

Political and constitutional liberty, preserved and achieved gradually and defined at least in part by tranquillity and stability for each person, is the first principle of this Montesquieuan jurisprudence.[22] Blackstone confirms this, four books later, with a final chapter of the work that praises the liberty achieved through more than a millennium of English constitutional progress, and which calls for further progress in that spirit (4.33). The central importance of liberty is evident throughout the work, beginning with the introductory lecture. Blackstone addresses himself to gentlemen, the nobility, and all commoners about why each needs some general knowledge of England's law of liberty, citing Locke's *Thoughts Concerning Education* on the necessity of at least basic training in law (1, "Intro.," sec. 1, *7–16). Two offices that gentlemen of "considerable property" may hold are jurors and, if "ambitious," members of Parliament. While no criticisms are made of jurors, sharp words are saved for the "mischiefs" caused by "rash and unexperienced" legislators tampering with the received common law. While the premise of the work is that Coke's, or even Hale's, traditional presentation of the common law is insufficiently scientific, here Blackstone calls upon Coke's criticism of alterations by "men of none or very little judgment in law." Blackstone makes the point more poetically: this noble fabric has had its "symmetry" destroyed, its "proportions" distorted, and "its majestic simplicity exchanged for specious embellishments and fantastic novelties" (*10). Perhaps Bentham, who heard Blackstone's lectures as a student, was so vehement a critic because Blackstone warned against such plans for reformation by legislative codification, dismissing them in Montesquieuan manner as likely to do more harm than good.

Indeed, Blackstone later criticizes the "visionary schemes" of the poor laws as "very imperfect, and inadequate to the purposes they are designed for," despite the efforts by judges to improve them—"a fate, that has generally attended most of our statute laws, where they have not the foundation of the common law to build upon" (1.9, *365). This praises the superiority of common-law reasoning, especially its judicial mode, to the more rationalist, visionary, and legislative method of a Bentham—or a Hobbes or Locke. It is no accident that in an opening lecture that criticizes legislators Blackstone emphasizes the importance of the nobility knowing the law, since the House of Lords is England's highest court of appeal. Judges in the "most subordinate" courts, too, must be competent in the law, including such magistrates as justices of the peace, who are rarely drawn from the legal profession—as is still the case in America today (1, "Intro.," sec. 1, *11–12).[23]

As Blackstone's lecture moves toward his important remarks on a map of the law, he cites Aristotle as teaching that knowledge of the laws is "the principal and most perfect branch of ethics," having just stated himself that jurisprudence employs "the noblest faculties of the soul" and exerts "the cardinal virtues of the heart" (1, "Intro.," sec. 1, *27).[24] Moreover, the common law itself will benefit from examination in universities, and he quickly turns from Aristotle to praise for one of the philosopher's greatest critics, Sir Francis Bacon, as one of those "wiser heads" who have proposed reforms or new digests of the common law. University students and faculty of law might come up with new ways, or simply execute Bacon's plans, for "improving its method, retrenching its superfluities, and reconciling the little contrarieties, which the practice of many centuries" necessarily create (*30). Bacon was Hobbes's mentor regarding the notion of a sovereign lawmaker and the autonomy of positive law, and Blackstone's opening discourse suggests that the Aristotelian practical wisdom of the common law, if understood as rooted not in Scholasticism but in Gothic and medieval British practice, can be improved by a moderate dose of Bacon's liberal penchant for uniformity and consistency. Again, Blackstone reveals the mixture of ancient and modern ideas in the service of liberty by his recourse, just after citing Aristotle and Bacon, to Montesquieuan terms. Even those training for the profession of law can benefit from his *Commentaries*, such is its improvement upon the apprentice method of the Inns, in which students are "uninstructed in the elements and first principles" upon which legal practice is founded. Students of the new liberal science of law, rather, will understand "arguments drawn *a priori*, from the spirit of the laws and the natural foundations of justice" (*34).

Blackstone's Complex Map of the Law

The structure of Blackstone's *Commentaries* is not only, then, the division into rights and wrongs, with further division of these into their private and public dimensions, as announced at the beginning of book 1 proper. The numerous discussions of whether this four-part structure is more indebted to Justinian or Hobbes, to Hale, or to some status quo are too swayed by either Bentham's critique or by an analytical cast of mind.[25] To understand Blackstone one must investigate his early and consistent indications that liberty is the animating principle of his jurisprudence and then examine his early statement on a general map of the law through the lens of this principle. Though we must take care not to reduce Blackstone's jurisprudence to Montesquieu's, proper attention to the influence of *The Spirit of the Laws* permits a more coherent and sympathetic reading. It is hard for the critical spirit of late modernity, whether manifested in liberal theory, legal realism, or postmodernist deconstruction, to understand why Montesquieu and Blackstone could have been so widely read and influential in the eighteenth and nineteenth centuries. The tacit assumption is that we have progressed beyond those backward jurisprudential days. We cannot truly make or defend that judgment, however, unless we first understand these seminal works.

Today's readers, not to mention those of the ilk of Destutt de Tracy and Bentham at the time, find it difficult to penetrate the complexity of presentation and reasoning in these two massive works. Such complexity either eluded or offended the analytical, systematic rigor of Bentham, who complained of Montesquieu's "pseudo-metaphysical sophistry" and criticized Blackstone more thematically as peddling a tradition-bound, incoherent view of law.[26] Subsequent jurisprudence, especially in America, has followed Bentham more than Blackstone or Montesquieu. This is true as to substance, in that our law of legislature, executive, bench, and administration now must be openly directed to social and political progress to be seen as legitimate, and must reform in the name of an abstract, sweeping principle, such as equality or utility. We also now are Hobbesian or Lockean in form or method, in that statutory codes have replaced common law and will grant authority to unelected judges only if they tacitly promise to legislate a progressive code anytime the legislature fails to do so. Given such Benthamite tendencies, it is important to recall, then, that the introductory sections of the *Commentaries* repeatedly state Blackstone's intention to bring an enlightened science to bear on the unsystematic state of the common law. He couples deferential references to Coke with criticisms, for while he was a "man of infinite learning in his profession," Coke was "not a little infected with the pedantry and quaintness of the times he lived in." Only one of Coke's four *Institutes* is "methodical," and the first, Coke-Littleton, presents common law merely "collected and heaped together" and is "greatly defective in method" (1, "Intro.," sec. 3, *72–73). Blackstone states this just after repeating his praise for Bacon's plan for a new digest of the law, one informed by a liberal spirit of science and not by Coke's artificial perfection of law through accumulated, refined practical wisdom (*64; cf. *30). Herbert Storing helpfully reminds us that, for Blackstone, "every science has its terms and rules of art, the reason of which may not be immediately visible."[27] Blackstone understood himself as undertaking a jurisprudence of rational progress—which suggests, paradoxically, that his fate at the hands of Bentham's demands for greater progress was prepared to some degree by his own more moderate plans for reform.

Understood in this way, Blackstone's general map of the elements of law, which concludes his lecture on liberal education in law, provides a more instructive guide to the *Commentaries* than does the explicit four-part structure of books. Just as Montesquieu supersedes his initial analysis of governments by nature and principle with his concerns about moderation, liberty, and the complex relations that constitute the spirit of the laws, so Blackstone's map of the elements of law and their relations reveals the true spirit of his analysis. He announces that his first principle of method will be to trace the elements of the law to their historic "fountains." These include the customs of the ancient Britons and Germans as recorded by Caesar and Tacitus, the codes of the northern nations or Goths, the rules of the Roman law, and, "above all," that "inexhaustible reservoir of legal antiquities and learning, the foedal law" (1, "Intro.," sec. 1, *35–36). This list comprehends the elements not only of British law but of the law of Western civilization, "the law of nations in our western orb," and Blackstone explicitly identifies these not just as historic artifacts but as the "primary rules and fundamental principles" of law itself. The first principles of law will not be found through philosophic abstraction or a single principle, such as utility. They are found by recognizing that a set of particular historical practices among peoples of northern Europe have provided a law and civilization of liberty found nowhere else in time or place. If Blackstone takes this history to be the fountain of the primary rules and fundamental principles of law, then he is guided not so much by Justinian or the Institutists, or by Bacon, Hobbes, or Locke, or by such continental jurists as Grotius or Pufendorf. Rather, this is a Montesquieuan jurisprudence and constitutionalism that blends the liberal and the Gothic, the Enlightenment and medieval tradition.

Blackstone's second, corresponding principle of method is to weigh and compare these fundamental principles "with the precepts of the law of nature, and the practice of other countries"; they should be "explained by reasons, illustrated by examples, and confirmed by undoubted authorities" (1, "Intro.," sec. 1, *36). Like Montesquieu, he argues for the fundamental, universal status of these Gothic principles of the law of liberty and does not assume the point. Philosophic analysis in light of a modern natural-law jurisprudence leads to rational explanation of why certain practices of law developed and why they should remain authoritative today, or what reforms may be needed. Here the "undoubted authorities" are not the customs themselves but the accepted writers on law and jurisprudence who will confirm the wisdom of Gothic law. After this philosophic interlude, however, Blackstone's map returns to his first principle of method and the specific character of these legal principles. In a sound map of the law, "their history should be deduced, their changes and revolutions observed, and it should be shewn how far they are connected with, or have at any time been affected by, the civil transactions of the kingdom" (*36). He implies, with Montesquieu, that an essential part of our nature is our historicity or development; thus, a natural law jurisprudence that examined human law in abstraction would not understand our nature. The closing stroke in this sketch thus reminds us that the Gothic, common-law spirit of English law has been mixed with a civil law element for centuries. No philosophic evaluation of English law could responsibly pass judgment unless it first grasped the principles of each strand, their intertwined historical development, and the consequent mixture that now defines the law and constitution of England.

Despite all the criticism of the *Commentaries'* structure and the perplexity as to why Blackstone composed it as he did, an examination of the introduction to the work reveals an animating principle that at once dictates that structure and instructs far beyond it. The genre of exhortation to liberal education in law through which Blackstone introduces his work is precisely the poetic, rhetorical mode most effective for instructing actual legislators, lawyers, and judges in a liberal spirit and moderate reform. The astounding influence of such works as *The Spirit of the Laws* and the *Commentaries* in their first centuries, and even beyond, proves the point. That genre, however, has caused the Benthamite, Austinian mind to undertake a frustrating search for a fundamental principle that a slightly more prudential, Aristotelian mind can grasp more readily. A case can be made that Blackstone faithfully journeys through his four books according to the principle of liberty and the corresponding map of the law sketched in the introduction. Unless one presumes, without argument, that a serious examination of law could not commence with elegant, inspiring rhetoric about why such study matters to practical minds, and should only commence in the Cartesian (or Hobbesian or Benthamite) mode of foundationalist abstraction, then the rationale for Blackstone's structure is not so mysterious. The three remaining sections of the introduction in fact discuss the law according to the two principles of method that Blackstone described in his map, albeit in reverse order. He turns first to a philosophic examination of the nature of laws in general (sec. 2), which includes references to such accepted authorities as Cicero, Justinian, Grotius, Pufendorf, and Locke. He then examines the laws of England and the countries subject to it (secs. 3, 4), including a historical analysis of the origins of the distinct parts of English law. Both in these sections and in the four-part structure announced in book 1, he employs these two principles of method. Every analysis of every part of the law in books 1 to 4 includes not only references to the history of the law and its development, but also an evaluation in light of natural law or universal principle, itself achieved partly through comparison to international laws and customs.

Only after this lengthy prolegomena does Blackstone announce that he will follow a great Roman lawyer and philosopher, Cicero, and the first of the great compilers of British law, Bracton (thirteenth century), in structuring his commentary. He employs their "very simple and obvious division" of the law into categories of rights and wrongs so as to analyze the law "methodically, under proper and distinct heads" (1.1, *121–22). He then divides each category again, analyzing rights in terms first of persons and then of things, and analyzing wrongs in terms of those that are private and those that are public. The consequent four-part structure moves from the rights of persons (including constitutional persons or offices, book 1), to the rights of things (property law, book 2), then to private wrongs (civil injuries, book 3), and finally to public wrongs (criminal law, book 4). After discussing law in general and English law in the introduction, and after providing the four-part structure of the books, the discussion in book 1 of the rights of persons discusses the rights of individual persons (ch. 1) and then begins a treatment of constitutional persons. Blackstone thus lays out the constitutionalism of the *Commentaries* in the introduction and the first seven chapters of book 1. The most important chapters are those on Parliament (ch. 2), the king and his title (ch. 3), and the king's prerogative (ch. 7), for in this last he completes his basic picture of judicial power. After commenting upon further details of certain constitutional persons, he concludes book 1 by examining various public and private estates of life, from the clergy and military to the family and corporations (chs. 10–18). This movement back and forth in Blackstone's constitutionalism between the rights of individuals and the rights of and limitations on offices, recalls Montesquieu's complex presentation of his liberal constitutionalism over the course of books 6, 11, and 12 of The *Spirit of the Laws*.

Indeed, perhaps it is the continuing perplexity over the organization of Montesquieu's own masterwork that has excluded him from the typical list of candidates for influences upon the *Commentaries'* structure, which ranges from Justinian to a seventeenth-century editor of the *Institutes*, Dionysius Gothofredus, and to Hale. Many scholars cite in passing that Montesquieu influenced Blackstone, but few explore the issue or grasp its import for liberal constitutionalism. Blackstone's principles and structure immediately seem less perplexing, however, if we recall Montesquieu's initial division of the kinds of right or law into the categories of international, political, and civil law (1.3), or the complicated relation he sketches between individual and constitutional liberty (books 6, 11, 12), or his emphasis throughout upon the Germanic roots of liberal progress (books 6, 11, 18, 28, 30, 31). Blackstone's general map of the law, analyzing both its history and its natural justice, is perhaps best understood not so much as a scheme laid on top of the fourfold structure but in terms of the spirit that not only chose such a typology of rights and wrongs but moves within it. Like Montesquieu, Blackstone balances his concern to achieve a rational, liberal science with an Aristotelian judgment that one must observe the particulars in action if one is to achieve a genuine science, let alone offer advice useful for reform. When analyzing the English law of civil suits and torts, he therefore insists that "the most natural and perspicuous" mode of examination is to "pursue it in the order and method wherein the proceedings themselves follow each other, rather than to distract and subdivide it by any more logical analysis" (3.18, *272; see also 3.23, *351).

Blackstone might judge that our late-modern penchant for analytical constructs and deductive rigor stands in need of tempering by attention to larger political and constitutional questions.[28] Moreover, the broader, Montesquieuan jurisprudence of the *Commentaries* need not reflect merely a modern historicism or a sociological jurisprudence, although such twentieth-century spirits as Holmes and Ehrlich have claimed Montesquieu as a predecessor. For all of Blackstone's devotion to a liberal science of law, and to individual rights to life, liberty, and property, his jurisprudence reflects something of an Aristotelian and Montesquieuan concern to understand law not as abstract principle but as the spirit or principle of a political regime. This larger, more political jurisprudence is evident just before he sketches his general map of the law, as he discusses those "qualities of the head" that students will need in order to profit from studying law in his "solid scientical method" and then addresses "those of the heart" as well. Amid references to the need for loyalty to the king, a sense of honor, and grounding in the principles of religion, he identifies the need for "a zeal for liberty and the constitution" (1, "Intro.," sec. 1, *34). Closer examination of Blackstone's debt to Montesquieu confirms that such "public spirit" mirrors the jurisprudence of *The Spirit of the Laws*—not least with regard to the role of the judicial power in a complex constitution of liberty.

six

A Gothic and Liberal Constitution: Blackstone's Tempering of Sovereignty

Bentham criticized the *Commentaries* as a merely traditional view of English common law, and its author as an apologist fearful of innovation. The analysis of religious heresy in book 4 embodied for him the work's antipathy to reform, and he mocked the "peremptoriness and complacency" which declared, "every thing is as it should be."[1] Bentham does note that in subsequent editions Blackstone modified the treatment of religious dissenters in response to criticisms by Priestly and Furneaux. Still, he gives Blackstone no credit either for consistently praising the decriminalizing of heresy, or for suggesting further reform. Blackstone lauds the confinement of heresy to ecclesiastical law and does note that all is "as it should be," but then continues, "unless, perhaps, that heresy ought to be more strictly defined, and no prosecution permitted, even in the ecclesiastical courts, till the tenets in question are by proper authority previously declared to be heretical."[2] Whether discussing particular statues, or legal principles, or larger constitutional forms, Blackstone is less apologetic and more philosophic than Bentham will admit.

William Holdsworth's dissent from the Benthamite view early in the twentieth century, in his comprehensive *History of English Law* and other essays, shifted from the academic line that Blackstone was a mere conservative. Holdsworth argued that Blackstone's views of equity, understood both as a mode of interpretation and as distinct courts of chancery, sought to infuse a spirit of reform into the common-law judiciary.[3] A reconsideration by the American judge and jurist Richard Posner, an avowed Holmesean, questions the Benthamite view even to the point of comparing Blackstone's innovations to the judicial legislating of the Warren Court era.[4] Bentham's view survives, however, in Grant Gilmore's argument that the *Commentaries* was written precisely to check the judicial activism prevalent in late-eighteenth-century England, especially that of the great and controversial Lord Mansfield.[5]

Whether finding the *Commentaries* incoherent or embodying a clear program, such views are variations of analyses by Bentham and Jefferson. Jefferson was among the first to disagree with Bentham's view that Blackstone fostered only legal and political stagnation. Rather, he feared that such English Tories as Hume, Blackstone, and Mansfield, and their American disciples Hamilton and Marshall, would turn modern freedom in a more commercial, quasi-aristocratic direction. When seeking a new law professor for the University of Virginia he emphasized to Madison that they find someone who would restore the "black-letter text" of Coke as the basic law book, rescuing students from "the honied Mansfieldism of Blackstone."[6] Does Blackstone advocate judicial legislating, or is he, as the analytic school and legal realists insist, the archetype of legal formalism and a static, declaratory theory of law that views judges as clerks? The *Commentaries* lays the seeds of this very question in its introduction, especially the discussion of English law (sec. 3). Blackstone raises it more clearly when he completes his portrait of British constitutionalism early in book 1—in chapters on the rights of individuals (ch. 2), parliament (ch. 3), and the king's prerogative, the literal source of judicial power (ch. 7). Neither the Benthamite nor Jeffersonian view captures Blackstone's intentions, however, whatever insight they might have regarding later consequences of his jurisprudence. Blackstone, like Montesquieu, advocates neither a mechanistic legal formalism and thorough subordination of judicial power, nor judicial usurpation of legislative power. Judges both explicate and foster the liberal spirit of common law and statutes, in an incremental manner, thereby distinguishing development in new circumstances from legislating anew. He reveals this in book 3 when comparing the common law to a Gothic castle gradually renovated, but not replaced, by respectful craftsmen. Unlike the Holmesean legal realists of the twentieth century who, like Bentham, have little regard for separation of powers, Blackstone places constitutional structures above immediate utility, both as a matter of the rule of law and to promote the ultimate utility for liberty and liberalism of such enduring principles.

The constitutional principles presented early in book 1 lay the groundwork for Blackstone's teaching on judicial power. His notion of subtle judicial reform of the laws does not yet see a tension, as Holmes and Woodrow Wilson will find, between the end of liberal security and the form of a separated, complex constitutionalism.[7] Having laid a constitutional foundation, the remaining books educate young gentlemen in England, its future lawyers, judges, and members of Parliament, in the use of the courts to serve gradual, orderly progress in the law. His remarks in each book on reforms needed in the parts of the law, both public and private, criminal and civil, suggest the possibilities of quiet judicial discernment of the law's rational and liberal spirit. The groundwork in book 1 for this cloaking of power includes a Montesquieuan and Gothic conception of constitutionalism, emphasizing historical development that achieves the complexity and balance necessary for liberty. This debt to Montesquieu qualifies one of the most widely studied and deeply complicated aspects of Blackstone's constitutionalism, his explicit statements on parliamentary sovereignty in English law and the subordination of judicial power. Indeed, strange as it sounds to jurisprudential ears attuned to abstract first principles, or to short-term utility, the key to Blackstone's jurisprudence—and thus to reconciling its many tensions—lies in the synthesis he finds between the doctrines of political and civil liberty, natural right, and the separation of powers.

The Trace of Montesquieu's Complex Liberalism

It is common to observe that both Blackstone's law lectures and his *Commentaries* were "very largely inspired by Montesquieu," but it is also the case that the extent of the debt often goes unexamined.[8] Bentham attests to this influence amid his usual severity: "The errors of Montesquieu were the errors of an original genius struggling under the heap of confusion accumulated by his predecessors. A great part of that heap he has contributed to remove. The husks of Montesquieu are dainties to our Author."[9] Montesquieu is not the sole influence on Blackstone, nor should one follow Bentham in dismissing Blackstone as unoriginal. One of the few studies of the relationship rightly notes that Blackstone's systematic exposition of English law began before publication of *The Spirit of the Laws* in 1748, and that Blackstone's first debt is to Locke: Montesquieu's work was "a reinforcement of Locke's influence, confirming Blackstone in a path he had already chosen." Still, Fletcher grants that, while Locke had taught him that stability requires separation of powers, he only learned its "full significance" from the Frenchman. To admit that in the *Commentaries* "everywhere the trace of Montesquieu is heavily pressed" implies that Montesquieu was both a source of independent ideas and a confirmation of Lockean ones.[10]

This view largely confirms a comparison of passages from *De l'esprit des lois* and the *Commentaries* published in 1824 by a French lawyer, Théodore

Regnault, as an appendix to a reduction of Montesquieu's work to analytical tables.[11] Beyond showing that Montesquieu's influence among French lawyers survived the Revolution, Regnault's analysis of Blackstone as "le Montesquieu de l'Angleterre" suggests that the *Commentaries* is indebted to *The Spirit of the Laws* not only when it is explicitly cited but even when not. Moreover, the tables reveal clear influence across a range of topics, beyond judicial power and due process to separation of powers, institutions, penal reform, and the principles of a moderate constitutionalism. Such influence tells much about Blackstone's broad, political conception of law and jurisprudence. Fletcher hints at a sound explanation for the many unacknowledged paraphrases of Montesquieu in the *Commentaries* in his discussion of a dispute in the House of Lords in 1806 when opponents to appointing the Lord Chief Justice to the Cabinet cited Montesquieu on the separation of powers. Although this spat occurred after the French Revolution, it suggests the degree of debt to a Frenchman that it was prudent to reveal in a work on English law even decades earlier:

> The mention of Montesquieu's name immediately put the ministeri-
> alists on their dignity. Were we to go abroad—and to France, of all
> places—to learn the principles of our Constitution? Lord St. John
> "did not mean to look into Montesquieu for the law and constitution
> of England; neither upon such a subject did he acknowledge such
> an authority." . . . Lord Hawkesbury declined to "look to any foreign
> writer for the principles of the British constitution," but for *general*
> principles of liberty he had no objection to consulting "so eminent a
> writer as baron Montesquieu."[12]

Blackstone largely adopts Lord Hawkesbury's less jingoistic but still pa-triotic mode, mostly citing Montesquieu for general principles of liberty, and when citing him on specific laws, French or otherwise, usually doing so in support of English law.[13] Still, he regularly and at times emphatically acknowl-edges Montesquieu, especially on constitutional liberty and penal reform. He cloaks the extent of his debt, especially regarding such potentially controversial points as his conception of judicial power, which closely tracks the French ju-rist's teaching. Blackstone's regular references to continental, Gothic, and other instances of foreign law further suggest Montesquieu's presence, even if the text cited is Stjernhook's *De jure Sveonum et Gothorum* (1672) or the *Modern Univer-sal History* (1745–66). He does explicitly criticize Montesquieu on a few points throughout the work, but he does not state some of the potentially more signif-icant differences. His discussion of judges later in book I, for example, seems to distance itself from Montesquieu's portrayal of English judges. Blackstone's account of the complexity of English courts and judging, in particular the primary role of professional judges in relation to juries, differs substantially from Montesquieu's initial remarks about England's "invisible and null" judges. Indeed, Blackstone's analysis of "the judicial power" in England is far more accurate than the early treatment in book 11 of *The Spirit of the Laws*. The jury indeed was a point of pride for English common law, and in eighteenth-century England professional judges were neither as numerous nor in such large bodies as the French *parlements*. Still, common-law and equity judges were not only important but dominant in the administration of English criminal and civil justice.[14] Blackstone does not labor to conceal this professional judging power, nor does he find such a judiciary threatening to liberty.[15] His analysis accords more with Montesquieu's descriptions of monarchical judging in the early and late books of *The Spirit of the Laws*, or with the qualifications on English judging later in chapter 6 of book 11, than with the initial remarks on republican judging in books 6 and 11. Blackstone's constitutionalism openly combines a republican devotion to liberty with a powerful, professional judiciary—elements that Montesquieu separates, at least on the surface. This occurs not only because the Englishman's monarchical yet liberal portrait is truer to English judging. Such complexity accords with the deeper refrain in Montesquieu's analysis of England, that there "the republic hides under the form of monarchy," and that one often sees "the form of an absolute government over the foundation of a free government" (*Spirit,* 5.19; 19.27). Such apparent differences about English judging only reveal the peculiar character of Montesquieu's initial treatment of judging in book 11. Moreover, Montesquieu more forthrightly advocates a powerful judiciary, even in its most republican form, by describing the English judicial power as fully independent of the other powers. Blackstone more accurately places judges under the throne, although he stresses *de facto* independence in a fully Montesquieuan spirit.

These considerations raise another apparent contrast, however, one arising from Blackstone's explicit repudiation of the notion that judges can correct acts of Parliament. Throughout his analysis of English law, he never anticipates the power of judicial review employed by American judges. Once again, however, the characteristic complexity of his jurisprudence suggests less disagreement with Montesquieu's conception of a cloaking of power than first appears. In the section of the introduction on the laws of England, Blackstone seriously considers a power similar to the right of remonstrance held by France's *parlements*, regularly praised in *The Spirit of the Laws*. He rejects the doctrine that "acts of parliament contrary to reason are void," which he explicitly links to the reasoning of Sir Edward Coke in *Dr. Bonham's Case* (1610) (1, "Intro.," sec. 3, *91, citing Coke's *Reports*). He agrees with Coke for interpreting a statute as not intending to violate the fundamental common-law principle that forbids an interested party from judging in his own case. However, he rejects any broader judicial power: "[I]f the parliament will positively enact a thing to be done which is unreasonable, I know of no power on earth that can control it." He repeats this apparent argument for parliamentary supremacy, although without reference to any judicial claim to void laws, early in book 1 in the chapter on Parliament (1.2, *160–61). These early dismissals of setting "the judicial power above the legislature" as "subversive of all government" suggest a significant debt to the legal positivism of Hobbes and Locke, and a departure from the spirit of Montesquieu (1, "Intro.," sec. 3, *91). Putting aside for now that these statements arise in Blackstone's ten rules for judicial interpretation of statutes, such an emphasis on human sovereignty seems to demote divine or natural law as a standard for positive law. On the other hand, Blackstone appeals to such a transcendent standard in his initial definitions of law given earlier in the introduction. His section entitled "Of the Nature of Laws in General" begins in Montesquieuan fashion by defining all law as "a rule of action," whether it governs the supreme being of the universe and all matter, or humans. He immediately adds, however, a more Hobbesian qualification: it is a rule of action "prescribed by some superior, and which the inferior is bound to obey" (1, "Intro.," sec. 2, *38).

This tone of legal and judicial positivism appears to be confirmed by the subsequent discussion of four kinds of law: first the laws of nature and revelation, and then the law of nations and municipal or positive law. The analysis of each type seems largely concerned with sovereignty and only occasionally moderates a Hobbesian, or Austinian, view. Blackstone does state that "no human laws should be suffered to contradict" the natural law and revealed law. Like Montesquieu, he moves from a Newtonian account of the laws of the universe to a God who ordains "relations of justice . . . in the nature of things antecedent to any positive precept" (1, "Intro.," sec. 2, *42, *40). However, these "laws of eternal justice" are equated with observing "the happiness of each individual," which reduces the natural and revealed laws to "one paternal precept," that "man should pursue his own happiness" (*40–41). The context suggests not Aristotelian teleology but modern liberal hedonism, providing only vague, subjective grounds for evaluating or challenging positive law. This dialectical spirit, blending legal naturalism and legal positivism, again is evident in the definition of the municipal law of a particular state as "a rule of civil conduct prescribed by the supreme power in a state, commanding what is right and prohibiting what is wrong" (*44). Blackstone cites no authority here, but in later iterations he attributes this definition to Cicero and Bracton (1.1, *122; 3.1, *1). Some scholars note that Blackstone's translation omits *justa* from Cicero's notion of law as a "just sanction" or command, distinguishing himself from Grotius, Pufendorf, and Burlamaqui by such positivism: the Hobbesian sovereign determines right or wrong and commands it so.[16] Blackstone's definition of the declaratory mode of law also strikes this note: declarations about rights and wrongs of individual action depend "not so much upon the law of revelation or of nature, as upon the wisdom and will of the legislator" (1, "Intro.," sec. 2, *54).

The jurisprudence of the *Commentaries* is too complex and balanced, however, to conclude that Blackstone is as much a positivist as Hobbes, or was "a forerunner of Austinian jurisprudence."[17] Again, while Blackstone is not reducible to one source, Montesquieu provided a model for this synthesis of classical natural law, common law, and modern legal positivism, a synthesis of fundamental principles of right with historical and current circumstances. Both jurists account for sovereignty, but both also appeal to the notion of antecedent relations of justice—"eternal, immutable laws of good and evil" that exist beyond any municipal law. This refrain occurs as regularly in Blackstone's volumes as in Montesquieu's masterwork, particularly on such questions as religious tolerance and penal reform. Blackstone states that rights and wrongs are not entirely creations of the legislature, for there are "rights which God and nature have established . . . natural rights, such as life and liberty" that "no human legislature has power to abridge or destroy." Some acts are "*mala in se,* such as murder, theft, and perjury," and in general there are actions that are "naturally and intrinsically right or wrong" (1, "Intro.," sec. 2, *54). Only "with regard to things in themselves indifferent" can the legislature have a freer hand. Herbert Storing captures the complexity of this jurisprudence when noting that it is "Blackstone's highest theme" to address "the relation between natural law and conventional law, as this relation presents itself to one who is a lawyer in the best and highest sense."[18] This is Montesquieu's theme throughout *The Spirit of the Laws,* especially in the historical jurisprudence and new "theory of laws" he develops in the last five books. This is the part of the work that Blackstone cites more than any other, and the jurisprudence it embodies has no counterpart in Hobbes or Locke. Blackstone begins his work with the approach to law that closes Montesquieu's work: to at once discover the origins of constitutional and civil law, the requirements of a humane natural right, the developments of history, and a legal prudence that can sort and balance this complex spirit of the laws. The general discussion of property that opens the book on the "rights of things" epitomizes Blackstone's middle position between modern positivism and a Scholastic, common-law naturalism. He declares that "there is no foundation in nature or natural law, why a set of words upon parchment should convey the dominion of land," and he scoffs that the dispute among such "writers on natural law" as Grotius, Pufendorf, and Locke about property rights "savors too much of nice and scholastic refinement" (2.1, *2, *8). It is hardly Lockean to note that "we often mistake for nature what we find established by long and inveterate custom" and thus to declare that property inheritance is "no *natural*, but merely a *civil*, right" (*11). This doubt about modern theoretical abstractions seems to echo the strongly qualified defense of private property in Aristotle and Thomas Aquinas, and Blackstone offers a Thomistic explanation that property laws have been developed by "the universal law of almost every nation (which is a kind of secondary law of nature)" (*10). On the other hand, he concludes the discussion on a Hobbesian note, declaring "the grand ends of civil society" to be "the peace and security of individuals" (*15).[19]

Blackstone dialectically establishes the view that there are some natural standards by which to judge the soundness of statutes or at least to guide judicial inferences about which possible intentions of the legislature would best accord with natural justice.[20] This is the spirit of Montesquieu's liberal philosophy, that the relations among things naturally constitute a balance or equilibrium, since both nature and mankind abhor an extreme. Purely Hobbesian sovereignty, with no check on the positive law or will of the lawmaker, is one such extreme. On the other hand, Montesquieu thought that a Scholastic natural law, understood as the inflexible source from which positive laws must be derived, adopted another extreme. The introduction and book 1 of the *Commentaries* indicate that Blackstone is not confused, as Bentham would have it, but seeks to be true to the nature of things by gradually accounting for the complexity and tendency toward equilibrium in human nature, politics, and law. Other passages in the work suggest that one institution he cultivates to undertake the role of balancing natural justice and positive sovereignty is a judiciary that can shape statutes in the right direction without explicitly declaring them void. Blackstone himself thus lays the groundwork for considering that his apparent doctrine of parliamentary supremacy is more qualified than it seems, and that his constitutionalism is more complex and Gothic than Hobbesian and modern.

A Complex Jurisprudence for a Mixed Constitution

As noted, in his first analysis of the laws of England, after preliminary discussions of legal education and law in general, Blackstone initially declares Parliament an "absolute authority" that "acknowledges no superior on earth" (1, "Intro.," sec. 3, *91). Few commentators note that these remarks arise amid the second of two discussions in the introduction on interpreting the law. This itself suggests not only the importance Blackstone placed upon judicial interpretation of law but also the crucial relation he saw between judicial power and the issue of parliamentary supremacy. His initial statement on such absolute authority indicates clear limits to the role of rationality in the law. Contrary to the example he cites of a nascent theory of judicial review, "there is no court that has power to defeat the intent of the legislature, when couched in such evident and express words, as leave no doubt whether it was the intent of the legislature or no" (*91). Blackstone's first word on the authority of Parliament in relation to judicial power is not, however, his last. His later treatment complicates these earlier statements enough to clear the way for a more complex constitutionalism, including an important role for an independent judiciary.

Blackstone's second analysis of parliamentary supremacy, in book 1, begins by citing Coke himself on its transcendent and absolute authority, although even here there is no mention of judicial checks on the legislature (1.2, *160). Still, it is worth noting that in later writings Coke himself affirmed the supreme power of Parliament and saw no contradiction between that affirmation and his reasoning in Dr. Bonham's Case.[21] Whatever Blackstone sought to imply by opening this second treatment with a citation not of Hobbes or Locke but of the great jurist and parliamentarian Coke, he states his own qualifications or concerns about legal positivism quite explicitly. He remarks that what some call "the omnipotence of parliament" is "a figure rather too bold" (*161). If such an "absolute despotic power" in fact exists—and Blackstone states, more in the spirit of his earlier remarks, that in all governments such a power must exist—then further measures must be discussed for the sake of "the liberties of this kingdom." The first of these safeguards is that members of Parliament should be "most eminent for their probity, their fortitude, and their knowledge." Doubts arise about this measure, however, in light of Blackstone's introductory lecture on the dire need for legal education among current and future parliamentarians. More explicitly, the sequel cites three authorities on the extreme danger such absolute power represents. The "great lord treasurer Burleigh," the common-law jurist Sir Matthew Hale, and "the president Montesquieu" all suggest that if England and its liberty are ever ruined, it would be by no other power but an absolute and corrupt Parliament (1.2, *161). Blackstone then repeats a reservation made about Locke's doctrine of popular revolution, the only recourse if an absolutely powerful Parliament becomes corrupt. In his introductory discussion of the nature of laws, Blackstone cautiously remarked that Locke "perhaps carries his theory too far" and that in revolution "the people would be reduced to a state of anarchy" (1, "Intro.," sec. 2, *52). By book 1, reservations have turned to criticism: "[H]owever just this conclusion [as to a popular right of revolution] may be in theory, we cannot adopt it, nor argue from it, under any dispensation of government actually existing" (1.2, *162). If political liberty is the most fundamental principle, however, then a principle of absolute parliamentary supremacy will need to be checked by a principle of popular revolution. Since Blackstone opens the *Commentaries* by citing Montesquieu to confirm that political liberty indeed is the first principle of English constitutionalism, these later remarks condemn the doctrine of popular revolution indirectly question parliamentary supremacy. Such revolution constitutes an extreme situation that would dissolve all government, repeal all positive laws, and indeed "destroy all law." While he repeats that, against a claim of revolution, "the power of parliament is absolute and without control," Blackstone's presentation quietly suggests that it is the Hobbesian claim of super-sovereignty itself that leads to "so desperate an event" as recourse to revolution.

His subsequent discussion of the Glorious Revolution deepens these concerns about Lockean revolution and adds a further teaching about constitutional moderation. Blackstone admits, in Lockean terms, that when a conflict arises between "the society at large" and the government's exercise of powers "originally delegated" by society, then "it must be decided by the voice of that society itself; there is not upon earth any other tribunal to resort to" (1.3, *211). He warns, however, against standing in judgment of what Parliament did in 1688, which is akin to "those dangerous political heresies, which so long distracted the state, but at length are all happily extinguished." Our "duty at this distance of time" is not to measure the events simply for their "justice, moderation, and expedience" but to accept them on "authority" (1.3, *212). These dangerous heresies apparently arose during what he earlier describes as "the times of madness and anarchy," referring to an act of 1648, the era of Cromwell. Indeed, Blackstone refers to the Cromwellian era just before he states his reservations about Lockean revolution in the chapter on Parliament (see 1.2, *160). The glory of the 1688 revolution was that Parliament avoided declaring "a total dissolution of the government, according to the principles of Mr. Locke," which would have "annihilated" all law, government, and tradition and reduced England to "a state of nature" (1.3, *213). Considering Parliament's "great wisdom" in avoiding the "wild extremes into which the visionary theories of some zealous republicans would have led them," Blackstone cannot help but evaluate the justice of what was done and praise it for the "temper and moderation which naturally arose from its equity." That extraordinary Parliament may have transcended "the letter of our ancient laws," but they did so "prudently." By declaring James to have attempted a subversion of the constitution, in effect to have abdicated the throne, they acted in accord with "the spirit of our constitution, and the rights of human nature" (1.3, *213, *212). In later remarks on such crises Blackstone reiterates these Montesquieuan warnings about extremism or utopia, paired with Montesquieuan praise for prudence and moderation. Those who might confront such constitutional conflicts should be guided by "the prudence of the times" and not any particular positive law, for such balanced judgment surely will maintain "the balance of the constitution." The extremes of "absolute power in the prince" and "national resistance by the people" should be shunned, despite the clamor of "the advocates of slavery on the one hand, and the demagogues of faction on the other" (1.7, *244–45, *250–51).

There are too many tensions, then, within Blackstone's analyses of legislative power and popular revolution to mark him an advocate of pure legal positivism and simple parliamentary supremacy. Nor is there evidence that these complex discussions are hastily composed by a mind sloppy about details or lacking a larger design for the work. The *Commentaries* praises neither royalism, nor legislative positivism, nor popular revolution, but rather moderate reform (and in a pinch, a duly authorized revolution) that preserves the fundamental law of liberty and natural rights through preserving balanced constitutional forms.[22] Moreover, Blackstone himself provides a key for deciphering the complexities and tensions of his jurisprudence, in the form of his unqualified praise for the separation of powers as the guarantor of both natural rights and political liberty. He first discusses this doctrine in his introductory analysis of the general nature of law, praising Britain for having the best form of municipal law, or constitution, yet known to man. That discussion of the separation of powers begins on a Montesquieuan, not Lockean, note by criticizing classical political philosophy for its limited focus on the distinct regimes of democracy, aristocracy, and monarchy and their corruptions. He cites only Cicero as an advocate of a mixed regime, with no reference to such great expositors as Aristotle or Polybius (1, "Intro.," sec. 2, *49–50). Both Hammond and Regnault note that this analysis of the three ancient governments paraphrases Montesquieu (citing 3.3 of *The Spirit of the Laws*, among other passages), and one can add that this odd treatment of the ancients implies that, for Blackstone, Montesquieu was the first to make an effective case for a mixed regime. Further, the subsequent praise of the unique balance of the British constitution draws upon neither Hobbes nor Locke but upon the Montesquieuan mode of discussing "three powers" in terms not only of governing functions but of a balancing of orders or claims to rule (see *Spirit*, 11.6; 11.12–19). For Blackstone, a separate monarchy gives England "all the advantages of strength and dispatch," while legislative power is "entrusted to three distinct powers," mixing monarchy, aristocracy, and democracy in King, Lords, and Commons. Each part is "actuated by different springs, and attentive to different interests"; thus, "in no other shape could we be so certain of finding the three great qualities of government so well and so happily united," namely, "virtue, wisdom, or power" (1, "Intro.," sec. 2, *50–51). Immediately after declaring that England's constitution "is so admirably tempered and compounded, that nothing can endanger or hurt it, but destroying the equilibrium of power," he declares the alternative of Lockean revolution a remedy that goes "too far" (*51–52).

Blackstone again emphasizes the separation of powers early in the chapter on Parliament in book 1, just prior to his second, more explicit doubts about Lockean revolution. Since he understands Parliament as "the King in Parliament," a complex version of parliamentary supremacy is compatible with the separation into King, Lords, and Commons (1.2, *146–47, *153–55). Moreover, the thrust of his praise for the separation of powers is precisely contrary to Hobbesian super-sovereignty. Once again, his concern is "the balance of the constitution," and he criticizes not only royal absolutism but also the Parliament under Cromwell for excluding the King from Parliament's authority and establishing "a worse oppression than any they intended to remedy" (*154–55). Thus, "the true excellence of the English government" is that "all the parts of it form a mutual check upon each other," because "every branch of our civil polity supports and is supported, regulates and is regulated, by the rest." The spirit here is Montesquieu's, as we should expect, given the opening of this chapter on Parliament, which paraphrases him on the absolute unity of tyrannical governments and the complex, articulated character of governments devoted to "the liberty of the subject" (1.2, *146–47). Montesquieu's hand also is present, paradoxically, in the curious omission of the judiciary as one of the three powers in this balance. The omission is not curious in one sense, since it accurately sketches the monarchical theory of the British constitution. Still, this initial view ultimately clashes with Blackstone's emphasis upon the *de facto* independence of judicial power from the monarchy (1.7). This is the mirror image of Montesquieu's treatment of the English constitution, which begins by listing judging as the third power but, by the middle of that famous analysis, practically drops it and replaces it with the upper house of a bicameral legislature. Montesquieu's analysis of the "three powers" initially refers to a modern concept of the separation of powers and then turns toward a classical, mixed-regime view of commons, lords, and monarch (*Spirit*, 11.6). In book 1 of the *Commentaries* Blackstone reverses this, moving from the more traditional mixed regime to the more prescriptive, modern analysis of separate functions. The three powers in the chapter on Parliament are the King-in-Parliament, and only later will he add another power, an effectively independent judiciary. It is in his initial focus on king, lords, and commons that Blackstone paraphrases Montesquieu's summation of his analysis of the English constitution, with its Newtonian theme of equilibrium: "Like three different powers in mechanics, they jointly impel the machine of government in a direction different from what either, acting by themselves, would have done; but at the same time in a direction partaking of each, and formed out of all; a direction which constitutes the true line of liberty and happiness of the community" (1.2, *155).

The sequel praises the House of Lords, the institution of "the body of the nobility," because in a "mixed and compounded constitution" it is necessary to have a third body that supports "the rights of both the crown and the people, by forming a barrier to withstand the encroachments of both" (1.2, *158). Without that middle branch, "stability" would be threatened, and the political order would be "precarious," since power would lurch "from one extreme to another." This is another passage that Regnault considered a paraphrase of Montesquieu (cf. *Spirit,* 3.7; 3.9). Blackstone already had noted in his introductory lecture that one function of the Lords, through which they presumably moderate and mediate the tensions of English politics, is to be the judicial power of last resort (1, "Intro.," sec. 1, *11). In book 1 he postpones analysis of this "judicial capacity," claiming it is more properly treated in analyzing civil and criminal procedure (see 3.4; 4.19). This obscures the extent to which the function of the Law Lords mixes legislative and judicial power, but, more important, it conceals another debt to Montesquieu. His later discussion cites and heavily paraphrases *The Spirit of the Laws* regarding the ultimate judicial power lodged in the Lords, which can protect individuals from popular hatred (4.19, *269–71).

The question arises as to how adequate this sketch of the constitution really is, since this aspect of the *Commentaries* often is criticized for either sloppiness or conservative obfuscation. Bentham and his followers argue that Blackstone knew, or should have known, that by the late eighteenth century the cabinet and prime minister—the executive committee of the Commons—had replaced the king as genuine executive. Similar criticisms are made of Montesquieu's analysis of the English constitution. Perhaps, however, both jurists deliberately omitted so obvious a topic as the cabinet. Blackstone, a member of Parliament since 1761, surely knew of this innovation, and Montesquieu would have observed its early stages during his 1731–32 visit to England, not to mention through his wide reading in and correspondence about English affairs. Such a deliberate omission accords with the fundamental importance each places on the separation of powers as the crucial Gothic foundation for a more modern, liberal conception of liberty. Giving the Cabinet the silent treatment signals that such complete fusion of legislative and executive power is dangerous to liberty. As noted, Blackstone is openly contemptuous of Cromwell's rule by Commons alone, but perhaps is circumspect in criticizing the leading governmental institution of his day. Recent voices echo such concerns, with late-twentieth-century British political scientists criticizing the Thatcher government of the 1980s as an "elective dictatorship" that used popular electoral support to consolidate power in the prime minister's office. In 1999 the House of Commons effectively abolished an upper house of hereditary and life peers, without having decided upon its replacement. With the monarch weakened in Blackstone's day, and the issue of British constitutional balance still alive two centuries later, one can understand his praise for the Lords as balancing the other powers, albeit perhaps more for its role of protecting the monarchy and tradition generally than protecting the people from the king.

Blackstone's views of parliamentary supremacy, sovereignty, and the nature of law—the elements of his constitutionalist jurisprudence—suggest that he is a more complicated and thoughtful jurist than initial appearances indicate. He mixes natural law principles with more positivist ones, and tempers this compound jurisprudence with a blend of separated powers and the classical mixed regime. He seeks to inculcate in future parliamentarians, lawyers, and judges a Gothic constitutionalism more effective at securing liberty than the simpler alternatives, and more capable of adaptation to that end. Given these foundations, the role of the judiciary and courts in Blackstone's jurisprudence is more of a question than Benthamite readers have recognized.[23] This is evident in the fact that, before thematically treating judicial power in its subordinate place in the constitution, as part of the king's prerogative (1.7), Blackstone mentions the importance of judges and courts out of order, so to speak. He discusses service on juries before service in Parliament when listing the offices for which students need a liberal education in law. Indeed, a lack of legal understanding by citizen jurors "has unavoidably thrown more power in the hands of the judges, to direct, control, and even reverse their verdicts, than perhaps the constitution intended" (1, "Intro.," sec. 1, *8–9). After mentioning the judicial function of the Lords, he turns to the judges in lower jurisdictions (*11–12, *14). When discussing laws in general, he states that the part of any law that constitutes "sanction" is either "expressly" defined by statute or is left "to the discretion of the judges" and those who execute the laws ("Intro.," sec. 2, *56). More important, the sections on the general nature of law and on English law in the introduction both conclude by treating legal interpretation and equitable discretion as exercised by judges (sec. 2, *58–62; sec. 3, *87–92). Blackstone's first discussion of interpretation begins by paraphrasing Montesquieu's criticism of imperial "rescripts," the idiosyncratic interpretations of law by a single executive (*59; see *Spirit*, 29.17). Not only is asking the executive's opinion "a bad method," but the alternative of asking "the legislature to decide particular disputes, is not only endless, but affords great room for partiality and oppression." What institution is to interpret the laws in "particular disputes"? Blackstone postpones an explicit answer, instead listing five "fairest and most rational ways" for discerning "the will of the legislator" and his "intentions." These are interpretation by (1) the words, (2) the context, (3) the subject matter, (4) the law's "effects and consequence," and, finally, (5) "the spirit and reason of the law." He implies that jurists and scholars of the law developed this five-part method, citing Pufendorf, Cicero, Grotius, and Latin legal maxims.

Not until discussing equity, discerning "the reason and spirit" of the law, does Blackstone mention a specific "power" to undertake such interpreting: "there should somewhere be a power vested of excepting those circumstances, which (had they been foreseen) the legislator himself would have excepted . . . as Grotius expresses it, '*lex non exacte definit, sed arbitrio boni viri permittit*'" (1, "Intro.," sec. 2, *62). Who are these "good men" whom the law permits to exercise judgment when the law is not exactly defined? Blackstone again addresses this indirectly, when cautioning against taking equity to an extreme, "lest thereby we destroy all law, and leave the decision of every question entirely in the breast of the judge" (*62). It is not clear that he means professional judges in courts of law until the close. Moreover, he makes no distinction between the Chancellor's courts of equity and the common-law courts, as he does when discussing these issues again at the close of the third section of the introduction. The Aristotelian function of moderating the severity of the law in particular cases, precisely so as to accord with the principle of justice intended by the lawmaker, is undertaken as much by common-law judges as by special courts of equity. All judges, however, must exercise this moderating power with the necessary moderation: "And law, without equity, though hard and disagreeable, is much more desirable for the public good, than equity without law: which would make every judge a legislator, and introduce most infinite confusion; as there would then be almost as many different rules of action laid down in our courts, as there are differences of capacity and sentiment in the human mind" ("Intro.," *62).

Blackstone, like Montesquieu, seeks balance in all things political and legal, and the relation of judicial power to the other constitutional powers is no exception. Still, the need to warn about abuse of judicial power arises because, by this midpoint of his introductory discourse on law and constitutionalism, he quietly has made the judiciary the central institution for interpreting the municipal law of any state. A question raised by the complexities of this Gothic constitutionalism, one that arises even before his most thematic and emphatic remarks on judicial power, is whether he recommends that courts be a truly coequal power, independent of Parliament, because they are necessary for moderating and balancing Britain's constitution of liberty.

A New Judiciary and the Cloaking of Power

Having explained his project for a liberal science of the law of liberty and discoursed upon law in general and rules for its interpretation, the third section of Blackstone's introduction turns to the laws of England. The implicit concern with judicial power continues by examining unwritten and written English law. The judicial theme only becomes explicit at the end of this third section, in a second discourse on legal interpretation. Here it becomes evident that Blackstone's basis for a quietly powerful judiciary is precisely that which Bacon and Hobbes sought to radically reform or repudiate, the English common law. The *lex non scripta,* or unwritten law, includes the common law proper, the "monuments and evidence" of which are found in "the records of the several courts of justice, in books of reports and judicial decisions, and in the treatises of learned sages of the profession, preserved and handed down to us from the times of highest antiquity." The common law is a form of unwritten law because the "original institution and authority" of its precepts "are not set down in writing, as acts of parliament are, but they receive their binding power, and the force of laws, by long and immemorial usage, and by their universal reception throughout the kingdom" (1, "Intro.," sec. 3, *63–64).

Two essential elements of common law so defined—the organic quality of arising from an ancient past while being consented to in the present, and its deposited presence in the decisions and writings of lawyers and judges—are antithetical to the liberal, analytical mind. Contrary to the Hobbesian concept of a sole human source of sovereignty, parliamentary statutes must compete with rulings, maxims, and writings from another body or institution. The Benthamite impulse for simplicity, uniformity, and codification, which are preconditions for statutory reform in the service of utility, must compete not only with divided power but with numerous sources of authority on the law, developed case by case. Both Hobbes and Bentham reject the notion that the antiquity of such rulings and maxims is in itself is a source of legal authority, and works like Hobbes's *Dialogue* or Bentham's *Fragment* embody the liberal repudiation of the common-law mind, including its Gothic, complicated constitutionalism. At the dawn of the twenty-first century one is tempted to say that the attack by Bacon and Hobbes on Coke largely has succeeded, as is evident in the decline throughout Anglo-American law not only of Coke's classic common-law jurisprudence but even of Blackstone's middle ground. Part and parcel of that decline is the rejection of any remaining root in Aristotelian practical wisdom or principled legal prudence by legal realism, which declares that there are no enduring, true legal principles, and that judging is therefore as much a matter of power politics as legislating and executing. Holmes and other realists effected this revolution, however, from within the judiciary, making a calculation neither Hobbes nor Bentham could accept—that the formal tools of common-law judging and an independent judiciary would now be used to pursue progressive, pragmatic, utilitarian reform.

One explanation for the way this revolution-from-within occurred is that Blackstone's partly liberal mind injects the seeds of radical transformation into an unsuspecting common law.[24] There is, as noted, a strong current of legal positivism in Blackstone's general jurisprudential remarks in the preceding section of the introduction, and here, in the sequel to his definition of common law, Bacon displaces Fortescue as the sounder authority on the historical origins of the common law (1, "Intro.," sec. 3, *64). The tone of liberal criticism of the common law continues with the remark that a "digest of laws" or "general digest" is lacking, which reiterates his opening lecture on the disorderly, unscientific state of the law. That lecture cited Bacon's wise proposal for a digest, and Blackstone repeats the approving citation here; his criticism of the "pedantry and quaintness" of Coke's learning lies just ahead in this section (sec. 3, *66, *64, *73; see also sec. 1, *30). Alternating with this undertone of the need for reform, however, is praise for the "political liberties" the ancient common law has preserved in England, while the Continent fell into renewed empire and despotism. This distinctive treatment of the common law then states that "the authority of these maxims rests entirely upon general reception and usage," implicitly demoting any grounding in the law of nature, practical wisdom, or right reason. The traditional view included consent as one principle of the common law, but Blackstone here incorporates into the common law of Fortescue or Coke a solid dose of the positivist critique by Hobbes. Perhaps the citizenry grants such consent, this newly prominent basis of the common law, because the law works to maintain liberty (sec. 3, *67–68).

Blackstone's exposition turns next to "a very natural, and very material question," namely, "[H]ow are these customs or maxims to be known, and by whom is their validity to be determined?" By the end of this section he offers his first remarks on parliamentary supremacy, declaring that statutes trump the unwritten law of the common-law courts. His answer here to the question of authority over the common law is, however, just as striking:

> The answer is, by the judges in the several courts of justice. They are the depositary of the laws; the living oracles, who must decide in all cases of doubt, and who are bound by an oath to decide according to the law of the land. Their knowledge of that law is derived from experience and study; from the "viginti annorum lucubrationes" [twenty years' laborious study], which Fortescue mentions; and from being long personally accustomed to the judicial decisions of their predecessors. And indeed these judicial decisions are the principal and most authoritative evidence, that can be given, of the existence of such a custom as shall form a part of the common law. (1, "Intro.," sec. 3, *69; citing Fortescue, De laudibus legum Anglie, ch. 8)

Blackstone gives professional judges pride of place regarding the common law, which he terms the "first ground and chief corner stone of the laws of England" in the sequel (*73). In so doing he echoes Montesquieu's account of monarchical judging—an author who twice claimed to have labored for twenty years over his masterwork (see *Spirit*, "Preface"). Though Blackstone does not cite the French jurist here, defining judges as the depository and oracles of the law recalls passages in books 2 and 6 of *The Spirit of the Laws*. Blackstone seeks an independent, authoritative source of the law that is separate from the turmoil of politics in judges who rule according to their studious learning and accumulated precedents. Proper change in the law comes from Parliament, although judges can incrementally bring the letter of the law into line with its spirit, if the latter is found through traditional modes of reasoning and is grounded in precedents at law. Still, Blackstone takes from Montesquieu an emphasis not found in Coke, for these remarks on judicial power and their sequel reiterate the more positivist tone of his initial definition of the common law. This is evident in his rationale for observing precedent:

> For it is an established rule to abide by former precedents, where
> the same points come again in litigation; as well to keep the scale
> of justice even and steady, and not liable to waver with every new
> judge's opinion; as also because the law in that case being solemnly
> declared and determined, what before was uncertain, and perhaps
> indifferent, is now become a permanent rule, which it is not in the
> breast of any subsequent judge to alter or vary from, according to his
> private sentiments: he being sworn to determine, not according to his
> own private judgment, but according to the known laws and customs
> of the land; not delegated to pronounce a new law, but to maintain
> and expound the old one. (1, "Intro.," sec. 3, *69)

The theme here is not judicial self-restraint, as if judges can freely decide when to legislate and when to hold back, but an inherently as well as externally limited judicial power. Blackstone states twice in quick succession that judges must rule not according to individual opinion but by the laws of the land, employing a venerable phrase from Magna Carta. He also states twice that judges are bound by their oath of office to do so, implying that failure could be grounds for losing office. The reasons given for adhering to precedent, then, stem less from a revealed or natural law separately conceived than from principles of proper procedure—fair treatment, restraint upon the idiosyncratic and possibly partisan opinions of judges, certainty and stability, and the separation of judging from legislating. True, keeping the scales of justice steady by treating like cases alike does tap a root in natural justice and is not merely procedural.

Still, there is little emphasis here upon Coke's notion that common-law judges possess an artificial reason or practical wisdom which, through generations of judging, perfects the law so that it is the embodiment of natural justice as discovered in particular cases.

Characteristically, however, this is but one statement in Blackstone's dialectical examination of precedent, judging, and legal interpretation that continues through most of this section on English law. Albert Alschuler notes that this passage was cited and criticized by the U.S. Supreme Court in 1963, when describing Blackstone as the "foremost exponent of the declaratory theory" of law, according to which judges find law rather than make it.[25] The judges cited Blackstone to repudiate this theory and then proceeded to break with the traditional common-law principle that, because judges find what the law requires rather than make new law, court precedents apply retroactively. A majority of the Court admitted that their recent landmark ruling about Fourth Amendment protections against government searches and seizures effectively legislated a new right of criminal due process, and then, also acting as a legislature, ruled that they would not apply the new standard to searches conducted before its announcement. Alschuler notes, however, that the Court omitted the sequel to Blackstone's statement that judges are not to "pronounce a new law, but to maintain and expound the old one," thereby missing the dialectal, complex character of his analysis:

> Yet this rule admits of exception, where the former determination
> is most evidently contrary to reason; much more if it be contrary
> to divine law. But even in such cases the subsequent judges do
> not pretend to make a new law, but to vindicate the old one from
> misrepresentation. For if it be found . . . manifestly absurd or unjust
> it is declared, not that such a sentence was *bad law*, but that it was *not
> law*. . . . And hence it is that our lawyers are with justice so copious
> in their encomiums on the reason of the common law; that they tell
> us, that the law is the perfection of reason, that it always intends to
> conform thereto, and that what is not reason is not law. (1, "Intro.,"
> sec. 3, *69–70)

This emphatic qualification of the nature of judicial power places Blackstone at odds not only with Coke but with Hobbes. Contrary to Coke, perhaps the most famous of the "lawyers" who declared English common law to be a perfection of reason, there is little hint of the traditional notion that the common law taps a root in natural law or is the perfection of right reason.[26] Blackstone does cite divine law, but not the notion of a natural law or right reason that links divine law and judicial reasoning, as found in Fortescue or Saint Germain. Hobbes, on the other hand, would not endorse the notion that an independent power could sit in judgment upon the reasonableness of the sovereign's law, especially when reason is only defined by the terms "manifestly absurd or unjust," which hardly add clarity. Blackstone's dialectical account proceeds to a third and fourth step, however, qualifying the declaration that "what is not reason is not law":

> Not that the particular reason of every rule in the law can at this distance of time be always precisely assigned: but it is sufficient that there be nothing in the rule flatly contradictory to reason, and then the law will presume to be well founded. And it hath been an ancient observation in the laws of England, that whenever a standing rule of law, of which the reason perhaps could not be remembered, hath been wantonly broke in upon by statutes or new resolutions, the wisdom of the rule hath in the end appeared from the inconveniences that have followed the innovation. The doctrine of the law then is this: that precedents and rules must be followed, unless flatly absurd or unjust: for though their reason be not obvious at first view, yet we owe such a deference to former times as not to suppose they acted wholly without consideration. (1, "Intro.," sec. 3, *70)

Blackstone cites only one authority in this passage, the Roman digests, or *Pandects,* of the civil law, but this does little to define reason other than to suggest a universal reason in which the common law participates, one not confined to time or place. He reiterates his admonition from the introductory lecture, as if he can sense a Bentham ahead, that legislators should not be so quick to reform what they don't understand. The fourth step in Blackstone's discourse is to declare that judges, too, are not to innovate or sit in judgment upon the reason of laws simply on the basis of contemporary opinion. He uses the example of a rule, established "time out of mind," that stepbrothers cannot inherit their brother's property, but that the property reverts to the king or another superior lord. This is a "positive law," fixed by "custom," and "evidenced by judicial decisions," and therefore a "modern judge" cannot depart from the rule "without a breach of his oath and the law." Recalling the traditional notion of things indifferent to natural law, he declares that the rule is not "repugnant to natural justice; though the reason of it, drawn from the feudal law, may not be quite obvious to everybody." Therefore, a modern judge who thinks it unjust must accept that "it is not in his power to alter it"; for, "*the law,* and the *opinion of the judge* are not always convertible terms" (1, "Intro.," sec. 3, *70–71).

The qualifications in this dialectical examination do not fit together easily: judges are the oracles of common law; judges are bound by precedent; judges are not so bound, however, if precedent is unreasonable; nonetheless, both legislators and judges musts defer to the ancient rules and customs of the common law and should not presume a rule irrational because it does not square with contemporary opinion. Blackstone confirms this dialectical character by his final statement, made just after warning of judicial legislating: "Upon the whole however, we may take it as a general rule, 'that the decisions of courts of justice are the evidence of what is common law:' in the same manner as, in the civil law, what the emperor had once determined was to serve for a guide for the future" (1, "Intro.," sec. 3, *71). This brings his subtle characterizations of judicial power full circle, to the view that judges are the depositories of the law. Blackstone's final word on the common law, in which he seems to quote himself as an authority, also provides the key to harmonizing these four propositions by recalling his regular distinction between common law and civil law. Rule by separated powers on the basis of custom and consent and dedicated to liberty is quite different from despotic rule by emperor and imperial rescripts. He confirms this theme when closing this entire discussion of custom, after remarking that Coke's *Reports* and *Institutes* are quaint, pedantic, and "greatly defective in method." Blackstone notes that Roman law, too, had an important place for custom "in the times of its liberty," but "when the imperial tyranny came to be fully established" the civil law abandoned custom and declared the emperor alone to be the source, and interpreter, of the law (*72–74).

Blackstone's initial discourse upon the unwritten common law concludes that "indeed it is one of the characteristic marks of English liberty, that our common law depends upon custom; which carries this internal evidence of freedom along with it, that it probably was introduced by the voluntary consent of the people" (1, "Intro.," sec. 3, *74). He emphasizes the theme of liberty both before and after his treatment of judicial power and *stare decisis* in common law because the only authority he cites on the presumptive rationality of common-law custom is the civil law. He could not cite Bacon or Hobbes, the forerunners of Bentham, Austin, and Holmes, who find nothing to respect in the thinking or practice of the past. While only Holmes among these liberal positivists was an advocate of strong judicial power, Blackstone should be given credit for seeing that not only legislators but judges could be the agents of rationalism, the repudiation of custom, and radical reform. Alternately, the fact that Blackstone ignores such masters of the common law as Fortescue, Saint Germain, or Coke regarding the presumptive reasonableness of custom suggests that his jurisprudence seeks liberal reform of the common law without repudiating the stability and protection for liberty that it had achieved. In light of his later discussions of the effective independence and importance of the judiciary, one can discern here the seeds of a view that judges can incrementally revise the law or shape its direction. Even his most emphatic qualification of or limit on judicial power in the introduction concludes by leaving "reason" vaguely defined and by noting that the law and the judge's opinion "are *not always* convertible terms"—implying that, at most times, they are (*70–71; emphasis added).

Blackstone's second treatment of legal interpretation develops this subtle innovation in the common-law mind. As noted, both the second and third sections of the introduction conclude with discourses on interpretation of the law, and both ultimately imply that judicial power is the main source of legal interpretation in the English constitution. After discussing the unwritten law of England in the bulk of the third section, then briefly analyzing civil law and ecclesiastical law as subordinate threads within the common law, Blackstone turns to the written law made by the King-in-Parliament. His main topic is ten rules for the construction of statutes, introduced by the distinction between statutes that are declaratory of the common law and those that are remedial (1, "Intro.," sec. 3, *86–91). Presumably, these ten rules supplement the five rules previously discussed, since these are more specifically relevant to, and arise from, English law. While Blackstone cites Justinian, Pufendorf, Cicero, and Grotius in the earlier account, here he cites mostly Coke, citing philosophic authors, Bacon and Cicero, only twice (sec. 3, *87–91; cf. sec. 2, *59–62). Separating these two discussions is Blackstone's long, subtle treatment of the common law and judicial power, but there are no fundamental differences in the two treatments of legal interpretation. Blackstone's introduction to the *Commentaries* thus lays the groundwork for interpreting Coke himself in a more liberal and scientific light, thereby turning the classic common law in a new direction.

The first rule of construction is that, regarding remedial statutes, one must understand the old common law, then the mischief it failed to address, and then what remedy Parliament devised through statute. Blackstone implicitly declares this a judicial function, while citing Coke for the relevant common-law maxim: "it is the business of the judges so to construe the act, as to suppress the mischief and advance the remedy" (1, "Intro.," sec. 3, *87). As Hamilton does in *Federalist* no. 78 when using common-law maxims to discern in the Constitution a power of judicial review, Blackstone implies that it is not the King-in-Parliament, not the Hobbesian sovereign, that supplies the very rules by which that sovereign's statutes are to be applied. The judiciary is a separate depository of legal understanding, and the authority cited throughout these rules of interpretation is Coke, both his *Reports* of judicial decisions and his *Institutes*, or treatise of the law. Still, Blackstone is keen to show the liberal character of common-law reasoning in the second, third, and fourth rules, for each would have judges interpret statutes so as to protect individuals from harm—whether loss of status, loss of security through criminal punishment, or loss of property through fraud. It is no accident that he cites Bacon's *Elements of the Law* here. Thus, "Penal statutes must be construed strictly," but "Statutes against frauds are to be liberally and beneficially expounded," and while the latter "may seem a contradiction to the [prior] rule," the implicit principle is maximum protection for the individual. This spirit is to govern the judges, whether penal or property law is at issue: "[W]here the statute acts upon the offender, and inflicts a penalty, as the pillory or a fine, it is then to be taken strictly: but when the statute acts upon the offence, by setting aside the fraudulent transaction, here it is to be construed liberally" (*88).

The last four rules turn to the more constitutional questions of authority and priority, and here Blackstone makes his initial statement on parliamentary supremacy, discussed above. Rule seven declares that when "the common law and a statute differ, the common law gives place to the statute," just as an old statute gives way to a new: newer laws abrogate older (1, "Intro.," sec. 3, *89). The ninth rule follows this line, stating that no Parliament can bind a future one by use of restraining clauses, for that would make the older one "sovereign" over the current one. To the contrary, a current Parliament "is always of equal, always of absolute authority: it acknowledges no superior on earth" (*90). This is the context for his striking remarks in the tenth rule, which repudiate any power of judicial review to nullify acts of parliament. The context, often overlooked, is crucial: "[A]cts of parliament that are impossible to be performed are of no validity; and if there arise out of them collaterally any absurd consequences, manifestly contradictory to common reason, they are, with regard to those consequences, void" (*91). Blackstone immediately recognizes the "restrictions" in this statement of the rule, and as noted, they restrict judicial power. His caveat begins, "I know it is generally laid down more largely" that statutes contrary to reason are void, and that judges can declare them so. He paraphrases Coke's reasoning from *Dr. Bonham's Case* and attributes the larger view of judicial power to it.

The same dialectic occurs here, however, as in the earlier discussion of judging in this section of the introduction. Blackstone gives the initiative to the judges, declares a severe limit on it, then reiterates that if something "unreasonable" flows from a statute "the judges are in decency to conclude that this consequence was not foreseen by the parliament, and therefore they are at liberty to expound the statute by equity, and only *quoad hoc* [as to this] disregard it" (1, "Intro.," sec. 3, *91). This last statement grants to the judiciary the evaluation of constitutional or legal decency and equitable interpretation, both of them discretionary powers. They are not unlimited, for judges can ignore the statute only as applied to this case, that is, in the narrowest way and without, apparently, setting a precedent. Indeed, the next movement in the dialectic reiterates that if Parliament did decide to do something unreasonable, such as allowing someone to be judge in his own case—"if we could conceive it possible" that they should do so—then "no court has the power to defeat the intent of the legislature, when couched in such evident and express words" (*91). Blackstone's final word, however, offers another discourse on equity: "These are the several grounds of the laws of England: over and above which, equity is also frequently called in to assist, to moderate, and to explain" (*91–92). He refers to his previous discussion of equitable interpretation, then confirms that this notion is not confined to the distinct courts of equity. Changes he made to later editions (italicized here) emphasize the discretion of common-law judges: "I shall therefore only add that (*besides the liberality of sentiment with which our common-law judges interpret acts of parliament, and such rules of the unwritten law as are not of a positive kind*), there are also *peculiar courts of equity* established for the benefit of the subject" (*92 [4th ed.]).

In the early editions of the *Commentaries* this passage might have implied that only in the Chancellor's equity courts were judges "to correct and soften the rigor of the law, when through its generality it bears too hard in particular cases" (1, "Intro.," sec. 3, *92). It is telling that he subsequently removed this phrase, which echoes the notion of equitable interpretation by all judges discussed in section 2 of the introduction, in order to explicitly confirm that common-law judges should interpret according to a liberal sentiment. This, coupled with the new definition of equity courts as "peculiar," marks only a change of emphasis, for in all the editions this passage lists limits on the jurisdiction of the courts of equity. He summarizes their function as "to relieve in all such cases as are, *bona fide*, objects of relief," and then immediately insists that this jurisdiction extends only to matters of property.

The third section of the introduction concludes, then, with yet another dialectical analysis. Having reiterated that all professional judges have equitable, discretionary powers, he reminds us of a limit on them:

> For the freedom of our constitution will not permit, that in criminal cases a power should be lodged in any judge, to construe the law otherwise than according to the letter. This caution, while it admirably protects the public liberty, can never bear hard upon individuals. A man cannot suffer *more* punishment than the law assigns, but he may

suffer less. The laws cannot be strained by partiality to inflict a penalty
beyond what the letter will warrant; but in cases where the letter
induces any apparent hardship, the crown has the power to pardon.
(1, "Intro.," sec. 3, *92)

Blackstone has not cited Montesquieu in this section, but his description of
common-law judges as the depositary and oracles of the law paraphrases passages in *The Spirit of the Laws* (see 2.4; 5.11; 6.1; 28.45). His emphasis on interpreting statutes, including criminal statutes, so as to protect individual liberty,
and on the general role of judicial equity in moderating the law betray further
influences (see *Spirit*, 6.3; 6.13; 11.6). While here it is only the crown that can
moderate criminal law, in book 4 Blackstone states that it is the discretionary
power of the judges that calls upon the crown to exercise that power. Indeed,
judges have several rules for exercising discretion, at least as to grounds for
temporary reprieves, some of which may last years (4.31). Moreover, the second, third, and fourth of his ten rules of interpretation specify the liberality
suggested in both discussions of interpretation, such that penal laws must always be construed, if possible, to the benefit of the criminal—which in that
case means strictly (1, "Intro.," sec. 3, *88). The reference to "partiality" here
also is telling, even if the immediate concern is partisan judges. If partisanship
is an issue with judges, certainly it also is a problem regarding legislators and
executives. It is all the more important to have independent judges interpreting,
applying, and moderating the law so as to avoid threats to liberty that might
arise from partisan criminal laws or prosecutions.

The bold notion here is that a judicial power of equity, exercised by all professional judges but most comprehensively in common-law courts, is to stand
"over and above" the laws of England, "to assist, to moderate, and to explain."
Blackstone softens any controversial edge by quickly defining limits. Still, the
very need for such qualifications, coupled with the reservations about parliamentary supremacy expressed earlier in the third section, suggest that Blackstone's introductory discourse quietly places judicial power at the center of his
theory of constitutional and statutory interpretation. Moreover, lying ahead are
the reservations in book 1 about absolute legislative sovereignty already noted,
as well as more emphatic statements about the independence of the judiciary,
both of which moderate these qualifications to judicial power. The structure
of Blackstone's *Commentaries* slowly moves the reader from the status quo theory of the monarchical or mixed constitution, in which judges are not fully
independent and sovereignty lies with the King-in-Parliament, toward a Montesquieuan conception of constitutionalism. The introduction lays the ground-

work for an exposition of English law and constitution in which judges must be independent enough to moderate the other powers if public and private liberty is to be preserved. The necessity of such a judicial power is fundamental, since political liberty is the very spirit of the constitution that Blackstone expounds.

seven

Blackstone, Lord Mansfield, and Common-Law Liberalism

The introduction and book 1 of the *Commentaries* lay the basis for a complex constitutionalism of separated powers, not simply of parliamentary sovereignty. On this Blackstone quietly builds a new conception of judicial power in British constitutionalism as the moderating, tempering element that ensures individual liberty and tranquillity. The means to this constitutional aim include liberalizing the common law of Coke and educating future statesmen in this legal spirit. By the work's end Blackstone follows Montesquieu in propounding not so much a liberalized common law but a liberalism qualified by common-law elements. Rather than adopt the abstract reason of Hobbes or Locke, he finds common-law means to the liberal ends of individual rights and tranquillity. Neither the utopian reason of sovereignty (or sovereignty and revolution) nor the Aristotelian reason of Coke's classic common law secures a humane liberalism. Still, the root of modern liberty lies in the Gothic spirit of common-law complexity, which can both temper and achieve modern aims.

Blackstone crowns these early, constitutionalist aspects of the work by depicting an effectively independent judicial power later in book 1. This subtly judicialized constitutionalism is the basis for his remarks, in the remainder of the *Commentaries*, on reform in particular areas of English law. This complicated, historical, and juridical approach to humane reform is inexcusably cumbersome and far too gradual for Bentham, but as noted, it has been extraordinarily successful in Britain and America among practical statesmen. If Blackstone is the root of American judicial power, however much the Holmesean revolution later transformed it, and if American judicial power is the model for a judicialized politics now spreading across the globe, then it is important to work through Blackstone's labyrinthine argument for a cloaking of power. It is not adequate to find Blackstone an advocate of a sovereign Parliament and a subordinate judiciary in book 1 and then fail to account for the legal reforms suggested throughout the voluminous details of the four books. These suggestions to judges and statesmen range from reforms of royal taxation and family law (book 1) to property law and commerce (book 2), to civil injuries and tort law (book 3), then to laws concerning toleration and capital punishment in the penal code (book 4).

Moreover, just as Montesquieu praises King Louis IX as a model for prudent reform of judicial power and the use of a new juridical spirit to moderate politics, so Blackstone has a model in mind, although one more contemporary (see *Spirit*, book 28). As the *Commentaries* moves from instructing in constitutional principle to inculcating a judicial prudence about particular areas of law, the spirit of Lord Mansfield, the most celebrated and controversial judge in eighteenth-century England, looms large. Nonetheless, Blackstone's novel, complex jurisprudential teaching not only adheres to, but derives from, a separation-of-powers constitutionalism. This suggests that the Holmesean model of judicial legislating in the twentieth century is not only radically different from Blackstone's judicial power, but at odds with the separation-of-powers constitution in which it resides. The genius of Mansfield and Blackstone is to adhere to fundamental principles of law, constitutionalism, and legal prudence while achieving reform toward liberal ends. This does not place courts at the center of legislating and policy, but seeks to moderate both legislating and executing by ensuring that a constitutional balance of power serves individual tranquillity. Were judges the absolute source of law, with no genuine separation of powers, both that balance and the liberal security that rests upon it would be endangered.

For Blackstone, then, judges are not visionary oracles of humane progress toward a later stage of societal evolution, either exercising self-restraint so as to allow the majority to evolve as it wills, or nudging society along a higher path. Rather, the primary metaphor Blackstone chooses for judges is that of renovating architects, who rearrange interior details within a sound, humane constitutional structure (book 3). Judges are not mere clerks or mechanics, but neither are they lawmakers, prophets of a new legal system. They are to be effectively independent of the executive and legislative powers, but all three are subordinate to the spirit of liberty and moderation evident in English constitutional history. Blackstone's model judge is his contemporary, Lord Mansfield, who used the forms and principles of English law to achieve a synthesis of common law and equity practice within the common-law courts. Mansfield and Blackstone thought this innovation at once consistent with fundamental principles of English law and a concrete, legitimate way to achieve humane legal reform. Moreover, it is consistent with this complicated balance of the rule of law and reform, of complexity and particularity, that Blackstone reveals his teaching on this cloaking of power in a subtle, complicated manner.

Rights, Constitutionalism, and an Independent Judiciary

Having stipulated that English law should be analyzed through a division into rights and wrongs, book 1 of the *Commentaries* discusses the rights of persons in English law and constitutionalism (1.1, *122). For Blackstone, "persons" encompasses individual and constitutional entities, and book 1 moves between these civil and political aspects of law, beginning with the absolute rights of individuals, then discussing the powers of institutions (constitutional persons), and then returning to the rights of private institutions and the family. The structure and content of the book clearly suggest influences from Hobbes and Locke. Its opening note, the discussion of individual rights, paraphrases the state of nature analyses of these earlier liberal philosophers. When Blackstone turns to constitutional analysis, the emphasis lies with Parliament and the king, and his dialectical examination could be read as laying out the tensions between Hobbesian sovereignty and Lockean separation of powers. Still, even these analyses of individual rights and constitutional complexities betray a Montesquieuan spirit that tempers other liberal influences. Since this element has been so consistently overlooked by Blackstone scholars, one might be forgiven for pressing to restore the balance. The very movement between categories of political and civil law, and the insistence upon a proper balance between them, suggests a Montesquieuan perspective on law, rights, and constitutionalism. Moreover, the fundamental principle that maintains coherence amid Blackstone's rich yet seemingly conflicting observations in book 1 is that only the English constitution has liberty as its end ("Intro.," sec. 1, *6). This principle of constitutional and individual liberty reconciles state-of-nature abstractions with a Gothic history of rights, and separation of powers with an effective sovereignty. Even early in the book 1, amid some of the most Hobbesian and Lockean moments in the work, Blackstone's constitutionalism suggests the necessity of a quiet prominence for judicial power. The balancing function of common-law judges might be the most effective way to reconcile these conflicting dimensions to both individual rights and constitutional powers, so as to secure both political and civil liberty.

The opening analysis of rights declares that "the principal aim of society is to protect individuals in the enjoyment of those absolute rights, which were vested in them by the immutable laws of nature" (1.1, *124). Since natural rights were not self-executing and required the historical act of forming "friendly and social communities," laws were established. There is a touch of Aristotle or Montesquieu in his remarks on peace, intercourse, and friendliness, but the Lockean emphasis prevails: "the first and primary end of human laws is to maintain and regulate these absolute rights of individuals." Still, amid this liberal theory, Blackstone insists that if these rights or "liberties" are "founded on nature and reason," they also are "coeval with our form of government" (1.1, *127). More than Lockean theory is at work, for he prefaces this synthesis of theoretical principle and historical confirmation with praise for the "spirit of liberty" that is "so deeply implanted in our constitution, and rooted even in our very soil" that no tyranny lasts, and even slaves are emancipated upon landing (*127). The sequel cites not Montesquieu but Gothic and traditional sources, ranging from Magna Carta to Coke, but this would please his French predecessor. Ernest Barker notes that Blackstone here provides the bedrock of the "declaratory" theory of law, arguing that these natural rights were declared, not invented, in fundamental documents.[1] This gives one pause about the dismissal of the declaratory view by modern legal realists in America as simplistic or mechanical, since when judicial review was established, the rights that judges secure were understood as defined in a Declaration of Independence. At any rate, before analyzing these absolute rights, which closely track Locke's trio of life, liberty, and property, Blackstone also echoes the Montesquieuan notion of English exceptionalism cited early in the introduction. Since in "most other countries of the world" these natural rights "now more or less [are] debased and destroyed," they can be called rights of "the people of England" (*129).

In the remainder of the chapter he specifies the three "principal absolute rights" of security, liberty, and property, and then five "auxiliary subordinate rights" that secure the principal ones (see 1.1, *140–41). Montesquieuan and common-law moments blend with Lockean liberalism throughout. The choice of the broader term "security" for the first absolute right, not simply the Lockean term "life," echoes Montesquieu's definition of liberty as that "tranquillity of spirit that comes from the opinion each one has of his security" (*Spirit*, 11.6). Such security includes "enjoyment" not only of life but of limb, and Blackstone broadens this to include a right to provision for welfare and thus relief for the poor. He deepens the Montesquieuan tone by declaring the Gothic legal tradition much more "humane" than Roman and civil law regarding this absolute right (1.1, *129, *132; see *Spirit*, 23.29). He also cites the importance of book 4's analysis of criminal law and penalties, and thus of judicial power and prudence, for understanding England's exceptional protection of rights. From Magna Carta to Coke it established that no punishment of life or limb can occur without "due process of law," and the ban on torture proves the mildness of English penal law (1.1, *133–34). Blackstone then defines the second principal right, liberty, as inextricably bound with the rule of law, specifically with juridical due process. He praises the writ of *habeas corpus* secured by courts independent of the royal power, and other requirements for "process from the courts of judicature," as bulwarks of personal liberty against despotism. He cites Coke's encomium from his second *Institutes* for this common-law writ, which affirms that it has been "so benignly and liberally construed for the benefit of the subject" as to ban exile as a criminal penalty. Blackstone praises "that second *magna carta*," the *Habeas Corpus* Act (1679), for fortifying this humane regime, and while a future Parliament could reverse this, his remarks imply a constitutional and juridical limit upon legislative power (*134–38). Montesquieu's spirit even appears in analyzing that most Lockean of rights, the right to property, for Blackstone states that protection for property is a "point of honor" as well as justice in English law. It is secured by "ancient statutes," "the great charter," and "the law of the land" that no person's property can be taken "unless he be duly brought to answer, and be forejudged by course of law" (*138–39).

Blackstone next observes that "the dead letter of the laws" alone could not protect these principal rights "if the constitution had provided no other method to secure their actual enjoyment"; thus, English constitutionalism includes five subordinate rights intended "to protect and maintain" those to security, liberty, and property (1.1, *140–41). The rationale for opening the first book on English law by analyzing individual rights now becomes clearer. The first three of the auxiliary rights are, curiously, institutions and the extent and limits of their powers, and they correspond to the three separate powers defined by Montesquieu and enacted in the American constitution. Blackstone merely mentions both the first right, the "constitution, powers, and privileges of parliament," and the second, the "limitation of the king's prerogative," since he discusses each later in this book (chs. 2 and 7, respectively). He briefly explains, however, their priority. The proper constitution of Parliament keeps legislative power "in due health and vigor," ensuring that no laws will be enacted that are "destructive of general liberty"; the second right guards executive power to ensure that it does not act beyond, or in contradiction to, law (*141). While the fourth and fifth auxiliary rights, to petition king or parliament for redress of grievances and to keep arms "under due restrictions," are not surprising, it is striking that the first three auxiliary individual rights are three institutional powers (*143–44). Barker notes how distinctly English, and Gothic, it is to define the constitution or regime of a people, and the chief institutions of that constitution, in terms of the individual rights of the subjects or citizens.[2]

The most extraordinary aspect of this analysis is that the third and central of the five rights, and the one treated at greatest length, is that of "applying to the courts of justice for redress of injuries." This prominence is odd, since Blackstone could have said of this right and power that it, too, would be discussed in its proper place, for he does devote part of a later chapter to it (1.7). Instead, he states that if in England the law is "the supreme arbiter of every man's life, liberty, and property," then the "courts of justice" provide the remedy and redress for any claimed injury to these rights, whether by a private or public person. As in the introduction, he insists upon a limit to judicial power, asserting that the law "depends not upon the arbitrary will of any judge" but is fixed in both common law and statute, unless changed by Parliament. Still, even Parliament is bound to leave standing "the old established forms of the common law," and neither king nor Parliament should diminish the independent, impartial power of "courts of justice" (1.1, *141–43). The effect of this rights discourse is to quietly establish Montesquieu's version of the separation of powers as the definitive account of English constitutionalism. Blackstone elevates judicial power to equal status—if third position—in relation to legislative and executive powers, and he does so even before he praises the separation of powers later in book 1 and then elevates judging more boldly. He cites only four authorities in treating these five auxiliary rights, and none are of Hobbesian provenance—Magna Carta twice, Coke once, and Montesquieu once. Moreover, the sequel reviews all the principal and auxiliary "liberties of Englishmen" and cites only Montesquieu. Blackstone calls upon *The Spirit of the Laws* one last time in this important chapter while defending the "gentle and moderate" restraints on natural liberty in English law, subsequently exhorting "the student in our laws" to delve further into these topics. He closes by citing not any English authority but "Father Paul"—apparently another foreigner, the seventeenth-century Venetian patriot Fr. Paolo Sarpi, who opposed Papal encroachments. The penultimate passage in this analysis of rights praises Montesquieu and recalls his verdict on English exceptionalism, thereby bringing the reader full circle, at the close of the first chapter of the first book, to the opening of Blackstone's introductory lecture:

> This review of our situation may fully justify the observation of a
> learned French author, who indeed generally both thought and wrote
> in the spirit of genuine freedom; and who hath not scrupled to profess,

even in the very bosom of his native country, that the English is the
only nation in the world, where political or civil liberty is the direct
end of its constitution. (1.1, *145–46, citing *Spirit*, 11.5; see "Intro.,"
sec. 1, *6)

Blackstone's next chapter examines the first auxiliary right, the powers of
Parliament, but in the guise of the rights of public persons (1.2). Here his important remarks on the separation of powers and parliamentary supremacy, already
discussed, begin a long analysis of constitutional law, defined as the political
or public law of government offices, institutions, and regulations concerning
public status (chs. 2–13). Only at the end of book 1 does he return to what
Montesquieu terms civil law, the legal status of private persons and relations
(chs. 14–18). It is significant that Blackstone employs "relations," a term from
book 1 of *The Spirit of the Laws*, to frame his entire analysis of the rights of public and private persons in book 1 of the *Commentaries*. The topic of Parliament
falls into this book on "the rights and duties of persons, as they are members of
society, and stand in various relations to one another," because the "most universal public relation . . . is that of government" (1.2, *146). This reflects Montesquieu's refrain that, despite the necessity of analytical categories, philosophers and statesmen must remember that all the parts of law and politics relate
to form a general spirit of laws, or general spirit of a nation. This fundamental
orientation allows Blackstone to place political or constitutional law under the
same "book" as the civil or private law of families and corporations—indeed,
to mix rights and institutions from the beginning. The rationale for doing so,
taken from Montesquieu, is to elevate civil law and its perspective of individual
tranquillity to equal status with political law. Both jurists suggest that the earlier liberalism of Hobbes and Locke, the one stressing sovereignty and the other
dual powers and a right of revolution, fails to keep its eyes on its stated prize
of individual rights. Such an emphasis on political law at the expense of the
private, civil sphere fails to protect liberty as tranquillity, so Blackstone follows
Montesquieu in elevating the institution that most emphatically views law and
politics in those terms, the judiciary. Blackstone has dissatisfied generations of
scholars who insist upon reading these chapters on constitutional law, on Parliament and king, through the lenses of Hobbesian concerns with sovereignty
or Lockean concerns with separation of powers and revolution. Book 1 of the
Commentaries argues, rather, that while there is some tension between the liberal concern with sovereignty and the liberal concern with separated powers, or
complexity, the problem is only theoretical, not necessarily practical. For Blackstone both the theoretical and actual tensions within English constitutionalism
are what keep it free, and any theoretical problem is resolved, or excused, by

the natural, historical confirmation that the system protects liberty. The same applies for any of Bentham's frettings about the jurisprudence and theory of rights in Blackstone's introduction. This recalls Montesquieu's ridicule of Harrington's utopian theories—that if the English constitution works, rooted in the Germanic woods and Gothic past, one shouldn't search for a fancy new model (*Spirit*, 11.5; 11.6). A further element of the common-law past overlooked by Hobbes and Locke is the new third power that rose in the Gothic lands even while the nobles declined in their capacity to balance king and commons, executive and legislative—namely, the judges and lawyers.

The thread connecting Blackstone's analyses of legislative and executive power in book 1 is the historical, constitutionalist lesson that moderation or balance, never extremes, is the best way to secure both political and civil liberty. In closing his analysis of the two main powers, just before thematically discussing judicial power, Blackstone chastises the extremes of "absolute power in the prince" and "national resistance by the people" as being "the advocates for slavery on the one hand, and the demagogues of faction on the other" (1.7, *251). These might be identified as the logical extremes inherent in the theories of Hobbes and Locke, respectively. Throughout his analysis of constitutional powers Blackstone leavens earlier liberalism with doses of Montesquieu's more complex conception. He opens the analysis of Parliament by tracing the institution to a Gothic past, and cites the very same passage from Tacitus, *On the Mores of the Germans,* that Montesquieu cites at the close of his analysis of England's constitution (1.2, *147; see *Spirit*, 11.6). Beyond the obvious debt in the analyses of separation of powers, the lawyer Regnault cites the analysis of the noble branch of Parliament as an unacknowledged paraphrasing of Montesquieu (see 1.2, *153–55, *157–58).[3] In mid-chapter Blackstone pauses to remark, just as Montesquieu does at the close of his analysis of England, that practice may not perfectly correspond with his sketch, thereby signaling that he is no mere apologist for existing laws and institutions: "This is the spirit of our constitution: not that I assert it is in fact quite so perfect† as I have here endeavored to describe it; for, if any alteration might be wished or suggested in the present frame of parliaments, it should be in favour of a more complete representation of the people" (1.2, *172). Later editions add a note (marked † here) that this qualification applies "to many other parts of the work" where England's laws are "represented as nearly approaching to perfection." His method is to elucidate "the clearness of the spring," implying Montesquieuan reform to remove corruptions and restore a better condition.

Blackstone's constitutional analysis next takes up executive power (1.3), and he devotes a considerable part of book 1 to analyzing the distinct dimensions of the king's title, family, councils, duties, prerogative, and revenue (chs.

3–8). In this section, under the topic of royal prerogative, Blackstone finally presents a thematic statement on judicial power in English constitutionalism. The Montesquieuan spirit animating this analysis suggests that his treatment of judicial power is not a footnote to royal power, but propounds a third, effectively independent power to balance legislative and executive. It is while examining the title to the throne that Blackstone criticizes the extremes of royalism and of Lockean revolution, as noted, and argues that England always has had a mixed, moderate constitution (1.3). The influence of book 30 of *The Spirit of the Laws*, which seeks moderation amid the similar extremes adopted by partisan historians of the French monarchy, is evident throughout. This is especially so at the chapter's close: "[I]n this due medium consists . . . the true constitutional notion of the right of succession to the imperial crown of these kingdoms. The extremes, between which it steers, are each of them equally destructive of those ends for which societies were formed and are kept on foot" (1.3, *217). In discussing the king's councils, he insists, as Montesquieu does repeatedly, that the privy council and other purely executive bodies such as the Star Chamber should not usurp the functions of the separate "judges of the courts of law" (1.5, *229–30). In the brief discussion of the king's duty, which is primarily to govern according to law, he cites Tacitus to remind us that "the constitution of our German ancestors" is the source of this constitutional conception of monarchy, and "has always been esteemed an express part of the common law" (1.6, *233–34). This prepares for the long discussion of royal prerogative, which itself opens by recalling that "our ancient constitution and laws" have always limited royal power, and that this was "a first and essential principle in all the Gothic systems of government" (1.7, *238).

This discussion of prerogative is usually read in light of Locke's seminal discussion, but Blackstone places great emphasis on "the balance of the constitution." Indeed, its very survival is at stake, and with it the liberty for which "the British constitution" is famous, if statesmen and jurists cannot achieve that balance (1.7, *243, *244, *237). He cites Locke's analysis of prerogative as "well defined," but does so only after warning against the extremes of republicanism and royalism regarding executive prerogative, and after citing the Italian jurist Gravina—the only modern authority approvingly cited in the opening book of *The Spirit of the Laws* (*250–52; *Spirit*, 1.3). Seeking guidance from Gravina's *Origine Roman juris* seems odd, since Blackstone cites an observation that in the Augustan revolution the emperor unified all the ancient magistracies of the republic. Blackstone acknowledges this oddity by asking that he not be deemed "an advocate for arbitrary power" when he stipulates that "in the exertion of lawful prerogative, the king is and ought to be absolute" (*250). It makes sense that the sequel takes up the foreign-affairs dimensions of executive power first. He expresses the same ambivalence that Plutarch suggests when criticizing Brutus's decision to kill Julius Caesar, or that Hobbes, Locke, and Montesquieu indicate when advocating a single sovereign in matters of state security, or that Hamilton expresses in defending a single holder of "the executive power" in the American Constitution. To one degree or another, none of these authors is shy about the ambitions they hold for great states, nor about the executive means necessary to such ends. Montesquieu, Blackstone, and Hamilton are distinctive, however, in insisting that such a power not only be bounded by law, but also be balanced by multiple powers and in multiple ways. As noted, this perspective may explain the silent treatment given to the innovation of blending executive and legislative powers in a Cabinet, since such simplification reduces the checks on both powers. Moreover, in discussing the executive's foreign-affairs powers, Blackstone cites "the learned Montesquieu" and *The Spirit of the Laws* three times, including the important remark that English policies demonstrate that they alone know how to enjoy simultaneously the benefits of religion, liberty, and commerce (1.7, *253, *260–61). This issue of a lawful executive power within a balanced, complex constitutional order provides the context for the most thematic discussion of judicial power in Blackstone's constitutionalism. Having analyzed the foreign-affairs powers of the executive, and then, on the domestic side, the king's power regarding legislation (the royal veto) and his exclusive power over military affairs, Blackstone turns to the king's capacity as "the fountain of justice," the "reservoir" of the "power of judicature" (1.7, *266).

He first analyzes judicial power historically, and this confirms, characteristically, a natural principle: "[B]y long and uniform usage of many ages, our kings have delegated the whole judicial power to the judges of their several courts, which are the grand depositary of the fundamental laws of the kingdom." This has produced "the dignity and independence of the judges in the superior courts," with their own "certain and established rules" of common-law and equity reasoning the king cannot alter. Blackstone emphasizes this by noting that the Act of Settlement (1701) confirmed the wisdom of "the old Gothic constitution" by guaranteeing judicial office not at the king's pleasure, nor during a single reign, but "during their good behaviour."[4] He quotes George III as viewing "the independence and uprightness of the judges, as essential to the impartial administration of justice; as one of the best securities of the rights and liberties of his subjects; and as most conducive to the honour of the crown" (1.7, *267–68). Blackstone then reiterates that the separation of powers is crucial to protecting rights, and he boldly declares that the English constitution's separation of powers is tripartite, not merely dual. In this "distinct and separate existence of the judicial power, in a peculiar body of men," he emphasizes, "consists one main preservative of the public liberty; which cannot subsist

long in any state, unless the administration of common justice be in some degree separated from both the legislative and also from the executive power"
(*269). He defends this depository of the laws—which has no counterpart in
Hobbes or Locke—by paraphrasing Montesquieu's analysis of the English constitution. If judicial power were wielded by the legislature, the rights of "life,
liberty, and property" would be controlled by "arbitrary judges" bound only
by their opinions and not by "any fundamental principles of law." Blackstone
contrasts judges who "are bound to observe" such fundamental laws by the very
character of their office and training, with legislatures marked more by shifting
opinions than legal principles. This is hardly a defense of legal positivism or
parliamentary supremacy. Similarly, when judging is joined to the executive, it
yields such arbitrary institutions as a "star chamber," and in general a fusing of
power that is "an overbalance for the legislative." If shifting opinions mark the
legislature, then sheer force defines the executive, and nothing is to be avoided
more in "a free constitution" than uniting judicial and executive power. This
lays the groundwork for Hamilton's characterization in *Federalist* no. 78 of the
three powers in the American federal constitution as marked by will, force, and
judgment.[5]

Blackstone's striking conclusion to his brief analysis of judicial power
leaves behind any royalist flavor to his defense of executive prerogative in
foreign affairs and confirms the stakes involved in securing judicial independence. He compares "the absolute power" of "a neighboring nation" to the
"despotic power" of "the eastern empires," Turkey in particular. The plight
of this unnamed neighbor is made "more tolerable" than the latter "in great
measure owing to their having vested the judicial power in their parliaments, a
body separate and distinct from both the legislative and executive." Moreover,
if that nation ever "recovers its former liberty, it will owe it to the efforts of those
assemblies" (1.7, *269). The comparison of a judicial depository of laws with
eastern despotism recalls passages from part 1 of *The Spirit of the Laws*, not to
mention the emphasis on independent judges within a complex constitution of
liberty.[6] Indeed, Blackstone's praise of *parlements* as bulwarks against Bourbon
absolutism says openly what the French jurist could only imply. He synthesizes
constitutionalist developments that Montesquieu's commentary on England
kept distinct on the surface, combining lessons about monarchical judging
with those on judging in republics. Blackstone's debt to this constitutionalist
argument appears not only in this analysis of judicial power but in the pattern
of topics around it. Just as Montesquieu's sequel to his books on constitutional
liberalism is a book on taxation, so the sequel to this analysis of prerogative
(with its lesson about judicial independence) is a chapter on royal revenue
and taxation, replete with warnings on royal power (*Commentaries*, 1.8; *Spirit*,

book 13). Blackstone observes that stealth can enhance power: the executive's "instruments of power are not perhaps so open and avowed as they formerly were, and therefore are the less liable to jealous and invidious reflections; but they are not the weaker on that account" (1.8, *335). Contrary to the boldness of Locke's advocacy of executive action, Blackstone is glad that the "stern commands of prerogative have yielded to the milder voice of influence," just as Montesquieu praised the shift from Machiavellism to moderation (*337; *Spirit*, 21.20). Blackstone's review of royal power repeatedly emphasizes the limits on prerogative gained by increased judicial independence, including the abolition of the Star Chamber, the *Habeas Corpus* Act, the Bill of Rights, and the provisions of the Act of Settlement on permanent tenure and salaries (*334).

Blackstone's adaptation of Montesquieuan subtlety appears in the fact that not until well into book 1 does he thematically discuss this most distinctive part of his complex constitutionalism. Perhaps he should have made an opening plea like that in *The Spirit of the Laws*, that one must read the whole work before criticizing any part of it, even if Bentham and those of his spirit would not heed it anyway. He does follow Montesquieu in arguing that if judicial power is to moderate politics and secure tranquillity, it cannot do so by stirring the envy of the legislative and executive. By postponing his bold statements on judicial power, Blackstone disguises the extent to which he expounded a genuinely tripartite separation of powers, Gothic in its roots but novel as an explicit doctrine. Perhaps he surmised that only judges, lawyers, and other partners in the humane project of cloaking power needed to be persuaded by such a constitutional analysis. He may even have thought it helpful for other readers to think he offered merely commentaries on the status quo, and muddled ones at that.

Blackstone's Castle, Mansfield, and Liberal Reform

Blackstone employs elements of both liberal philosophy and classic common law to expound his own constitutionalism of liberty, adopting neither school wholesale. The entire argument of book 1 of the *Commentaries* suggests that he draws upon Coke and Locke while transcending each. If an unscientific common law is prone to traditionalism, the remedy is not revolutionary preparation for a liberal utopia, built upon clear, precise axioms. Aristotelian right reason and scholastic natural law do impede liberal progress, not to mention personal liberty and tranquillity regarding morals and conscience. Still, Blackstone endorses neither pure legal positivism nor liberal skepticism about traditional moral and religious aims for politics. Following Montesquieu, he warns that a law which serves only pleasure and freedom produces an unstable, extreme politics among individuals left radically separate from each other, and from any tradition (see *Spirit*, 19.27). Blackstone thus uses elements of both liberalism and common law so that they balance each other, guided by a complex constitutional tradition and the prudential maxims arising from it about how to achieve humane, liberal justice. The very complexity of politics and law reveals the natural propriety of a quasi-Newtonian equilibrium of forces, doctrines, and practices, casting doubt upon any one abstract theory, whether Scholastic or Lockean. This Montesquieuan jurisprudence recommends that common-law judges, concerned with both the rights of particular individuals and more general principles, should be repositories of such legal, moral, and political balance. Blackstone's analysis of a constitutionalism of liberty, and the role of judicial power in it, does not state this explicitly until book 3, in the often-cited passage that the common law is "an old Gothic castle" needing renovation. He praises the common law for retaining its medieval exterior while judges gradually convert its interior to afford modern convenience (3.17, *268).[7] This discussion confirms that Montesquieu's project for a cloaking of power is a central theme of Blackstone's jurisprudence. He first described the common law in architectural terms in the 1753 lecture on legal education that became the foundation for the *Commentaries*, comparing the common law to "the venerable edifices of antiquity" (1, "Intro.," sec. 1, *10). Speaking to England's Benthams, the heirs of Hobbes and Locke, he cites the "great and well-experienced judge" Coke to admonish radical legislators about the inherent wisdom in such a structure: "The common law of England has fared like other venerable edifices of antiquity; which rash and unexperienced workmen have ventured to new-dress and refine, with all the rage of modern improvement. Hence frequently its symmetry has been destroyed, its proportions distorted, and its majestic simplicity exchanged for specious embellishments and fantastic novelties" (*10).

Blackstone preempts the charges of Bentham, perhaps fanning the eventual ire of such critics, by criticizing the confident progressivism of the modern legislative mind.[8] He contrasts the visionary aims yet practical failure of the late seventeenth-century poor laws as "a fate that has generally attended most of our statute laws, where they have not the foundation of the common law to build on" (1.9, *365). From the first, the *Commentaries* quietly praises the possibilities for reform opened up by common-law judging infused with a liberal spirit. Several remarks in the preface and introduction feature a judicial model at once respectful of common law yet developing its more liberal possibilities, blending the spirit of the courts of equity with the common law. It becomes clear that the epitome of this model is William Murray, first Earl of Mansfield (1705–1793), Lord Chief Justice of the King's Bench from 1756 to 1788, often termed the greatest English judge of the eighteenth century. Mansfield's Scottish descent exposed him to both the Roman and continental law as well as the common law, as Blackstone explains when praising legal training in "the northern parts of our own island" (1, "Intro.," sec. 1, *4). He had been the king's solicitor general and attorney general, and had an extensive private practice in the equity courts of the Chancery.[9] Blackstone opens the *Commentaries* by praising the sort of judging for which Mansfield, by 1765, was known both nationally and internationally, saying that "a masterly acquaintance with the general spirit of laws and the principles of universal jurisprudence," combined with knowledge of the "original, reason, and history" of modern laws and constitutions, "hath given a beauty and energy to many modern judicial decisions, with which our ancestors were wholly unacquainted" ("Preface," xxxvii). This Montesquieuan praise of Mansfieldean judging, in terms foreshadowing Blackstone's subsequent criticism of Coke's quaintness and parochialism, rests on both personal experience and philosophic authority. Blackstone knew Mansfield well—it was Mansfield who suggested the lectures on English law at Oxford—and he notes that Montesquieu himself had praised Mansfield.[10] When treating maritime courts in book 3, Blackstone praises a judge on England's commission of appeals for international disputes for his service to national and international law during the Seven Years' War (1756–63). He cites a letter by Montesquieu, and remarks by the jurist Emerich de Vattel, specifically praising this judge's reply to a Prussian challenge against prize captures in the war of Austrian succession (1740–48):

> [D]uring the whole of that war, the commission of appeals was regularly attended and all its decisions conducted by a judge, whose masterly acquaintance with the law of nations was known and revered by every state in Europe.† (3.5, *70)
>
> † See the sentiments of the President Montesquieu, and M. Vattel (a subject of the King of Prussia) on the answer transmitted by the English court to his Prussian Majesty's *Exposition des motifs*, etc., A.D. 1753. (Montesquieu's Letters, 5 Mar. 1753. Vattel's *Droit de gens. l.* 2 *c.* 7 § 4.)[11]

Blackstone's remarks on the Gothic castle of the law, later in this book on torts and civil procedure, epitomize reform by judges and suggest the influence of Mansfield's mostly quiet judicial statesmanship. The context for this earlier, explicit praise of Mansfield also suggests the influence of Montesquieu. Since both jurists sought to moderate liberal constitutionalism by elevating civil law to parity with political law, it is no surprise that Blackstone's bold remarks on judges occur when discussing civil procedure. Indeed, his analysis here concerns both political and civil law, since the castle in question represents civil remedies for torts (3.17). He thus cites the 1688 Bill of Rights and the complex procedure of writs developed by common-law courts as limits on the king's remedies that are "part of the liberties of England, and greatly for the safety of the subject" (*259; see also *263–64). This recalls his earlier defense in book 3 of the *Commentaries* of the widespread use of legal fictions by common-law judges, which Bentham considered a pestilence in the law.[12] In laying out the various courts of common law and equity Blackstone discusses a fiction by which the Court of King's Bench extended its original jurisdiction. This occasions a defense, calling upon Coke, of the many such devices to be encountered throughout this book:

> [T]hese fictions of law, though at first they may startle the student, he will find upon further consideration to be highly beneficial and useful: especially as this maxim is ever invariably observed, that no fiction shall extend to work an injury; its proper operation being to prevent a mischief, or remedy an inconvenience, that might result from the general rule of law. So true it is, that *in fictione juris semper subsistit aequitas* (a fiction of law is always founded in equity). (3.4, *43)

In the sequel Blackstone laments that the common law of an earlier era lacked just that "little liberality in the judges" that would have gained for its courts the just remedies of equity courts. He then discusses the famous dispute between Bacon and Coke over the rank of common-law and equity courts (3.4, *51, *53–54). He states that Coke was wrong, since the Chancellor indeed could trump common-law courts, but adds that Coke "acted a very noble part" in another case that genuinely threatened judicial independence, by swearing that where the king intervened in the judicial process he would not obey but, rather, would "do his duty" (*54 n. *h*).[13] Blackstone then praises the seventeenth-century court of Chancery under Sir Heneage Finch, who exercised "a pervading genius" that discovered and pursued "the true spirit of justice" regardless of obstacles in "the narrow and technical notions which then prevailed in the courts of law." This great judge built "a system of jurisprudence" upon "wide and rational foundations" because he recognized the "reason and necessities of mankind" stemming from the decline of feudalism and the rise of modern commerce (3.4, *55). The sequel praises "the masterly hands of our forefathers" who established a complex judicial system that so effectively secures justice, and he is grateful that its "great and original lines are still strong and visible." He distinguishes reforms by judges who respectfully renovate the castle of the law from the "fanciful alterations and wild experiments (so frequent in this fertile age)" undertaken by more legislative spirits. Necessary reforms should be achieved by "closely adhering to the wisdom of the ancient plan" and

by "attending to the spirit, without neglecting the forms, of [our forefathers']
excellent and venerable institutions" (*60).

This analysis, and several others that distinguish the legislative and judicial
spirits, provide crucial context for the remarks later in this book on the Gothic
castle of the law. Blackstone prepares for this famous metaphor by summarizing several chapters on the common-law system of writs and admitting the
difficulty caused by their "great variety" and "immethodical arrangement." He
defends this "intricacy of our legal process" as "one of those troublesome, but
not dangerous, evils which have their root in the frame of our constitution,
and which therefore can never be cured, without hazarding everything that is
dear to us" (3.17, *265–66, *267). This distinctly Montesquieuan point is that
in "absolute governments" simplicity of the laws is paramount, and political,
economic, or social changes are accommodated in the law in a quite illiberal
way: "[T]he prince by his edict may promulgate a new code."[14] Blackstone even
warns that a "legislative revolution," with a legislature completely redrafting a
code, is no better than edicts from a prince. The legislature's handiwork would
be too simple, too arbitrary and legally imprudent, failing to harmonize with
the remainder of the intricate, common-law system (*267). He does speak of
reform, but insists that the excellence of England's complicated system is that
it is not a code of civil law traceable to the Empire. The common law, intricate and confusing, better protects the liberties of all because no arbitrary or
despotic power can easily move through its complicated web. It was better
for liberty, for example, that the common-law judges reformed the feudal laws
on property. Indeed, "the judges quickly perceived" that, with feudalism gone,
the "forms and delays" of the old writs were "ill-suited to that more simple
and commercial mode of property" newly rising. Such judicial reform by "a
series of minute contrivances" was so gradual that the judges "wisely avoided
soliciting any great legislative revolution." Blackstone regrets that the "dread of
innovation" characteristic of common-law judges prevented this gradual reform
from achieving its full potential, but he insists that it nonetheless prepared the
way for "more liberal and enterprizing judges" in the courts of equity to make
greater reforms and innovations. Both tracks of judicial reform had to be undertaken indirectly, by "fictions and circuities" that maintain the forms of feudal
procedure and terms of art, for if not, such a complicated, liberty-protecting
system would collapse (3.17, *268).

Blackstone preempts Benthamite criticisms by admitting that the more liberal spirit of the equity courts prodded the more conservative courts of law,
while also insisting that this complex system provides for "speedy and substantial justice, much better than could now be effected by any great fundamental alterations." Moreover, with a guide like Blackstone giving one "the

proper clew," this "labyrinth" of judicial renovations to the common law "is easily pervaded": "We inherit a Gothic castle, erected in the days of chivalry, but fitted up for a modern inhabitant. The moated ramparts, the embattled towers, and the trophied halls are magnificent and venerable, but useless. The inferior apartments, now converted into rooms of convenience are cheerful and commodious, though their approaches are winding and difficult" (3.17, *268).

This defense of the medieval, Germanic spirit of law as the best basis for modern liberty echoes the closing books in *The Spirit of the Laws*, which begin with an epigraph from Ovid about metamorphosis (book 28). Montesquieu, too, speaks of feudal law as a "labyrinth full of paths and detours," confident he has found "the end of the thread" and can walk through (*Spirit*, 30.2). Both jurists seek reform toward a commercial liberalism and view the case-by-case acts of judges as more liberal than the Machiavellian efficacy of new codes.[15] The *Commentaries* reiterates these themes through a final survey of the origins and gradual progress of English law, culminating in another architectural metaphor. Blackstone collects the argument of the four books with a "history of our law and liberties" ranging from its Gothic roots through four subsequent periods to the "perfection" enjoyed since the Glorious Revolution (4.33, *442). A constitution "so wisely contrived, so strongly raised, and so highly finished" contains "the accumulated wisdom of the ages." Still, he insists that its faults have not "been concealed from view," problems which chiefly arise from "the decays of time" or "the rage of unskillful improvements in later ages" (*442–43). He has examined its "solid foundations," laid out its "extensive plan" and its parts, and from the harmony among the parts demonstrated "the elegant proportion of the whole." Noble structures of "ancient simplicity" and "the more curious refinements of modern art" have been noted. His closing words strike the basic chords of his opening lecture regarding liberty, the debt to Gothic benefactors, and further prudent reform toward humane aims:

> To sustain, to repair, to beautify this noble pile is a charge entrusted principally to the nobility and such gentlemen of the kingdom as are delegated by their country to parliament. The protection of THE LIBERTY OF BRITAIN is a duty which they owe to themselves, who enjoy it; to their ancestors, who transmitted it down; and to their posterity, who will claim at their hands this, the best birthright and noblest inheritance of mankind. (4.33, *443, emphasis in original)

Bentham, if he read this far, must have thought this more rhetoric, artfully concealing Blackstone's defense of things familiar or the privileges enjoyed by his class. Rhetoric can serve noble or sinister ends, as Thucydides and

Aristotle, among others, carefully demonstrated long ago, and it achieves either effect through its power to persuade. One great student of the *Commentaries*, Abraham Lincoln, seems to have been struck by Blackstone's peroration, since its phrases and cadences appear in some of that common-law lawyer's great speeches and writings; Hamilton's constitutional arguments bear a similar imprint. One aim of Blackstone's rhetoric might be to conceal from some, while urging upon others, the extent of the reforms he thinks the noble castle requires if liberty is to be preserved or expanded. Does he further seek to conceal from some yet urge upon others the extent to which gentlemen outside Parliament, especially in the courts, should undertake such reforms? Beyond the evidence already submitted, further proof lies in the great wealth of detailed legal commentary in the four books. Since this excavation of Blackstone's constitutionalism already has covered much ground, one can justly recall Montesquieu's metaphor of an archaeologist who only scratches the surface of his destination after much preparatory labor (*Spirit*, 28.45). Even a partial survey of Blackstone's remarks advocating liberal reform by judges amply indicates a project to cloak British politics and law with the moderating power of the judiciary.

Liberal Instruction in Common-Law Prudence

Albert Alschuler's recent argument that lawyers and judges should rediscover Blackstone notes that Boorstin's classic study included a list of the many proposals for legal reform in the *Commentaries*.[16] Boorstin belittles these for being couched in terms of a mysterious, automatic progress, as if Blackstone chronicles reform but discourages reformers, since all is swept along by some Hegelian tide of history.[17] Holdsworth notes, more soberly, that Blackstone was a reformer and renovator of not only his college and university but his town, and that both as parliamentarian and judge he proposed such measures as prison reform and better pay for judges. He also catalogues the reform proposals, and while his reply to Bentham is sounder, he still endorses Gibbon's critique that the "pious son" could not criticize English law with an open mind.[18] What few commentators note, whether finding Blackstone a conservative or reformer, is the quiet argument throughout the *Commentaries* that judges should shape the letter of common law, and even statutes, to accord with the essential spirit of liberty and humanity in English constitutionalism.[19] Even before passing out of book 1, on the rights of constitutional and civil persons, Blackstone discusses judicial reform of family law, citing Montesquieu twice. Judges have interpreted already humane statutes so as to extend the natural right of children to parental protection, since heirs and children "are favorites of our courts of justice" (1.16, *448, *450).[20] The stream of comments about judicial reform of the law increases, however, as Blackstone moves inward from the grand constitutional outlines of political law toward the details of civil law administered by courts, in the books on property, torts and civil procedure, and criminal law. The final chapter of the work reminds reformers, whether legislative or judicial, of the great principles of constitutional liberty that any reforms must work within and preserve, and among those principles is the distinction between a proper role for judicial power and an aggrandizing judicialism that would violate separation of powers and constitutional balance.

Upon stating in book 2 that one can't understand Britain's constitution without studying "the antiquities of our English jurisprudence," Blackstone recounts how feudal judges restored the sound old common-law principles of property after incompetent statutory meddling (2.4, *44). Judges, by a "subtle finesse of construction," had adapted the law of real property to remedy "inconveniences" that made possession uncertain over generations. In 1285 the Lords countered these judicial practices with the statute *De Donis*, more favorable to nobles than freeholders. Blackstone then applauds the "pious fraud" of common recoveries, a fiction invented by judges in the fifteenth century to evade the statute, noting that Edward IV and later Parliaments endorsed a reform that judges had "clandestinely begun" (2.7, *112, *116–17; see also 2.18, *271; 2.21, *357). Judges were "*astuti* (cunning) in inventing" reasons to uphold these recoveries, and this recourse to "such awkward shifts, such subtle refinements, and such strange reasoning" promoted free property holding. He notes that "modern courts of justice have indeed adopted a more manly way of treating the subject" by openly stating their circumvention of the ancient statute as the formal conveyance of property rights. He calls for statutory reform to clarify the common law, but there is no doubt that judges led the way (2.21, *360–61).

Regarding inheritance law, Blackstone mostly defends a feudal rule favoring blood relatives over kin through marriage, yet he "must be impartial enough" to admit it may cause "hardship." This is especially so if "in practice" judges carry the rule "farther than the principle" of it warrants. He insists that "it is not for me to determine" a remedy, but suggests either that "the legislature [should] give relief" or that "a private inconvenience be submitted to, rather than a long established rule should be shaken" (2.14, *230–33).[21] Here he is not so bold as Mansfield, who in *Perrin v. Blake* (1770) undertook his most controversial ruling in seeking to displace a feudal rule on inheritance from *Shelly's Case* (1581) with a more equitable one, friendlier to the wishes of individual property holders. Mansfield's decision in the King's Bench was overruled on appeal in the Exchequer Chamber (1772), with Mr. Justice Blackstone taking the lead in justifying the medieval rule.[22] Still, Holdsworth considers this disagreement an exception, noting the deep influence on the English legal profession of Mansfield's efforts to infuse the spirit of equity courts into the common law. Blackstone substantially revises for the *Commentaries* the treatments of equity, commercial law, and other topics from his lectures dating to 1753—changes that Holdsworth traces to Mansfield.[23] Perhaps in *Perrin* Blackstone thought Mansfield had done too openly, and in a controversial case litigated for decades, what otherwise could be achieved without real or perceived harm to the separation of judicial and legislative power. Montesquieu's "maxim" in such cases is that the prudent statesman should act "in a secret and imperceptible manner" to moderate the hardship "in the most pardonable particular case, until he could come to modify it in every case" (*Spirit*, 6.13). Blackstone seems to add that a fundamental reform, with great weight of case precedent against it, is not the kind that judges can or should undertake ahead of the legislature.[24]

As noted, the book on torts and civil procedure prepares for the Gothic castle passage near its close by commending the liberality of certain equity jurists and by citing the praise of both Vattel and Montesquieu for Mansfield's judicial acumen (3.4; 3.5). Blackstone makes a more oblique reference to judicial statesmanship in discussing a special court that Mansfield transformed into the source of modern commercial and insurance law (3.6, *74–75). Book 1 examined such "law merchant" under the king's prerogative power over commerce, and Blackstone substantially revised later editions by claiming that such law now was "a part of the law of England" and not a separate body of law (1.7, *273). Thus, while both this area of law and the judicial power itself nominally fall under royal prerogative, in fact it is Mansfield's incorporation of special merchant juries into the common-law courts that independently develops a whole new body of law.[25] Montesquieu's advocacy of the benefits of commerce for modern liberty and for liberalizing despotic regimes praised just such a commercial jurisprudence presided over by a small set of competent judges (*Spirit*, 20.18). Blackstone further prepares for his Gothic castle metaphor by praising the judicial prudence that devised common-law remedies for disputes about real property, including fictions in the writs of ejection and possession borrowed from the equity courts as a "method of doing complete justice" (3.11, *200–201). He defends such judicial development of civil procedure as a "modern way" of settling disputes that is "infinitely more convenient for attaining the end of justice." He quotes a unanimous 1758 ruling that such a fiction was "invented, under the control and power of the court, for the advancement of justice in many respects" (*202, *205–6).

After his encomium on the Gothic castle and its judicial renovators, he defends a judicial discretion, contrived through their own view of judicial power, to change the venue of civil trials "so as not to cause but to prevent a defect of justice" (3.20, *294; see also *303, *305–6). The last part of the book examines the history, principles, and procedures of civil trials, elaborating a Montesquieuan defense of juridical complexity as the best way to protect a large, commercial, civilized nation and, "above all, the liberty and property of the subject" (3.22, *327). This complexity also arises because judges are "only to *declare* and *pronounce*, not to *make* or *new-model* the law" (*327; emphasis in original). This is consistent with all that precedes it only if Blackstone genuinely means that judges are not making a new spirit of the law but adapting the letter to comply with its existing spirit. Indeed, Blackstone cites *The Spirit of the Laws* twice in this first chapter on trials, on the theme of the origins in feudal procedure of a more modern, liberal judicial process (*339, *342). He openly praises the judges through whom "new remedies were devised, and new forms of action were introduced," including the judicial fiction of trespass (*347; see 3.4, *42–43, *51). A Montesquieuan tone percolates through the rest of book 3, with *The Spirit of the Laws* cited even in introducing that central institution of the common law, trial by jury, knowledge of which is "most absolutely necessary for every gentleman in the kingdom" (3.23, *349, *350, citing *Spirit,* 30.18). He paraphrases Montesquieu's praise of professional judges throughout this first discussion of jury trials, which has a later counterpart in the book on criminal law, and he attributes the success of "this best preservative of English liberty" to its balancing of judge and jury (*381). He obscures this debt to Montesquieu by criticizing the latter's remark that England, like Rome, Sparta, and Carthage, will someday lose its liberty when Parliament grows corrupt, since the "celebrated French author" should have recalled that none of these regimes enjoyed trial by jury (*379, citing *Spirit,* 11.6). He surrounds this objection, however, with paraphrases of Montesquieu on the dangers of purely popular judicial power, on the need for legal principles to "be deposited in the breasts of the judges," and on limiting juries to questions of fact (3.23, *356, *361, *366, *373, *375, *379–80, *385). Moreover, this praise for a depository of laws leads to a typically Montesquieuan suggestion that, while encomium is due, even this great institution of jury trial could be improved by several reforms (*381–85).[26]

The book's final chapter, on equity courts, confirms this treatment of civil trials at common law, as Blackstone propounds a renovation of the common-law castle to incorporate more of the spirit of equity (3.27; see 3.24, *396). He summarizes the book by citing Montesquieu's distinction between despotic simplicity and liberal complexity, defending the confusing ways of England's castle of liberty (3.26, *424, citing *Spirit,* 6.2). The extraordinary final chapter then seeks to fuse common-law and equity courts regarding principles if not procedure, an effort indebted to Mansfield's judicial statesmanship (3.27).[27]

Blackstone cites his own analyses of equity in the introduction to argue that common-law courts no less than equity ones adjudge "according to the spirit of the rule," delineating a larger theme throughout these first three books (*429–30). Both kinds of courts, if "courts of justice," must adopt whatever rule is "best" according to "the nature and reason of the thing"—a phrase Hamilton will borrow in discerning a power of judicial review in the American constitution (*434).

Having journeyed this far through Blackstone's suggestions for judicial reform to achieve liberal security for individuals, we can only glance at the final pyramid, the book on criminal law. Brevity is fitting here, since Blackstone is more candid in noting his debt to Montesquieu's notion of reform toward a humane liberalism. His analysis of criminal law characteristically begins by discussing the general principles of natural right and positive law, as well as some historical references to earlier views of law. He cites Montesquieu and Beccaria as the "ingenious writers" who documented the "inhumanity" and severity of European penal law, and he openly adopts them as models for a few needed reforms of English law (4.1, *3). England's penal law, comparatively speaking, is nearly perfect, since crimes and penalties are accurately defined, prosecutions and trials are public, torture is unknown, and defendants enjoy trial by jury. Still, "we shall occasionally find room to remark some particulars, that seem to want revision and amendment," to include "too scrupulous an adherence to some rules of the ancient common law" by judges, when the reasons for them have ceased (*3–4). Obsolete or absurd laws need repealing, but, as Blackstone has lamented from the opening lecture of the work, greater care is needed in framing new ones. Perhaps legislators can learn something from jurists and judges.

Blackstone's general introduction to criminal law cites Bacon, Grotius, Pufendorf, the book of Genesis, Cicero, Solon, and Demosthenes, while citing Beccaria's *On Crimes and Punishments* (1764) four times and *The Spirit of the Laws* twice. Having opened the first book of the *Commentaries* by discussing the rights of persons in terms of natural right and then analyzed the positive law of constitutional powers, property, and torts, Blackstone once again dialectically examines the relationship between natural right and positive law. A sound criminal law "should be founded upon principles that are permanent, uniform, and universal; and always conformable to the dictates of truth and justice, the feelings of humanity, and the indelible rights of mankind." Still, at times "it may be modified, narrowed, or enlarged, according to the local or occasional necessities of the state" it governs (4.1, *3). This Montesquieuan blending of universal truths and local modifications is characteristic, yet book 4 reemphasizes natural right in a manner particularly indebted to Montesquieu's analysis of the civil law about crimes, criminal due process, and security for individuals. Knowledge of such matters is "of the utmost importance to every individual in the state," and to know the criminal law of one's own country is "a matter of universal concern" (*2; see *Spirit*, 12.2). As it does for his predecessor, this topic causes Blackstone to drop his guard and openly instruct both legislators and judges in humane, liberal reform. On capital punishment he states that "[e]very humane legislator" will be "extremely cautious" in establishing such a penalty, and will be guided by "the dictates of conscience and humanity" (4.1, *10–11). While there can be no single rule for determining what punishment is appropriate for a given crime, he does provide several rules of prudence and "general principles" that may aid lawmakers and aid judges in assessing penalties fitting for particular circumstances (*14–17). The final maxim, that excessive severity in penal laws is counterproductive and reduces security, cites the chapter in *The Spirit of the Laws* in which Montesquieu directly advises legislators and judges to reform law openly when they can and gradually or quietly when they cannot (*17, citing *Spirit*, 6.13). The sequel notes Beccaria's proposal for a precise scale of crimes and punishments, but calls it "too romantic." He then turns to the more moderate Montesquieu to confirm that a "wise legislator" nonetheless can mark some "principal divisions" between more serious and lesser offenses (*18).

Having laid this foundation, Blackstone surveys the categories of criminal law, grouped as crimes against religion, the law of nations, the government, public order and safety, and individuals (4.4–17; see 4.4, *42–43; 4.14, *176–77). After briefly treating the means for preventing crime, which occasions a liberal pronouncement that the purpose of penal law is not retribution but security and prevention, the second half of the book examines the courts of criminal law and criminal procedure (4.18, *251–52; 4.19–32). The great theme of the first half of book 4 is moderation in prosecution and punishment, for both political and private crimes. Blackstone emphasizes religious toleration, freedom of thought and speech, and moderation in the severity of punishments—especially replacing capital with corporal, and corporal with fines, whenever possible (see 4.4, religious toleration; 4.6, treason; 4.10, perjury). On these and other topics he advises legislators and judges through regular citations to, and substantial paraphrasings of, books 6 and 12 of *The Spirit of the Laws*, as well as the analyses of England in books 11 and 19. He informs judges about predecessors who mitigated the operation of severe laws, praising one chief justice for resigning rather than assenting to an inhumane penalty. He lauds the fraudulent extension of "benefit of clergy" to lay people as a mitigating device that brings the law more in accord with Biblical mercy, and defends the "pious perjury" of merciful juries. Still, he praises limitations on judicial discretion when they prevent judges from being more severe (4.6, *80, *85; 4.14, *193, *198, *201–2; 4.17, *238; 4.18, *256). Regarding criminal courts, Blackstone cites Montesquieu's justification of the great power of the Law Lords as the trial court for impeachments, to temper popular passions with legal learning (4.19, *261).[28] His discussion of the gradual extension of benefit of clergy to lay people, so as to mitigate capital punishments, is a Montesquieuan narrative of the seeds of liberal progress found amid medieval barbarity (4.28; see, e.g., *371). Blackstone's analysis of judgment at trial is characteristically complex, in part praising the fixed penalties that assure rule of law rather than arbitrary decisions of judges or juries, yet praising "the almost general mitigation" by judges of the cruelest aspects of many punishments. Such judicial temperings have been "authorized" by the "humanity of the English nation" through their "tacit consent." By the close of the chapter he is bolder, suggesting outright abolition by Parliament of corruption of blood for convicted criminals and their descendants (4.29, *377–78, *388).[29]

Blackstone then announces, having journeyed through four books from the rights of persons to public wrongs, that he "cannot dismiss the student" without a final survey of the constitution in terms of the "revolutions" in English law from its origins to the present (4.32, *406). Montesquieu, too, closes his masterwork by treating the "revolutions," or gradual evolutions, in France's constitutional monarchy, and this spirit informs Blackstone's final chapter on the rise, progress, and gradual improvement of England's laws (4.33). Indeed, the chapter draws upon all the historical books at the close of The Spirit of the Laws, for at the center of Blackstone's summary narrative, both literally and figuratively, is the great jurist-king Edward I (d. 1307). Edward's reforms of courts and of both civil and criminal justice planted the seed for modern due process and the equitable uses of judicial power, and thus for a humane constitutional liberty—an echo of Montesquieu's praise for what Louis IX achieved, a generation earlier, in France (4.33, *425–30; cf. Spirit, book 28). Blackstone's narrative of "juridical improvement" and "juridical history" then discusses the perfection of Edward's reforms during the reign of Henry VIII, through the growing power of the equity courts to ameliorate the "narrowness and pedantry of the courts of common law." He boasts that one of the judicial inventions of that era can be "molded to a thousand useful purposes by the ingenuity of an able artist," leaving it open as to whether that artist is a common-law or equity judge, or a lawyer (*429, *430, *430–31). He indicts political extremism—the absolutism of Henry VIII or Charles I, the "confusion" and chaos characteristic of Cromwell and republican utopianism—while praising the eloquence and moderation practiced by a Sidney, a Locke, a Milton (*434–35, *438). The statutory reforms of property law and civil liberties under Charles II constitute a "second *magna carta*," and whatever statute reform has not achieved has been secured by "gradual custom, and the interposition of our courts of justice" (*438–39). Since the Glorious Revolution, the Act of Settlement has "made the judges completely independent of the king, his ministers, and his successors," and Blackstone concludes his panoramic sketch with some reforms subsequently achieved in "the administration of private justice." The final two reforms point to the work of Chief Justice Mansfield:

> the great system of marine jurisprudence, of which the foundations have been laid, by clearly developing the principles on which policies of insurance are founded . . . and, lastly, the liberality of sentiment which (though late) now has taken possession of our courts of common law, and induced them to adopt (where facts can be clearly ascertained) the same principles of redress as have prevailed in our courts of equity . . . and this, not only where especially empowered by particular statutes . . . but by extending the remedial influence of the equitable writ of trespass on the case, according to its primitive institution by King Edward the First, to almost every instance of injustice not remedied by any other process. (4.33, *441–42)

Blackstone's final commentary thus pronounces the cloaking of power, epitomized by Mansfield's judicial statesmanship, as a crowning achievement of a constitutionalism of liberty first established by the Saxon Alfred and then restored, after the Norman conquest, by Edward the First. His peroration on "the noble pile" of the English constitution echoes both the Gothic castle metaphor and his introductory lecture, reiterating his aim to educate gentleman of the law, whether at bar, or bench, or in Parliament, in sustaining and renovating this edifice of liberty (4.33, *442–43). He portrays Mansfield, and implicitly himself, as continuing Edward's use of judicial power to achieve a moderate politics and security for individuals, just as Montesquieu implicitly portrays himself as the heir to Louis IX. Since the question lingers as to whether this Montesquieuan project entails what today is termed judicial activism, a closer look at the relation between Mansfield's practice and Blackstone's jurisprudence is fitting.

Much commentary on Lord Mansfield compares him to Holmes or reads him in a Holmesean light, since both jurists address the challenge to received legal wisdom from the pressures of "progress." Mansfield is famous for declaring that principle and not precedent defines English law, and Holmes for declaring that "it is revolting to have no better reason for a rule of law than that so it was laid down in the time of Henry IV."[30] What separates Montesquieu, Blackstone,

and Mansfield from Holmes, however, is the insistence that natural right undergirds positive law and guides legal prudence, and the concomitant insistence
upon separation of powers in Montesquieu and Blackstone. As will be noted,
Holmes is famous for dismissing natural law jurisprudence, and infamous for
his cold rejection in *Buck v. Bell* (1927) of a natural rights defense against forced
sterilization of mental institution inmates. Mansfield cited both natural justice
and English law when he ruled in the Lords in *Chamberlain of London v. Evans*
(1767) that a Protestant dissenter could not be fined, and in the King's Bench in
Sommersett's Case (1772) that a slave brought to England must be freed.[31] Still,
regarding both the rule on property in *Shelly's Case* and slavery, Blackstone is
more cautious about the legitimacy of courts making new law without tacit consent of the legislature or at least of the professional legal community. Mansfield
did praise the *Commentaries* and recommended it as better for educating future
lawyers than the "uncouth crabbed" Coke-Littleton, for this new text pleas-
ingly inculcates "the first principles on which our excellent laws are founded."[32]
Mansfield must have sensed that the respect was mutual, but whatever may be
true of Mansfield's own conception of judging, Blackstone interprets judicial
power as subordinate to a constitutionalism of separated powers.

Blackstone is no Holmesean, therefore, not because his is a mechanical
or formalistic view of judging, but because both constitutionalism and natural
right or equity stand above and guide judicial discretion. Moreover, the fusion
of equity into the common law sought by both Mansfield and Blackstone was
consistent with their principle of rule by law, since they understood equity to
be neither historicist nor a vehicle for the contemporary moral preferences of
judges. Equity in a judicial sense meant a body of rules and principles used to
meliorate the hardship of the law. In its larger sense, it meant a search within
the law for a balance, if there was room for maneuver, that would err on the
side of natural right. In many instances Blackstone and Mansfield declared they
could find no room to exercise equitable judging, adopting the principle that a
hardship in one case was excused by adherence to the rule of law and separation of powers.[33] Their Montesquieuan balance of law and equity thus retained
some element of Aristotelianism and of Coke's classic common law. Holdsworth
comes close to noting this when identifying the importance for a common-law
constitutionalism of "a learned self-governing profession, responsible only to
itself"—in effect, a judicial depository of practical legal wisdom. Holdsworth
also notes the affinity between Burke, Blackstone, and Mansfield in opposing
Bentham's legislative dominance and progressivism while avoiding mere historicism; these common-law lawyers endorse a moderate reformism predicated
upon "principles of natural reason and justice." He cites Burke's praise of Mansfield's legal statesmanship, for holding the balance between legal positivism and

legal naturalism: "His ideas go to the growing melioration of the law, by making its liberality keep pace with the demands of justice, and the actual concerns of the world; not restricting the infinitely diversified occasions of men, and the rules of natural justice, within artificial circumscriptions, but conforming our jurisprudence to the growth of our commerce and of our empire."[34]

Finally, Blackstone's conception of judging includes the declaratory principle that judges claim not to make law but to indicate what the law is, knowing that on appeal or by statute their judgment can be declared erroneous. In the Montesquieuan model, judicial initiative and judicial prudence do not entail either activism or supremacy. Blackstone's skepticism about the implications of the broad reading of *Bonham's Case*, or Mansfield's reform in *Perrin v. Blake*, is qualified by other passages in the *Commentaries*, but it is not merely rhetorical. The chasm between Blackstone's view and the prevailing conception of judicial power and constitutionalism in twentieth-century America, one opened up by Holmes long after that power was founded, is the great problem confronting the judiciary and American constitutionalism in the twenty-first century. Nonetheless, there is a kernel of truth to the Holmesean reading of Mansfield and to Richard Posner's reading of Blackstone as a Warren Court judicial legislator. One can detect the seed of Holmesean realism in Blackstone, however small it may be, if one considers how it was that Holmes could have used existing aspects of jurisprudence and professional legal understanding in nineteenth-century America to so effortlessly effect a revolution from within. Other philosophical and jurisprudential revolutions intervened, to be sure, and neither Montesquieu nor Blackstone intended Holmes's brash insistence on progress in law and society, nor his demotion of law and reason to devices for masking a brutal social struggle. Still, their tendency to narrow the scope of natural right to the Hobbesian ends of security and tranquillity, paired with their emphasis on judicial procedure in service of such liberal ends, ultimately divorces common law from its scholastic and Aristotelian roots. Their aim was humane and moderate, since each thought of their jurisprudence as developing the liberal tendencies with the Gothic legal and constitutional tradition. It is now taken for granted in Anglo-American jurisprudence that they were moving in the right direction, and that Bentham and Holmes were generally correct to radically reform law and constitution; such is the paradoxical close-mindedness of a project, or party, of enlightenment. We would profit from measuring our conceptions of law and mores, and our breathtaking view of judicial power, against the understanding of Montesquieu and Blackstone, to ask whether in all ways we have become more humane and decent, more reasonable, more law-abiding.

We also would do well to recall that these Enlightenment jurists are not the only benchmarks for American constitutionalism and jurisprudence. The nature of judicial power as first established in America also hinges on the importance of the framers' early training in Coke, of a Declaration of Independence emphasizing both natural right and common-law prudence, and of a written Constitution embodying fundamental law. The question is whether this complex legal culture tempered the aims of Montesquieu, Blackstone, and their liberal forefathers, making American constitutionalism not a common-law liberalism but a liberalized version of a more fundamentally common-law jurisprudence.

PART THREE

Montesquieu's Judicial Legacy in America

The heirs to Montesquieu's thought have interpreted or implemented his project for the cloaking of power along three distinct lines, developing three different views of modern judicial power which, nonetheless, are Montesquieuan. The judicial power epitomized by Lord Mansfield in England and quietly propounded by Blackstone is the first legacy, but judicial power takes a somewhat different form in the American constitutional order. Hamilton, Marshall, and the lawyers who framed and developed judicial power under the 1787 Constitution were students as much of Coke as of Montesquieu and Blackstone; thus, their studies yielded a common-law jurisprudence that is liberalized but still significantly Aristotelian. Informing this American conception of judicial power are doctrines of fundamental law, natural right, and the rule of law understood as deposited in the Declaration and the Constitution, a view not purely liberal. In this second strain of the Montesquieuan legacy, both Hamilton and Tocqueville find in American constitutionalism a novel yet necessarily implied power of judicial review. More fundamentally, they find a judicial capacity to temper the rationalism and positivism of liberal philosophy with the more Aristotelian elements of classic common law. It is only with Oliver Wendell Holmes, embodying the third version of Montesquieu's legacy in modern judicial power, that any traces of Coke and even of the moderating elements in Blackstone's common-law liberalism are repudiated. Larger conceptions of moderation and separation of powers fall to an openly positivist, legislative, and evolutionary conception of judging.

The variations among these views of judicial power confirm the inherent complexity of Montesquieu's philosophy; strongly divergent views arise from his work, depending upon which strain in it is developed. Examining Hamilton (1757–1804) and Tocqueville (1805–1859) in particular permits a turn from excavating the Montesquieuan cloaking of power to evaluating it. Tocqueville's emphasis on the common-law dimension of American judging seeks to counteract the tranquil individual security actively sought by his French predecessor, making him a sound interpreter of the Hamiltonian spirit of judicial power. This is not to doubt that the political science of *The Federalist* and of *Democracy in America* share, among other things, a significant debt to Montesquieu. Still, Tocqueville amplifies Hamilton's doubts about the viability of a liberal order devoted solely to popular sovereignty and individual security, suggesting a need to shore up human greatness and the rule of law in modern liberal democracy. Oliver Wendell Holmes (1841–1935) openly repudiates this original conception of American law and judging. The paradox is that his new jurisprudence of legal realism, which has no more of a place for separation-of-powers constitutionalism than for any other fixed legal or moral principle, nonetheless has some root in Montesquieu's project for a cloaking of power. These three views of modern judicial power do not constitute a linear path from Montesquieu to Holmesean judicial legislating and legal skepticism, since the middle strain, embodied by Hamilton and Tocqueville, is the least liberal or Montesquieuan among them. Moreover, the recognition of a debt to Montesquieu's conception of judging diminishes as the story progresses, even if Holmes still recognizes some influence. The comparison among these jurists does reveal, however, that the classic common-law conception of law and judging in Coke is similar to the views of Hamilton and Tocqueville, and that this American common-law jurisprudence marks some departure from the more liberal views of Montesquieu and Blackstone. Moreover, the judicialized view of law and politics in Holmes is an extreme development of the Montesquieuan teaching, one that simultaneously repudiates the more balanced, classical common-law view of judicial power in Coke, Hamilton, and Tocqueville.

Holmes's own view, and that of the predominantly pragmatic, realist spirit in American jurisprudence today, is that legal realism rejects Blackstone's jurisprudence in the same manner that Bentham had—as outdated and as an impediment to the realistic study of and progress in the law. Unlike Bentham's remedy of a new legislative code, however, the project of Holmesean realism places courts and judges at the center of political and legal reform. In this way the spirit of liberal judicializing that began quietly in Blackstone's law school, which then was moderated or brought back toward Coke by Hamilton and Tocqueville, was developed by Holmes in its most radical possible direction. Judges are not invisible and null, nor is judging distinct from legislating, although judges might occasionally, for some reason, discern that they should permit rather than the check the dominant forces of the day. Some of the jurisprudential consequences of this transformation come to light through examination of Holmes's influence upon both the proponents and critics of the current right of privacy and abortion jurisprudence of the Supreme Court. The paradox is that Montesquieuan objections arise to the judicial legislating that is the ultimate, if unintended, development of Montesquieu's quest for liberal tranquillity, given the French jurist's equally basic concerns with the distinctness of judicial power, the moderating effect of the rule of law, and the perpetuation of a sound constitutional order.

The brief analyses of Hamilton, Tocqueville, Holmes, and the late-twentieth-century Supreme Court that follow are, if taken individually, inadequate treatments of complicated and controversial topics. Taken together, however, they suggest some interesting consequences of a Montesquieuan conception of judicial power. One connecting thread is the answer these sketches provide to a larger constitutional question about judicial review in America. A fundamental puzzle raised by the growth of American judicial power, and by the spread of that model around the world, is why such a powerful judiciary arose in the face of a nineteenth- and twentieth-century trend toward democratization. This is not directly addressed by most recent theoretical or jurisprudential debates about judicial review, although Bickel's concern about a "counter-majoritarian difficulty" approaches it. How did it become conceivable that a state or federal court could so easily presume to decide, for example, the winner of a presidential election contest? How could leaders of the legal profession think of either level of court as their first resort in settling such a momentous political dispute, and how could the judges so readily find it a justiciable, as distinct from political, issue? The democratic trend which this seems to buck is evident in the purging of such "mixed constitution" or republican elements in the American Constitution as indirect election of the president and Senate, or, in Britain, the purging of a powerful House of Lords. Perhaps the twentieth-century rise of the administrative state, which grants great power to unelected bureaucracies, suggests that a powerful judiciary is not exceptional. Nevertheless, the American Supreme Court is unrivaled in its comprehensive power, independence, and constitutional command, even by the Federal Reserve Board. Moreover, a constitutionalist would insist that, in both theory and practice, public administration does not raise the same level of questions as do the powers of the constitutional branches. Still, the recent rise of a powerful bureaucracy in the European Union might confirm what the New Deal already suggested, namely, the prescience of Tocqueville's concern that a shift to populism ultimately brings the silent tendency toward a pervasive administrative state. Perhaps judicial power, under the Holmesean conception, has become just another branch of public administration, partly delegated by and partly taken from the executive and legislative powers—as with the "private attorney general" provisions in many late-twentieth-century statutes that encourage the use of courts as public policy forums.

The administrative state, however, did not significantly shape American politics until the end of the nineteenth century, although the framers and John Marshall had established the Court as a genuinely significant branch by the first third of that century. Further, it was not until Holmesean positivism had pervaded the legal profession that the judiciary became the ally of the administrative state, and here it is interesting to note the parallel rise to prominence of Holmes in law and Woodrow Wilson in political science. The exceptional rise of a professional judiciary in America predates the Wilsonian and Weberian revolutions in political science, and nothing in the original spirit of the American bench and bar entails support for those transformations. While Hamilton was a great advocate of both judicial power and "administration," he propounded the Montesquieuan constitutionalism that Wilson later criticizes as impeding efficient administration. Tocqueville's opposition to centralized administration, paired with his strong advocacy of judicial power, also is better explained by a Montesquieuan legacy, especially if one recalls the reluctance of both Montesquieu and Blackstone to depict the power of the Cabinet in their sketches of English constitutionalism. Hamilton advocates administration as a dimension of executive power, not as the hybrid legislative-executive-judicial power endorsed by Wilson. This typifies the deep debt of the American framers to the separation-of-powers principle that led Montesquieu and Blackstone to omit a fused power from their analyses of England. Conversely, from Blackstone to Tocqueville these Montesquieuans endorse judicial power as crucial to the separation of powers and a proper constitutionalism, even as they warn against the fused power of an administrative state.

The first cause of an independent judiciary and its subsequent rise to power in eighteenth- and nineteenth-century America seems to be the blending of Montesquieu's complicated liberal constitutionalism with the common-law tradition of mixed constitutionalism, something undertaken nowhere more extensively than in America. Such judicial statesmen as Blackstone, Hamilton, and John Marshall did not intend and would not endorse Holmesean legal realism or its thoroughly judicialized constitutionalism, nor the bureaucratizing of politics. Hamilton and Marshall argued for judicial independence, a common-law profession, and judicial review so as to establish judges as guardians of constitutional tradition and limited government. They understood themselves as adapting Montesquieu and Blackstone to the new circumstances of a Declaration of natural right, a written fundamental law, and a complex republican government. As I will argue, Tocqueville expounded the American framers' achievement in just this spirit. There is a tale to be told, however, about the seeds within Montesquieu's moderate conception of constitutionalism and judicial power that permitted the rise of Holmesean realism, with its immoderate repudiations of natural right, a stable constitutionalism, and the separation of powers.

eight

Hamilton's Common-Law Constitutionalism and Judicial Prudence

Much recent scholarship about the American founding has debated the prevalence of its liberal philosophical or classical republican elements, implicitly criticizing the older view of Corwin and McIlwain that traced the American conception of natural rights to a constitutional tradition dating from Magna Carta.[1] Other contestants have entered the debate as well, claiming that the Whig opposition tradition, or Protestant Christianity, or the Scottish Enlightenment, or the English common-law tradition, lie at the root of the ideas encapsulated in the Declaration, the Constitution, and the Bill of Rights. Recent efforts at a new synthesis or amalgam, explaining the relationships among these influences, have shifted the debate away from stark alternatives to sorting out relative weights, although some now argue that the founding is simply incoherent, with no dominant political ideas defining its plethora of views.[2] While discussion of judicial power in the American founding cannot avoid this lively debate, the arguments here are more suggestive than exhaustive, even on the narrower but still complicated issues of the framers' views on jurisprudence and judging. Since judging is the least Hobbesian or Lockean of the powers in American constitutionalism, a *prima facie* case arises for reconsidering American judicial power in light of not only early liberalism, or Coke's classic common law, but also a Montesquieuan conception that blended these elements.[3] This raises

larger issues about the distinctive adaptation of Montesquieu's capacious, syn-
thesizing philosophy by the framers. We should ask whether political circumstance and political principle, embodied in the Declaration of Independence
and the 1787 Constitution, led such framers of American judicial power as
Hamilton to read Montesquieu and Blackstone as much through the lens of
Coke as that of Locke.

A discussion of judicial power in the American founding also enters, of
course, the contentious partisan and scholarly debate about judicial review
as practiced by the twentieth-century Supreme Court, and even by the late-
nineteenth-century Court regarding a due process liberty of contract. Most recent scholarship views American judicial review in Holmesean terms, taking
up either the theme of the living constitution or that of judicial restraint in
his complicated, even contradictory jurisprudence. This mistakenly confines
the Constitution and the framers' conception of judicial power to a universe
of Holmesean positivism. While the leading jurisprudential lights among the
framers would recognize such legal skepticism, they would disown it, whether
in its historicist mode of judicial activism or its strictly positivist mode of judicial restraint. Examining Hamilton and Tocqueville on judicial power permits
the recovery of a pre-Holmesean perspective that advocates a strong but limited judicial power, in which the central debates about judging relate to the
separation of powers, a republican constitutionalism, natural right, and legal
prudence. Our recent concerns about positivism, historicism, or postmodern
indeterminacy in legal interpretation overlook these issues because they are
later imports, arising not from the framers' constitutionalism but from later
jurisprudential quandaries of the nineteenth century.

Unlike the judicial restraint and judicial activist schools of the twentieth
century, the original American understanding defined judges neither as legislators nor as mere clerks, but as powerful officers in a constitutionalism of
separated and limited powers. Recourse to Hamilton is crucial, since he makes
the most thematic case for Article III power during the debates over the Constitution, and lays the ground for a constitutional review power intimated by
earlier American courts and later secured by Chief Justice Marshall. Hamilton,
one of the leading statesmen-jurists of the American founding, owes a significant debt to Montesquieu, albeit one tempered by other influences. Hamilton's
perspective reveals that the dominant views of judicial power today are latter-
day versions of either Jefferson's majoritarian criticism of federal judicial power
or the overt political activism of a Justice Chase (for ends different than those of
a Justice Brennan, of course). In contrast, Hamilton and Tocqueville propound
judges who are neither functionaries unable to account for the judgment they
in fact exercise, nor willful prophets of a new egalitarianism and psychologi-

cal security. Their judges resemble the complex model found in Montesquieu and Blackstone, which has no counterpart in Hobbes or Locke. The deeper complexity to American judging, for both Hamilton and Tocqueville, lies in their recourse to traditional common-law jurisprudence beyond the confines of Montesquieuan liberalism.

Montesquieu, Common Law, and the Complexity of the American Founding

The American founders knew Montesquieu in part because Blackstone's *Commentaries* was replacing Coke-Littleton as the basic law text, and Hamilton seems to have discerned the quiet emphasis that both English jurists placed on an effectively independent, moderating judiciary. Primarily, however, the Americans knew Montesquieu in his own right prior to the Blackstonean channel that disseminated his jurisprudence. There is wide agreement about the importance of "the celebrated Montesquieu" to the founding generation, especially during the framing of the 1787 Constitution and the early years of the new federal government. In terms of published citations to Enlightenment authors, Montesquieu was most influential as America turned from Revolution to preserving liberty through new constitutional forms. Montesquieu rivaled Locke even during the 1770s but became the most frequently cited author in the 1780s, being surpassed in the 1790s only by authors upon whom he exercised no small influence, Blackstone and Hume.[4] From at least 1760 it is evident that Americans of all parties and points of view were well acquainted with Montesquieu. On separation of powers and political liberty, as well as federalism and republican virtue, his authority was so fundamental that often the debate concerned a proper understanding of *The Spirit of the Laws*.[5] His influence upon leading statesmen survived even Jefferson's later antipathy to a republicanism the Virginian found too conservative and aristocratic. John Adams's *Defence of the Constitutions of Government of the United States* (1787–88), an apology for mixed constitutions against simple republican forms, explicitly relies upon Montesquieu's defense of complex government.[6] Leading Federalists and Anti-Federalists marshaled Montesquieu's support for their view of the Constitution, as is evident in Hamilton's debate with the Anti-Federalist reading of *The Spirit of the Laws* in *Federalist* no. 9. His distinctive political philosophy pervades *The Federalist*, often in explicit citations on federalism (nos. 9; 43), separation of powers (no. 47), and an independent judiciary (no. 78). This extends to the blending of a realist political psychology with a factional political dynamic in nos. 10 and 51. *The Federalist* cites Blackstone almost as much as Montesquieu, but Hobbes, Locke, Sidney, or Harrington not once. Indeed, its reliance upon

Montesquieu was internally more consistent, and more accurately reflected *The Spirit of the Laws*, than did the Anti-Federalist writings.[7]

In establishing a special place for courts and judging in American constitutionalism, however, Hamilton and Marshall drew upon both Coke's classic common law and the common-law liberalism of Montesquieu and Blackstone.[8] Robert Faulkner emphasizes Locke's influence upon Marshall's constitutional jurisprudence, and reads Blackstone, too, as a Lockean liberal, but he hardly portrays Marshall as one-dimensional. He notes "traces of an older and nobler aristocratic republicanism that has a distinct place in Marshall's thinking," including the somewhat Aristotelian and Ciceronian character of Marshall's admiration for Washington, and his own judicial statesmanship and magnanimity.[9] Faulkner also argues that Marshall expected courts to engage questions of "policy," at least regarding "the legitimacy of the political departments' exercise of their powers" under the Constitution, a judgment informed by "that liberal jurisprudence with which Courts educated by Blackstone were familiar."[10] Hobbes and Locke, however, largely influence the founding of American judicial power in a negative way, given their emphasis on sovereigns and legislators over judges, and the lowered ends their courts would serve.[11] The success of Lockean liberalism in orienting politics toward individual tranquillity and security is indeed one cause of greater power and stature for the judiciary, the institution that more than any other guarantees such rights to actual individuals.[12] Still, the degree of power and prominence granted courts in America then and now, and the robust constitutionalism advocated by such defenders of an independent judiciary as Washington, Hamilton, and Marshall, suggest a more robust conception of judicial power at the founding. Most scholars have underplayed the Montesquieuan dimension here, with its blending of classic common-law elements into a more complex liberalism.

James Stoner approaches the debates about the liberal, or republican, or liberal-republican principles of the American founding by arguing that, while we cannot ignore the importance of Hobbesian and Lockean liberalism, we must recognize the principled complexity of the founders' political thought. Among the other elements we must account for is their training in, and experience with, the English common-law tradition. He suggests that a common-law mind best characterizes the distinctive complexity of American constitutionalism, since this jurisprudence emphasizes practical judgment over grand theory and the assimilation of disparate ideas rather than analysis and division. The blend of Lockean and common-law elements in the Declaration itself confirms this; in that document, revolutionary but constitutionalist statesmen synthesized principles that philosophers or academics find incompatible. Jefferson looked back on the Declaration as resting upon "the harmonizing sentiments of the day," including "the elementary books of public right, as Aristotle, Cicero, Locke, Sydney, etc."[13] The four references in the Declaration to a divinity, which anchor its more famous natural rights principles, encompass broadly providential conceptions of divinity, including Biblical ones, but not a strictly Hobbesian state-of-nature theory nor a strictly deist, watchmaker god. Lockean interpretations view these references as embellishments, but this begs the question as to whether the state-of-nature and natural-rights principles—announced in terms of the laws of Nature and Nature's God, and of endowments by a creator—govern or are governed by this philosophical theology. The phrase "our constitution" (in the first charge where the king has "combined with others") refers to something other than the colonial "charters" mentioned later, and further suggests a common-law constitutionalism as the fundamental disposition into which Lockean ideas about rights are welcomed. The 1774 Declaration and Resolves of the First Continental Congress already had traced the rights of Americans to the English constitution and the common law, and lawyers steeped in Coke and Blackstone understood that the very title of the 1774 and 1776 documents cast them as legal remonstrances. To entitle each a "declaration" announces within the Anglo-American legal community that each is a pleading of principles and grievances before a higher bar, one to which all law-abiding persons, including king and Parliament, must submit.[14] A common-law legal prudence, augmented by invocations of a providential divinity and sacred honor, blends with and tempers the state-of-nature appeal to revolution and natural rights in these documents.

Classic common-law thinking is both renowned and criticized for such assimilation of new ideas and circumstances into older principles and procedures. It is this legal orientation that blended Lockean, Montesquieuan, republican, and Christian ideas with its own practical jurisprudence to forge a distinctive American constitutionalism.[15] Awareness of the jurisprudential complexity of the founding better explains both important details and such larger phenomena as the moderation of America's revolution compared to the French Declaration and revolution a generation later. From Fortescue and Saint Germain to Coke, classic common law embodies not just mechanical devices but a tradition of political and jurisprudential thought, one that blended with liberalism in the jurisprudential thoughts and deeds of Blackstone, Hamilton, Marshall, Kent, and Story. If liberalism is now the dominant element in the mix, we should not close our minds to a different relationship existing at America's founding. The syncretism of these Anglo-American jurists reflects the inclination of Fortescue and Coke, as they strove to balance right and efficacy in explicating the common law, to cite a range of minds from Plato, Aristotle, and Cicero to Aquinas and Bracton as seamlessly justifying its fundamental principles. Drawing upon classical and medieval philosophy, the common-law jurists define justice and right in its most exalted, or fundamental, sense in terms of virtue, a characteristic shared by Fortescue, Coke, and Tocqueville. The American jurists, more distanced from pure liberalism than Blackstone was, are drawn to the classical standards Coke sets for their profession, as when he wished for fellow lawyers "the gladsome light of jurisprudence, the loveliness of temperance, the stabilitie of fortitude, and the soliditie of justice."[16]

Awareness of a common-law dimension to the founding, by balancing but not canceling Locke's deep imprint, also accounts for the framers' great reliance upon Montesquieu. Both the classic common law of Coke and the Gothic liberalism of Montesquieu and Blackstone contrast with the analytical cast of Hobbes, Locke, and rationalism generally. The complex constitutionalism of Montesquieu and of the classic common law, including the emphasis on judicial power, also explains the repeated charges in the Declaration concerning courts and common-law rights, not to mention the subsequent constitutional novelty of independent judicial branches in the state and federal constitutions. The arguments of *The Federalist*, especially Hamilton's case for a federal judiciary with life tenure and a constitutional review power, further reveal a new constitutionalism that adapts the Montesquieuan teaching on judicial power to the context of a Declaration and written Constitution, federalism, and a complex republicanism. Even the Anti-Federalists tempered their distrust of an aristocratic federal judiciary with their successful insistence on a Bill of Rights, and of all people it was Jefferson who most clearly foresaw, and initially endorsed, the likely institutional consequences of such provisions. He later loathed the Hamiltonian conception of judicial power and sought to subordinate the federal judiciary, but he initially suggested that one argument for a bill of rights that had "great weight" with him was "the legal check which it puts into the hands of the judiciary."[17]

The Judicial Power and Hamilton's Complex Constitutionalism

Hamilton's defense of a "next to nothing" federal judiciary in *Federalist* no. 78 epitomizes the American adaptation of Montesquieu's cloaking of power. His importance in the original conception of American judicial power is broader and deeper, however, than this one essay in the ratification debate over the Constitution. Hamilton's contribution to this dimension of American constitutionalism often is overlooked, as is the importance of judicial power in his own constitutional thought. So significant were his words and deeds for the original conceptions of American federalism and executive power—ranging from war and foreign affairs to political economy and taxation—that studies of his political thought almost exclusively concern these important topics.[18] His profession as a lawyer and advocate in court was not merely preliminary, however, to his executive ambitions, nor merely a consolation after his national political career ended; it is rightly said that he "deserves a statue in front of the Supreme Court almost as much as his statue at the Treasury Department."[19] He worked to establish judicial power not only in *The Federalist* (1787–88) but also in making the first widely noted argument for judicial review, citing Coke, in *Rutgers v. Waddington* (New York, 1784), and later in his criticisms of Jefferson's plan to repeal the 1801 Judiciary Act.[20] A recent reconstruction of Hamilton's political thought studies these discourses on judicial power as well as his defense of both newspapers and courts as forums for discerning truth and for protecting justice against majority tyranny, in *The People v. Croswell* (New York, 1804). There, in the spirit of Coke, Hamilton defined common law as "Natural law and natural reason applied to the purposes of society," and urged an appellate court to view Blackstone's speech-restrictive doctrine of libel as "being against reason and natural justice, and contrary to the original principles of the common law."[21] Many great dramas of General Hamilton's life did concern war, commerce, and executive statesmanship, and he did decline Washington's entreaty to become chief justice in 1795. Still, the extraordinary claims made for judicial power in *The Federalist* are consistent with important thoughts and deeds throughout his life.[22] Before serving in Washington's army his essay "The Farmer Refuted" (1775) defended America's cause as grounded in "natural rights" and "the law of nature," as expounded by "Grotius, Puffendorf, Locke, Montesquieu, and Burlemaqui." At age eighteen he repudiates the legal positivism of "Mr. Hobbs" for denying "a supreme intelligence, who rules the world, and has established law to regulate the actions of his creatures." Such phrases, and references to the "despotic kingdoms" of Turkey, Russia, France, and Spain, confirm his early study of Montesquieu at King's College (later Columbia), and the essay quotes Blackstone twice, at length, on natural law and the rights of individuals.[23] Having argued for independence in Blackstonean terms, it is no surprise that after fighting as an artillery officer, aide to Washington, and battlefield commander, he renewed his study of law. His subsequent liberal studies and legal training bore fruit not only in a distinguished practice but in a succession of state and national political offices, as well as prominent writings. His thought and experience reveal a political and constitutional mind colored not only by liberalism but classic common-law training, coupled with a premodern spirit oriented to civic duty and human greatness.

After the Constitutional Convention Hamilton conceived the idea for a series of essays in the New York papers to defend the proposed Constitution, and upon securing the collaboration of John Jay and James Madison, he wrote two-thirds of the eighty-five essays that became *The Federalist*.[24] By writing as Publius Publicola, celebrated by Plutarch for establishing the Roman republic in 509 B.C., Hamilton parried New York Anti-Federalists who had attacked the Constitution under such names as Cato and Brutus. Moreover, the names Federalist and Publius reveal his strategy regarding the Constitution's rhetorical weak points—its purported consolidation of power and its distrust of the people. The one signals that the Constitution embodies true federalism, with a federal government that genuinely can balance the states, while the other tells a citizenry schooled in Plutarch that Federalists were as devoted to the people as Publicola, the "cherisher of the people."[25] This spirit also accords with Hamilton's request in *Federalist* no. 1 that the Constitution be debated in a manner proving that people could be governed by "reflection and choice," balancing "candor" and "moderation." These appeals to the worldwide fate of rational governance and to political moderation open the series on a Montesquieuan note.[26] This larger spirit to *The Federalist* also made it useful in the Virginia ratification debate, and Hamilton's 1788 preface even apologizes for the repetition and lack of literary unity in the set. This ambitious scope of argument in the essays and their publication as a book signal a design suited not only to battle but for a more enduring exposition of American constitutionalism.[27] Jefferson praised it, while implying that Madison was the primary author, not only because it "establishes firmly the plan of the government" but as "the best commentary on the principles of government, which ever was written." Washington, with characteristic sobriety, wrote to Hamilton that, having canvassed Federalist and Anti-Federalist writings, he had seen none better calculated to "produce conviction," and that *The Federalist* would endure: "When the transient circumstances and fugitive performances which attended this crisis shall have disappeared, that work will merit the notice of posterity because in it are candidly and ably discussed the principles of freedom and the topics of government, which will always be interesting to mankind so long as they shall be connected in civil society."[28]

Hamilton, Madison, and Jay all were black-letter, common-law lawyers, trained in both Coke and Blackstone, and Jay would become the first chief justice of the United States. It is not surprising, then, that the importance of an independent, federal judicial power arises early in the essays and percolates throughout *The Federalist*, culminating in Hamilton's exposition in nos. 78 to 83.[29] Jay, then foreign secretary of the Confederation, opens the defense of the Constitution in nos. 2 to 5 by arguing that it alone can secure the Union, and only a strong Union can provide Americans with security. The absence of a federal judicial power will perpetuate disharmony within American foreign policy regarding compliance with treaties and international law, while thirteen different court rulings on such matters will deliver to foreign nations both unjustified and justified causes for war.[30] Hamilton underscores the importance of a federal judiciary in *Federalist* no. 9 while arguing that the Constitution's superiority to ancient republics rests upon the "great improvement" achieved in the "science of politics" in modern times. This bold claim sounds Machiavellian or Hobbesian, but the improvements Hamilton cites in "modern" political science reflect the complex, common-law liberalism of Montesquieu and Blackstone. Four of these remedies for the ills of republicanism that were unknown or imperfectly known by the ancients are hallmarks of American constitutionalism, from the separation of powers and legislative bicameralism to elected representation and the federalism that permits an extended republic. The central principle of the five that define, for Hamilton, the new political science and American constitutionalism, is "the institution of courts composed of judges holding their offices during good behavior" (no. 9, 48). All five remedies directly stem from Montesquieu's constitutionalism, while only the notion of legislative representation is specifically evident in Locke, as part of his simpler separation of powers. This emphasis on a Montesquieuan separation of powers is a fitting introduction to the main topic of Hamilton's essay, the true nature of federalism and thus the true meaning of the most authoritative text on the principles of a federal republic, *The Spirit of the Laws*.

Hamilton further emphasizes independent judging when arguing that the Constitution at last establishes the proper rule of law in America's federal republic (no. 15). The Confederation had left Congress legally powerless in the face of the states' disregard for national authority. The crucial missing element for civilized, effective governance is "the agency of the courts and ministers of justice" in enforcing laws. The lack of "the COERCION of the magistracy" left Congress to choose between lawlessness and "the COERCION of arms," and Hamilton scoffs that this does not "deserve the name of government, nor would any prudent man choose to commit his happiness to it" (no. 15, 91; see no. 16, 97–98). He reinforces the importance of the judiciary in domestic affairs, just as Jay had done regarding foreign affairs, by arguing in no. 17 that the administration of justice is the "great cement of society." The state governments have "one transcendent advantage" over the federal government in keeping the attachments of the people and preventing any encroachments by national authority, namely "the ordinary administration of civil and criminal justice." Hamilton declares this function, the province of executives and judges, "the most powerful, most universal, and most attractive source of popular obedience and attachment." Still, he notes that the people's attachment to closer governments might be weakened by "a much better administration" of government at the national level (no. 17, 102; see no. 46, 301).

Hamilton raises the stakes concerning judicial power when summarizing in no. 22 the defects of the Articles of Confederation and amplifies the concerns already raised by Jay:

> A circumstance which crowns the defects of the Confederation remains yet to be mentioned,—the want of a judiciary power. Laws are a dead letter without courts to expound and define their true meaning and operation. The treaties of the United States . . . must, like all other laws, be ascertained by judicial determinations. To provide uniformity in these determinations, they ought to be submitted, in the last resort, to one SUPREME TRIBUNAL. . . . The faith, the reputation, the peace of the whole Union are thus continually at the mercy of the prejudices, the passions [of each state]. Is it possible that foreign nations can either respect or confide in such a government? Is it possible that the people of America will longer consent to trust their honor, their happiness, their safety, on so precarious a foundation? (no. 22, 137–38)

Hamilton tempers the Montesquieuan concern with individual safety and tranquillity by emphasizing, in the Declaration's words, the larger political ends endangered by the lack of a proper judicial power, to include the good faith, reputation, honor, and happiness of the nation and its citizens. Madison later develops these arguments when noting that laws always are "more or less obscure or equivocal until their meaning be liquidated and ascertained by a series of particular discussions and adjudications" (no. 37, 226). Not unrelated to these quiet defenses of an Article III power is Hamilton's argument in no. 35 about the adequacy of the limited representation provided by a small House of Representatives, since "the learned professions" will moderate any imbalances of class or interest among such a small body. Law was the predominant profession among office holders during the founding era, and Hamilton affirms that since such professionals "truly form no distinct interest in society," they will be "the objects of the confidence and choice" of other, more partisan elements (no. 35, 210–11). This professional pride in serving as honest broker and best citizen of a law-governed community hardly seems credible two centuries later, when one can gauge the power of and resentment toward lawyers in America by the steady supply of lawyer jokes. The praise for lawyers here and in no. 78 does not exempt them, however, from the sober judgments about human nature in such essays as nos. 6 and 51, just as Montesquieu criticizes judges and lawyers in both *The Persian Letters* and *The Spirit of the Laws*. The larger point taken from Montesquieu is the vital contribution to liberty made by a Gothic or common-law bar and bench, not as Platonic guardians, but in keeping other political powers and parties within the bounds of law, even while the latter would check any excesses from the bench.

With nos. 47–51, Publius shifts to an exposition of the separation of powers in the new government, and while these important essays rarely mention judicial power, even the few references here foreshadow the commentary on Article III that Hamilton begins in no. 78. After consulting "the celebrated Montesquieu" in no. 47 on the theory of the separation of powers, Publius examines in no. 49 how to enforce a constitutional distribution of powers against attempted encroachments by one branch or another. In nos. 47 and 48 Madison argues, citing Jefferson's *Notes on Virginia* (1784), that because the legislature is closest to the people, it represents the greater danger to any constitutional limits. In no. 49 Publius—probably Madison, perhaps Hamilton—criticizes Jefferson's proposal in the *Notes* for ensuring separation through recourse to popular conventions, which could alter a constitution or correct breaches of it (no. 49, 321–22). The first objection echoes Aristotle and the common-law doctrine of precedent, arguing that frequent changes in the laws, especially the fundamental law, will undermine that reverence for laws so crucial for developing the political habit of being ruled by law. Publius then more openly criticizes plebiscitary government, since the passions of the American people might overwhelm their more considered judgment now that the dangers of revolution have passed and more self-interested, partisan passions have arisen. Perhaps the crucial objection, however, is that popular appeals will not restore the constitutional "equilibrium" endangered by any encroachments. The legislature is most likely to breach such limits, and the people likely will concur with any legislative majority, it being the most populist power. Publius thus associates the executive and judiciary with the "*reason*" of the people and the legislature with the "*passions*" that can overwhelm both reason and those branches (no. 49, 322–25).

The extraordinary argument of no. 49 strongly criticizes Jefferson's Rousseauian trust in the moral purity of the people, but postpones to no. 51 an explanation of just how to enforce a constitutional separation of powers. Here some oblique references to the judiciary usually are lost amid analysis of the more famous phrases by Publius (probably Madison) about human nature and the need to counteract ambition with ambition. He notes that each branch might be truly independent only if none were permitted a role in appointments or selections for the others, which would require direct popular selection. He immediately cites "the judiciary department" as an obvious exception to such a design. This analysis develops the praise for the learned professions from no. 35, by arguing that "peculiar qualifications" are the "essential" and defining characteristic of judicial office—quietly presuming the common-law tradition of selecting the bench from the practicing bar (no. 51, 330–31). Publius also announces in no. 51 the not-so-Jeffersonian principle that a sound constitutional order "must first enable the government to control the governed; and in the next place oblige it to control itself." Dependence on the people is the root of republican government, but the constitutional framework needs "auxiliary precautions" and "inventions of prudence" to ensure that both citizens and officials are governed by law (331–32). The legislature, again, is most likely to threaten constitutional limits, and Publius suggests that the Constitution makes a "qualified connection" between the least populist legislative branch, the Senate, and the generally weak Executive. Publius thus defines the three least obviously republican branches, the unelected judiciary and the indirectly elected Senate and Executive, as keeping the House—and, one infers, the more populist governments of the states—within the bounds of the constitutional order (332–33).

Federalist no. 51 closes with a reprise of the extended-sphere argument of no. 10, and Publius quietly warns of the consequences when, in a political order where "justice is the end of government," the government cannot check majoritarian encroachments on the Constitution and its protection of rights. Some might have recourse to "a will in the community independent of the majority—that is, of the society itself," either a "hereditary or self-appointed authority" that is "altogether independent of the people" (no. 51, 333–35). This is inimical to "the *republican cause*," and Publius calls upon the extended sphere with its plurality of factions to ensure that majority factions never cause such injustice as to provoke this reaction. Still, in the remainder of The Federalist Publius expounds not the popular politics of multiple factions but precisely the least republican branches as the core of American constitutionalism, in impressive essays on the Senate (nos. 62–63), Executive (nos. 70–71), and Judiciary (no. 78). He construes these powers as intended to maintain equilibrium in the government and the supremacy of constitutional limits in the face of turbulent popular politics. Indeed, no. 63 (probably Madison, possibly Hamilton) criticizes the pluralist faction remedy of nos. 10 and 51 as insufficient and calls for "auxiliary precautions" such as the Senate to check majority faction (404). Publius ultimately suggests that a simply negative view of power checking power does not adequately answer the question left open by no. 49 regarding how to ensure legal protections for rights or the rule of law more generally. The answer given by no. 51 in itself, without the constitutional argument developed in the essays on Senate, executive, and judiciary, would tend toward gridlock or crisis, thus increasing the likelihood of either recourse to powers outside the community or government, or a collapse into populism.

The analysis of the separation of powers in nos. 47 to 51 thus quietly prepares for the more positive conception of the principle developed in the essays on the Senate, executive, and judiciary, largely written by Hamilton. The positive conception calls upon the principle of a division of labor to argue that distinct powers will perform each function better. This complex constitutionalism also contains the negative conception of separation usually termed checks and balances. Within the confines of republicanism, *The Federalist* ultimately emphasizes the positive view, rooted in Aristotle's conception of separate functions in a polity, having initially emphasized the negative conception drawn more from Locke and Montesquieu.[31] The shift occurs quietly, but, as noted, Publius lays a foundation in the early essays for the apex of this positive conception of separation of powers, the analysis of judicial power in no. 78. In addition to early remarks on the importance of a competent federal judiciary, Madison provides another pillar in no. 37. He defends the Constitutional Convention for moderating the more populist qualities of "republican liberty" with offices marked by "stability and energy" so as to achieve a fundamental requisite of liberty, "good government" (223–24). This emphasis upon sober, constitutional government under law is at the heart of Hamilton's effort in no. 78, the first thematic, unequivocal argument for judicial review in Anglo-American jurisprudence.

"The Integrity and Moderation of the Judiciary": Bulwark, Depository, Schoolmaster

Hamilton states that his topic in no. 78 is not the utility and necessity of a federal judiciary, since earlier essays have demonstrated this (495). Still, his defense of the not-so-republican appointment and tenure of federal judges entails an argument about the utility and necessity of this extraordinary institution, based on its implicit powers of constitutional review and legal moderation. The exposition of judicial power in no. 78 thus has three main strands, which interweave throughout. First, Hamilton defends an independent judiciary with a negative conception of the separation of powers, on the Montesquieuan premise that professional judges must be bulwarks against the populist abuses likely to come from the legislative power in a republic. The second draws upon Coke as much as Montesquieu, arguing that the Constitution implies a distinctly common-law character for the federal judiciary, a body of lawyers elevated to the bench and serving as a depository not of force or will but legal judgment. The first strand proposes the novel power of judicial review, but it is the second that explains why common-law judges in a republic could have such a power and be entrusted with it, a shift from negative to positive conceptions of the separation of powers. The third strand, often overlooked, amplifies both of these elements through a more fully positive conception of the separation of powers. Hamilton ultimately blends Montesquieu's juridical liberalism with an Aristotelian appreciation for practical legal wisdom, defining the judiciary as not only the guardians of the Constitution but the schoolmasters of moderation and constitutionalism.

Hamilton begins modestly, however, by citing Montesquieu on liberty and a tripartite separation of powers and then defining a quietly influential judiciary as crucial to individual security and tranquillity. This is the most obvious link between the American judiciary and *The Spirit of the Laws*, for no. 78 quotes "[t]he celebrated Montesquieu" to insist that, of the three powers, "the judiciary is next to nothing" (496, quoting *Spirit*, 11.6). Hamilton perhaps exaggerates about the helplessness of the federal judiciary, but today we take for granted an independence and potency in America's courts that he could not assume. Echoing the arguments of nos. 9, 49, and 51, he declares appointment of judges during good behavior a crucial advance in the science of politics, not least because an independent judiciary is, in a republic, an "excellent barrier to the encroachments and oppressions of the representative body." Indeed, even before citing Montesquieu, Hamilton invokes a comprehensive conception of professional judging, naming it "the best expedient which can be devised in any government, to secure a steady, upright, and impartial administration of the laws" (496). He justifies this with his second quotation from Montesquieu in no. 78, agreeing that "there is no liberty, if the power of judging be not separated from the legislative and executive powers" (497, quoting *Spirit*, 11.6). These premises lead him to argue that Article III and the entire Constitution imply a power to examine laws for constitutionality that we now call judicial review, although he never uses the term. Such a power was mentioned favorably in the 1787 Convention but not debated at length there, and Hamilton's argument did have some Anglo-American antecedents in Coke and in earlier American legal practice, including his own.[32] Nevertheless, his thematic case in no. 78 for a robust power of constitutional review, in a fully independent judiciary, largely is novel.[33] Earlier in 1788 Brutus criticized the Constitution as anti-republican for granting such a controlling power over elected officials, both federal and state, to a handful of unelected, practically life-tenured judges. Hamilton could take cold comfort that a prominent Anti-Federalist also found an implied power of judicial review in the Constitution. Here as elsewhere in *The Federalist*, however, he turns the Anti-Federalist concern with too much government into an argument that greater protection for liberty requires competent government. Publius defends independent, powerful judges as crucial to good government and good government as crucial to liberty and tranquillity, much as he has just defended the not-so-republican Senate and Executive.[34]

Hamilton's brief for judicial review begins by arguing that independent courts are "peculiarly essential in a limited Constitution," defined as "one which contains certain specified exceptions to the legislative authority" (no. 78, 497). While it seems Lockean to emphasize a written constitution, only the likes of Coke, Montesquieu, or Blackstone would suggest that the very integrity of constitutionalism and the rule of law in a republic hinge upon the right kind of judicial power. Constitutional limits on the legislature "can be preserved in practice no other way than through the medium of the courts of justice, whose duty it must be to declare all acts contrary to the manifest tenor of the Constitution void." It soon is clear that the reasoning which discerns such a power in the Constitution stems largely from common-law jurisprudence, as is evident through repeated characterizations of certain legal maxims and premises as natural or reasonable. Still, the initial argument serves the Montesquieuan ends of a balanced constitution that protects individual security. The "natural" presumption of a written constitution is not the coordinate review propounded by Brutus and later by Jefferson and Jackson, with each department the final judge of the constitutionality of its own powers. This would merely permit legislatures to "substitute their *will*" for that of the people deposited in the Constitution (498). Nor does a power of review place unelected judges above the legislative power, as the Anti-Federalists, and later Jefferson, charge. Rather, it is "far more rational to suppose, that the courts were designed to be an intermediate body between the people and the legislature, in order, among other things, to keep the latter within the limits assigned to their authority" (498). Judicial review of statutes for compliance with the Constitution ensures not judicial supremacy over the legislature but that "the power of the people is superior to both," since the fundamental power of the people is deposited in the Constitution (499).

Hamilton summarizes this first, Montesquieuan line of argument by declaring truly independent courts of justice to be "the bulwarks of a limited Constitution against legislative encroachments" (no. 78, 500). He elaborates this by declaring judicial independence "equally requisite to guard the Constitution and the rights of individuals from the effects of those ill humors, which the arts of designing men, or the influence of particular conjunctures, sometimes disseminate among the people themselves." This echoes the concern with majority tyranny in nos. 10 and 51, but Hamilton proposes a remedy that reaches beyond pluralist faction to the principles of energy, stability, and good government, as expounded in no. 37 and the essays on the Senate and Executive. There is a hint, then, of the positive view of separation of powers even in this Montesquieuan exposition of judicial power as the best line of defense for rights, especially minority rights, against majoritarian and legislative threats. To expect judges to check popular moves toward either "dangerous innovations in the government" or "serious oppressions of the minor party in the community" is to expect "an uncommon portion of fortitude in the judges to do their duty as faithful guardians of the Constitution" (no. 78, 500–501).

Hamilton's bridge to a more positive, quasi-Aristotelian view of an independent judiciary is the common-law jurisprudence found in Coke and in those elements of Blackstone's *Commentaries* that preserve the classic common-law tradition. This second line of argument arises early in the essay as Hamilton is defining judicial power in terms of professional legal judgment, precisely the sort of judgment Hobbes criticized and Locke ignored. The very "nature of its functions" always will make the judiciary "least dangerous to the political rights of the Constitution," since "it may truly be said to have neither FORCE nor WILL, but merely judgment." Having power from neither sword nor purse, but merely pen and books, the judiciary "must ultimately depend upon the aid of the executive arm even for the efficacy of its judgments" (no. 78, 496). This distinctiveness suggests that Hamilton's rationale for examining only judicial tenure here, and not mode of appointment, may be as much effective rhetoric as scrupulous literary organization. He claims that since previous essays have discussed appointment of all civil officers, it would be "useless repetition" to examine judicial appointment, but this underplays the qualitative difference between judges and, say, Representatives in the House, let alone ordinary citizens. Hamilton had argued, echoing no. 51, that executive nomination and Senate confirmation of officers is the best way to secure good administration since it promotes "a judicious choice" of men, the crucial concern being "to investigate with care the qualities requisite to the station to be filled" (no. 76, 484–85). In no. 78 Hamilton thus omits the fact that judges serving a tenure more monarchical or aristocratic than republican are neither elected by the people nor appointed by their House, but appointed by the two branches of the federal government already distanced from the people.

Hamilton emphasizes the argument, drawn not only from Coke but also from Montesquieu and Blackstone, that judges represent the rule of law, as depositories of legal learning and of those impartial benchmarks that guide the political order. Only if federal judges are truly independent can they be "the citadel of the public justice and the public security" which the Constitution intends (no. 78, 497). This assures a republican citizenry that such remote judges can be trusted with a power of constitutional review. It is fitting, then, that the bulk of the reasoning for judicial review draws deeply from the common-law tradition.[35] There must be a power of judicial review implicit in the Constitution because the "interpretation of the laws is the proper and peculiar province of the courts," and Hamilton's general reasoning here about "a constitution" clearly reveals his debt to a jurisprudence with roots beyond America itself. If interpretation of the laws is peculiarly and properly judicial work, and "a constitution is, in fact, and must be regarded by the judges, as a fundamental law," then judges must be not mere clerks but must exercise judgment in interpreting the meaning of both statutes and the Constitution (498). Neither Hobbes nor Locke, Bentham nor Austin, could provide such reasoning. Hamilton's explanation of how judges will determine whether a statute violates the Constitution simply states an analogy to a conflict between two statutes, and assures us that such "exercise of judicial discretion, in determining between two contradictory laws, is exemplified in a familiar instance." What follows would be familiar primarily to lawyers trained in the common law, and perhaps to citizens who breathed the legal and political air in America suffused with that jurisprudence. "The rule which has obtained in the courts for determining [the] relative validity" of two conflicting statutes is that a later statement of legislative will trumps an earlier one. This may sound Hobbesian, but Hamilton emphasizes that courts are not beholden to any other power for such rules. This analogy, and the defense of review for constitutionality that it serves, is the statement of a classic common-law mind, echoing the confident pronouncements of Coke more than the subtle qualifications of Montesquieu or Blackstone:

> But this is a mere rule of construction, not derived from any positive law, but from the nature and reason of the thing. It is a rule not enjoined upon the courts by legislative provision, but adopted by themselves as consonant to truth and propriety, for the direction of their conduct as interpreters of the law. They thought it reasonable that between the interfering acts of an equal authority, that which was the last indication of its will should have the preference. (no. 78, 499)

The repeated references to "will" and the analogy between a constitution as fundamental law and ordinary statutes suggest to some that Hamilton is a legal positivist who reduces even "fundamental law" to a human law that has no basis in nature, or at least none beyond human will. His classic common-law training and experience, and both the manner and substance of his argument here, suggest otherwise. Hamilton gives due weight to the positive, legislative will, but also to an Aristotelian, prudential appeal to principles of natural right that undergird human laws, an appeal made not just by jurists but by any people who frame a constitution. Since America is a republic, Hamilton emphasizes the common-law grounding of such a judicial power in the active and tacit consent of the people to long-standing precedents that secure their liberty and happiness. Such arguments define the common-law tradition from Fortescue to that Whig defender of liberty against monarchical encroachments, Coke.[36] In the same vein, the common-law constitutionalism of no. 78 does not emphasize the Declaration of Independence or other documents of abstract right, but the constitutionalizing of the people's consent in a fundamental document of written law. Both the people who ratify the Constitution and the judges authorized to interpret it would be bound by a written law, yet would understand that written law as itself informed, and justified, by unwritten principles of nature, reason, truth, and propriety. Such a blending of unwritten law, partly natural and partly customary, with positive law is more characteristically Aristotelian than Hobbesian, although Montesquieu and Blackstone also inform this complex jurisprudence.

This common-law complexity yields Hamilton's ultimate conclusion to the argument that judicial review is inherent in a limited constitution, which he reaches by applying the analogy of statutory conflict to a clash between a constitution and a statute made under it. Once again he argues that "the nature and reason of the thing" decides the question, namely, that "the prior act of a superior ought to be preferred to the subsequent act of an inferior and subordinate authority" (no. 78, 499–500). Not only the will of temporary legislative majorities but even the temporary will of the people that undergirds elected legislative and executive authority are subordinate to the Constitution. This completes the argument of nos. 37 and 49 that a sovereign republican people will realize that justice and interest are best secured by ordaining and then subordinating themselves to a fundamental law that establishes good government.[37] Hamilton implies that this is what a reasonable people already has done in separate state constitutions, and will do again if still reasonable. This confidence is particularly evident in his reply to the Anti-Federalist objection that such powerful judges are likely to rule by sheer will. If courts could deploy spurious constitutional objections simply to oppose their will to the legislature, why would they not do so in the less dramatic mode of simply bending every statute to their will, case by case? The Anti-Federalist concern, "if it proved anything, would prove that there ought to be no judges distinct from [the legislature]" (500). Hamilton stops here, having recalled the authoritative principles implicit in Coke's common law, pronounced by Montesquieu, and accepted by the Anti-Federalists—that there must be separation of powers, specifically an independent judiciary, if the rule of law and thus liberty are to be secured (see nos. 47–51 and no. 81, 514–16).

Hamilton responds further to this concern about unchecked judges when he later cites the legislature's powers of impeachment and removal for "malconduct," insisting that "[t]his is alone a great security" (no. 79, 505–6; no. 81, 518). Here, however, he allays this legitimate republican fear by emphasizing the security inherent in the common-law training of judges. This final recourse to the common law comes near the essay's close, in making a "weightier" argument for "permanency of the judicial offices," one "deducible from the nature of the qualifications they require" (no. 78, 502). As elsewhere in this second line of analysis, his common-law reasoning borrows from Montesquieu and Blackstone, here by noting that it is "frequently remarked" that "a voluminous code of laws is one of the inconveniences necessarily connected with the advantages of a free government." He emphasizes the protections for liberty and the rule of law that come with such professional training, doing so with the authority of a common-law lawyer: "To avoid an arbitrary discretion in the courts, it is indispensable that they should be bound down by strict rules and precedents, which serve to define and point out their duty in every particular case that comes before them." Given the depravity of mankind, which leads to numerous legal controversies, "the records of those precedents must unavoidably swell to a very considerable bulk, and must demand long and laborious study to acquire a competent knowledge of them" (502–3). It is unquestioned that this legal depository will be a common-law, not civil law, judiciary. This understanding was so universal among drafters and ratifiers alike that, in contrast to Articles I and II there is not a word in Article III about qualifications for office. The matter is left safely with the Senate and executive, since the common-law tradition of drawing the bench from the professional bar was the state practice already and implicitly would apply to the new federal judiciary. Indeed, the brevity of Article III as a whole confirms this presumption about the specifically common-law character of the federal judiciary. Hamilton's immediate point in all this is that "but few men" will have "sufficient skill in the laws to qualify" as judges, and then, "given the ordinary depravity of human nature," there will be a still smaller number "who unite the requisite integrity with the requisite knowledge." Even these few honorable, learned lawyers are human, however, since to entice such "fit characters" away from "a lucrative line of practice" they must be offered more security than a temporary tenure provides (503).

This emphasis on the extraordinary legal training and presumed moral integrity of federal judges points to the third strand in Hamilton's analysis of judicial power. Upon concluding his argument for judicial review, and just before these remarks on qualifications, he refers several times to the "duty" that such independent judges will have "to adhere to" the Constitution over a statute that contravenes it, "their duty as faithful guardians of the Constitution" (no. 78, 500–501). These ennobling references prepare for an argument that combines the more negative concern for a check on legislative and popular usurpations with the more positive conception of professionals needing independence or space to do their job well:

> But it is not with a view to infractions of the Constitution only, that the independence of the judges may be an essential safeguard against the effects of occasional ill humors in society. These sometimes ex-tend no farther than to the injury of the private rights of particular classes of citizens, by unjust and partial laws. Here also the firmness of the judicial magistracy is of vast importance in mitigating the severity and confining the operation of such laws. . . . This is a circumstance calculated to have more influence upon the character of our governments, than but few may imagine. The benefits of the integrity and moderation of the judiciary have already been felt in more states than one. (no. 78, 501–2)

Such a judiciary "serves to moderate" more than the "immediate mischiefs" caused by unjust laws, thereby protecting particular individuals case by case, as Montesquieu or Blackstone would expect; it also "operates as a check upon the legislative body in passing" such laws at all, since partisans will see that "the scruples of the courts" pose obstacles to their aims. The integrity and moderation of the entire body of common-law judges has greater consequence for the character of American politics than most citizens realize. This argu-ment surpasses any claims openly made for judicial power by Montesquieu or Blackstone, although it shows their influence. Hamilton extols the benefit of a judicial ability to curb the will of the elected legislature and executive, as embodied in statutes, even if a law is not "contrary to the manifest tenor of the Constitution"—the standard earlier defined in the argument for judi-cial review (no. 78, 497). Will and force, the purse and the sword, may have the sanction of popular election, direct or indirect, and may have the support of majority sentiment at any given moment. Judgment, however, can oppose such power quietly and incrementally when a common-law judicial prudence discerns that laws, even if constitutional, are unjust, partial, or violate private rights. Moreover, such judicial moderation of politics in the states already "must have commanded the esteem and applause of all the virtuous and disinter-ested," of "[c]onsiderate men of every description" (502). Such a "temper in the courts" will check any "spirit of injustice" that might arise, if only by the subtle, indirect method of mitigating and confining unjust laws.

The context of the separation of powers and natural right remains, how-ever, and nothing here replaces that constitutionalism with judicial legislating or activism. Rather, the judiciary can instruct the legislature in subtle ways, through its rulings, reasonings, and remedies, on the true standard of not only legal constitutionality but of justice as discerned by common-law prudence. Even further, common-law judges set the standard for virtuous, disinterested, and considerate thoughts and deeds in republican politics. This transcends any liberal concern with rights defined in Hobbesian or Lockean terms. There is much evidence throughout *The Federalist* of Publius's aim to balance concerns of interest and advantage with higher and nobler aims, even if at moments the latter might be less appreciated in themselves than as means to more pedestrian ends. When Publius (Madison) turns from criticizing the Articles to expositing the Constitution, he states that its form is republican not only because that is entailed by the "genius" of Americans and "the fundamental principles of the Revolution," but also because of "that honorable determination which animates every votary of freedom, to rest all our political experiments on the capacity of mankind for self-government" (no. 39, 239). Hamilton's third strain of argument in no. 78 contains a hint of the need for the highest citizens and office holders in republics actually to take their bearings by such nobler qualities, animated simply by the virtues of rule of law, legal prudence, and justice. In this complex republicanism that blends Hobbesian realism with regard for higher human qualities, lawyers and especially judges become more than leading citizens and officials. In Hamilton's liberalized, common-law constitutionalism they become republican schoolmasters.[38]

In the remaining essays on the judiciary Hamilton refines the arguments of no. 78 and further displays a common-law mind. He assures republicans that such a judiciary will abide by the strict notion of constitutional review he has laid out and will not abuse this privilege of interpretation, since recourse to impeachment always lies with Congress (nos. 79; 81). This also endorses an external inducement for judges to moderately exercise the capacity for tempering unjust and partial, if constitutional, laws. A discussion of the "equity" clause in Article III, section 2 then construes it in a narrow, technical sense, as the judicial capacity to relieve suitors of "hard bargains" in civil cases (no. 80, 511–13; see no. 83, 540). By vesting courts with jurisdiction over all cases "in law and equity," the Constitution fuses common-law and equity jurisdiction more fully than even Lord Mansfield and Blackstone had sought earlier in the eighteenth century. Hamilton thus anchors American jurisprudence in a known, if ever gradually evolving, legal tradition that prescribes rules and maxims, precedents and authorities, to govern judicial rulings in both law and equity. This discussion of equity prepares for his reply to another Anti-Federalist charge against Article III, which Hamilton implicitly draws from essays 11 to 15 of Brutus (no. 81, 515). Brutus claimed that equity jurisdiction, coupled with an implied power of constitutional review, would encourage federal judges to interpret the Constitution according to its "spirit" and thus to effectively thwart other federal branches, the states, and the people (see, e.g., essay 15). Hamilton's reply begins awkwardly, affirming that "there is not a syllable in the plan under consideration which *directly* empowers the national courts to construe the laws according to the spirit of the Constitution," although he adds that judges in the states so interpret the laws already. Moreover, he not only reiterates that the principle of judicial review, understood strictly as discerning "an evident opposition" between statute and constitution, is necessary in a limited constitution but that, "as far as it is true, [it] is equally applicable to most, if not all the State governments." He again confronts these defenders of the state constitutions with the fact that nine states have independent judicial bodies, suggesting a contradiction between their opposition to the Constitution and their avowed adherence to Montesquieuan separation of powers and federalism. Only a separate judicial body, however, can "temper and moderate" the laws, or gather men with the knowledge, studious history, and qualifications "which fit men for the stations of judges" (no. 81, 515–17).

As Hamilton's exposition of judicial power concludes, it shades into a treatment of the final topic addressed in *The Federalist*, the absence of a Bill of Rights. Essay no. 83 employs considerable legal learning and rhetorical effort to suggest that, while Article III guarantees the right of trial by jury in criminal cases, the absence of a similar clause regarding civil cases does not implicitly preclude such protection. Moreover, Hamilton argues that, while this is an important question, jury trials are not always as essential to liberty and the protection of rights in civil cases as they are in criminal ones. The protections in the Fourth through Eighth Amendments of rights regarding both criminal and civil cases manifest that Hamilton was on the wrong side of history, and some of his reasoning in nos. 83 and 84 is strained. Nevertheless, his argument regarding civil trials and his general response in no. 84 about a Bill of Rights reveal an important disposition, and it is not hostility to the specific rights espoused by Anti-Federalists. In both cases Hamilton argues that the general constitutionalism of federalism, separation of powers, elections, and representation specified in both the Constitution and the state constitutions will more adequately protect individual rights than any additional parchment provisions in the federal charter. The capstone of this line of argument is that "the Constitution is itself, in every rational sense, and to every useful purpose, A BILL OF RIGHTS" (no. 84, 551). Hamilton's exposition of judicial power thus begins by citing Montesquieu, while its sequel, on constitutionalism and bills of rights, cites "the judicious Blackstone" (no. 84, 548). Hamilton's core principles are shaped by the larger constitutionalism these authors embody and by the classic common-law tradition they sought to revise. His orientation in politics is not only to liberty, but also to a kind of political and human dignity, as he displayed in a life spent writing for and fighting in the Revolution, framing and governing under the Constitution, and defending minority speech and rights in the *Croswell* case. His arguments here for an independent, ennobling judiciary portray the Montesquieuan cloaking of power as an extension or development of the common-law constitutionalism embodied in Coke. Hamilton's judiciary, at once benchmark for and schoolhouse of constitutional government, echoes the Aristotelian status claimed by Coke for those grave and learned men of the common law who, through long study in and development of the legal tradition, were depositories of a kind of perfection of practical reason.

Hamilton's Judiciary and the Modern Mixed Regime

The demise of Hamilton's constitutionalist understanding of the judiciary, eclipsed by more partisan views of bench and bar, now is considered among the most prescient of the Anti-Federalist concerns about the Constitution. As Jefferson foresaw, a Bill of Rights places greater power in the hands of the judiciary, and while he may have thought this would empower the state bench, the record of two centuries suggests that the political power and prominence of both federal and state judges has increased substantially. The judiciary has achieved this in part by rejecting the larger understandings of constitutionalism and common law that Hamilton considered as anchors of the American polity and as the justification for judicial review. While the federal judiciary was a powerful presence in American life once Marshall assured it of its intended place, Marshall could not have foreseen its dominant presence in a sweeping range of political, social, and economic matters into the twenty-first century. The American legal profession increasingly has followed the Holmesean path, in which judges keep law and constitution in tune with the times, or the sentiments of the majority, or an expansive conception of individual autonomy which ensures that there will always be a diversity of viewpoints and never either consensus or any higher common aim. This Holmesean revolution explains the further paradox that the Anti-Federalists, in whom such scholars as Gordon Wood and Herbert Storing find elements of classical republicanism or communitarian thought, become, through their insistence on further specific guarantees of individual rights, one source of the apathetic individualism that Tocqueville feared.

Hamilton's conception of judicial power throughout *The Federalist* blends his common-law commitment to courts and lawyers with his Montesquieuan understanding of a complex, separation-of-powers constitutionalism. His account of the new federal judiciary praises judges who are not strictly re-publican, since their source of authority is not solely the consent of the people. This is in part a Montesquieuan approach, employing a not-so-republican office for the republican and liberal ends of the rule of law and individual tranquillity. However, when Hamilton extends judicial power to moderating the partisan or illiberal excesses of a free politics, and then to the role of benchmark for and educator in the civic virtues, he emphasizes a quasi-Aristotelian concern with the qualities and merits of office holders. Coordinate review is for him no remedy for constitutional crises, because it yields either legislative or executive supremacy, or perhaps anarchy, thereby reducing constitutionalism to either force or will.[39] Hamilton's defense of judicial review thus responds to fears of an antirepublican judicial supremacy by emphasizing not only the judiciary's weakness but also the training and character of judges. This represents the peak of Hamilton's positive separation-of-powers doctrine, with the judiciary being one of the three powers and also, as Harvey Mansfield notes, "the one above the others, the only one with its eye steadily on the whole, monitor of the separation of powers and guardian of the Constitution."[40] They serve above the others, however, only on those rare occasions when they are more genuinely under the authority of the Constitution than are the others, and duty calls them to bring others back into line—a line not of their own making.

Because the lawyers called to the bench will not be ordinary in character or training, the Hamiltonian defense of judicial review implicitly links judging and the rule of law with some version of a balancing of orders or virtues. One evident sign of this is the fact that, as James Bryce noted more than a century ago, judges in America lost the wigs but kept the robes of the English monarch's judges.[41] The case for the rule of law over rule by persons, as first made by Aristotle, stems from recognition of the unreliability of human character, but Aristotle also refines an older understanding that the rule of law depends in part upon the character of men.[42] The American framers understood these principles in a roughly similar way, despite other fundamental differences with classical phi-losophy. Aristotle intertwines his analysis of and defense of the rule of law in the *Politics* with his account of a mixed regime, the classical constitutionalism that balanced different social orders and claims to civic virtue in the differing parts of a polity. While the republicanism of the American framers foreclosed this in its classical sense, they sought to remedy the defects of republicanism by repub-licanizing certain aristocratic functions, virtues, and characters. This dimension of American constitutionalism stands between, or transcends, the current lib-eral and classical republican schools regarding the American founding. James Wilson, later a Supreme Court Justice, captured the complexity of this new constitutionalism when arguing in Pennsylvania's ratifying convention that, in contrast to Britain's mixed government, the proposed government was "in principle . . . purely democratical. But that principle is applied in different forms, in order to obtain the advantages, and exclude the inconveniences, of the simple modes of government."[43] The Anti-Federalist concerns about aristocratic ambition explain why this understanding would not be loudly announced either then or later.[44] Still, Federal Farmer's arguments regarding the "natural classes of men" or "several orders of men in society," which he generally divided into the "natural aristocracy" and "natural democracy," provide some support for Hamilton's positive separation of powers.[45] Wilson, once again, captures the tension between these two views of a constitutional republic when arguing in the Federal Convention that "[h]e was for raising the federal pyramid to a considerable altitude, and for that reason wished to give it as broad a basis as possible."[46] Federal Farmer objected to the Convention's hierarchical constitutional arrangement of the different orders, but he did so based upon a similar understanding of the differences in talents, virtues, and effort among individuals.[47] Given the enduring conflict over these putative differences among men, Publius's use of separation of powers to quietly achieve the effects of a mixed regime recalls Aristotle's teaching that a good such regime is one so well mixed that it cannot be readily identified as predominantly a democracy or oligarchy. Such a constitutional order moderates or blends the separate claims of, and thus the competition between, the rival virtues or classes so as to make the differences less noticeable and less problematic.[48]

The modern, republicanized version of a mixed or balanced constitution works through the modern theory of the separation of powers, not the entrenchment of different classes or claims to virtue. Still, the modern mixed regime is similar to its classical counterpart in having an intrinsic connection to, and import for, the rule of law as constitutionalism. Implicit in the employment of aristocratic characters or virtues in a republican order is the recognition that the rule of law is meant to improve, not utterly replace, the rule of men. This is especially evident in Publius's argument for judges of special character and training, elevated and robed both literally and figuratively, which is a theme throughout The Federalist, even if boldly developed only in no. 78. The judicial power embodies a quasi-aristocratic character as a not strictly republican yet not anti-republican remedy for the passion-induced injustices that republicanism can inflict upon itself. In the language of Federalist no. 37 (Madison), if the judiciary is intended to be a reliable influence for "good government" within the structure of "republican liberty," then attention should be paid to the sources and nature of the judiciary's special virtue and to the scope of its special role. A comparison between Holmes and either Hamilton or Tocqueville indicates that it is the classic common-law element in the framers' jurisprudence, and not solely the Montesquieuan conception of judging, that provides this ennobling, quasi-aristocratic character to the original American conception of judicial power. Holmes repudiates exactly this moral element of American law, or any law. Given the phenomena of prominent American jurists worrying about a pervasive legal nihilism that rejects any legitimacy to or autonomy of the law, and the phenomena of both originalists and living constitutionalists on the Supreme Court openly declaring adherents of the other school to be illegitimate judicial activists and legislators, there are grounds for questioning what we have gained from a century of sophisticated legal skepticism.[49]

Evident in both Publius and Tocqueville, and tempering their modern liberalism, is a concern for virtue in the law and legal profession, which, especially in the case of Publius, necessarily remains hidden within constitutionalist arguments about separation of powers, representation, and the need for good government. In 1787 Charles Pinckney encapsulated this view in defending the eligibility of Congressmen for other offices of the government, which the Convention endorsed once it was clarified to require a Congressman's choice between a congressional seat and civil office. Pinckney "considered the eligibility of members of the Legislature to the honorable offices of Government, as resembling the policy of the Romans, in making the temple of virtue the road to the temple of fame." In Publius this constitutionalist concern for personal and professional virtues is evident in the defense of the least democratic offices of the government, the Senate, Executive, and Judiciary.[50] Hamilton qualifies the narrower liberalism or concern for negative liberty in Montesquieu and Blackstone, partly through his explicit defense of natural right both by pen and sword during the Revolution and after, and partly through an attachment to the classical common-law constitutionalism of Coke. This is evident both in his forthright exposition of a power of judicial review and judicial prudence, and in his suggestion that the judiciary should perform higher, ennobling functions in the American political order. If natural right and common law together form a core in Hamilton's constitutionalism that is qualified by his subscription to Montesquieuan liberalism, it is striking that these are precisely the core elements of the Western legal tradition and the founders' constitutionalism that Holmes repudiates in the late nineteenth century. The paradox of Montesquieu's legacy in modern constitutionalism is that the transformation of liberal politics about which Tocqueville warned—the rise of the populist leader, the administrative state, the isolated individual, and a corrosive moral skepticism—perhaps finds its seed in Montesquieu himself. His own philosophy, or its implications and consequences, may be one cause of the threat to the viability of liberal constitutionalism, a threat which is Tocqueville's larger theme.

nine

Tocqueville's Judicial Statesmanship and Common-Law Spirit

Alexis de Tocqueville's *Democracy in America* (1835–40) analyzes and praises America's experiment in self-government, while discerning problems in democratic life not noticed by many Americans at the time, or later. Its diagnoses of the soul of not just America but of modern liberal democracy have earned it great praise, but also the scorn and even neglect often shown by Americans toward a work dubbed a classic, especially one at all critical of democracy.[1] Tocqueville would not be surprised by this, having begun the second volume of *Democracy* with an analysis of America's characteristic pragmatism and its disregard for tradition or respected authorities. While he acknowledged his debt to Montesquieu, and scholars regularly note that influence, his political philosophy ultimately questions whether the largely negative view of politics and liberty in Montesquieu and other liberals can sustain either a decent polity or the human soul. Communitarians and liberals in recent decades have debated his warning about an isolating, apathetic "individualism" caused by modern democracy, a phenomena that deepens itself over time. An often-overlooked dimension to Tocqueville's diagnosis, however, is his emphasis upon judges and lawyers as a remedy for the problems of individualistic mass democracy. Whether or not Tocqueville discerned the project for a cloaking of power in Montesquieu and Blackstone, it is significant that a political science substantially indebted to Montesquieu would question the aims of his constitutionalism yet concur with his emphasis upon judicial power and the spirit of law.

Recent debates about American constitutional interpretation have noted the evergreen quality of Tocqueville's observations about judicial power in our constitutional order. Whether to praise him or bury him, scholars often cite his observation that "there is almost no political question in the United States that is not resolved sooner or later into a judicial question." Even further, he argues that Supreme Court Justices "must not only be good citizens, educated and upright men—qualities necessary for all magistrates—one must also find statesmen in them."[2] A few voices even have praised Tocqueville's idea of a judicial prudence guided by the Constitution's original principles as a proper model for constitutional interpretation and adjudication. In doing so, they implicitly or explicitly criticize the predominant opposing schools in the twentieth-century American debate—a legal positivism that seeks a sovereign will in the text's "original intent," and a historicism that seeks a "living constitution" through "contemporary ratification."[3] An originalist argument counters that Tocqueville's conception of judges would have been "strange and revolutionary" to the framers and is "not only ungrounded in the framers' thought" but would have been "an impeachable offense."[4] This is not implausible, especially as an Anti-Federalist view of federal judicial power, but it ultimately rests on a misconception of Tocqueville. His endorsement of America's original constitutionalism of limited powers readily appears if, along with his emphasis upon the judiciary, one grasps his praise of the classic common-law training that shaped America's bar and bench well into the nineteenth century.[5] This response to originalist concerns does not impress the historicist, progressive school, however, which might ask how Tocqueville's formalism is relevant to a "living constitution" today, given the seismic changes in law and society that have occurred during the last 170 years. Two distinguished law professors, however, recently have recommended him to American lawyers and judges, testifying to Tocqueville's legal acumen and jurisprudential richness. Both Anthony Kronman, dean of Yale Law School, and Mary Ann Glendon, Learned Hand Professor at Harvard Law School, argue that the "failing ideals of the legal profession" or "the crisis in the legal profession" consists in the loss of the legal spirit and character that Tocqueville praised.[6] Each compares his conception of aristocratic, ennobling judging with *Planned Parenthood v. Casey* (1992), in which a fractured Supreme Court upheld its original abortion ruling, *Roe v. Wade* (1973).[7] Kronman and Glendon draw this comparison for different reasons, however, one arguing that Tocqueville would have praised the defense of *Roe* by the *Casey* plurality, and the other that he would criticize it.

Understanding this abortion debate, and the issues of constitutional interpretation that inform it, ultimately requires engagement with the legal realism embodied by Oliver Wendell Holmes Jr., which informs both of the main voices in twentieth-century constitutional jurisprudence. That engagement in turn requires comparison with what Holmes rejected, namely the original American conception of judicial power and jurisprudence in Hamilton or Marshall. To surmise how the founders might respond to the Holmesean revolution and twentieth-century jurisprudential debates, it is helpful to examine a thinker who shared their legal and constitutionalist principles but who also addresses later political developments and schools of thought. Tocqueville is the indispensable figure here, endorsing the founding principles of American constitutionalism while addressing deeper issues about the American polity and what its prevailing character or inclinations might be. *Democracy in America* discerned several issues and problems before even the most insightful of Americans, even the founders, wrote of them. An examination of his jurisprudence and a comparison to Montesquieu, Blackstone, and Hamilton illuminate not only the original American understanding of judicial power but also the Montesquieuan project for a cloaking of power, which Tocqueville seeks to modify. Such an inquiry also confirms that Tocqueville offers not just political sociology or accurate prognostications, but a complex political philosophy.

The American "Lawyer Spirit" and Judicial Statesmanship

Like Montaigne and Montesquieu before him, Tocqueville was a French nobleman and a jurist. Living in the wake of the French Revolution, he was acutely aware, however, of deep questions raised not only about the meaning of aristocracy but about the meaning of law and right. Like Montesquieu, he wrote a massive work of political philosophy that is rich, complicated, and the source of much debate, a work intending to address the dilemmas and possibilities of the moment while also contributing to enduring philosophic understanding. Perhaps because of the richness of *Democracy in America* in both size and substance, little attention is paid to its emphasis upon the role of lawyers and judges in both the rise and perpetuation of modern democracy. In the introduction to volume 1 Tocqueville cryptically mentions "a mother thought that so to speak links all its parts." Rather than being a single abstract concept, this fundamental thought may be his concern to ensure that the new "equality of conditions" remains a democratic liberty and not a democratic "tyranny."[8] If so, then *Democracy* argues that a properly constituted legal profession and judiciary are indispensable means to maintaining human liberty in the modern world. In the opening historical portrait, Tocqueville lists "jurists" and the growing complexity of civil law as primary causes of the rise of democracy out of

European feudalism, appearing to draw upon the jurisprudential-political histories of Montesquieu and Blackstone. It is no accident, then, that in the closing pages of the work he recommends "judicial power" as one of the "democratic procedures" for securing liberty against despotism (1, "Intro.," 4; 2.4.7, 668–69). In volume 1, about American constitutionalism, he pays special attention to the "justices of the peace" in his important discussion of communal or town government in New England. He analyzes American judicial power in itself, both state and federal, before discussing the federal Constitution and government. He remarks of the federal judiciary that "a more immense judicial power has never been constituted in any people" (1.1.5, 68–79; 1.1.6; 1.1.8, 130–42, at 141). Tocqueville's concern with the role of lawyers and judges in modern government remained a theme in his writings, as is evident in his study of the old regime and revolution in France and his 1848 report to the Academy of Moral and Political Sciences on democracy in Switzerland.[9]

Tocqueville further emphasizes lawyers and judges by extensively discussing how the "lawyer spirit," especially through judges and juries, "tempers the tyranny of the majority" in America (1.2.8). He argues that lawyers form "the most powerful" and "the lone counterweight to democracy." The lawyer spirit (*l'esprit légiste*) counteracts "the vices inherent in popular government" through both its virtues and its defects: "When the American people let themselves be intoxicated by their passions or become so self-indulgent as to be carried away by their ideas, the lawyers make them feel an almost invisible brake that moderates and halts them" (1.2.8, 256). This "aristocratic body" of judges and lawyers, and the jury system that is "the main source of its power," "tempers the tyranny of the majority" precisely because courts and the legal profession educate citizens in a common-law lawyer spirit. This spirit includes mental habits inclined toward order, forms, and precedent, as well as such principles as "equity," "responsibility," "duties toward society," and a "respect for the thing judged and the idea of right" (1.2.8, 263, 250, 256, 262).[10] Tocqueville identifies the fundamental character of the American *esprit légiste*—more literally the "legal specialist" or "jurist" spirit—as that of English common law, the English and American "law of precedents." He contrasts this with the French lawyer's inclination for abstract rationalism, since the Anglo-American lawyer combines "taste and respect for what is old" with "love of what is regular and legal." He observes, with some criticism, the "timid habits" and "static penchants" that common-law lawyers derive from attention to "the opinions and legal decisions of their fathers." Still, he is even more critical of the French civil law lawyer who always brings in "his own system of ideas" and "the constitutive principles of the laws" when deciding even the most trivial matter (254–55).

Because American lawyers embody common-law reasoning, with its peculiar inclinations and habits, and, more important, because this lawyer spirit
gives the legal profession a special power to shape the character of the citizenry and politics, Tocqueville concludes that the "American aristocracy is at
the attorneys' bar and on the judges' bench" (1.2.8, 256). The implication,
confirmed by his use of the term in other works, is that such an aristocracy
is a "governing body" of the "leading men" of politics and society, an "open
aristocracy" as distinct from a landed, hereditary caste.[11] Common-law lawyers
form such an open aristocracy in America because the merit evident in their
learning, and the vital function of resolving disputes according to law, quietly
confer a form of rule. Jefferson, too, hoped that a "natural *aristoi*" of "virtue
and talents" would govern in America.[12] Tocqueville, however, emphasizes that
common-law lawyers have a further quality essential to any aristocracy, a respect for the wisdom of the past. These are the qualities of bar and bench that
Hamilton praises in *The Federalist* as crucial for moderating factional conflict
and elevating political life in America (nos. 35; 78; see also no. 49). While
Tocqueville does not refer to Montesquieu, Blackstone, or Hamilton to buttress
these notions of law and judging, he does cite each of these authors elsewhere
in *Democracy*. His debt to Hamilton on this topic is perhaps the easiest to establish, since he declares *The Federalist* a "fine book" that, beyond its specific
importance for understanding America, "should be familiar to statesmen of every country" (1.1.8, 108 n. 8). Tocqueville notes that his own book consults it
regularly, and he openly praises the defunct Federalist party as having contained
men of "virtue" and "wisdom"—indeed, "all the great men" of the Revolution.
His regular warnings about a decline from constitutionalism to populism, and
from populist government to despotism, concern as much the deterioration
he saw in Jacksonian America as the descent of the French Revolution into
the Terror and Napoleon. The Federalists' brief ascendance at the American
founding thus is "one of the most fortunate events that accompanied the birth
of the great American Union," and he recommends John Marshall's biography
of George Washington on the theme of the statesman's resistance to popular
passions (1.2.2, 168–69; 1.2.5, 219–20; see also 1.1.8, 128–30).[13] Given the
similarities between *Democracy in America* and *The Federalist* on many such
issues, one suspects that Tocqueville draws upon Publius more often than he
cites him.[14] As to the influence of Blackstone, Tocqueville explicitly draws upon
Chancellor Kent's *Commentaries on American Law* (1826–30) and Joseph Story's
Commentaries on the Constitution (1833) for matters of law, judging, and jurisprudence. Both Kent and Story owe an obvious debt to Blackstone, whose
masterwork is the model for their works on American law. Their debt to Montesquieu is less obvious, arising largely through Blackstone, but any lawyers

or well-educated citizens of their era would have studied *The Spirit of the Laws* to some degree. Each of these works—so important for American legal understanding throughout the nineteenth century, and so important for Tocqueville's grasp of American jurisprudence—largely follows the principles of Hamilton and Marshall, respectively, the great figures of American law with whom Kent and Story worked and whom they deeply admired.

Tocqueville's analysis of judicial power, and its place in his diagnosis of modern self-government more generally, appears to be an elaboration of Hamilton's common-law jurisprudence and constitutionalism. In an early discussion of the "elevated rank" held by the Supreme Court among the powers of American government, Tocqueville argues that such a judiciary is crucial in a federal order. Indeed, the fate of American democracy ultimately rests not with the president or Congress but with the Court: "In the hands of seven federal judges rest ceaselessly the peace, the prosperity, the very existence of the Union" (1.1.8, 141–42). Without their arbitration of the tensions among the various powers and principles of a complex constitutional order—executive and legislative, union and states, public interest and private, "the spirit of conservation against democratic instability"—the Constitution "is a dead letter." Such power to preserve the constitutional order entails, however, the capacity to destroy it, and he believes that the president or Congress might falter without the union suffering or perishing. Of the Court alone, Tocqueville observed, two decades before *Dred Scott* (1857), that "if the Supreme Court ever came to be composed of imprudent or corrupt men, the confederation would have to fear anarchy or civil war" (1.1.8, 142; see also 108). Tocqueville then praises the framers of the Constitution for making the judicial power independent of the legislative, since one of the "[t]wo principal dangers" threatening democracies is the "[c]oncentration in the legislative power of all the other powers of government." He thus cites "the power granted to American courts to pronounce on the constitutionality of laws" as "one of the most powerful barriers ever erected against the tyranny of political assemblies" (1.1.8, 146; 1.1.6, 98).

Tocqueville's portrait of judges and lawyers praises them for two crucial functions in our constitutionalism. They preserve the union from a destructive competition of powers both within the federal government and between it and the states. Less dramatically but more significantly, they educate the citizenry in the habits and virtues that "best prepare the people to be free" (1.2.8, 262). This is an "immense" power, but only if "the people consent to obey the law"— noting that, since judicial power rests not on force but "opinion," for judges it is "as dangerous to fall short of [it] as to exceed" public opinion. The judicial power must be, then, not only the monitor of the separation of powers and federalism but also the educator in the mores required for republican rule. The latter involves at once persuading and commanding the people to obey the law, and assessing how best to achieve either aim on a given legal issue. He concludes not only that federal judges must have the qualities of citizenship, learning, and moral integrity necessary for all magistrates, but that "one must also find statesmen in them; they must know how to discern the spirit of their times, to confront the obstacles they can defeat, and to steer out of the current when the flood threatens to carry away with them the sovereignty of the Union and the obedience owed to its laws" (1.1.8, 142). This is one of several emphatic statements Tocqueville offers regarding judicial power in America. Such pronouncements have few if any counterparts in his analyses of legislative or executive power, or the state governments, or any other source of authority in the American polity, save religion. They recall the extraordinary judgments made about judicial power by Montesquieu, Hamilton, and, Blackstone. Each of these constitutionalists underscores, in their efforts to understand free government, the paradox that a crucial, potent power should be held by the least dramatic, least active, and least democratic of powers. Moreover, each finds that efforts to educate and reform modern constitutionalism require a quiet, complicated advocacy of the legal profession and the judiciary that forms its peak. In *Democracy* Tocqueville deepens Hamilton's largely common-law conceptions of law, judging, and constitutionalism, and even more clearly transcends the more liberal and narrow conceptions of Blackstone and Montesquieu. It is telling that Tocqueville thinks only religion is as potent and fundamental an influence in guiding a modern democratic people as is the lawyer spirit and its judicial epitome.

A Common-Law Remedy for the Democratic Soul

The reasons for Tocqueville's emphasis upon judging, and for his notion of statesmanship regarding "the spirit of the times" that advocates neither judicial supremacy nor historicism, ultimately stem from the opening argument of *Democracy* that a "new political science is needed for a world altogether new" (1, "Intro.," 7). This bold remark merits consideration, for during the writing of both volumes of *Democracy*, and especially after 1835, Tocqueville undertook extensive reading in ancient, medieval, and modern political philosophy in the Western tradition. If he understood himself to be offering a new political science not per se, but for a new world, he did so amid study ranging from Plato, Aristotle, and Plutarch, to Thomas Aquinas, and on to Machiavelli, Montaigne, Bacon, and Descartes.[15] Moreover, he remarked to his cousin Kergolay that, while writing volume 2, there were "three men with whom I commune a bit every day, Pascal, Montesquieu, and Rousseau. A fourth is missing: you."[16]

Considerable ink has been spilt in the attempt to discern which philosopher is the primary influence upon Tocqueville's works. Specifically regarding *Democracy*, its extraordinary commitment to modern equality has suggested to some the predominant influence of Rousseau.[17] One should take Tocqueville at his word, however, and be alert to the strains of each thinker found in his arguments, all the while respecting his capacity to rise above any single predecessor.[18] The influence usually overlooked here is Tocqueville's cousin, a philosophic friend upon whom he depended for conversation throughout his life, as he did with Beaumont, to assist his insights and investigations. This suggests Tocqueville's capacity to employ ideas of earlier philosophers to aid his philosophic understanding in new circumstances, and to develop new syntheses from diverse thinkers. Whatever the differences in substance, this is at least the stated method of Aristotle's *Ethics* and *Politics*, not to mention other great philosophers in the Western tradition.

Though we cannot discount the Rousseauian moments in Tocqueville's work, it may be that, by applying the methods and spirits of both Montesquieu and Pascal to the new phenomenon of widespread equality, *Democracy* undertakes a modern version of Aristotle's political science.[19] Montesquieu clearly informs the complex, massive structure of the work, its opening chapter on terrain and climate, and its emphasis on mores or political culture, as well as a typology of regimes indebted to Aristotle yet adapted to modern phenomena.[20] Still, Tocqueville's emphatic concern with the state of the human soul in modern democracy, and his serious attention to the questions of religion and revelation, suggest the influence of Pascal. The foundation for his analysis of American mores in the second volume of *Democracy* is Pascalian skepticism about the ability of Cartesian philosophy to achieve certainty regarding humanity's most fundamental questions.[21] Nevertheless, just as Montesquieu is more confident about reason than Montaigne, Tocqueville tempers such Augustinian doubts by insisting that he can formulate a political science that captures this new political and social condition of man. He synthesizes the political scientific method of Montesquieu, itself described by several modern scholars as the closest thing to Aristotle in modernity, with the larger questions posed by Pascal to modern man and to the modern philosophic, political project. A fundamental departure from Aristotle's philosophy, even with a Pascalian influence to elevate his view, is Tocqueville's insistence that historical change dictates the inadequacy of relying solely upon conceptions about an unchanging human nature. His new political science, for what he argues are radically new conditions for humanity, nonetheless echoes Aristotelianism in its central concern with human nature, the human soul, and its higher destiny. He develops an Aristotelian method that combines observation of particulars with prescription in light of fundamental philosophic principles of natural right and constitutionalism. Such a political science is more concerned with the higher potentiality of politics and the soul than is Montesquieu's new science, while nonetheless arguing for the need to depart from the ancients. This leads Tocqueville to take a twofold stance toward the phenomenon of modern democracy, for uppermost in his mind is the fate of the human soul itself, "the natural greatness of man," in the conditions of modern democracy (1, "Intro.," 5).[22] Montesquieu and Rousseau, even given their concerns with the degradation of man in modernity, are more concerned with the idiosyncratic "self" than with the soul. Neither philosopher could have stated, as Tocqueville does, that in aristocracies one finds "inequality and misery," but "souls were not degraded" (8). This complicated political science informs Tocqueville's descriptions and prescriptions regarding judges and lawyers in modern democracy.

On the one hand, Tocqueville argues that the revolution which replaced feudal aristocracy with modern democracy is "a providential fact," since the "gradual progress of equality" or "the equality of conditions" is "universal," "enduring," and "daily escapes human power" (1, "Intro.," 6, 3). On the other hand, he is neither a determinist nor a fatalist about modern democracy. He warns that egalitarianism "lends itself almost as readily" to "the sovereignty of all and the absolute power of one alone." His main fear is the power of modern equality to homogenize and enervate human souls, to produce not citizens but subjects who would "fall below the level of humanity" (1.1.3, 52; 1.2.9, 301; see also 1, "Intro.," 12; and 2.4.6, 665). A leading voice in France's recent rediscovery of Tocqueville argues that his greatness lies in "his capacity at one and the same time for promoting the clear hope that democracy entails while deepening a sense for its doleful secret"—that "the question of ends is pushed back" until "the silence becomes deafening."[23] On the basis of this one pregnant thought, Tocqueville's political science practices the kind of statesmanship he commends to judges, to "discern the spirit of their times" so as to "confront those obstacles they can defeat" while steering "out of the current when the flood threatens to carry [them] away." As Aristotle argued, political science as a practical science must seek to achieve what good it can in light of both philosophic principle and actual circumstances.[24] Tocqueville thought equality was an irreversible fact of "the times" but he also insisted that a choice confronted mankind, between equality in liberty and "equality in servitude" (1.1.3, 52). If modern man is to secure liberty and whatever political virtue is possible, then statesmanlike steering is needed, a practical wisdom rooted in the philosophic ability to look beyond any current party and to speak stern truths to democracy in a spirit of friendship (1, "Intro.," 15; 2, "Notice," 400). Like Montesquieu, he sprinkles his philosophic analyses with prudential advice, as in his efforts from the opening of *Democracy* to elevate the democratic soul by linking liberty and religion and tempering the extremes of Christian fundamentalism and rationalist atheism: "One still encounters Christians among us, full of zeal, whose religious souls love to nourish themselves from the truths of the other life; doubtless they are going to be moved to favor human liberty, the source of all moral greatness" (1, "Intro.," 11).[25]

Tocqueville's new science of politics aids modern democracy by emphasizing not only the theme of religion and liberty but also the theme of law, right, and the juridical spirit. A common-law, properly aristocratic legal profession and judiciary is a crucial remedy for the prime ills he diagnoses, which stem from the change in our souls produced by equality of conditions. This connection between the legal profession and his concern with the soul is not immediately clear in *Democracy in America*, and today the thought of looking to lawyers and judges for serious moral or political guidance is counterintuitive, to speak mildly. The fundamental importance of the common-law lawyer spirit for the work comes to light as Tocqueville reveals the deep problems inherent in the points of departure, or fundamental principles, he discerns for American constitutionalism in volume 1, and for American mores in volume 2. At the beginning of volume 1 Tocqueville describes the point of departure for American constitutionalism and politics as the "marvelous combination" achieved by the Puritans of "the *spirit of religion* and the *spirit of liberty*" (1.1.2, 43; emphasis in original). However, he subsequently judges that, by the 1830s, this founding principle no longer can maintain democratic freedom as opposed to equality under tyranny: "Do you not see that religions are weakening and that the divine notion of rights is disappearing? Do you not find that mores are being altered, and that with them the moral notion of rights is being effaced? Do you not perceive on all sides beliefs that give way to reasoning, and sentiments that give way to calculations?" (1.2.6, 228; see 1.2.9, 281–88, 299).

He does not identify the cause for this eclipse of religious faith until, early in volume 2, he searches for the origins of American mores and sentiments in the philosophic spirit of Enlightenment rationalism. He discusses the "philosophic method of the Americans" as a new point of departure flowing from America's original Protestant one, identifying not Descartes but Luther and the "sixteenth-century reformers" as the root of this radically modern philosophy (2.1.1). The Protestant Reformation is the seed of a Cartesian skepticism or rationalism that eschews all tradition and common sense, all forms and natural ends. The new philosophy favors reliance on "the individual effort of [one's] reason," one consequence of which is that each person "withdraws narrowly into himself and claims to judge the world from there" (2.1.1, 403–4). Such modern rationalism isolates individuals from one another and cuts off succeeding generations from traditional reasoning and judgments. A half-century before American thinkers had coined the term *pragmatism,* Tocqueville essentially described and diagnosed the problems with this combination of skepticism and progressive, historicist principles.[26] The paradoxical result of such individualism is that equally weak minds or souls look to the democratic mass, to public opinion, for guidance: "The same equality that makes him independent of each of his fellow citizens in particular leaves him isolated and defenseless against the action of the greatest number" (2.1.2, 409). Tocqueville suggests no inevitability or Hegelian "end of history" to this modern drama, for democracy can yield either liberty or tyranny. Long before Nietzsche or Kojève, he grasped that any such end point entailed the eclipse of humanity, the "last man," suggesting that the historicist repudiation of natural-right principles for humanity and politics is not necessarily either progressive or humane. The unintended consequences of America's blend of pragmatism and skepticism include corrosion of the fundamental link between religion and liberty achieved in the original point of departure and its replacement by a democratic inclination toward "pantheism." Tocqueville foresees American Transcendentalism and its erasure of distinctions or hierarchy between the "microcosm" of the individual and the "macrocosm," celebrating homogeneous man, democratic society, and the merging of humanity and divinity in a single existence (2.1.7).[27] Ultimately, since pantheism in turn yields a democratic "instinct for centralization" and centralized administration, volume 2 concludes with a warning as to "what kind of despotism democratic nations have to fear." This new, soft despotism "reduces each nation to being nothing more than a herd of timid and industrious animals of which the government is the shepherd" (2.4.5, 659; 2.4.6, 661, 663).

It is while examining the consequences of this philosophic foundation that Tocqueville reveals his extraordinary hopes for Anglo-American lawyers and judges. When suggesting that Puritan liberty cannot counteract the skeptical individualism caused by democratic philosophy, since Protestantism is the seed of that philosophy, he proposes two other antidotes. After diagnosing pragmatism, and thereby explaining why Americans are deeply Cartesian but never read Descartes, Tocqueville immediately praises both English empiricism and traditional Catholic Christianity (see 2.1, chs. 3, 4, 5, 6). He contrasts the empiricism and attention to particulars of English thinking with the French taste for philosophic abstraction and generalization, worrying that American thinking is becoming more abstract and rationalist. His endorsement of Catholicism in America deepens the point, since Luther's search for a clean, radically personal foundation for faith similarly rejects the tradition and hierarchy implicit in the English common law. The only remarks that anticipate and make sense of his qualified praise of English empiricism are those in volume 1 on Anglo-

American legal reasoning, the common-law *esprit légiste*. Moreover, Tocqueville closes the entire work on this theme, examining the importance of courts and then of forms and formalities, even urging an "enlightened and reflective worship" of the latter (2.4.7, 668–69). His extraordinary emphasis on lawyers and judges in American constitutionalism serves, then, a larger purpose beyond any sociological or institutional analysis of an American elite. The lawyer spirit and its judicial epitome are a crucial antidote to the skeptical, isolating rationalism of democracy that leads, he fears, to both pantheism and despotism.[28] He dwells upon the American lawyer's ways and habits of thinking, his characteristically English love of particulars and precedents, of forms and regularity. The contrast between this common-law spirit and the civil law taste for Enlightenment rationalism and abstraction is stark: "The English or the American lawyer inquires into what has been done, the French lawyer into what one ought to wish to do; the one wants rulings, the other reasons" (1.2.8, 255). Tocqueville also declares his awareness of "the inherent defects of the lawyer spirit," since its "conservative" spirit makes Anglo-American lawyers resemble "the Egyptian priests" who are "the lone interpreter[s] of an occult science." Still, he suggests that an American common-law statesmanship can balance this with appropriate attention to securing what is "good," even if prudence teaches that one should expect to secure only as much good as is possible given "the spirit of the times" (1.2.8, 254–56; 1.1.8, 142). The American common-law lawyer avoids French abstraction, which tends toward utopian revolution, but Tocqueville also thinks he can avoid the conservative historicist tendencies of English law that divorce organic tradition from right. His jabs at the cultist aspects of English jurisprudence seem to warn American lawyers to moderate these very tendencies. While "English law is like [the trunk of] an ancient tree," and its lawyers would "rather depart from reason and humanity than from the law," one of the great benefits of American democracy is its emphasis on not only law but also right (compare 1.2.8, 256 with 1.2.6).[29]

Tocqueville's most widely noted remark on the judiciary and politics, read in context, thus concerns the deep influence that a properly balanced common-law spirit achieves in America's democratic political order. Such an influence is antithetical to the judicial activism or supremacy claimed by Holmesean judges in the twentieth century:

> There is almost no political question in the United States that is not resolved sooner or later into a judicial question. Hence the obligation under which the parties find themselves in their daily polemics to borrow from the ideas and language of justice. . . . Judicial language thus becomes in a way the vulgar language; the lawyer spirit, born inside the schools and the courts, therefore spreads little by little

beyond their precincts; it so to speak infiltrates all society, it descends into the lowest ranks, and finally the whole people contract a part of the habits and tastes of a magistrate. (1.2.8, 257–58)

Tocqueville's linking of the common-law lawyer spirit with his central concern for the soul and with his warnings about the corrosive effects of modern philosophy is buttressed by the striking omission in *Democracy in America* of any discussion of the Declaration of Independence.[30] Moreover, his one thematic treatment of rights adopts the classic common-law view of Fortescue and Coke, excluding the Hobbesian, Lockean notions of self-preservation or interest and recalling the terms of classical and medieval philosophy: "After the general idea of virtue I know of none more beautiful than that of rights, or rather these two ideas are intermingled. The idea of rights is nothing other than the idea of virtue introduced into the world of politics" (1.2.6, 227).[31] This section of *Democracy*, on "the idea of rights," and its sequel, on "respect for the law," fall within the five "real advantages that American society derives from democratic government" (1.2.6). Such views of law and rights develop Tocqueville's emphasis upon judicial power early in this first volume, and lead to the striking analysis of judging, law, and rights that follows. By treating such juridical topics in terms of virtue and beauty, and a legal aristocracy in terms of statesmanship guided by integrity, right, and liberty, Tocqueville seeks to pull American law and democracy toward its highest, most principled potential.

Tocqueville reinforces such notions when he ponders why the ancients could not discern "the equal right to liberty that each bears from birth," explaining that it was Christ who first taught that all men are "naturally alike and equal." This turn to Biblical religion, not to the American Declaration of Independence or the French Declaration of the Rights of Man, occurs when contrasting English empiricism with rationalist abstraction early in volume 2 (2.1.3, 413). His concern is that modern rationalism and skepticism exacerbate the individual isolation that in turn threatens democratic liberty, human greatness, and human dignity. This dictates a series of choices, both prudential and philosophical, about how to at once analyze and influence the soul of modern democracy. His concern with rationalism leads to an initial emphasis on the Puritan origin of American liberty, however flawed, at the expense of the Declaration. Since, however, he finds the Puritan point of departure in need of buttressing, he recommends the common-law spirit and judicial enforcement of individual rights—rights understood in a more virtuous, public-spirited sense—as among the prime supports for both Christian mores and liberty. Abraham Lincoln, both in his formulations in the 1830s of the threats to American liberty and decency, and in his subsequent rhetorical efforts as president to address such threats, strikes similar themes about a civil religion that reconciles the rule of law and religious devotion.[32] *Democracy* itself does not suggest that Tocqueville ever considers the American Declaration as both a common-law statement of grievances within a shared constitutionalism and an Enlightenment statement of abstract, Lockean rights. Still, the realities of the ways the document has been perceived offer some justification for his cautious approach to it. Lincoln used the Declaration as a source of abstract principles as well as of revered American tradition, and both the popular and academic understanding of the document today tend to overlook its common-law form and grievances in favor of its ringing Enlightenment phrases. If Tocqueville's larger aim was to check the growth of abstract rationalism in America, with its tendencies to undermine natural right, liberty, and human decency in favor of pantheism and soft despotism, then his silent treatment of the Declaration seems to have been his prudent choice in the service of right.

Tocqueville's hope is that the lawyer spirit will work with township government, associations, parties, and other institutions that combat apathetic individualism—each of these an element of his effort to preempt the role of the modern, rationalist intellectual. It is with this goal in mind that he says of the judge's broader effect on jurors and citizens that "his power makes itself felt on all habits of mind [or spirit] and even the very souls of those who have cooperated with him in judging" (1.2.8, 264). This fundamental concern for the soul's fate in modern democracy led him to conclude that, while he was "aware of the inherent defects of the lawyer spirit," nevertheless this kind of common-law influence was indispensable for the very survival of American democracy. Even further, it is crucial for self-government everywhere: "[W]ithout this mixture of the lawyer spirit and the democratic spirit, . . . I doubt that democracy could long govern society, and I cannot believe that in our day a republic could hope to preserve its existence if the influence of lawyers in its affairs did not grow in proportion with the power of the people" (1.2.8, 254). Tocqueville finds America's common-law judges performing the crucial function of instructing jurors and all citizens in "the idea of right" and in "equity," "responsibility," "political virtue," and "duties." By thus "forcing men to occupy themselves with something other than their own affairs," the legal profession and judges combat that "individual selfishness which is like the blight of societies" (1.2.8, 262).

The Cloaking of Power, Judicial Statesmanship, and Constitutionalism

As Kronman, Glendon, and other leading lawyers suggest, members of the Anglo-American legal community today have deep concerns about the loss of integrity or fundamental principles in our bar and bench.[33] Tocqueville's very language about lawyers and judges, not to mention his larger argument about their crucial role as republican schoolmasters, seems foreign to the American polity today. The judicialization of politics, the rise of untempered interest-group pluralism, and an ever-increasing emphasis on material prosperity have combined to yield great power to lawyers both in and out of political office. For a litigious America, with few prominent models of lawyers in public life who serve the higher purposes of the legal profession, Tocqueville's suggestion that we look to lawyers and judges to ennoble American life seems either odd or anachronistic.

By examining Tocqueville's constitutionalism and jurisprudence in light of the writings of Montesquieu, Blackstone, and Hamilton, each of whom he cites in *Democracy*, we can hope to explain why such a change occurred and what it portends. Tocqueville's praise of a professional legal spirit and its judicial acme recalls Montesquieu's conception of a depository of the laws (e.g., *The Spirit of the Laws* 2.4; 6.1; 12.2). In his first thematic discussion of American judicial power, Tocqueville attempts to establish how distinct the American version is from any other judiciary by comparing it to the French *parlements*, specifically the Parlement of Paris (1.1.6, 93–94). He does not refer to Montesquieu here, nor later when praising American courts as more effective at curbing abuses of government power than are France's old parlements—and as more effective than France's new republican courts, which, on crucial issues, are not independent of the legislature and executive (99).[34] His French predecessor may well have approved of these remarks and of a general emphasis on judicial power. Still, only Tocqueville incorporates a distinct element of classical virtue and natural right in his jurisprudence and analysis of judging. His reasons for doing so delineate the crucial difference between the two. Tocqueville's common-law lawyer spirit aims to leaven egalitarian and individualistic qualities in modern democracy, among which perhaps the most worrisome, since least noticed, is the quiet flattening of the human soul toward exclusive concern with individual security, tranquillity, and physical comfort. He emphatically describes and commends a legal orientation to order, forms, and precedent, and to such principles of justice as equity, responsibility, and duties toward society. He praises American judges, having cited the works of such figures as Marshall, Kent, and Story, for inculcating respect for the judgments of courts and for the idea of right. The American version of common law not only avoids French rationalism through its English taste for the old and regular, but also elevates such traditional notions toward higher ideas of justice and human purpose.

Tocqueville hopes such a judicial power and legal spirit will counteract the concern with individual tranquillity, but this concern is centrally important to Montesquieu's constitutionalism and his project for a cloaking of power.

Tocqueville's broad agreement with Montesquieu and Blackstone regarding liberty, separation of powers, a professional and independent judiciary, and the need for a jurisprudence largely modeled upon English common law coincides with fundamental disagreements about the ends which these constitutionalist principles and institutions serve. The debt that both Hamilton and Tocqueville owe to Coke and the classic common law balances the evident influence of Montesquieu and Blackstone upon their analyses of constitutionalism. Neither Hamilton nor Marshall would consider Tocqueville's conception of a statesman-like role for judges strange and revolutionary, although each might find his own theory and practice of common-law prudence more fully expounded by the Frenchman. It is not surprising that American officeholders could not afford to be as candid as Tocqueville in elaborating an openly aristocratic account of professional expertise and judicial power. Even Hamilton in *Federalist* no. 78 probably exercised such prudence, for its bold suggestions about judicial power are not as thematically developed as they might be. While the American common-law conception of judicial power is not as cloaked as the accounts of Montesquieu and Blackstone—who never endorse a notion of judicial review, and who disguise their moderating of traditional moral standards—this does not mean the Americans can be so open as Tocqueville. Marshall's complicated, cautious argument establishing the constitutional status of judicial review in *Marbury v. Madison* (1803) seems to understand that, as Robert Faulkner notes, one cannot "preach democracy's limitations to democrats and expect thus to leaven democracy."[35]

The relations between the conceptions of judicial power given by Hamilton, Marshall, and Tocqueville deserve further consideration, especially through analysis of Tocqueville's citations to *The Federalist*, Hamilton, Marshall, Story, and Kent. Tocqueville's appeal to the common-law prudence and educative role of judges amplifies Hamilton's common-law arguments in *The Federalist*, which sought to justify both a power of judicial review and the broader benefits of "the integrity and moderation of the judiciary." A congruence with the decisions of Marshall and Story also merits study. In several landmark cases Marshall appealed to "equity," or to the "spirit" of, or the "general principles" implicit in, the Constitution as the best way to interpret the document. Nonetheless, Marshall's classic common-law disposition cautioned, unlike the "living constitution" school of today, that such a spirit nonetheless is "to be chiefly collected from its words."[36] The constitutionalism of *Democracy* also joins Hamilton in implicitly criticizing a Madisonian conception of the Constitution as a structure for competing interests, as is evident in its similarities to Hamilton's emphasis on the "more permanent branches" and his more positive, constructive reading of the separation of powers.[37] Tocqueville's common-law constitutionalism thus accords with the jurisprudence of the founders to the extent that they incorporated an Aristotelian concept of legal discretion that embraced faithfulness to the Constitution's letter and spirit and was informed by attention to the requirements of the constitutional order. This may explain why, at least regarding chief justices, Washington and Adams sought lawyers such as Jay, Hamilton, and Marshall, all of them experienced statesmen in elected office and international diplomacy.[38] As Faulkner notes, Marshall's judicial statesmanship in crucial constitutional opinions thus offered "practical discourses on liberal government," with *Marbury* in particular being "a brief essay on what the rule of law is to mean" in America.[39]

If one compares the conceptions of judicial power in Montesquieu and Tocqueville in light of the contrast between ancient and modern constitutionalism, Tocqueville's view lies closer to the ancients. In contrast to Montesquieu's distinctly modern and liberal account, Tocqueville "reproduces in democratic conditions the Aristotelian notion of the independence of judging, according to which it represents a check on human government, or a calling to account in light of an external standard, either law or nature."[40] This does not mean there is a call to or even an intimation of judicial activism or judicial supremacy in *Democracy in America*. While Tocqueville disagrees with Montesquieu's emphasis on negative liberty and individualism, he retains Montesquieu's fundamental concern with constitutional forms and separation of powers. Few judges, jurists, and lawyers in America today share such a concern, and still fewer subscribe even to the mild formulations of natural right in Montesquieu and Blackstone. This is one sign of the fundamental transformation in our conceptions of judicial power and jurisprudence during the past century. Woodrow Wilson's more democratic, Rousseauian notion of a living constitution has replaced the constitutionalist legacy of Montesquieu, Blackstone, Hamilton, Marshall, and Tocqueville. A constitution must be made to adapt to the felt needs of the people of the day and to the new programs of their leaders, at the expense of its original forms, principles, and precedents. More specifically, the judging power should be not the depository of laws but a prophetic voice of pragmatic policy making, the vanguard of evolving meanings of law. This shift toward a radically independent, potent judicial power in modern liberal constitutionalism is largely traceable to the efforts of Holmes and the jurisprudence of legal realism he embodied.

Because an Aristotelian concern with the prudent application of sound theory informs both Hamilton and Tocqueville, their writings readily offer broad principles for formulating a distinct alternative to today's dominant views, a jurisprudence of judicial statesmanship that yields neither a strictly positivist originalism nor a historicist judicial legislation. As will be discussed, not all "original intent" arguments subscribe to the legal skepticism or positivism evident in Holmes or in Judge Robert Bork.[41] Some originalists might be persuaded, then, that both Tocqueville and the framers of American judicial power prescribe a common-law judicial statesmanship as crucial to the proper functioning of our constitutional order. This still leaves the question of what such a jurisprudence would practically advise in our Holmesean era of pragmatism, legal and moral skepticism, and eschewal of the jurisprudential tradition that in fact gave rise to an independent judicial power. One rule of thumb is that today's judiciary should not attempt "statesmanlike" adjudications, since in the wake of the Holmesean revolution these most likely would be made without regard to the Constitution's fundamental principles. Further, the common-law legal prudence practiced by Lincoln, in the defense of more traditional rights, is helpful in discerning what lessons can be distilled from the founders and Tocqueville. Lincoln's principled but prudent opposition to the constitutional authority of the Supreme Court's *Dred Scott* decision is a model of common-law reasoning and statesmanship. He argued that the constitutional reasoning of Taney's majority opinion lacked those "claims to the public confidence" which make judicial decisions "precedents" and "authorities," as evaluated by "common sense" and "the customary understanding of the legal profession." He applies such common-law criteria as "the unanimous concurrence of the judges" and whether the decision is "in accordance with legal expectation, and with the steady practice of the departments throughout our history." Alternately, even if an opinion lacked these qualities, Lincoln ultimately would accept its legal authority if "it had been before the court more than once, and had there been affirmed and reaffirmed through a course of years."[42]

The eclipse in the twentieth century of traditional common-law jurisprudence eschews, of course, Lincoln's very appeal to "customary" understandings or to any greater stability in the law than can be secured by consolidating the most recent doctrinal revolution. Still, a common-law constitutionalism, emphasizing a properly judicial reason, tempers custom with a concern for natural justice, as is evident in the Preamble to the Constitution and reaffirmed in *Federalist* no. 51, declaring that "[j]ustice is the end of government." The orientation to practical moral wisdom in the common-law tradition—confirmed by much Anglo-American practice and justified by the continued presence of moral concerns, explicitly or implicitly, even in realist and postmodernist jurisprudence—exposes moral skepticism as an abstraction from the reality of political communities, political thought, and law.[43] This is especially true of a people whose constitutionalism is, as Lincoln reminded us, based upon the laws of Nature and Nature's God and dedicated to truths. Still, even originalists who reject legal realism and moral skepticism might worry that the American framers intended not judges but elected legislatures and judges to exercise independent moral judgment in the making of law. Natural-law jurisprudence, for example, might enter current debates over constitutional interpretation to argue that, for Thomas Aquinas, the task of discerning the natural law in the positive law is primarily legislative and not judicial.[44] The American founders and Tocqueville would concur, and while their common-law jurisprudence is not strictly Thomistic, there is some link between these schools, in the form of the Scholasticism still evident in the jurisprudence of Fortescue, Saint Germain, and Coke. Putting aside the immense complexities of such lineages, the separation-of-powers constitutionalism of Montesquieu and Blackstone, to which Hamilton and Tocqueville largely subscribe, does confirm that the task of translating natural right into positive law is primarily a legislative and executive task. Still, those primary determinations often are imprecise, as Madison, no advocate of judicial activism, observed in *The Federalist*: laws always are "more or less obscure or equivocal until their meaning be liquidated and ascertained by a series of particular discussions and adjudications" (no. 37). Moreover, Hamilton and Tocqueville suggest that the framers of a constitution and the people who ratify their work are in a sense superlegislators. A common-law conception of an independent judicial power within that constitution suggests that a crucial function for such judges is to serve the constitution by enforcing its plain meaning, as Hamilton and Marshall might say, against any later attempts to subvert or elude it. The difficult question always remains of whether and to what degree a judge in a given case should correct, not permanently displace, a current legislator by discerning the fundamental principles and requirements of the Constitution for that case, or that area of law.[45]

Hamilton and Tocqueville suggest that a jurisprudence oriented to the perpetuation of republican constitutionalism should arise from the judge's regular exercise of a judgment guided by binding precedent and fundamental, established principles. This attention to custom and precedent should guide, in turn, judicial discretion where the precise meaning of the law as applied to new cases or controversies is initially not clear. Such classic common-law interplay between legal interpretation and judicial statesmanship would signal at least a partial restoration of our original constitutionalism, and this could help to return judges and lawyers to the stabilizing, ennobling role that both the founders and Tocqueville endorsed. Tocqueville also knew, however, that our expectations for securing the political good must be tempered, given the spirit of the times. The American legal profession throughout the twentieth century and at the dawn of the twenty-first seems dominated by one spirit more than any other, whether openly recognized as such or not, namely, the sophisticated legal realism of Holmes. Regardless of whether one thinks the framers' jurisprudence is best described as liberalized common law or as common-law liberalism, the ambitious jurist from Boston largely repudiated their understanding of law.

ten

Holmes and Judicialized Liberalism

Like any effort by a philosopher to reform politics, Montesquieu's project for a cloaking of power may have had unintended consequences. The writings and judicial opinions of Oliver Wendell Holmes Jr. (1841–1935) and the extraordinary influence he achieved in twentieth-century legal thought in America spring in part from the effort by Montesquieu and Blackstone to moderate law by divorcing judicial procedure from jurisprudential essence. The legal realism of Holmes certainly makes judging more important to, indeed essentially indistinguishable from, partisan politics. His project to redefine law epitomizes, however, philosophical and constitutional immoderation by claiming to uncloak the real nature of politics and judging. The subtle French jurist and his circumspect disciple Blackstone hardly could endorse the style or substance of the project. *The Spirit of the Laws* opens by emphatically warning that proposed political reforms must be weighed against ills they might cause, and Blackstone's adherence to that spirit frustrated Bentham. Nonetheless, the efforts of these jurists to achieve liberal tranquillity through a subtle judicializing of politics may have prepared the way for a radical jurisprudential transformation, one that ultimately repudiates their conceptions of constitutionalism and a stable rule of law.

Holmes's skepticism about any fixed legal principle yields an explicit concept of judicial legislating intended to achieve a new social and legal order, one more attuned to either current majority will or an evolutionary progress of the species. While legal pragmatists today might emphasize his occasional pronouncements on judicial self-restraint, his bold legal realism in fact envisions great judges as oracles of social and legal progress, indirectly instructing the majority through what Holmes called "interstitial change" in the law. One ground for this revolutionary notion is Montesquieu's elevation of liberal tranquillity to be the fundamental human concern, paired with his reconception of bar and bench as gradually reforming the law to this end. This influence is evident even if a naked judicialization of politics—captured in Holmes's famous definition of law as what *courts* can be expected to do—was not intended by the original program for a cloaking of power. Indeed, such judicial legislating disregards the careful equilibrium of powers essential to Montesquieu's constitutionalism, among other principles of a supposedly outdated, original Constitution. The separation of powers is thus, paradoxically, a victim of a cloaking of power that initially rested upon liberal and somewhat skeptical premises about law and natural right. The liberal project for a cloaking of power, if not tempered, sacrifices constitutional forms and principles to the ends of liberal progress and individual tranquillity.

One way to rediscover the liberalized common-law jurisprudence of America's framers and Tocqueville is to examine later legal controversies in light of it, since familiar quandaries might well arise because of departures from the older understanding. Among the most controversial products of the Holmesean revolution is the right-of-privacy doctrine established by the twentieth-century Supreme Court. If the roots of the Court's most recent abortion jurisprudence lie in Holmes, then interesting contrasts arise between this novel development in our constitutional law and the jurisprudence of the American founders and Tocqueville. Such a broad comparison raises, of course, as many questions as it answers. Nevertheless, examining the abortion case *Planned Parenthood v. Casey* (1992) in light of the framers and Tocqueville suggests that our judiciary no longer remedies but in fact exacerbates the abstract reasoning and isolating individualism that Tocqueville thought harmful to real liberty and to the perpetuation of the rule of law. A comparison to Hamilton and Tocqueville also reminds us of how different American jurisprudence prior to Holmes was from either of the versions of legal realism dominant today, the judicial restraint and living Constitution schools. Before examining Holmes's jurisprudence and its consequences for but one area of American constitutional law the question arises as to how such a transformation from the constitutionalism of Hamilton and Tocqueville could have occurred. How did the American common-law consensus, which moderated the Montesquieuan cloaking of power, produce such an immoderate view of law and judging and elevate a man with a "brutal worldview" to be the "great oracle of American law"?[1] The declining fortunes of Montesquieu's philosophy in America during the nineteenth and twentieth centuries correspond with the rise of this jurisprudence that repudiates notions of natural right and enduring legal principle.

The Fate of Montesquieu's Constitutionalism in America

Montesquieu's fundamental influence on the most influential of modern constitutions has been obscured by time as well as by doctrinal censure. The consequence is that, like Bolivia's two capital cities, America governs itself partly under a new constitution and partly under the old. Since the height of his influence in the 1780s and 1790s, advocates of a more democratic, Lockean republicanism have deemed Montesquieu insufficiently devoted to popular liberty and equality. Jefferson propounded this view late in the founding era, and subsequent liberal political theory and social science amplified it. Although Jefferson copied extensive passages from Montesquieu into his *Commonplace Book*, he later helped to translate and publish a commentary on *The Spirit of the Laws* by Destutt de Tracy, which criticized Montesquieu from a more purely liberal, analytical perspective. Jefferson's letters express his own verdict on Montesquieu's work, including a reference to its "heresies" and the clear implication that Destutt de Tracy's commentary is superior to the original.[2] A similar spirit informed his dislike for Blackstone, evident in his discussions with Madison regarding the proper "political principles" for the first professor in law at the University of Virginia.[3]

To note only the milestones of Montesquieu's fate in America, Jefferson prepared the soil for Woodrow Wilson's not dissimilar criticism a century hence. The crucial difference is that Wilson takes aim not only at Montesquieu but quite openly at the very Constitution informed by this supposedly anachronistic philosophy. The chapter on the presidency in his *Constitutional Government in the United States* (1908) opens with a severe critique of the Newtonian, mechanistic paradigm informing Montesquieu's separation of powers and the 1787 Constitution. Such a political science is outdated in the wake of Darwinian evolution, Hegelian liberal progress, and Rousseau's more democratic vision for constitutional government. Wilson's new political science thus defined the presidency in the nonconstitutional terms of popular leadership and scientific administration, making it the key to moving the Constitution beyond its obsolete doctrines to a higher plane of democratic politics. Such a presidency would liberate the organic, living Constitution from its bondage to the "Whig" or "literary" theory of the text embodied by *The Spirit of the Laws*, and this call for emancipation from Montesquieu's influence later informed Wilson's conduct as president.[4] From the mid-twentieth century, readers of a widely used translation of *The Spirit of the Laws* were introduced to the work through a blend of these Jeffersonian and Wilsonian criticisms. Franz Neumann deems Montesquieu's attempt at "a system of politics" a failure, since "[p]romise and performance are not in proportion"; indeed, it is not "a great book." Montesquieu's errors partly stem from his "aristocratic prejudices," and he even is named a chief influence upon the "anti-democratic wing of German liberalism" in the nineteenth century. Neumann closes this extraordinary effort with a Wilsonian call for emancipation from Montesquieu's emphasis on constitutionalism, although he claims the Baron himself would change tack if he had observed "mass democracy in action." The notion that "administration is the primary instrument for the utilization of political power for social purposes" unfortunately must labor against old prejudices, and "[m]odern political science must emancipate itself from the deadweight of the separation of powers doctrine which, much against Montesquieu's conception, has been transformed into a dogma."[5]

The story of Montesquieu in America is thus one of a direct and fundamental influence that has waned, largely because his philosophy and constitutionalism have been considered too conservative—whether as insufficiently democratic, or as insufficiently pragmatic regarding the evolution of constitutional principles. The intervening centuries also have seen the rise of a more analytical, deductive mode of political philosophy that finds *The Spirit of the Laws* unsystematic, even chatty. However, such criticisms of Montesquieu, and of constitutionalism more generally, have failed to completely transform the Constitution, producing a layer of democratic populism and progressive intellectualism over a complex system of separated offices and powers. This confusion or internal tension in our politics is evident upon comparing the more populist selection processes for both the Executive and Senate today with the original understanding of these offices, especially in light of the duties still imposed upon them by the Constitution regarding international relations, national security, and appointment of officers, including judges. One reason for studying Montesquieu today is that his influence on these and other American institutions has been not erased but reduced and garbled. Regarding judicial power, he informs our jurisprudence both directly and through Blackstone, then through Hamilton and Marshall, and later through Chancellor Kent's *Commentaries on American Law* (1826–30) and Joseph Story's *Commentaries on the Constitution* (1833). Constitutionalist and common-law jurisprudence was eclipsed in the twentieth century largely through the transformation achieved by Holmes and his legacy in legal realism. Still, Montesquieu's blending of noble and republican elements in the judicial power, and his blending of judicial power with the upper house of the legislature, survives in the American Constitution and in our revisions of English common-law customs. In addition to the fundamental characteristics of the judges governed by Article III, as analyzed by Hamilton in *The Federalist,* the Senate serves as court of impeachment; the chief justice presides over presidential impeachments; and judges still wear robes, but not wigs. Moreover, through America's influence on the world's liberal democracies, whether they are parliamentary or separation-of-powers governments, Montesquieu's imprint is evident in the prominence of pluralism or moderate faction, of federalism, and of judicial power—and thus of lawyers and litigation. Indeed, the prominence of judicial power is among the leading exports of American constitutionalism today.

Holmes eschewed Montesquieu's constitutionalism while admiring other ends or aims of his philosophy, generally viewing it as a cosmopolitan, historicist humanism that survived its outdated efforts at a science of politics. As a consciously self-styled man of letters from a newly distinguished American family of letters, Holmes prominently displayed his wide reading in private correspondence and public writings alike. Catherine Bowen portrays him as discovering Montesquieu when he studied law just after his harrowing service in the Civil War:

> Holmes was fascinated by Montesquieu. Here was a lonely scholar,
> sitting in a library—yet his book had done as much to remodel the
> world as any material product of the eighteenth century. . . . Holmes
> was struck anew with the awful power of ideas to change the world.
> Montesquieu commanded the future more surely from his study than
> Napoleon from his throne. A valid idea was worth a regiment any
> day. The man of action has the present, yes—but does not the thinker
> control the future?[6]

In his references to and writings about Montesquieu that occasionally arise throughout his mature life, Holmes appears to have styled himself after the combination of thinker and man of action that he found in this famous predecessor. This is particularly evident in an essay published in 1900, even though his analysis clearly considers many of Montesquieu's ideas to have passed their prime. Still, if Wilson openly attacked Montesquieu's anachronistic science of politics and boldly proposed its replacement, Holmes found an essence in his thought that might be useful for projects beyond the ken of the old French jurist. The consequences for Montesquieu's political science and constitutionalism, and especially for the aim to subtly judicialize politics, were hardly more benign than those of Wilson's more explicitly hostile stance. Holmes saw in him a thinker who sought to change the world, an emphasis on ceaseless historical change in all ideas and practices, and realism about the conflict of forces and interests in human life—and not much more. He read into Montesquieu's philosophy a full-blown historicism that is there only in seed, but such historicism was pervasive in a late-nineteenth-century America fascinated with evolution and progress.[7] All that remained, after Holmes was through, were the immoderate elements of Montesquieu's complex thought—the ambition to influence practical affairs, the attention to historical change and particularity, the hints of Machiavellian realism. In effect, Holmes thought he had found a predecessor for his own radically historical, amoral jurisprudence of legal realism. It is paradoxical that this jurisprudence would tear down the constitutionalism and conception of judicial power that Montesquieu in fact had propounded, but Holmes had been schooled in the cruelties of fate during combat in America's Civil War. Such a fate might befall any thinker. For Holmes, this view did not preclude his own entitlement to change the future path of the law while the field of battle was his to influence.

Holmes and the Transformation of American Law and Judging

The introduction that Holmes wrote to a 1900 edition of *The Spirit of the Laws* evinces both his affinity with Montesquieu the lonely if transforming thinker, and his contempt for the details of his political science—a contempt not exactly bred by excessive familiarity.[8] While noting that the French philosopher had been a judge, Holmes says nothing about Montesquieu's conception of judicial power. Even Max Lerner, a Holmes disciple, remarks that "for all its fluid quality and its insight," the essay is "without political depth," and he notes the dissent registered by Holmes's friend Sir Frederick Pollock regarding its view of Montesquieu on separation of powers.[9] The essay gives much more space to *Persian Letters*, and to Holmes's own remarks on the fate of thinkers in the winds of time, than to *The Spirit of the Laws*, offering only a dismissive glance at the separation of powers and its influence on modern constitutionalism. Holmes characterizes Montesquieu's analysis of the English constitution, with its three separate powers, as "a fiction invented by him, a fiction which misled Blackstone and Delolme," and then rests content with a reference to the criticism of separation of powers by Walter Bagehot in *The English Constitution* (1867). Pollock's letter, written three decades later, defends Montesquieu, Blackstone, and the American founders on the grounds that the distribution of power between a bicameral Parliament and the Crown, as well as the status of the Cabinet, were fluid until the nineteenth century. Holmes curtly replies that "the little I ever knew" about "Montesquieu and the balance of political powers" is "pretty well forgotten"; thus, "I accept your remarks in respectful silence."[10]

This terseness may be a sign of advanced age and the passing of many years since the essay's writing, but it also may signal an extraordinary incongruity that characterized Holmes—that between his significant power to influence law and constitutionalism and his meager interest in and knowledge of actual politics.[11] Bowen's portrait of the young lawyer discovering Montesquieu thus would be astounding were it not a paraphrase of Holmes's conclusion to this later essay. After belittling Montesquieu in several ways, Holmes concludes that this classic work, outdated after a short time like all human thought, is valuable as a "precursor" to numerous reforms in law, politics, and philosophy: "There is not space even to point out how many seeds it sowed." *The Spirit of the Laws* was "a dazzling success at the moment, and since then probably has done as much to remodel the world as any product of the eighteenth century, which burned so many forests and sowed so many fields." All this, Holmes impresses upon the readers, stemmed from a "scholar sitting in a library," but, "[l]ike Descartes or Kant, he commanded the future . . . more than Napoleon" did.[12] If this does not in itself indicate ambition to be such a figure, Holmes's concluding remarks, describing the Preface to *The Spirit of the Laws* as "that immortal cheer to other lonely spirits," seems unmistakable. As if all this were not extraordinary enough for an introduction to a classic work—although, admittedly, Holmes had begun by calling *The Spirit of the Laws* "as dead as the classics"—he concludes by quoting at length from Montesquieu's close to his Preface. Holmes, with the Baron, can say, "I do not think that I have been wanting in genius."

At this time of his life Holmes was making a genre of such hubris. In a 1901 speech from his seat on the Massachusetts Supreme Judicial Court commemorating John Marshall's swearing in as chief justice of the U.S. Supreme Court, Holmes unequivocally if subtly announces his own clear superiority to Marshall as a jurist and thinker. After announcing that *The Federalist* represents a "finite" range of thinking, Holmes pronounced his "doubt whether, after Hamilton and the Constitution, Marshall's work proved more than a strong intellect, a good style, personal ascendancy in his court, courage, justice, and the convictions of his party." The tone suggests extraordinary condescension by a high-ranking judge toward those qualities of character, judgment, and prudence that, even after Holmes's corrosive realism had begun to leave its mark, still epitomized public service by common-law professionals in America. The sequel further belittles that tradition and Marshall by leaving him altogether, in order to define a new standard for American law and judging:

> My keenest interest is excited, not by what are called great questions
> and great cases, but by little decisions which the common run of selec-
> tors would pass by because they did not deal with the Constitution or

a telephone company, yet which have in them the germ of some wider theory, and therefore of some profound interstitial change in the very tissue of the law. The men whom I should be tempted to commemorate would be the originators of transforming thought. They often are half obscure, because what the world pays for is judgment, not the original mind.[13]

In these essays on famous predecessors Holmes mostly announces his own superiority. Montesquieu may represent the transforming thinker, but his ideas have spent their force. Marshall was a legal minion in the service of the real commanders of life's battlefield, the original thinkers. Holmes as an originator of transforming thought finds himself superior even to the Constitution, for great cases concern not the Constitution but changes in the interstices of American law that will undermine, or transform, or leave behind the document. If this radical jurisprudential view entailed that some day other lonely spirits and their original theories would supersede him in turn, then Holmes accepted this with the fatalism or existentialism that increasingly marked his writings throughout his life. His writings on and off the bench combine his father's poetic, Transcendentalist inclination with the "soldier's faith" of a Civil War officer wounded three times in the most brutal war fought by humankind to that time. This background produced a theoretical inclination toward Darwinian struggle and evolution, and an existentialist acceptance of a world defined by power and devoid of genuinely transcendent meaning.[14] This fatalism clearly informs some of his more famous opinions on the U.S. Supreme Court from 1903 to 1932, as well as his other speeches and writings of this period. His dissent in *Lochner v. New York* (1905) argues that the Constitution is "made for people of fundamentally differing views" and, having no substantive principles in itself, provides only an arena for the struggle of forces. His pioneering opinions in First Amendment free speech jurisprudence further argue that American law and constitutionalism should view all of human life, including ideas, as contending forces. This is most evident in his dissent in *Abrams v. U.S.* (1919), that men should realize that "time has upset many fighting faiths" and that the highest principle of our constitutionalism should be "free trade in ideas." His dissent in *Gitlow v. New York* (1925) argues that "every idea is an incitement" and that "the dominant forces of the community" must have their way.[15] This bleak, skeptical, but somewhat poetic and existentialist view also marks the perorations to such extra-judicial speeches and writings as "Law and the Court" (1913) and "Natural Law" (1918).[16]

Such skeptical views of law, morals, and politics hardly seem traceable to Montesquieu, who argues for natural right and the rule of law as the framework for his prudential remarks encouraging humane political reform. Still, Holmes's affinity to Montesquieu, expressed in his 1900 essay and in later years, does not rest on an entirely willful, implausible reading. There is no indication in that essay that Holmes perceived Montesquieu as a forerunner to his own judge-centered conception of modern law and politics. Still, it is interesting that Holmes and Laski agreed that these thoughts on Montesquieu were sufficiently important to warrant inclusion in the *Collected Legal Papers*, the first attempt to collect Holmes's legal writings.[17] His one thematic comment on Montesquieu's political science is telling, moreover, for suggesting the root similarity between his own legal realism and his predecessor's philosophy. He cites the definition of "the most perfect government" from the *Persian Letters*, that the "government most conformed to reason" and "most perfect" is one that "attains its goal with the least friction," and therefore "leads men along paths most agreeable to their interests and inclinations."[18] Holmes never refers here to the mature account of government in *The Spirit of the Laws*, and offers only a brief criticism of it later in the essay, thereby masking the repudiation of constitutionalism and separation of powers inherent in his skeptical realism. He does heartily endorse Montesquieu's remarks from the *Persian Letters*, even as he places his own imprint on them: "What have two hundred years added? What proximate test of excellence can be found except correspondence to the actual equilibrium of force in the community—that is, conformity to the wishes of the dominant power?" Perhaps Holmes is not unwarranted in admiring Montesquieu's liberal realism, even while rejecting his constitutionalism. The redefinition of natural right in the *Persian Letters* and *The Spirit of the Laws* in terms of natural affections and passionate, familial attachments does open itself to reductionist, morally skeptical lines of thought not originally intended. Similarly, an emphasis on individual tranquillity and security may have cleared the way for an individualism that undermines the very constitutionalism Montesquieu propounds.

Laski regularly mentioned Montesquieu in his correspondence with Holmes from 1916 to 1935, at one point suggesting that the person who edited Montesquieu "with an attempt to suggest contemporary applications would do a great work."[19] Apparently those applications would not include the adherence to a separation-of-powers constitutionalism and stable rule of law so evident in Montesquieu. Laski recounted to Holmes a dissertation on Montesquieu he examined, in which the candidate "made a great fuss about the separation of powers." Laski responded by reading an excerpt from Holmes's dissent in the *Jensen* case (1917): "I recognize without hesitation that judges do and must legislate, but they can do so only interstitially; the are confined from molar to molecular motions." The student replies that it is "the business of judges to preserve and not to betray the principles of the American constitution," but

Laski reports this in a mocking tone that implies Holmes, too, will find this defense of an older jurisprudence naive.[20] By regularly praising Montesquieu as a thinker, while disparaging the core of his constitutionalism, Holmes and his admirers suggest that only a suitably pruned Montesquieu was a forerunner to their own full-blown historicism and legal realism. Another episode in this strange relationship with Montesquieu arises through an essay by a founder of the sociological jurisprudence school. Eugen Ehrlich reports that in "a highly flattering letter Mr. Justice Holmes has suggested a criticism of my book on the sociology of law . . . in that he finds there no reference to Montesquieu."[21] Protesting at once his "reverence" for Montesquieu and his desire to "pay due honor to the illustrious American jurisconsult," Ehrlich states that The Spirit of the Laws was "the first attempt to fashion a sociology of law." Montesquieu had at least partially moved beyond "the law-of-nature school" to discern that "law depends on multifarious conditions and varies at once with these conditions." By reducing the law of nature to "the natural instincts of mankind"—to live in peace, to be sexual, to search for food, to be modest if a woman—he replaced the "ought" of natural law with the "is" of prevailing sociological conditions.[22] While Holmes's analysis of Montesquieu is not this sophisticated, the two essays share such a view. The elements of historicism and empiricism in Montesquieu's philosophy, coupled with his reductive account of natural right, expose him to being viewed as a forerunner to what these early-twentieth-century thinkers consider a mature, sophisticated, morally skeptical conception of law as an ever-changing bundle of historical forces.

Arguably, these legal realists exaggerate certain elements of Montesquieu's philosophy and ignore not only the seriousness of his concern for natural right but the seamlessness he saw between a stable constitutionalism and the protection of natural right. Nonetheless, contrary to Woodrow Wilson's repudiation of Montesquieu as the Muse of an outdated Constitution, these jurists consider him a precursor to their break from the traditional common-law jurisprudence of Hamilton and Marshall in favor of legal positivism and skepticism. However plausible this may be as an understanding of Montesquieu, one of its consequences is the transformation by legal realists of a subtle cloaking of power into an open argument for judicial legislating and, indeed, a judicializing of all law and politics. Holmes's jurisprudence itself clarifies this connection between legal realism and judicial activism.

Legal realism eschews any natural law or right reason at the core of law, and for Holmes, law is the posited will of the dominant forces of the community at a given moment. This legal and philosophical skepticism is the thread uniting his prolific work over more than a half-century, on the state and federal bench and in other writings.[23] His most famous essay, "The Path of the Law"

(1897), propounds such skepticism as the most scientific theory of law: "every word of moral significance [should] be banished from the law altogether," washed out by a "cynical acid," because "[i]f you want to know the law and nothing else, you must look at it as a bad man, who cares only for the material consequences which such knowledge enables him to predict."[24] One notorious judicial consequence of this jurisprudence is his opinion for the Court in *Buck v. Bell* (1927), upholding state legislation requiring the forced sterilization of "imbeciles." His belief in eugenics amplified the brutality of his *obiter dicta* and the holding, calling such acts "lesser sacrifices" reasonably demanded of "those who already sap the strength of the State," so as to "prevent our being swamped with incompetence." Over the silent dissent of only one justice, Holmes concluded: "Three generations of imbeciles are enough."[25] As early as 1881, in the opening to his influential book on the common law, he proposed a pragmatic, realistic liberation from traditional legal naïveté. Law is not about "logic" but "experience," since "the felt necessities of the time, the prevalent moral and political theories, intuitions of public policy, avowed or unconscious, even the prejudices which judges share with their fellow men" are more characteristic of law than "the syllogism." This entails that "the substance of the law at any given time pretty nearly corresponds . . . with what is then understood to be convenient," and only its "form and machinery" are dependent upon "its past."[26] He rejected the classical common-law understanding, embodied for America's founders in Coke's *Institutes* (1628), and even scorned the common-law liberalism of Blackstone's *Commentaries*. He also criticized the American version of Blackstone's jurisprudence and constitutionalism, inspired by Hamilton and Marshall, and digested for nineteenth-century lawyers by Kent's *Commentaries on American Law* and Story's *Commentaries on the Constitution*.[27] According to such common-law jurists as Coke, Kent, and Story, the judge, in settling specific disputes, discovers the law in particular cases in accord with positive law and with right reason as refined in maxims and precedents. There is need for judgment, or professional legal prudence, but such discovery is understood as essentially distinct from making new law. The more realistic, progressive conception declares this naive. Judges actually make new law, in large or small doses, case by case. Montesquieu and Blackstone mark a step toward this novel conception of judging, but for them judges still serve fundamental principles of natural right and separation of powers. They further maintain a distinctive judging function by emphasizing long-established precedent and traditional legal training. Holmes repudiates each of these distinguishing, limiting concepts, essentially fusing judging and legislating, juridical law and raw politics, constitutionalism and Darwinian struggle.

Holmes and such early students as Pound (*The Spirit of the Common Law,*

1921) and Cardozo (*The Nature of the Judicial Process*, 1921) were so effective in this transformation that today we cannot conceive of the common law as being anything other than "case law" and "judge-made law." This is the standard view presented by such works as Llewellyn's *The Common Law Tradition* (1960), Calabresi's *A Common Law for the Age of Statutes* (1982), and most discussions of common law today by judges, professors, and scholars. James Stoner argues for a rediscovery of the original American conception of law and judging by recognizing that classic common-law reasoning fundamentally defined the founders' constitutionalism. This jurisprudence allowed them to recognize the basic authority of a written constitution as a declaration of constitutionalist principles, and to assimilate the elements of liberal, Lockean theory therein. American jurists produced, through this synthesis, an American "common-law constitutionalism" distinct from both English common law and the liberal positivism of Hobbes and Locke.[28] A central element of that constitutionalism is the separation of powers, vesting parcels of legal authority in three branches while making the Constitution supreme above all; this is what marks such constitutionalism as "the rule of law." The proposal by Montesquieu and Blackstone for quiet judicial reform to achieve a law's liberal spirit does shift from Coke's classical conception of law and judging. Still, Holmes propounds a seismic shift beyond anything contemplated in the Montesquieuan tradition, forsaking both cloaking and moderation. The fate during the twentieth century of the separation of powers, a principle central to both Montesquieu's political science and our original constitutionalism, confirms this break. Holmes's pronouncement of a new path for the law encapsulates a transformed understanding of constitutional, statutory, and common law: "The prophecies of what *the courts* will do in fact, and nothing more pretentious, are what I mean by the law."[29]

The increasing dominance of Holmesean skepticism defines the revolution in twentieth-century American law, avowedly or unknowingly defining nearly all schools, left, right, or center, with the exception of the minority of natural-law jurists.[30] This is evident in the quandaries regarding constitutional law and interpretation that increasingly have defined the Supreme Court, from federalism to religion, separation of powers to freedom of speech, commerce to due process. This is the case perhaps in no area of constitutional law more emphatically than the Court's right of privacy doctrine and jurisprudence of abortion.

Holmes, *Casey,* and the Jurisprudence of Individualism

For some theorists of liberalism and law, the extraordinary power of American judges is part of their enlightened, statesmanlike role consistent with the American vision of individual liberty and equality. If we did not permit judges this expansive role in interpreting statutes and the Constitution, then how would we ensure that every individual had his day in court? What recourse for protection of rights would individuals and political minorities have against the majority tyranny occasionally perpetrated by legislatures or executives? To others, this amounts to government by an imperial judiciary: an abusive broadening of constitutional powers and a violation of the principle of democratic consent. How can the law remain a neutral framework for political competition if unelected judges think they can make better policy judgments than elected officials and others with practical experience? How can it be legitimate for the referee to violate the separation of powers, join one of the partisan sides of an issue, and change the meaning of the basic rules of the game found in the Constitution?[31] This debate, dominant in late-twentieth-century constitutional law scholarship, is itself one legacy of Holmes's transformation of American law. In essence it is a dispute between two branches of Holmesean pragmatism over the discretion to be exercised in judicial review and constitutional interpretation. Those "original intention" and "judicial restraint" advocates who descend from Holmes—many, but not all—argue that skepticism about the moral or rational status of law is grounds for judicial restraint and deference to the majority will. Such a binding will is found in the original constitutional text or in statutes of a democratic legislature, and judges are competent only to discern that will, not to evaluate its justice. The "living Constitution" branch argues that skepticism about nature and reason reveals the time-bound, historicist character of law, but that this requires judges to discern the majority will of today, or what the majority should believe as it evolves toward the most recent notions of human dignity. Judges, therefore, must bring constitution and statute up to date by calling legislative majorities to live by a vision of what these laws mean today.

The fact that both schools largely stem from Holmes is evident in *Roe v. Wade* (1973) itself, in which a majority of the Court ruled for the first time that the Constitution included a right to abort a human fetus largely free of legal restrictions. One of the first justifications Justice Blackmun's Court opinion provides for this novel constitutional right is a citation to Holmes's argument in *Lochner* that the Constitution "is made for people of fundamentally differing views." However, Justice Rehnquist's dissent then claims that Holmes would support judicial deference toward the law banning abortion, since his *Lochner* opinion was a dissent from the Court's use of substantive due process reasoning to invalidate a labor law.[32] This paradoxical situation paved the way for a similar confusion evident in *Roe*'s most important progeny, the Court's abortion ruling in *Planned Parenthood v. Casey* (1992). As noted, such leading American lawyers as Anthony Kronman and Mary Ann Glendon recently have argued that the "failing ideals" of, or "crisis" in, America's legal profession is evidenced in the loss of the legal spirit and character that Tocqueville praised.[33] Each compares Tocqueville's conception of ennobling, prudential judging with the *Casey* decision, which upheld *Roe* while substantially revising the rationale for, and permissible regulations about, legalized abortion.[34] Kronman praises the plurality opinion in *Casey* for its "judicious search for a middle course and wise balancing of principle and precedent," suggesting a kinship between Tocqueville's jurisprudence and the living Constitution school. Glendon, in contrast, depicts the *Casey* plurality's "grandiose pretensions of judicial authority" as another case of legal professionals "shedding the habits and restraints that once made the bench and the bar pillars of the democratic experiment." This disagreement by leading scholars over how their chosen exemplar of legal prudence would rate today's judges provides, so to speak, probable cause for further proceedings.

Since Tocqueville's ideas of judicial statesmanship fundamentally accord with the jurisprudence of Hamilton and Marshall, both of the views represented in *Casey* in fact owe more to the revolutionary conceptions of law and judging espoused by Holmes than to the founding ideas of American law. While the *Casey* majority is properly alert to perpetuating the rule of law, their historicist, pragmatic reasoning undermines that very law. On the other hand, while Justice Scalia properly criticizes the *Casey* majority's departures from text and tradition, his legal skepticism and consequent deference to legislative majorities undermine any such traditional authority, including the grounds for judicial independence and judicial review.[35] The defects of these main voices in our contentious jurisprudence of individual autonomy, and the consequent narrowness of our debate over constitutional interpretation, stem from the change in American law and jurisprudence achieved by Holmes. Sketching these links between *Casey*, Holmes, and Tocqueville explains why, as some leading lawyers suggest, Tocqueville provides a judgment lacking in recent debates over judicial review—and further, why a philosophic argument for traditional jurisprudence should be pursued.

When *Planned Parenthood v. Casey* was decided in 1992, the previous three abortion cases had produced no Court opinion, and the complex *Casey* decision—five opinions, at over 80 pages in the *Supreme Court Reporter*—did not resolve the Court's debate.[36] *Casey* split the Court into three blocs on two main constitutional issues, the status of Pennsylvania's five abortion regulations and of *Roe* itself. The Court upheld *Roe* by a vote of five to four but upheld four of the five regulations by a larger margin. A "joint opinion" by three justices revised *Roe* by at once narrowing its holding, thus upholding four of the regulations, while reformulating and even expanding its constitutional foundation. This dual revision achieved by Justices O'Connor, Kennedy, and Souter is at points a Court opinion and at others not even a plurality opinion. By preserving "the essential holding" of *Roe* while discarding such parts as its trimester analysis of the competing constitutional rights involved in pregnancy, the joint opinion held a middle ground between four justices who would overrule *Roe* and two who would leave it unchanged.[37] In this confusing manner the *Casey* decision continued the debate over constitutional interpretation, in the courts and beyond, that was rekindled by the announcement in *Griswold v. Connecticut* (1965) of a right of privacy, and further fueled by its extension in *Roe*.

   Casey also stirred up the issue of judicial statesmanship, since a prominent section of the joint opinion finds five justices agreeing that a defense of *Roe* turns upon the role of *stare decisis* in judicial review and upon the Court's role in our constitutional order. Adherence to precedent is deemed essential to the Court's authority, and overruling *Roe* would "seriously weaken the Court's capacity to exercise the judicial power and to function as the Supreme Court of a Nation dedicated to the rule of law."[38] *Roe* is one of the "rare" cases when "the Court's interpretation of the Constitution calls the contending sides of a national controversy to end their national division by accepting a common mandate rooted in the Constitution." Having "staked its authority" in such a "watershed decision," overturning it would do "profound and unnecessary damage to the Court's legitimacy" and to "the Nation's commitment to the rule of law."[39] Legitimacy, defined as "a product of substance and perception that shows itself in the people's acceptance of the Judiciary as fit to determine what the Nation's law means and to declare what it demands," is said to be "the source of this Court's authority." This discussion of the rule of law shifts the argument from a strictly legal to a more political terrain, a reading confirmed by the opinion's insistence that "[t]he Court's concern with legitimacy is not for the sake of the Court but for the sake of the Nation to which it is responsible."[40] The opinion reassures those who might disagree with a watershed decision such as *Brown v. Board of Education* (1954) or *Roe* but "nevertheless struggle to accept it, because they respect the rule of law." The justices declare that "[t]o all those who will be so tested by following, the Court implicitly undertakes to remain steadfast."[41] This discourse on *stare decisis* and legitimacy concludes by affirming what it sees as the Court's role in shaping the character of our constitutional order:

> Like the character of an individual, the legitimacy of the Court must
> be earned over time. So, indeed, must be the character of a Nation
> of people who aspire to live according to the rule of law. Their belief
> in themselves as such a people is not readily separable from their un-
> derstanding of the Court invested with the authority to decide their
> constitutional cases and speak before all others for their constitutional

ideals. If the Court's legitimacy should be undermined, then, so would the country be in its very ability to see itself through its constitutional ideals.[42]

This conception of legitimacy, shorn of its Holmesean, inspirational prose, looks to immediate efficacy more than enduring substance. As a version of philosophic pragmatism, it emphasizes evolving meanings in contrast to fixed principles, discerning what works in a given, near-term situation in lieu of abiding rules and principles. This dimension to the opinion was anticipated by a prominent law review essay which argued that "departure from precedent may sometimes threaten the stability and continuity of the political order and should therefore be avoided: *Roe* provides a ready example."[43] The root of such pragmatism is a skepticism about reason, morals, and law that departs from both the liberal philosophy and classical common law informing the original notions of legitimacy and stability in American constitutionalism. The joint opinion endorses an expansive conception of liberty but pragmatically admits to "the reservations any of us may have in reaffirming the central holding of *Roe*." The issue is not "whether each of us, had we been Members of the Court" when abortion came before it "as an original matter, would have concluded, as the *Roe* Court did." *Roe* can be at once defended and substantially revised simply because "there is a limit to the amount of error that can plausibly be imputed to prior courts."[44] Locke and Montesquieu emphasize individual security and political stability but secure these through a constitutional separation among the powers that make and administer a fixed law, not by the supremacy of an ever-changing, judge-made constitution. Montesquieu, arguably the source of an independent, prominent judicial power in liberalism and an advocate of individual tranquillity, argued that, in republics, "judgments should be fixed to such a degree that they are never anything but a precise text of the law." Only then could all know what the law required. If his notion of a subtle judicializing of politics suggests more discretion than strictly republican judging allows, it nonetheless works by gradual change according to the spirit evident in a law, and within a constitution defined by separation of powers and natural right.[45] For the architects of liberal constitutionalism, this new conception of a sovereign judiciary, ever updating the constitution, could not secure a stable, just political order.

The pragmatism and judicial legislating evident in the *Casey* plurality also depart from the very common-law tradition that yields the maxim *stare decisis et non quieta movere*. Common-law reasoning, as understood by such classical expositors as Fortescue, Saint Germain, and Coke, works from precedent cases and maxims with a judgment informed by both particulars and generalities.

Coke defined this judgment as a "perfection of reason gotten by long studie, observation and experience," and "fined and refined by an infinite number of grave and learned men."[46] For Coke, as for Aristotle, refining our understanding of an enduring natural right does not entail the historicist notion that all ideas are radically time-bound.[47] This traditional view informed the framing of America's constitutionalism and was prominent throughout the nineteenth century, but was effectively erased by Holmes, Pollock, Pound, and their pupils. Legal realism largely succeeded in reducing common law to a conception of case law and judge-made law compatible with its legal skepticism. By its departure, however, from both liberal political philosophy and classic common law, not to mention from the natural-rights principles and self-evident truths of the Declaration, the joint opinion's skeptical account of legitimacy places in question the very meaning of constitutionalism, precedent, and the rule of law.

Related to these theoretical difficulties are the practical problems posed regarding a noble lie about legitimacy which, given its focus on short-term stability and security, has little nobility to recommend it to the governed, and struggles to conceal its departure from the genuine legitimacy of legal text and tradition. The original conception of judging in the supposedly outdated constitutionalism was grounded in principles of natural rights, popular consent, separation of powers, and the common-law tradition. The repudiation of most of these principles by historicist visions of progress still leaves unelected judges confronting popular consent, as captured in Alexander Bickel's formulation of the "countermajoritarian difficulty." Further, with judges having no common page from which to read, it is no surprise that efforts to supplant text and legal tradition yield increasingly long and fractured decisions. The *Casey* joint opinion sought to give a right to abortion a firmer textual basis and wider foundation in constitutional law by removing it from the shadowy realm of the right of privacy, a right grounded by the *Griswold* decision only in the "penumbras" of various textual guarantees of rights. The right to abort now is said to be part of the "liberty" protected by the "substantive" dimensions of the due process clauses in the Fifth and Fourteenth Amendments.[48] This stretches the conceivable boundaries of "liberty," and of whatever legal process or substance might be due, in violation of state common law and statutes, just as *Roe* had done before it. It is not surprising that it is harder to find agreement among a majority of justices as to the precise contours of this evolved meaning of the text. Adjudicative principles, or tests like *Casey's* "no undue burden" on the right of abortion, control such cases without having the support of a current Court majority, not to mention support of tradition, precedent, evidently sound reasoning, or the plain meaning of the text.

Justice Scalia's dissent, alert to such difficulties, rejects the joint opinion's

reasoning on *stare decisis* and quotes it to caricature its conception of a statesmanlike role for the Court:

> The Imperial Judiciary lives. It is instructive to compare this Nietz-
> schean vision of us unelected, life-tenured judges—leading a Volk
> who will be "tested by following," and whose very "belief in them-
> selves" is mystically bound up in their "understanding" of a Court
> that "speak[s] before all others for their constitutional ideals"—with
> the somewhat more modest role envisioned for these lawyers by the
> Founders [or] with the more democratic views of a more humble
> man. [49]

Scalia quotes Hamilton's statement from *Federalist* no. 78 that the judiciary has
"neither FORCE nor WILL but merely judgment." He also cites Lincoln's warning,
in opposing *Dred Scott* (1857), that "if the policy of the Government upon vital
questions affecting the whole people is to be irrevocably fixed by decisions of
the Supreme Court . . . the people will have ceased to be their own rulers." [50]
The plurality or majority reasoning about a constitutional right to abort thus
conceals "raw judicial policy choices" and is based not upon law but upon
"philosophical predilection and moral intuition." [51] Moreover, Scalia compares
the joint opinion's reasoning on the role of the Court with Chief Justice Taney's
decision on slavery in *Dred Scott*: "I expect that . . . [Taney], too, had thought
himself 'call[ing] the contending sides of a national controversy to end their national division by accepting a common mandate rooted in the Constitution.'" [52]
These and similar criticisms are sound to the extent that the fundamental error of the *Casey* majority is its departure from legal text and tradition in favor
of evolved meanings. If, however, Scalia adheres to such traditional legal authorities simply from a democratic skepticism about any others, then the difficulty arises that such skepticism about reason and law would apply to such old
sources themselves. The old understandings of truths and rights, so conceived,
would fail to supply a properly constitutional response to the historicist claim
that, to use Jefferson's phrase, the earth belongs to the living. [53] The skepticism
and moral relativism implicit in Scalia's repeated distinction between "legal"
judgments and "value judgments" places him more in the company of Justice
Holmes than of Hamilton or Chief Justice Marshall. [54]

James Stoner argues that the fracture between the *Casey* majority and dissenters stems from "a severing of two elements that once were united in the
classic form of common-law adjudication." On the one hand lies the principle
of "development of law from precedent to precedent in the name of reason,"
and on the other "the anchoring of law in custom and tradition freely attested

and consented to."[55] The severing of reason from tradition, of the rational use of precedent from the customary character of the law, explains why the *Casey* plurality has failed in its aim to "cal[l] the contending sides of a national controversy to end their national division by accepting a common mandate rooted in the Constitution."[56] A historicist notion of judicial statesmanship prescribes an isolated, autonomous individual, while the positivist alternative lacks the deeper reasoning needed to counter the pragmatic individualism of the living Constitution school. While the Court claims to revise *Roe*, the conflicting citations to Holmes by both the opposing sides in *Roe* still define the problematic debate in *Casey*. The living Constitution view informs the justices who endorsed the joint opinion and upheld a revised *Roe*, while the view of judicial deference to a positivistic original intent and democratic majorities informs those who would have overturned *Roe*. Each side follows Holmes in departing from the constitutionalism and jurisprudence shared by the founders and Tocqueville.

The Holmesean element in the *Casey* joint opinion is most evident in the very mixture of pragmatism and rationalism that Tocqueville hoped judges would resist. This produces the opinion's defining contradiction. Its pragmatic pole defends *Roe* only for the sake of legal stability, while its rationalist pole offers a sweeping definition of the liberty inherent in the due process clauses. The opinion cites several precedents that afford "constitutional protection to personal decisions relating to marriage, procreation, contraception, family relationships, child rearing, education." It then draws from these, however, the most abstract principle possible:

> These matters, involving the most intimate and personal choices a person may make in a lifetime, choices central to personal dignity and autonomy, are central to the liberty protected by the Fourteenth Amendment. At the heart of liberty is the right to define one's own concept of existence, of meaning, of the universe, and of the mystery of human life. Beliefs about these matters could not define the attributes of personhood were they formed under compulsion of the State.[57]

This jurisprudence is abstract in two senses, both of which are antithetical to classical common-law reasoning and to any but the most recent, novel developments in American jurisprudence. Notions of "personal dignity and autonomy" as defining "personhood" reflect the neo-Kantian moral theory and analytical liberalism of John Rawls and his school.[58] Consistent with this abstract moral theory, the justices replace the severe, traditional morality that Kant postulated as necessary for autonomy of the will—thus true moral freedom—with the libertarian version offered by John Stuart Mill in *On Liberty* (1859).[59] Justice Scalia asks, of course, what basis in any legal text and tradition, apart from judicial legislating, exists for this atomistic view of the liberty protected by due process. How, if this is what the Constitution commands, can there continue to be any state regulation of "homosexual sodomy, polygamy, adult incest, and suicide," as well as numerous other actions—for, since they occur among consenting adults, they would not violate Mill's "harm" principle.[60] Moreover, this abstract "self" cut off from the complex reality of political life—from nature, family, community, and legal and moral tradition—is theorized as free to engage in the paradoxical act of self-creation *ex nihilo*. In fact, experience tends to confirm Tocqueville's prescient concern that this lonely self is likely to be all the more dependent upon the shifting opinions of mass society and upon government.[61]

The joint opinion's reasoning is also abstract, legislative, and not properly judicial in drawing a strikingly general rule from a precedent only by ignoring the reasoning and facts of the prior case. This is evident in the contradiction between the opinion's reasoning and that of the case it identifies as the root of the modern right of privacy and substantive due process precedents. The opinion quotes three times from Justice Harlan's dissent in the contraception case *Poe v. Ullman* (1961), which became the basis for the Court's announcement of a constitutional right of privacy in *Griswold*. The *Casey* plurality quotes Harlan's argument that in such cases judges must be guided by "the traditions" of the nation and "restraint." However, it omits his specific argument that the need for judicial balancing of "the liberty of the individual" and "the demands of organized society" should not simply negate state laws regarding the "moral welfare of its citizenry."[62] Harlan does mix Holmesean pragmatism and activism with this defense of tradition, since his concern for marital and family privacy arises in a case in which no couple had proper legal standing, and his endorsement of tradition is hardly unequivocal. Nonetheless, the *Casey* opinion displays a degree of Millian abstraction from the moral concerns of communities and from traditional legal understanding that is sharply opposed to Harlan's reasoning:

> It is in this area of sexual morality, which contains many proscriptions
> of consensual behavior having little or no direct impact on others,
> that the State of Connecticut has expressed its moral judgment. . . .
> Certainly, Connecticut's judgment is no more demonstrably correct
> or incorrect than are the varieties of judgment, expressed in law, on
> marriage and divorce, on adult consensual homosexuality, abortion,
> and sterilization, or euthanasia and suicide . . . [t]he very controversial
> nature of these questions would, I think, require us to hesitate long

before concluding that the Constitution precluded Connecticut from choosing as it has among these various views.[63]

The joint opinion's abstraction from the facts and reasoning of Harlan's *Poe* dissent, finding in it an evolving, individualistic conception of liberty, brings to mind Bertrand Russell's insight that pragmatism "is like a warm bath that heats up so imperceptibly that you don't know when to scream."[64] It is fitting that such reasoning would defend but revise *Roe*, since a pragmatic evolution of legal reasoning, in the service of a near-term policy goal, produced that decision itself. The *Roe* Court opinion cites a then recent contraceptive case, *Eisenstadt v. Baird* (1972), in which Justice Brennan transformed the marital right of privacy discovered by the Court in *Griswold*. In *Eisenstadt*, it became "the right of the *individual*, married or single, to be free from unwarranted governmental intrusion into matters so fundamentally affecting a person as the decision whether to bear or beget a child."[65] Brennan's complete abstraction from the marital context of the *Griswold* reasoning and from the common-law tradition of family law was achieved by a novel use of the equal protection clause to deconstruct marriage in the eyes of the Constitution. For Brennan, "the marital couple is not an independent entity with a mind and heart of its own, but an association of two individuals each with a separate individual makeup."[66] The jurisprudence of individualism, from *Eisenstadt* to *Casey*, elevates autonomy as the defining essence of constitutionally protected liberty. This isolated individual is judicially decreed through twin modes of abstraction—a rationalism that ignores the moral requirements and complex realities of political communities, and a distorting abstraction from legal and moral precedent in the name of progress. The Court now mandates the moral result Tocqueville thought it would counteract, by the jurisprudential means he thought it would reject.

The legal positivism of Justice Scalia's dissent, however, makes it an inadequate alternative. Here and in other opinions Scalia states that questions of "values" not directly addressed by the Constitution should be left to democratic majorities, since no answer to them is more rational than another. In one case he refers to "value judgments" that are "neither set forth in the Constitution nor known to the Justices of this Court any better than they are known to nine people picked at random from the Kansas City telephone directory."[67] Such skepticism undermines the notion of tradition to which he appeals, for if there is no rational basis for, no truth to, the "value judgments" embodied in the Constitution and laws, and if democratic majorities should decide such questions, why should dead majorities rule living ones? Why should there be an independent judiciary with the discretionary legal judgment inherent in judicial review? Scalia is correct that in our constitutionalism many questions have been left to the legislative and executive powers. For the classic common-law jurist, however, a court need be neither a philosophy seminar nor a usurper of legislative power for judges to exercise a distinctively legal judgment that justifies their black robes and life tenure in a republican regime.

The common-law constitutionalism of Hamilton and Tocqueville seems a necessary supplement to Justice Scalia's positivist judicial restraint, as well as a necessary corrective to the historicism of the *Casey* majority. Such jurisprudential resources reveal, for example, that neither of the current Holmesean conceptions justifies judicial review. The framers discovered this power not in the literal text of the Constitution but in, as Hamilton argued, "the nature and reason of the thing." Neither contemporary school could endorse Hamilton's further conception that "the integrity and moderation of the judiciary" benefits "the character of our governments" more than most will realize.[68] He was concerned to avoid, nonetheless, "an arbitrary discretion in the courts," a view echoed in Tocqueville's critique of French judges who indulged the most abstract rationalisms. Such common-law judicial statesmanship is closer to the original intention of the framers than is a skeptical majoritarianism. A further similarity to the founders arises from Tocqueville's awareness that it is "an astonishing thing what authority is accorded to the intervention of courts by the general opinion of mankind" and that this constitutes "a moral force in which tribunals are clothed."[69] Justice Scalia's opinions occasionally evince sympathy for tradition and the classic common law, but his predominant legal positivism cannot fully explain why judges should be restrained and defer to legislators, or why the rule of law is to be perpetuated. Such principles require judges, or at least leading judges, to adopt the perspective of the constitutional statesman, not the legal clerk. Both Hamilton and Tocqueville sought to check arbitrary judicial discretion, but neither took the path of skepticism to do so.

Beyond Holmesean Judicial Power?

The fundamental difficulty of the Holmesean view of judging is that, since every constitution must intend its own stability and perpetuation, it requires judges who, even if properly termed oracles, serve in that capacity as depositories of enduring legal principles and practices. The radical skepticism of American legal realism and pragmatism raises serious doubts about the continued viability or perpetuation of such a shifting, unanchored legal and political order. If law has no anchor in a claim to justice beyond the idiosyncratic moral intuitions of a given academic or judge, and no anchor in certain enduring rules and practices, what makes it law? Why obey judges who see themselves as legislators, transformers, imaginative oracles of some vision of the future path of the law?

The desire to mold law according to our fundamental passions and interests, so as to achieve our tranquillity and security—or, in Holmes's brutal world, the domination of our forces over competing forces—ultimately undermines the forms and principles required for the maintenance of any law at all. The fact that the legal realism that largely defines American jurisprudence is in this way so unrealistic produces troubling consequences for our law and politics. While the broad comparison of Hamilton, Tocqueville, Holmes, and *Casey* attempted here is by no means exhaustive, I hope it is at least provocative.

As noted, one great problem facing American constitutional jurisprudence today is the contradiction inherent in a legal positivism that encompasses rival strains of Holmesean realism, evident in the fact that neither school can justify the power of judicial review.[70] Tocqueville praises our constitutionalism as "simpler and more rational" than that of either England or France because it makes the constitution "a work apart," a law above law, precisely through judicial review of legislation for conformity with the constitution (*Democracy*, 1.1.6). He also understands, however, that to maintain such a law above law requires a special function from—and thus a special character or spirit in—the judicial power, as guardians and servants of the Constitution and its fundamental principles. Our now characteristic American inability to justify undemocratic institutions such as the Court, or the Senate, or the presidency unless they are transformed into tribunes of the people is not unrelated to the individualism that finds no mystery or sanctity in human life, no fixed or elevated meaning to law. The common root is a modern skepticism leading us to eschew any meaning or order in nature independent of the human will, any reality to the traditional distinctions regarding what is higher or virtuous in human life. The consequences of our liberation from even searching for natural standards of human good were anticipated by Tocqueville and are abundantly evident. We mask our condition with a democratic moralism that urges upon us the seemingly high-minded goals of liberating individual choices, individual dignity, fairness, and toleration from any traditional moral or political restraints. Tocqueville saw such thinking in germ, and exhorted the legal profession and all citizens to appreciate the usefulness of the blend of natural rights and a traditional legal prudence in America's common-law spirit for counteracting the slide toward modern nihilism and individualism. Whether the legal profession can restore an Aristotelian element to temper the current blend of Hobbesian skepticism and egalitarian liberation, by recovering a common-law appreciation for both enduring precedent and the relation of law to morals, is an important question. Efforts to rediscover a classic common-law jurisprudence will reveal the principled complexity of the founders' jurisprudence, balancing concern for the natural rights of individuals with larger political and moral aims, and balancing the separation of powers and the consent of the governed with the benefits of principled, moderate judging.[71]

Examining Holmesean realism in light of the liberalized common law of the founders and Tocqueville also exposes the supposed neutrality of recent liberal theory. Rawlsian liberals and various kinds of communitarians have debated whether an expansive conception of individual liberty or autonomy actually keeps the government neutral as to value judgments. The classic common-law perspective reminds us that all laws educate about substantive moral judgments in some fashion or other. The Supreme Court certainly has pronounced since *Roe* when human life begins, even while explicitly disavowing that role, giving rise to what some call an "abortion culture."[72] Across the academic and political spectrum in recent decades one could hear concerns about "defining deviancy down," "bowling alone," and "democracy's discontent," about the need for a "politics of meaning" or "habits of the heart," for "personal responsibility" or "family values." Only recently, however, have these widely noted problems been traced to our systemic legal positivism and the individualism it enforces.[73] The fact that Americans, like any people, are concerned with the deeper meanings of human life and politics, and not simply relativist "values," makes the skepticism of legal realism not very convincing. This universal human concern with moral meaning is what makes much originalist argument about judicial restraint a hollow opponent to the more inspirational rhetoric of historicist judicial discretion, epitomized by the opinions of Justice Brennan and the writings of Ronald Dworkin. Many in the bar and bench have accepted Holmes's scorn for any effort at discerning enduring, natural truths in law and constitutionalism. The moral aspiration still evident in American jurisprudence mostly finds voice in the call for equal dignity and a progressive vision of what the individual rights in the Constitution can mean for today. The *Casey* plurality opinion epitomizes the theoretical and practical problems with such a conception of constitution, law, and judging, suggesting the need to examine sounder alternatives.

As for the Hamiltonian, Tocquevillean alternative, this broad-brush comparison of different schools of constitutional jurisprudence raises the obvious question of what a common-law statesman might do today regarding our contentious right-of-privacy cases. Hamilton or Tocqueville might advise that the distinction between judicial statesmanship and judicial legislating particularly applies to these moral issues. Judicial promotion of individual autonomy has forbidden communities from doing what even Justice Harlan recognized they have always done: regulating and educating on matters of sexuality, marriage, and the family. Statesmanlike discretion, informed by the Constitution's letter and spirit, would promote the community's concern for such issues in a way that fosters deliberation and a comprehensive public policy. Our constitutionalism long has recognized the relationship of law and mores, but now tries to enforce the new morality that claims they can be divided. One statement on the traditional relationship, from which Holmes dissented, is made in *Meyer v. Nebraska* (1923), in which the Court found the liberty protected by due process to encompass unenumerated rights regarding business, education, marriage, family and children, and worship of God. They defined these liberties as "rights long freely enjoyed" and "privileges long recognized at common law as essential to the orderly pursuit of happiness by free men."[74] In *Snyder v. Massachusetts* (1934), the Court stated that the benchmark for discerning a constitutional right was to be "a principle of justice so rooted in the traditions and conscience of our people as to be ranked as fundamental," appealing to the principles of the Declaration and the judicial prudence of the common law. Such judgments were replaced by the kind of abstract "rationalizing principle" fashioned by Justice Cardozo, a disciple of Holmes, in *Palko v. Connecticut* (1937), who defined a constitutional right as involving "the very essence of ordered liberty" and a "fair and enlightened system of justice."[75]

Both Montesquieuan jurisprudence and the classic common-law spirit offer grounds for criticizing Holmesean realism, since it poses grave obstacles to perpetuating the rule of law in a sound constitutional order. These fundamental aims suffer amid a judicialized politics that fosters instability in constitutional law, amid the partisanship in both law and politics bred by that instability, and amid a skeptical individualism that provides, in fact, one of the few fixed goals in the Holmesean legal landscape. If Blackstone's metaphor for law was a country to be mapped or a castle to be maintained, then Holmes gives us a meandering path with few fixed destinations and low horizons. After a century of this novel conception of constitutionalism and judicial power, we have gained enough distance to take a look at where it has brought us and to be pragmatic about our pragmatism. Such examination also suggests, however, that the origins of this unfortunate path partly lie in dimensions of the Montesquieuan project itself, which in turn recommends renewed inquiry into other resources available in our jurisprudential tradition.

Conclusion

The Cloaking of Power and the
Perpetuation of Constitutionalism

Our judicialized liberalism raises large questions about the views of politics, law, and rights favored by the original, Montesquieuan project for cloaking power and ultimately by the legislative judiciary of Holmesean legal realism. If nobler conceptions of humanity and law fail to moderate its emphasis upon individual security, Montesquieuan jurisprudence is vulnerable to a legal skepticism that eschews all enduring legal principle, including the separation of powers and natural rights. Does Montesquieu's project to subtly judicialize politics inevitably harm the judiciary and constitutionalism, as well as the individuals these institutions sought to protect, or do later thoughts and deeds depart from the plan unnecessarily? At stake is the perpetuation of such a judicialized constitutionalism, and perhaps of modern liberal constitutionalism itself. The judicial statesmanship of Hamilton and Tocqueville achieves a sounder, more principled moderation of power by blending the liberal constitutionalism of Montesquieu and Blackstone with a more traditional jurisprudence. The classic common-law spirit corrects the skeptical, atomistic tendency in liberal jurisprudence, while being open to a liberal concern with individual liberty and toleration. Moreover, because the minds of traditionally trained jurists achieve this synthesis, free of rationalist abstraction or moral skepticism, its theoretical and practical tensions are surmountable.

The predominant view in American law and academia, however, sees no such problems in our constitutionalism and thus has little regard for such remedies. From the starkness and brutality of Holmes's legal realism came milder versions of his revolutionary doctrine, so that by the middle of the twentieth century, ideas about legal pragmatism, the indeterminacy of meaning, and judicial legislating were becoming commonplace. After the initial ruling in *Brown v. Board of Education* (1954), Robert Dahl argued in 1958 that, empirically, the Supreme Court makes national policy just as the Congress and president do. Its case procedure and legal reasoning obscure the fact that "the policy views dominant on the Court are never for long out of line with the policy views dominant among the lawmaking majorities of the United States."[1] John Rawls's theoretical formulation of judicialized liberalism, in which the Supreme Court embodies public reason itself, is in this sense indebted to Holmes, Dahl, and other realists in law and political science. Rawls elevates philosopher-judges above the Constitution because he elevates an evolving consensus over enduring right and principle. The highest court in a liberal democracy epitomizes public reasoning about "the good of the public and matters of fundamental justice," as informed by "the ideals and principles expressed by society's conception of political justice." Breaking from his philosophy in *A Theory of Justice* (1971), Rawls claims now that only liberal reason, not reason simply, is the ground for justice as fairness: "[A] plurality of reasonable yet incompatible comprehensive doctrines is the normal result of the exercise of human reason within the framework of the free institutions of a constitutional democratic regime." A supreme court is the "institutional exemplar" of such tolerant, pluralistic reasoning.[2] For Rawls, as for Ronald Dworkin, judges must do more than adjudicate particular cases according to a largely settled law; thus, the rights they secure are more than the traditional protections from political and civil threats to life, political liberty, and private property.

A range of contemporary political theorists has challenged this reconception of liberalism, warning about a judicialized politics that reduces any higher civic and moral aims to litigious disputes about individual claims and entitlements.[3] Michael Sandel argues that in the twentieth century American judicial power, under the guise of securing rights, effectively instructed individuals to reject the duties and principles imposed by representative political communities and their richer conceptions of politics. "More explicitly than any other institution, the [modern] Supreme Court presides over the priority of right" at the expense of notions of the good life or the common good, by defining these rights "in a way that does not presuppose any particular conception of the good life." The Court "has come to view the Constitution as a neutral framework of rights within which persons can pursue their own ends, consistent with a similar

liberty for others," and it "increasingly interprets the requirement of neutrality as expressing or advancing a conception of persons as free and independent
selves."[4] Only recently have civic republican or communitarian concerns about
the decline of liberal democracy singled out the modern judiciary as a prime
cause of the ills so diagnosed. Sandel in particular argues that this jurisprudence
of individualism and autonomy breaks with both the constitutionalism of the
American founders and the liberal tradition as a whole.[5]

   Sandel does not clarify, however, that his criticisms only have weight if they
presuppose not just any "conception of the human good" but one justified as
the proper development of our nature, in terms of that state of soul necessary
for citizens of a self-governing republic; otherwise, they mirror the groundless
coherentism they would criticize. This dilemma points to the Aristotelian argument that human beings must be members of a political, moral community if
they are to lead a good life. Liberal individualism and skepticism about natural
right have cooperated in recent centuries to eschew such traditional moral realism about human nature and the good, undermining any fuller, higher formulations of the means and ends for liberal politics. Jurists from Ronald Dworkin to
Michael Moore and John Finnis have sought to restore moral principle or moral
realism to recent jurisprudence, but like Sandel, few will venture to reestablish
a genuine moral realism rooted in the reality of nature. Various degrees of debt
to Cartesian skepticism produce efforts at moral realism rooted merely in epistemological constructs of varying sorts; few jurists today refer to the principles
and language of Coke, Hamilton, or Tocqueville. The modest suggestion of this
book's inquiry into modern constitutionalism is that our jurisprudence would
do well to guide its theorizing by something other than the extremes of near-
term pragmatism and abstract epistemology. A more balanced, comprehensive
jurisprudence would temper these elements of law with concern for the institutional realities of regimes and real political communities, especially the requirements of separation of powers and legal stability propounded by the founders
of modern judicial power.[6] If the rule of law, as implemented by independent
courts and a professional bar, is to moderate the brute force of political conflict,
then it must strive to be a fair, neutral arbiter. Such legitimacy rests upon the
efforts of judges and lawyers to abide by, not invent anew, the fundamental
principles of law. The leading philosophers of law in the Western tradition,
from Plato and Aristotle to at least Montesquieu and Tocqueville, weighed the
magnitude of these requirements and determined that the very notion of law
rests upon a conception of natural right or natural law. The many skeptics and
sophists who have always dissented from these efforts cannot be given credit
for the civilizing achievements of constitutionalism, the rule of law, a legal profession, and independent courts, all in service of responsible liberty and the

pursuit of happiness. We should be realistic about the price we continue to pay for legal realism, admitting that traditional common-law jurisprudence, far from being "formalistic," embodied more understanding of the requirements of judging and politics than our sophisticated legal pragmatism.

A salutary descent from the heights of political philosophy and jurisprudence, one that stops short, however, of the depths of rootless pragmatism, would locate in American constitutionalism this contrast between jurists who have established or perpetuated these juridical achievements and those who have undermined them for the sake of the consensus of the moment, the policy aims of the near-term, or intellectual hubris. Rediscovery of the Montesquieuan legacy in modern constitutionalism, which in turn raises the question of the classic common-law tradition, therefore points to an intrinsic relation among a complex constitutionalism, republicanism, and principles of natural right. Holmes and such later theorists as Dahl and Rawls have little room for the separation of powers in their jurisprudence and democratic theory, given their focus on the needs and consensus of the moment, on majoritarian struggle, and on individual interests and narrowly conceived rights. These recent theorists of liberal democracy also repudiate, either boldly or mildly, any notion of a natural anchor for the rights secured by liberal law. Montesquieu's philosophy, in contrast, propounds a complex constitutionalism of separated powers as indispensable for securing natural rights. The works of Blackstone, Hamilton, and Tocqueville further affirm within liberal constitutionalism the intrinsic relations among these principles. In this sense Montesquieuan constitutionalism reflects some debt to the founder of political science and constitutionalism, Aristotle, who simultaneously teaches the importance of natural right and the soundness of dividing regimes into distinct functions—the deliberative body, the offices, and the law courts.[7] In the story of judicial power sketched here, it is only Holmes and his descendents who repudiate a stable constitutional order, separation of powers, and natural right. The difficulty for modern constitutionalism is that Holmes owes something to Montesquieu, even given his willful distortions of his predecessor. The subtler, psychological conception of natural right in *The Spirit of the Laws*, emphasizing individual tranquillity, may eventually undermine the liberal jurisprudence and complex constitutionalism intended to serve that desire for security. At the least, it opens a path for corrosive skepticism among jurists and judges about the competing individual interests lurking behind all law and politics. The boldness with which Holmesean realism blurs judging and legislating, and discards natural right for evolving and expansive conceptions of individual rights, suggests the need to temper even the moderate liberalism of Montesquieu and Blackstone with Aristotelian legal principles, as Hamilton and Tocqueville do. Alexander Bickel eventually pointed his views of constitutionalism and jurisprudence in this direction, moving from earlier affirmations of historicism and a quiet kind of judicial legislating to a search for fundamental constitutional principles that would restore the distinctiveness of, and enduring legal principles for, judicial power.[8] His successors have developed his search for a jurisprudence and conception of judicial power that accords with fundamental principles of American constitutionalism, to include explicit affirmations of traditional notions regarding natural rights, separation of powers, and genuinely stable legal precedent.[9]

The role of *The Spirit of the Laws* and its legacy in developing a judicialized politics matters not only for American constitutionalism but for the liberal, democratic politics and law that have been dominant in much of the world since the collapse of communism in Europe and the Americas. Separation of powers and a distinct judicial power have suffered not only in America but elsewhere, through our exporting of judicial activism. Debates about "the judicializing of politics" are more widely prominent, as is evident from controversies over the Pinochet case in Britain's House of Lords, the newly energetic European Court of Human Rights, and the permanent International Criminal Court for war crimes and crimes against humanity. The concern arises that the spreading of liberal democracy has not in itself cured the defects of this modern form of political life and governance, either among those long familiar with it or among its new adherents. This judicializing aspect of modern liberalism deserves as much attention as other aspects of the process of democratization. A recent analysis argues that, while "judicial activism" is distinct from "judicial review," activism has been spreading among judiciaries influenced by the American model. Judges are "increasingly important players in the process of policy formation in more than one polity," ranging from the United States and Canada to Israel and Japan. While the comparative evidence indicates that "judicial activism, generally speaking, serves the ends of liberalism," it also suggests that "judicial activism tends to erode both the parliamentary system and majoritarian democracy." The entire phenomenon "raises serious questions about the future health of liberal democracy and responsible government in Japan and the West."[10] Such concerns resonate anew for Americans, given the presidential election of 2000 and the foreign terrorist attacks of 2001. Both in a national election, and in providing for national security after the initial attacks upon the World Trade Center in 1993, we judicialized matters that, while in need of moral principle and order, nonetheless properly lie either largely or completely outside the competence of courts of law, in the domains of legislative and executive power.

The challenges facing a judicialized liberal democracy involve not only such obvious conflicts over separation of powers but also deeper problems caused, in part, by a jurisprudence of individualism. One can be a friend to liberal republicanism, grateful for modern gains ranging from individual liberty and general prosperity to military prowess, while nonetheless observing its problems and prominent analyses of them. The range of concerns registered by Rousseau, Hegel, Tocqueville, Marx, and Nietzsche have been developed by theorists from Durkheim, Voeglin, and Strauss to Arendt, Sandel, and Elshtain. A Pope resolutely opposed to communism in the name of human freedom lectures the prosperous liberal democracies, after their victory in the Cold War, about a culture of death and materialism. Such concerns traverse the contemporary academic and political spectrum today and are not easily dismissed as conservative or polemical. They animate diverse discussions of the moral decay, isolation from community, and discontent affecting individuals, families, and communities in the modern West. Less widely observed is that an increasing judicialization of politics either causes, or undermines possible remedies for, such problems. Even courts informed by a more traditionally Montesquieuan view of judging cannot be the primary forum for addressing these problems. Montesquieu's original formulation for a cloaking of power moderated politics by transforming private vices into public virtues, but such a judicializing of life tends to increase the appetite for individual security and vice. Whatever the benefits yielded in early modernity, our current condition of self-government, both individual and communal, is so threatened by selfishness and disorder that its prospects become troubled. If the immediate response to a war on terrorism suggests robust resources in individual and civic virtue, it is less clear that we can sustain the greater and more widespread sacrifices that may be required, since these concerns hardly are new. An isolating individualism or loss of civic virtue was one of Lincoln's focal concerns in his 1838 Perpetuation Address and in such presidential speeches as the Gettysburg Address and Second Inaugural.[11] Tocqueville's similar analyses indicate that even a moderate liberalism like Montesquieu's is unable to provide the individual tranquillity it promises, because the atomistic, amoral political order it fosters ultimately is untenable.

None of this suggests that Montesquieuan moderation or the separation of powers is hopelessly problematic, but it does suggest that some of the complex resources of our constitutional and philosophical tradition must be called upon to balance the shortcomings of others. Montesquieu, Blackstone, Hamilton, and Tocqueville provide us with a constitutionalism that is moderate both as to what human reason can achieve and as to the limits of human nature and politics. Regarding judicial power, both the United States and the countries that have adopted our conceptions of judging and jurisprudence would do well to recover these lessons of a moderate constitutionalism and jurisprudence. The indirect mode of tempering politics proposed by Montesquieu and

Blackstone, through gradual judicial reform of the laws, avoids the problems that a century of Holmesean legal realism has brought to our constitutional law and jurisprudence. Few in the law schools or the courts today believe that there is a fundamental reason or rationality behind law and judging, and as a consequence most either accept or proclaim that judging is politics by other means. The bitter fruits of such pragmatism now range from an increasing boldness in legislating from the bench, with its familiar displays of judicial squabbling and legal uncertainty, to a growing discussion of a crisis of legitimacy in the courts and in law generally.[12]

Perhaps the widespread, bipartisan criticism of the Supreme Court ruling in *Bush v. Gore* (2000) will restore a more sober view about the need to conceive of judging in less transient and more properly legal terms. Still, the largely one-sided criticism among legal and academic commentators about judicial activism by the U.S. high court, with little concern raised about the greater ardor shown by the Florida Supreme Court and by both presidential campaigns to judicialize an electoral and political dispute, suggests that this episode may not provide lasting lessons in itself. We will need to deliberately recall that one reason for Montesquieu's subtlety in proposing a cloaking of power lies in the very advantages of judicial weakness and invisibility. Blackstone, Hamilton, and Tocqueville confirm his view that judges can moderate the conflict between the two more visible powers, and better secure justice for individuals, only if their interventions remain gradual and imperceptible. A recent echo of this friendly warning reminds judges that "the secret of their power" lies in the difficulty of conceiving of them as part of law enforcement or government, as "busy administrators and busybody legislators." Judging, rather, is at its best when "kept out of sight, when its actions are supported by judgments and the source of judgment is seen to be the will of the lawmaker," or when judges discern evident principles of legal tradition "as 'the living oracles' of the law."[13] A rediscovery of Montesquieu, Blackstone, and their original legacy in American jurisprudence provides us with a constitutionalism based upon natural right and reason, a moderate conception of law and rights amenable to our modern, liberal sensibilities. This jurisprudential tradition restores to us full and serious analyses of the separation of powers and other fundamental principles of our political order. It also offers reasons to subscribe to such principles, rooted in commitments to human liberty and a decent, humane politics. American judges, lawyers, and legal and political theorists who have lost either an understanding or an appreciation of these principles should investigate these jurists both for such higher reasons and, more immediately, to help restore the foundations of our judging, law, and jurisprudence. If we are not willful enough to abandon reason for postmodern critique or parody, yet weary of the apparent

groundlessness of American legal and political pragmatism, then these constitutionalists and jurists of our past might speak to us still. Montesquieu and his
disciple Blackstone might understand, too, if we sought to balance their views
with resources of our jurisprudential tradition that moderate their weaknesses
while making the most of their virtues.

Notes

Introduction

1. See Donald Lutz, "The Relative Influence of European Writers on Late Eighteenth-Century American Political Thought," 193.

2. Jan-Erik Lane and Svante Ersson argue in *The New Institutional Politics* that "the analysis of political institutions that Montesquieu set forth in 1748 remains the best framework for comparative institutional analysis" (115, 286–87). Steven Fish offers similar praise in "Social Science and Democratization in East Europe and Eurasia," 805.

3. Judith Shklar, *Montesquieu*, 81; see also 88–91, 113, 124–25.

4. Alexander Hamilton, John Jay, and James Madison, *The Federalist*, ed. Robert Scigliano, no. 78, 501–2.

5. Alexis de Tocqueville, *Democracy in America*, ed. and trans. Harvey Mansfield and Delba Winthrop, vol. 1, pt. 1, ch. 8, 141 (hereafter cited as follows: 1.1.8, 141); 2.2.8, 257.

6. Recent works include Kenneth Holland, *Judicial Activism in Comparative Perspective*; C. Neal Tate and Torbjorn Vallinder, eds., *The Global Expansion of Judicial Power*; Alec S. Sweet, *Governing with Judges: Constitutional Politics in Europe*; and Herman Schwartz, *The Struggle for Constitutional Justice in Post-Communist Europe*. See also Lane and Ersson, *New Institutional Politics*, 147, 166–78.

7. See Alexander Bickel, *The Least Dangerous Branch: The Supreme Court at the Bar of Politics, The Supreme Court and the Idea of Progress,* and *The Morality of Consent.* See also Soterios Barber, *On What the Constitution Means*; Robert Nagel, *Constitutional Cultures: The Mentality and Consequences of Judicial Review*; Mary Ann Glendon, *Rights Talk: The Impoverishment of Political Discourse,* and *A Nation under Lawyers: How the Crisis in the Legal Profession Is Transforming American Society*; and Robert Clinton, *God and Man in the Law: The Foundations of Anglo-American Constitutionalism.*

8. See John Rawls, *Political Liberalism*, Lecture 6, 231–40, 212–13. See also Ronald Dworkin, *Freedom's Law: The Moral Reading of the American Constitution.*

9. Michael Sandel, *Democracy's Discontent: America in Search of a Public Philosophy,* 28; see also 39–47, 92–101, 279–80, 286–88.

10. Compare the Lockean views in Rogers Smith, *Liberalism and American Constitutional Law,* and Michael Zuckert, *The Natural Rights Republic: Studies in the Foundation of the American Political Tradition,* with those of James Stoner, *Common Law and Liberal Theory: Coke, Hobbes, and the Origins of American Constitutionalism.*

11. See Peter Conroy, *Montesquieu Revisited.* See also Pierre Manent, *The City of Man,* and the range of views in David Carrithers, Michael Mosher, and Paul Rahe, eds., *Montesquieu's Science of Politics: Essays on* The Spirit of Laws.

12. For similar rediscoveries of complex Enlightenment philosophers, see Charles L. Griswold Jr., "Enlightenment and Counter-Enlightenment in the Work of Adam Smith," in *Adam Smith and the Virtue of Enlightenment,* 7–21; and John Danford, *David Hume and the Problem of Reason: Recovering the Human Sciences.*

13. D'Alembert, *OEuvres complètes,* 5 vols., 3:450–51; quoted in Thomas Pangle, *Montesquieu's Philosophy of Liberalism,* 11–12. See also David Lowenthal, "Book I of Montesquieu's *The Spirit of the Laws,*" 485–86.

14. See W. B. Gwyn, *The Meaning of the Separation of Powers;* and M. J. C. Vile, *Constitutionalism and the Separation of Powers.*

15. Montesquieu, *De l'esprit des lois,* book 11, ch. 6, in the Pléiade edition of the *Œuvres complètes,* 2:398. Subsequent references to *The Spirit of the Laws* are cited parenthetically by book, chapter, and page (e.g., 11.6, 398).

16. Matthew Franck offers a Lockean view of modern judicial power in *Against the Imperial Judiciary: The Supreme Court versus the Sovereignty of the People.*

17. Hamilton, *Federalist* no. 78, 496.

18. See Tocqueville, *Democracy,* ed. Mansfield and Winthrop, 1.1.8; 1.2.8; 2.2.2–3. I initially made this argument in "Judicial Statesmanship, the Jurisprudence of Individualism, and Tocqueville's Common Law Spirit."

19. Anthony Kronman, *The Lost Lawyer: Failing Ideals of the Legal Profession,* 1–3; Glendon, *Nation under Lawyers,* 3–5.

20. Reprinted as "Montesquieu," in Oliver Wendell Holmes, *Collected Legal Papers.*

21. A model for such recourse to traditional political science and jurisprudence in order to protect fundamental constitutional and liberal principles not adequately secured by more recent thinking is presented by James Ceaser in *Liberal Democracy and Political Science.*

One

1. On Montesquieu and Aristotle, see Courtenay Ilbert, "Montesquieu," 417, 432; Robert Shackleton, *Montesquieu,* 265–66; Mark Waddicor, *Montesquieu and the Philosophy of Natural Law,* 102–3, 127–28; Thomas Pangle, *Montesquieu's Philosophy of Liberalism,* 42–43, 47–51, 59–66, 118–23, 161–62, 188–90; and Simone Goyard-Fabre, *Montesquieu.* For David Lowenthal, Montesquieu blends "the natural philosophies of Descartes and

Newton with a political philosophy reviving the comprehensive variety and prudent flexibility of Aristotle"; see "Montesquieu and the Classics," 259.

2. See Elie Carcassonne, *Montesquieu et le problème de la constitution française au XVIII siècle*, chs. 4–6; and Franklin Ford, *Robe and Sword*, 238–45.

3. Rebecca Kingston, *Montesquieu and the Parlement of Bordeaux*, 219–71.

4. Louis Althusser, *Montesquieu*, 98–103.

5. Mauro Cappelletti, "Repudiating Montesquieu? The Expansion and Legitimacy of 'Constitutional Justice,' " especially 12 n. 28.

6. Simone Goyard-Fabre, "Le Réformisme de Montesquieu," 66–67; emphasis in original, my translation. Goyard-Fabre argues for Montesquieu's debt to the common law, especially to Fortescue, in "L'idée de représentation dans *L'Esprit des lois*."

7. James Stoner, *Common Law and Liberal Theory*, 160, 154, 158. Brief discussions of Montesquieu on judicial power include those of Judith Shklar, *Montesquieu*, 81, 88–91, 113, 124–25; Paul Rahe, *Republics Ancient and Modern*, vol. 2, *New Modes and Orders in Early Modern Political Thought*, 212–13, 414 n. 173, and 413 n. 165; Diana Schaub, *Erotic Liberalism*, 149; René Cassin, "Montesquieu et la protection juridictionelle des libertés," 249–56; Georges Vlachos, "Le Pouvoir judiciaire dans *L'Esprit des lois*"; Anne Cohler, *Montesquieu's Comparative Politics and the Spirit of American Constitutionalism*, 168; and Matthew Bergman, "Montesquieu's Theory of Government and the Framing of the American Constitution," 17, 26, 35.

8. See also his remark on a "chain" of meaning ("Preface," 229). He described *Persian Letters* as seeking to "link the whole by a chain that is secret and, in some fashion, unknown" (see "Reflections," Pléiade ed., 1:129). In his "Notice" to *The Spirit of the Laws*, he states, "I have had new ideas; new words have had to be found or new meanings given to old ones" ("Avertissement" [1757], 2:227–28); see Pangle, *Montesquieu's Philosophy*, 11–19; and David Lowenthal, "Book I of Montesquieu's *The Spirit of the Laws*," 485–86.

9. Pangle, *Montesquieu's Philosophy*, 217.

10. I discuss these fundamental principles of Montesquieu's philosophy and of the structure of *The Spirit of the Laws*, briefly treated in subsequent pages, in "Montesquieu's Complex Natural Right and Moderate Liberalism." My analysis has benefited from study of Michael Zuckert, "Natural Law, Natural Rights, and Classical Liberalism: On Montesquieu's Critique of Hobbes." See also my dissertation, "The Cloaking of Power," ch. 1. I discuss Montesquieu's debt to Machiavelli in "The Machiavellian Spirit of Montesquieu's Liberal Republic."

11. See Lowenthal, "Book I"; and Pangle, *Montesquieu's Philosophy*, 2–47. Alternately, see Shklar, *Montesquieu*; Cohler, *Montesquieu's Comparative Politics*; Goyard-Fabre, *Montesquieu*; and my essay, "Montesquieu's Complex Natural Right and Moderate Liberalism."

12. See Harvey Mansfield, *Taming the Prince*, 214 ff. Montesquieu satirizes abstract thinking throughout *Persian Letters*; see letters 45, 72, 73, 109, 128, 134–37, and 145. See also *The Spirit of the Laws*, 11.5, 396; 11.6, 407; 29.19, 882–83; and 30.12, 898.

13. Plutarch, "To an Uneducated Prince," *Moralia* 780c. See Thomas Pangle, ed., *The Laws of Plato,* 690b and note 24 to book 3, 522–23.

14. See Lowenthal, "Book I," 495, and *passim*. See also Pangle, *Montesquieu's Philosophy*, 20–47. Alternately, see Cohler, *Montesquieu's Comparative Politics*, 34–65.

15. On the structure of *The Spirit of the Laws*, see Schaub, *Erotic Liberalism*, 136–44; Cohler, *Montesquieu's Comparative Politics*, 11–33; and Rahe, *Republics Ancient and Modern*, 2:210–14. On his typology of regimes, see Pangle, *Montesquieu's Philosophy*, 103; Mansfield, *Taming the Prince*, 229 and n. 12; and Paul Rahe, "Forms of Government: Structure, Principle, Object, and Aim," 69–108.

16. Another important figure is Sir Francis Bacon; see Robert Faulkner, *Francis Bacon and the Project of Progress,* especially "Law as Effectual Security," 209–24.

17. See, in particular, Thomas Hobbes, *The Elements of Law,* and *Leviathan*; John Locke, *An Essay Concerning the True Original, Extent, and End of Civil Government (Second Treatise).*

18. Locke, *Second Treatise*, ch. 7, sec. 87; Hobbes, *Leviathan*, part 1, ch. 13, 185 [p. 62 of 1651 edition]. St. Augustine laments the tragic quality of human judging, in light of a transcendent standard, in *Concerning the City of God against the Pagans*, 19.6, 859–61.

19. Locke, *Second Treatise,* ch. 7, sec. 87, 323–24.

20. See Leo Strauss, "Modern Natural Right," in *Natural Right and History,* 165–251; see also Michael Zuckert, *Natural Rights and the New Republicanism,* chs. 7–10. Alternately, see John Dunn, *The Political Thought of John Locke*; and Richard Ashcraft, *Revolutionary Politics and Locke's Two Treatises of Government.*

21. Hobbes, *Elements*, pt. 2, ch. 10, sec. 8, 188; compare his analysis of natural law as merely "dictates of Reason" in *Leviathan*, pt. 1, ch. 15, 216–17 [80]; Locke, *Second Treatise*, ch. 9, sec. 124, 351; ch. 11, sec. 136, 358.

22. See Strauss, *Natural Right and History*, 190 n. 30.

23. At the close of *The Elements of Law,* where Hobbes rejects any premodern notion of "right reason," he also dismisses the equity judging and "*responsa prudentum*" (learned opinions) of the common law. See also Stoner, "From General Science to Singular Case," in *Common Law and Liberal Theory*, 110–11.

24. Locke, *Second Treatise*, ch. 7, sec. 93, 328.

25. Ibid., ch. 9, sec. 131, 353; see also ch. 11, sec. 136, 358.

26. Ibid., ch. 14, sec. 168, 379; ch. 19, sec. 240, 427.

27. Stoner, *Common Law and Liberal Theory*, 138, 147.

28. St. Thomas Aquinas, *Summa theologiae,* 1–2, q. 90, a. 4: Law is "an ordinance of reason made for the common good, by him who has care of the community, promulgated." Translated from the Latin text in *Aquinas: Selected Political Writings,* 112.

29. See Mansfield, *Taming the Prince*, 261.

30. See Aristotle, *Politics*, 1285b34–1288b2 (bk. 3, chs. 15–18).

31. John Fortescue, *In Praise of the Laws of England*; see, for example, chs. 4, 5, 9, 13, and 16.

32. J. G. A. Pocock, *The Ancient Constitution and the Feudal Law*, chs. 1 and 2. Challenges to Pocock's dim view of reason in the common law include those by Glenn Burgess, in *The Politics of the Ancient Constitution*, and J. W. Tubbs, in "Custom, Time, and Reason," 363–406. See also Ellis Sandoz, "Fortescue, Coke, and Anglo-American Constitutionalism"; and Christopher Brooks, "The Place of Magna Carta and the Ancient Constitution in Sixteenth-Century Legal Thought." Gary McDowell emphasizes Coke's Scholasticism in "Coke, Corwin, and the Constitution."

33. Sir Edward Coke, *The First Part of the Institutes of the Lawes of England* (Coke-Littleton), 2.6, sec. 138, p. 97b. Note also the "Epilogus," on reason as "the soul of the law," pp. 394b–395a; 1.1, sec. 3, pp. 10b–11b, on twenty "fountains" of the common law and fifteen kinds of law; also pp. 67a, 183b, 232b, and 235a. See Stephen Siegel, "The Aristotelian Basis of English Law, 1450–1800"; and James Stoner, "Common Law and Natural Law."

34. See Stoner, "Coke's Life and Law," and "The *Dialogue* and Common Law," in *Common Law and Liberal Theory*, 13–26, 116–34; and Joseph Cropsey, "Introduction."

35. See Stoner, *Common Law and Liberal Theory*, 150–51; and David Resnick, "Locke and the Rejection of the Ancient Constitution."

36. Stoner, *Common Law and Liberal Theory*, 157.

37. The comprehensive range of Coke's jurisprudence and constitutionalism, from his *Reports* and *Institutes* to his conflicts with James I (e.g., the Prohibitions del Roy, 1607) and his later speeches in Parliament, is captured in *The Selected Writings and Speeches of Sir Edward Coke*.

38. Montesquieu, *Pensées*, no. 1964 (Barckhausen; no. 1664 Nagel), Pléiade ed., 1:1477–79; my translation. See Shackleton, *Montesquieu*, 278, 287 n. 5, 383–84; see also J. Churton Collins, *Voltaire, Montesquieu, and Rousseau in England*, 165; and John Campbell, *Lives of the Lord Chancellors*, 7:75–76.

39. *Spicilège*, no. 523, Pléiade ed., 2:1369; *Pensées*, no. 75, 1:995. Montesquieu twice calls his own masterwork "a labor of twenty years" (*Spirit*, "Preface," 229, 231). Fortescue says the knowledge necessary for a judge is "scarcely attainable in the laborious studies of twenty years" (*In Praise*, ch. 8, p. 16). See also Blackstone, *Commentaries*, ed. W. C. Jones, bk. 1, "Introduction," sec. 1, *37; sec. 3, *69. For the traditional "star page" (with asterisk) citation method for the *Commentaries*, see chapter 5 in this volume, at note 16.

40. Christopher Saint Germain, *St. German's Doctor and Student*; cf. Aquinas, *Summa theologiae*, 1–2, 90–95.

41. Perhaps the most Scholastic of Coke's judicial writings is his opinion in *Calvin's Case, or the Case of the Postnati* (1608), published in volume 7 of Coke's *Reports*, 1a ff.; the second, and most crucial, of the five parts of the opinion discusses the law of nature and cites Aristotle's *Ethics* and *Politics*, Cicero, St. Paul, Bracton, Fortescue, and Saint Germain.

42. Stoner, *Common Law and Liberal Theory*, 154.

43. See Franklin J. Pegues, "Parlement de Paris" and "Law and Justice."

44. Ibid.

45. Montesquieu first developed these themes decades earlier; see *Persian Letters*, nos. 92 and 140, Pléiade ed., 1:267–68, 340–41.

46. See also 5.6; 11.6; 19.27; and the books on commerce, 20–22.

47. See Michael Mosher, "The Particulars of a Universal Politics," 178–88, and "Monarchy's Paradox," 159–229; see also Sharon Krause, *Liberalism with Honor.*

48. For a comparison of Smith's doctrines of "emulation" and the "invisible hand," in *Theory of Moral Sentiments,* 4.1, and *Wealth of Nations,* 4.ii, see Joseph Cropsey, "Adam Smith."

49. *The Spirit of the Laws* cites Mandeville's *Fable of the Bees* (1766) twice, in 7.1 and 19.8, but never cites its subtitle: *Private Vices, Public Benefits.*

50. Oliver Wendell Holmes, "Montesquieu," in *Collected Legal Papers,* 257–58; see *Persian Letters,* no. 80, Pléiade ed., 1:252.

Two

1. On lawyers and litigation see also 28.35; on judicial excess, 29.1; see also *Persian Letters,* nos. 68, 100, Pléiade ed., 1:237–38, 279–80.

2. I discuss this further in "The Machiavellian Spirit of Montesquieu's Liberal Republic."

3. Niccolò Machiavelli, *Discourses on Livy,* 1.7, par. 1, 3, 4, 24–25. I have slightly revised the translation, consulting *Discorsi sopra la prima deca di Tito Livio,* 1.7, in *Tutte le opere.*

4. Later in book 6 Montesquieu cites his remarks in the *Considerations* about Constantine's severity (6.15, 326). See *Considerations,* chs. 14, 15, 17, and 20.

5. Aristotle, *Nicomachean Ethics,* 1128b.

6. See Daniel Patrick Moynihan, "Defining Deviancy Down."

7. One meaning of the cognate *ressortir* is "to be under the jurisdiction of."

8. See Sergio Cotta, "Montesquieu, la séparation des pouvoirs, et la Constitution fédérale des Etats-Unis"; W. B. Gwyn, *The Meaning of the Separation of Powers*; and Sharon Krause, "The Spirit of Separate Powers in Montesquieu."

9. Compare Aristotle's *Nicomachean Ethics,* 1095a–b, on the various meanings of "happiness." Montesquieu earlier had defined happiness as a political "harmony" that "alone is true peace" (*Considerations,* 9, Pléiade ed., 2:119).

10. See Lowenthal, "Montesquieu and the Classics"; and David Carrithers, "Not So Virtuous Republics."

11. Locke, *Second Treatise,* secs. 87–93, 127–31, and 143–48; on judging, secs. 87–88, 125, 131, and 219. See Stoner, "Montesquieu's Liberal Spirit," in *Common Law and Liberal Theory,* 155, citing Gwyn, *Separation of Powers,* 101.

12. Stoner, "Montesquieu's Liberal Spirit," 156.

13. In his *Athenian Regime* Aristotle describes judging and the law courts as democratic; see *The Politics of Aristotle*, ed. Ernest Barker, app. 4, 377, from *Athenaion Politeia* 9.1, 383; *Ath. Pol.* 68.1.

14. I am indebted to Diana Schaub for this phrasing, referring to recent science fiction about invisible spacecraft.

15. Plato, *Republic*, 359d ff., 612b; Herodotus, *Persian Wars*, 1.8–14.

16. Montesquieu uses "soul" sparingly in the work (e.g., 12.18; 24.19; 28.41); see Lowenthal, "Book I," 498 and n. 35.

17. Montesquieu had indicated his preference for a more republican kind of senate in *Considerations*, 8.

18. I discuss this further in "The Machiavellian Spirit of Montesquieu's Liberal Republic."

19. Montesquieu strongly criticized the tribunes in *Considerations*, 8 and 14.

Three

1. Compare the Preface: "I have not drawn my principles from my prejudices but from the nature of things" (229). See Thomas Pangle, *Montesquieu's Philosophy of Liberalism*, 260–305, especially 271–79.

2. See Pangle, *Montesquieu's Philosophy*, 155–60: Montesquieu defines *esprit* (mind) in terms of prudence and good judgment, but also philosophy and genius.

3. The six parts divide the books as follows: 1–8; 9–13; 14–19; 20–23; 24–26; and 27–31.

4. See Harvey Mansfield, *Taming the Prince*, 328 n. 5.

5. Leo Strauss argues that *The Spirit of the Laws* is "directed against the Thomistic view of natural right" and that "Montesquieu tried to recover for statesmanship a latitude which had been considerably restricted by the Thomistic teaching" (*Natural Right and History*, 164). Strauss does not note the discussions of prudence in the *Summa Theologiae*, in both the questions on law (I-II, q. 90–108) and the questions on prudence (II-II, q. 47–56).

6. Cesare Beccaria, *Dei delitti e delle pene*, 10; and Marcello Maestro, *Cesare Beccaria and the Origins of Penal Reform*, 17–18.

7. John Stuart Mill, *On Liberty*, 13. Steven Kautz contrasts Montesquieu and Mill on the theme of moderation in criminal law in *Liberalism and Community*, 70–71.

8. See Pangle, *Montesquieu's Philosophy*, 161–99. On the six-part structure, see Anne Cohler, *Montesquieu's Comparative Politics and the Spirit of American Constitutionalism*, 11–33; Diana Schaub, *Erotic Liberalism*, 136–44; and my essay "Montesquieu's Complex Natural Right and Moderate Liberalism."

9. See Schaub, *Erotic Liberalism*, 142–44; Sharon Krause, "The Spirit of Separate Powers in Montesquieu"; and Paul Rahe, "Forms of Government: Structure, Principle, Object, and Aim."

10. Schaub, *Erotic Liberalism,* 144. Montesquieu refers to *Os Lusiadas* (1572) by de Camões (or de Camöens). I discuss the philosophic import of his frequent recourse to poetry in "Montesquieu's Complex Natural Right and Moderate Liberalism."

11. Compare Machiavelli, *Discourses on Livy,* bk. 1, "Proem"; and Bacon, *New Organon,* sec. 129, as quoted in Robert Faulkner, *Francis Bacon and the Project of Progress,* 55.

12. A prominent advocate of this view is Joseph Nye; see "Soft Power," and *Bound to Lead: The Changing Nature of American Power.*

13. See Pangle, *Montesquieu's Philosophy,* 200–248; and Catherine Larrère, "Montesquieu on Economics and Commerce."

14. See Harold J. Berman, *Law and Revolution: The Formation of the Western Legal Tradition,* 346, 375.

15. Compare Hobbes, *Leviathan,* ch. 42. In general, see Rebecca Kingston, "Montesquieu on Religion and the Question of Toleration"; Robert Bartlett, "On the Politics of Faith and Reason: The Project of Enlightenment in Pierre Bayle and Montesquieu"; and Diana Schaub, "Of Believers and Barbarians: Montesquieu's Enlightened Toleration."

16. Compare Locke, *A Letter Concerning Toleration* (1689) and *Reasonableness of Christianity* (1695).

17. See Bacon, "On Judicature," *Essays,* no. 56; Hobbes, *Leviathan,* "Introduction"; Locke, *Second Treatise,* ch. 13, sec. 158. In general, see Faulkner, *Bacon and the Project of Progress,* 214.

Four

1. Roger B. Oake criticizes this in "*De l'esprit des lois,* Books XXVI–XXXI." Cf. Thomas Pangle: the historical books "form the background or context" for book 29, even if they are of "far greater importance than the typical appendix"; see *Montesquieu's Philosophy of Liberalism,* 279–80, and see also 281–301.

2. The first-edition title reads, *On the spirit of the laws, or the relation which the laws ought to have with the constitution of each government, mores, climate, religion, commerce, etc., to which the author has added some new researches on the Roman laws touching successions, on the French laws and on the feudal laws.* Montesquieu struck the subtitle from the final edition; see *De l'esprit des lois,* ed. Robert Derathé, 1: "Introduction"; Shackleton, *Montesquieu* (1961), 225–43; Pangle, *Montesquieu's Philosophy,* 289; see also notes 5 and 6 below.

3. See Eugen Ehrlich, "Montesquieu and Sociological Jurisprudence," 582 (discussed subsequently in chapter 10 in this volume).

4. Michael Oakeshott cites Montesquieu on moderation and law, judicial power, and historical experience as the best guide for jurisprudence in "The Rule of Law," 156–57, 165, 169, 177–78.

5. See Oake, "Books XXVI–XXXI"; Iris Cox, *Montesquieu and the History of French Laws,* 4; and Cox, "Montesquieu and the History of Laws," 409–29. For the "appendix"

thesis, see Montesquieu, *De l'esprit des lois*, ed. Jean Brethe de la Gressaye, 4: "Introduction," xi–xii.

6. Shackleton's manuscript researches on the book on Roman law buttress the view that part 6 is no appendix; see *Montesquieu*, 320, 239–40, and on part 6 generally, 320–36.

7. Diana Schaub, *Erotic Liberalism*, 175 n. 13.

8. See also 6.10; 6.17; 10.3; 10.14; 11.18; and cf. *Persian Letters*, no. 131, in Pléiade ed., 1:329.

9. See also 10.3; 15.17; and 26, chs. 4, 6, 8, 19.

10. See also 13.5; 19.25; 21.20; 22.2; and 26, chs. 6, 15.

11. Pangle emphasizes only Montesquieu's concern with German barbarism, overlooking the theme of legal development or reform here; see *Montesquieu's Philosophy*, 180–83.

12. Cox, *History of French Laws*, 21, 151–72; Pangle, *Montesquieu's Philosophy*, 280–81, 294–97; see also Cox, "History of Laws."

13. See Pangle, *Montesquieu's Philosophy*, 288.

14. Montesquieu substantially revised 28.38 after 1748; see Callois's notes, Pléiade ed., 2:1532–33.

15. Montesquieu seems to describe *The Spirit of the Laws* itself here: "What is this obscure, confused, and ambiguous code where one constantly mixes French jurisprudence with Roman law; in which one speaks as a legislator and reveals a jurist; where one finds a whole body of jurisprudence covering all situations, all the points of civil right?" (28.38, 852).

16. The Pléiade edition silently corrects Montesquieu's apparent error, obscuring this possibly deliberate signal of a deeper issue.

17. See Pangle, *Montesquieu's Philosophy*, 291–301; and Cox, *History of French Laws*, 151–72; see also Elie Carcassone, *Montesquieu et le problème de la constitution française au XVIII siècle*, chs. 1 and 4; and Franklin L. Ford, *Robe and Sword: The Regrouping of the French Aristocracy after Louis XIV*, especially 238–45.

18. See Harvey Mansfield, *Taming the Prince*, 232–33; and Herodotus, *Persian Wars*, 4.144.

19. See Mansfield, *Taming the Prince*, 214–20; see also chapter 1 in this volume, and my essay, "Montesquieu's Complex Natural Right and Moderate Liberalism."

20. See Oake, "Books XXVI–XXXI," 168.

Part Two

1. Darien McWhirter, *The Legal 100: A Ranking of the Individuals Who Have Most Influenced the Law*; Sir Courtenay Ilbert, "Montesquieu."

2. Cesare Beccaria, *Dei delitti e delle pene*; and Marcello Maestro, *Cesare Beccaria and the Origins of Penal Reform*.

3. See Albert Alschuler, "Rediscovering Blackstone"; more generally, see Robert Faulkner, *The Jurisprudence of John Marshall*; and Albert Alschuler, *Law without Values: The Life, Work, and Legacy of Justice Holmes*.

Five

1. See William Twining, *Blackstone's Tower: The English Law School*. On American legal education, see A. V. Dicey, "Blackstone's Commentaries," 300–301, citing James Bradley Thayer, "The Teaching of English Law at Universities" (1895); and Dennis Nolan, "Sir William Blackstone and the New Republic," 311–21.

2. Sir William Blackstone, *Commentaries on the Laws of England*, ed. W. C. Jones, bk. 1, "Preface," xxxvii; and see bk. 1, "Introduction," 1. See also the note on texts in the frontmatter of this volume, and notes 14 and 16 below. Hereafter cited by book number, chapter number or section, and page number.

3. Jeremy Bentham, *A Comment on the Commentaries and a Fragment on Government*. Subsequent references cite *A Fragment on Government* (1988).

4. Rupert Cross argues that Bentham mostly "deliberately misrepresented parts of what Blackstone wrote" and engaged in "willful misreading and inept comment"; see "Blackstone v. Bentham," 517, 520, 521.

5. Bk. 1, "Preface," xxxvii–xxxviii.

6. See Arthur Sherbo, *Shakespeare's Midwives: Some Neglected Shakespeareans,* 67–85; and G. P. Macdonnell, "Blackstone, Sir William (1723–80)," noting Blackstone's poem "A Lawyer's Farewell to His Muse" and his treatise on architecture. See also W. S. Holdsworth, "Some Aspects of Blackstone and His Commentaries," 263–64.

7. Bentham, preface to *A Fragment on Government*, 23–24.

8. See Charles Warren, *A History of the American Bar,* 177–80; Nolan, "Blackstone and the New Republic"; Donald Lutz, "The Relative Influence of European Writers"; Albert Alschuler, "Rediscovering Blackstone," 3–19; and Robert Ferguson, *Law and Letters in American Culture,* 11–15, 30–33. As late as 1915 a basic American text anthologized the *Commentaries* under the title *Essentials of the Law* (see Marshall D. Ewell, ed., *Essentials of the Law*).

9. Daniel Boorstin, *The Mysterious Science of Law,* iii, iv.

10. Ibid., 189–91; see, for example, the discussion of property as "approaching the high altar of Blackstone's legal theology" (166); see also Dicey, "Blackstone's Commentaries"; and Ernest Barker, *Essays in Government*, 120–53. The most audacious, impressive misreading since Bentham's is that of Duncan Kennedy, "The Structure of Blackstone's Commentaries."

11. See W. S. Holdsworth, *A History of English Law*, 12:91–101, 702–37.

12. In addition to essays by Alschuler, Holdsworth, and Nolan already cited, see Paul Lucas, "Ex Parte Sir William Blackstone, 'Plagiarist': A Note on Blackstone and the Natural Law"; Herbert Storing, "William Blackstone"; John Finnis, "Blackstone's Theoretical Intentions"; Gerald Stourzh, "William Blackstone: Teacher of Revolution"; Michael

Lobban, "Blackstone and the Science of Law"; David Lieberman, "Blackstone's Science of Legislation"; Alan Watson, "Comment: The Structure of Blackstone's Commentaries"; Matthew Franck's chapter, "The Political Science of Blackstone's *Commentaries*," in *Against the Imperial Judiciary: The Supreme Court vs. the Sovereignty of the People,* 200–207; George Anastaplo, "Nature and Convention in Blackstone's *Commentaries.*" See also the sympathetic treatment of Blackstone in David Lieberman, *The Province of Legislation Determined.*

13. Boorstin notes that before Blackstone, "nearly all general works on the common law had been called 'Institutes' or 'Abridgments'"; see *Mysterious Science,* 34–35, 199 n. 14, citing P. H. Winfield, *The Chief Sources of English Legal History* (1925). However, Coke highly praises Plowden's *Commentaries* (*Les Commentaries, ou Reportes de Edmunde Plowden,* London, 1571), and, before writing his *Institutes,* calls his own *Reports* "Commentaries" on the common law; see the preface to 1 *Reports* (1602) and the preface to 8 *Reports* (1611) in *Selected Writings and Speeches of Sir Edward Coke.*

14. The Jones edition omits the dedication; see the University of Chicago's edition of Blackstone's *Commentaries* (1979), bk. 1, facing the preface. On editions of the *Commentaries,* see the note on texts in the frontmatter of this volume; see also Storing, "William Blackstone," 622–34 n. 1; and Alschuler, "Rediscovering Blackstone," 3 n. 4.; see also note 16 below.

15. Blackstone announced his "Lectures on the Laws of England" as suited for those preparing for careers in law and those "desirous to be in some Degree acquainted with the Constitution and Polity of their own Country"; see the Jones edition, "Concerning the *Commentaries,*" xv.

16. Bk. 1, ch. 1, *122–23. The recent Chicago reprint omits the "star page" citation method (with asterisk), based upon the pagination of the tenth edition (1787) and used by scholars for two centuries. I retain the star page citation, but depart from the traditional legal form (e.g., 1 Bl. Comm. *122–23), which implies a legal reference encyclopedia without a coherent design; Blackstone himself cites passages of his work by book, chapter, and page. Subsequent references to the *Commentaries* are made parenthetically in the text, abbreviating this three-part citation (e.g., 1.1, *122–23).

17. See Kennedy, "Structure," 211, 231 ff.; for criticism of Kennedy, see Watson, "Structure of Blackstone's *Commentaries.*"

18. Bentham, pref. to *A Fragment on Government,* 6–7.

19. Citing *The Spirit of the Laws,* 11.5. Blackstone adds "civil liberty" to Montesquieu's "political liberty." Still, in 1.3 Montesquieu defines both political and civil law; and books 11 and 12 link the protection of political (or constitutional) and civil (or individual) liberty.

20. Bentham, pref. to *A Fragment on Government,* 6, 4, 16.

21. On Blackstone and Hale, see Finnis, "Theoretical Intentions"; Lieberman, "Science of Legislation"; and H. J. Berman and C. J. Reid Jr., "The Transformation of English Legal Science."

22. Through critical legal studies, Kennedy perceives that Blackstone's aim is both legal and broadly political, but he reduces this to irrationalism. Blackstone and all legal philosophers—the critical, postmodern school excepted, apparently—pursue not truth but propaganda in defense of a status quo. See "Structure," sections 1 and 2, B. On liberty in Blackstone, see Lieberman, "Science of Legislation," 126–28; Alschuler, "Rediscovering Blackstone," 16 n. 89 and sections 3 and 5 (28–36, 44–55); and Anastaplo, "Nature and Convention," 161–76, 167–68.

23. See Paul Lucas, "Blackstone and the Reform of the Legal Profession," especially 456–62, 482–89, on a political-legal education for gentlemen.

24. Blackstone quotes the Greek from Aristotle, *Nicomachean Ethics*, book 5. The citation is incorrect, at least by editions considered standard since the nineteenth century. I am grateful to Susan Collins for clarifying that the passage occurs in 5.1, at 1129b30, not in 5.3 as Blackstone indicates: "Justice is complete virtue because it is the use [or practice] of complete virtue." Blackstone's interpretation seems less odd upon recalling that Fortescue comments upon precisely this passage from Aristotle in *In Praise of the Laws of England*, ch. 4, 9. Later in *Ethics* 5 Aristotle argues that equity is the just, but is better than the just, since it modifies the law to achieve the lawgiver's intent in specific circumstances. On the importance of equitable discretion for Blackstone and Mansfield, see chapter 7 in this volume.

25. See A. W. B. Simpson, "The Common Law and Legal Theory," contrasting common law with liberal, positivist minds; see also James Stoner, *Common Law and Liberal Theory*.

26. Bentham, *A Fragment on Government*, 56 (sec. 42 n. x). See Gerald Postema, *Bentham and the Common Law,* especially ch. 1; and Timothy Fuller, "Jeremy Bentham, James Mill."

27. Storing, "William Blackstone," 630. See also Stephen Siegel, "The Aristotelian Basis of English Law, 1450–1800," 56–58, on Blackstone's repudiation of the Aristotelian method of a legal prudence.

28. Alan Watson criticizes scholars who expect too much analytical rigor from Blackstone: "[A] legal historian who is interested in law both as cultural phenomenon and as social reality is less disconcerted"; see "Structure of Blackstone's *Commentaries*," 805. Watson suggests Gothofredus as a prime influence, but he does not discuss Montesquieu.

Six

1. Jeremy Bentham, *A Fragment on Government,* 18, citing *Commentaries* 4.4, *49.

2. *Pace* Bentham, Blackstone carefully preempts the charge that toleration entails disestablishment: he seeks "to illustrate the excellence of our present establishment, by looking back to former times," then suggests further reforms (4.4, *49).

3. William S. Holdsworth, "Blackstone's Treatment of Equity." See also *A History of English Law*, 12:588–605.

4. Richard Posner, *The Economics of Justice*, 13–47, especially 23–27. Posner's Holmesean argument is that Blackstone's "judge-made law" is a more effective means to implement Bentham's utilitarian calculus than the latter realized.

5. Grant Gilmore, *The Ages of American Law*, 5. See Albert Alschuler, "Rediscovering Blackstone," sec. 4, "The Role of Judges."

6. Letter to Madison, Feb. 17, 1826, in *Thomas Jefferson: Writings*, ed. Merrill D. Peterson, 1513–14. See also Julian S. Waterman, "Thomas Jefferson and Blackstone's *Commentaries*"; and James Stoner, "Sound Whigs or Honeyed Tories?" 103–17.

7. On the end of liberal rights undermining constitutional forms, see Harvey Mansfield, *America's Constitutional Soul*, 1–17, 101–14.

8. F. T. H. Fletcher, *Montesquieu and English Politics, 1750–1800*, 24 n. 1, 29, 121. See also James Stoner, *Common Law and Liberal Theory*, 62–75.

9. Jeremy Bentham, *A Comment on the Commentaries and a Fragment on Government*, 278. Bentham also remarked, "The Englishman copied: but the Frenchman thought."

10. Fletcher, *Montesquieu*, 123, 127. Matthew Franck emphasizes Blackstone's debt to Hobbes and Locke in *Against the Imperial Judiciary*, 200–207. Stoner, in *Common Law and Liberal Theory*, compares the influences of Hobbes, Locke, and Montesquieu on Blackstone.

11. Théodore Regnault, *Tableaux Analytiques de L'Esprit des lois de Montesquieu, suivis de la Comparaison de plusieurs principes et passages de Montesquieu et de Blackstone*.

12. Fletcher, *Montesquieu*, 127, 147, citing House of Lords Debates, Feb. 24, 1806 (emphasis in original). Fletcher finds no evidence for "a curious legend" that in the eighteenth century a copy of *The Spirit of the Laws* lay open on a table in the Commons (31).

13. Alan Watson similarly explains Blackstone's concealment of his debt to Justinian's *Institutes* and its seventeenth-century editor Gothofredus for the *Commentaries*' structure; see "Comment: The Structure of Blackstone's Commentaries," 810.

14. See Theodore Plucknett, *A Concise History of the Common Law*, 231–51, 131–38; Edward Jenks, *A Short History of English Law*, 71–82, 187–209, and *The Book of English Law*, 46–62.

15. For praise of superior court judges in jury trials, see 3.23, especially *355–56, *361, *373, *375, *379–81.

16. Paul Lucas, "Ex Parte Sir William Blackstone, 'Plagiarist,'" 145–47; see also H. L. A. Hart, "Blackstone's Use of the Law of Nature"; and Michael Lobban, "Blackstone and the Science of Law."

17. Lucas, "Ex Parte," 156–58. Ernest Barker argues that Blackstone was "a votary of confusion of ideas" in *Essays on Government*, 143–46. This is doubtful, but Barker confirms the complexity of Blackstone's analyses of law and constitution, including separation-of-powers limits on royal prerogative.

18. Herbert Storing, "William Blackstone," 623; also, the "plan or organization of the *Commentaries*" indicates "a movement or progression from the natural to the conventional."

19. Robert Clinton notes a debt to Scholastic views, but overlooks the modern, liberal elements of Blackstone's discussion of property, in *God and Man in the Law: The Foundations of Anglo-American Constitutionalism,* 158, 254, nn. 7–8.

20. On Blackstone coherently balancing natural law and positive law, see David Lieberman, "Blackstone's Science of Legislation," 125–27; Alschuler, "Rediscovering Blackstone," section 2 (19–27); and George Anastaplo, "Nature and Convention," *passim.* See Harold Berman and Charles Reid on Kent and Story: "[T]hey implicitly combined, as did Hale and Blackstone, a positivist, or analytical, theory of law with a natural-law theory and a historical theory" ("The Transformation of English Legal Science," 511). For Blackstone as intending to clarify natural law but failing to do so, see John Finnis, "Blackstone's Theoretical Intentions," *passim.*

21. See James Stoner's chapter entitled "*Dr. Bonham's Case* and Lawyers' History," in *Common Law and Liberal Theory,* esp. 48–62.

22. Hamilton's "The Farmer Refuted" (1775) cites Blackstone on natural rights; see *Selected Writings,* 19–22. See Gerald Stourzh, "Blackstone: Teacher of Revolution," 184, 197–200; and Dennis Nolan, "Sir William Blackstone and the New Republic," 294.

23. For Lobban, Blackstone never bothers to reconcile natural law with parliamentary supremacy because "more important for him was the role of judges who, as oracles of the law, explained what the law was by putting into practice a law which already existed in the mists of time and the people's consciousness"; see "Blackstone and the Science of Law," 327–28. This portrays Blackstone as too strictly of the "ancient constitution" view, but it recognizes the import of his conception of judicial power.

24. Stephen Siegel, in "The Aristotelian Basis of English Law," finds Blackstone shifting from an Aristotelian to a Cartesian epistemology of legal certainty (56–61). Stoner finds Blackstone a mixed case, employing common-law methods and principles for liberal, rationalist ends; see *Common Law and Liberal Theory,* 162–75.

25. Alschuler, "Rediscovering Blackstone," 36–37, citing *Linkletter v. Walker,* 381 U.S. 618 (1963), 636–40.

26. Later Blackstone cites Coke's distinction between "every unlearned man's reason" and that "artificial and legal reason" which is "warranted by authority of law" (1, "Intro.," sec. 3, *77). The context, however, concerns particular customs that obtain only in specific areas, not the general notion of custom essential to the common law. Blackstone demotes Coke's authority on this central question to a secondary status.

Seven

1. Ernest Barker, *Essays on Government,* 139–40.

2. Ibid., 141–42.

3. Théodore Regnault, *Tableaux Analytiques de L'Esprit des lois de Montesquieu* (1824).

4. The Act also states the need for further securing "our religion, laws and liberties"; see George B. Adams and H. Morse Stephens, eds., *Select Documents of English Constitutional History,* 478–79.

5. Harold Berman and Charles Reid suggest that a "constitutional transformation" already was afoot, with Blackstone not innovating but consolidating; see their "Transformation of English Legal Science," 506.

6. W. S. Holdsworth characterizes this discussion of "an independent judiciary" as revealing "clearer traces of Montesquieu's influence"; see "Aspects of Blackstone and His Commentaries," 282–83.

7. See Herbert Storing, "William Blackstone," 630–32, and James Stoner, *Common Law and Liberal Theory,* 174–75.

8. See David Lieberman, *The Province of Legislation Determined.*

9. W. S. Holdsworth, *History of English Law,* 12:464–69; see 464–78 on his life and work. See also James M. Rigg, "Murray, William"; Cecil Fifoot, *Lord Mansfield*; Edmund Heward, *Lord Mansfield*; Bernard Shientag, *Moulders of Legal Thought,* 99–158.

10. Holdsworth, *History,* 12:91. In 1752 Murray nominated Blackstone for a chair at Oxford, and when this failed, he suggested a lecture topic.

11. Montesquieu does not cite Mansfield by name, but calls the judgment a "response without reply"; see *Œuvres complètes de Montesquieu,* ed. André Masson, 3:1452–53 (no. 672); my translation. See Holdsworth, *History,* 12:469, 476. For Mansfield's opinion, see Van Vechten Veeder, ed., *Legal Masterpieces: Specimens of Argumentation and Exposition by Eminent Lawyers,* 1:20–32; see also 1–19.

12. "Fiction, tautology, technicality, circuity, irregularity, inconsistency remain. But above all the pestilential breath of Fiction poisons the sense of every instrument it comes near"; see Jeremy Bentham, *A Fragment on Government,* 21, commenting on 3.21, *322.

13. Blackstone cites this as the Bishop of Winchester's case; according to the Acts of the Privy Council of 1616, Coke alone of the judges stated to James I that "when that case should bee, hee would doe that should bee fitt for a Judge to doe"; see *The Selected Writings and Speeches of Sir Edward Coke,* vol. 2, *Commendans and the King's Displeasure.*

14. Boorstin notes that this defense of complexity in 3.17 is "summarizing Montesquieu," citing book 11 of *The Spirit the Laws*; see *The Mysterious Science of Law,* 219 n. 81. To Boorstin, this is mere "aesthetics," portraying a "sublime" image of the Gothic so as to discourage reform (102–5).

15. See also 2.4, *44; and 3.10, *196–97.

16. Albert Alschuler, "Rediscovering Blackstone," at notes 204–5; Alschuler cites Boorstin, *Mysterious Science,* ch. 3 and 213 n. 65.

17. Boorstin, *Mysterious Science,* 78–84. Duncan Kennedy, too, notes passages where Blackstone's judges independently shape law, while also suggesting that his judges are agents of the status quo. Compare his "Structure of Blackstone's Commentaries," 244–46, 249–55, 264, 266–67, 351, 363–64, with 268–69, 371.

18. Holdsworth, *History,* 12:708, 728–29, 732–36; see also the *Dictionary of National Biography* 2:600–601, and Barker, "Blackstone on the British Constitution," 132–33.

19. Again, exceptions include Storing, "Blackstone," 628–32; Alschuler, "Redis-covering Blackstone," sec. 4, "The Role of Judges"; Stoner, "Liberalized Common Law," in *Common Law and Liberal Theory*; and David Lieberman, "Blackstone's Science of Legislation," 134, 139, 141, 145, 147–49.

20. See also 1.9, *365; 1.14, *427–28. Robert Ferguson notes in the treatment of marriage in 1.15 Blackstone's uneasiness about the inegalitarian legal status of women; see *The American Enlightenment, 1750–1820,* 160, 162.

21. John Finnis defends Blackstone's treatment against Hart, although he overlooks Blackstone's tone of reform; see "Blackstone's Theoretical Intentions," 172–73.

22. See Holdsworth, *History,* 12:553, 558–59, 707; Fifoot, *Mansfield,* 158–97; Shientag, *Moulders of Legal Thought,* 112–13; Heward, *Mansfield,* 125–38; and William R. Leslie, "Similarities in Lord Mansfield's and Joseph Story's View of Fundamental Law," esp. 279–84.

23. W. S. Holdsworth, "Blackstone's Treatment of Equity," 11; see also 7–13 and the appended "Note" at 28–32 (reprinting one of Blackstone's lectures on equity).

24. On equitable judicial reform of alienation by deed, the source of the modern law of trusts, see 2.20, *332–37.

25. Holdsworth, *History,* 12:536–40, 723. Holdsworth also notes changes regarding bills of exchange and law merchant from the law lectures to the *Commentaries,* after Mansfield had joined the King's Bench.

26. See also 3.24, *389–90, on judicial reforms of judgment at trial, ratified by popular consent.

27. For Holdsworth, Blackstone "does little more than reproduce" Mansfield's views on fusing the rules of law and equity, and he notes the speculation that Mansfield wrote this section of the *Commentaries*; see "Blackstone's Treatment of Equity," 7–13.

28. For judicial reforms of criminal procedure, especially in capital cases, see 4.27, *349–50, *355–58.

29. For Blackstone's endorsement of judicial discretion regarding pardons, compare 4.31, *388, citing *Spirit,* 6.5, with subsequent qualifications at *394, *396, *402.

30. See *Jones v. Randall* (1774), and *Rust v. Cooper* (1777), both cited in Fifoot, *Mansfield,* 220–21. See also the essay entitled "The Path of the Law" in Oliver Wendell Holmes, *The Mind and Faith of Justice Holmes,* 83. Shientag, in *Moulders of Legal Thought,* praises Holmes, Cardozo, and Mansfield as "modern" judges (1, 99, 153); see also Heward, *Mansfield,* 173.

31. On *Evans,* see Shientag, *Moulders of Legal Thought,* 121–23; Mansfield's opinion is in Veeder, *Legal Masterpieces,* 1:9–19.

32. Cited in John Holliday, *The Life of William, late Earl of Mansfield,* 89–90.

33. For Mansfield's adherence to precedent over principle, see Fifoot, *Mansfield,* 208–11. Heward notes this in a less Holmesean moment, in *Mansfield,* 171.

34. Holdsworth, *History,* 12:157, 550, 554; see also 723. See Burke's report on the impeachment of Warren Hastings in *The Works of the Right Honourable Edmund Burke,* 4:481.

Eight

1. Comprehensive assessments of these debates include those of Thomas Pangle, *The Spirit of Modern Republicanism,* esp. 7–8; Michael Zuckert, *The Natural Rights Republic,* esp. 1–8, 202–43; and Hans Eicholz, *Harmonizing Sentiments: The Declaration of Independence and the Jeffersonian Idea of Self-Government.*

2. For a review of recent scholarship, see Alan Gibson, "Ancient, Moderns, and Americans"; and Paul Carrese, "The Complexity, and Principles, of the American Founding: A Reply to Alan Gibson." For the "plethora of views," see Isaac Kramnick, "The Great National Discussion."

3. Recent scholarship about the framing of American judicial power includes the work of Raoul Berger, *Congress v. the Supreme Court;* Rogers Smith, *Liberalism and American Constitutional Law;* Gary Jacobsohn, *The Supreme Court and the Decline of Constitutional Aspiration;* James Stoner, *Common Law and Liberal Theory;* Matthew Franck, *Against the Imperial Judiciary;* and Robert Clinton, *Marbury v. Madison and Judicial Review,* and *God and Man in the Law: The Foundations of Anglo-American Constitutionalism.* See the bibliography, and notes 32 and 33 below.

4. Donald Lutz, "The Relative Influence of European Writers on Late Eighteenth-Century American Political Thought."

5. Paul Spurlin, *Montesquieu in America, 1760–1801,* 258–61. On the judiciary, see Spurlin, *The French Enlightenment in America,* 86–98; and Sergio Cotta, "Montesquieu, la séparation des pouvoirs, et la Constitution fédérale des Etats-Unis."

6. John Adams, *The Works of John Adams,* esp. vol. 4 (the first volume of the *Defence*).

7. See Herbert Storing, *What the Anti-Federalists Were FOR,* 6; and James Muller, "The American Framers' Debt to Montesquieu," 87–102, esp. 92–93, 98, 235 n. 2. See also Nannerl Keohane, "The President's English: Montesquieu in America, 1776"; Anne Cohler, *Montesquieu's Comparative Politics and the Spirit of American Constitutionalism,* 148–69; Thomas Pangle, "The Philosophic Understandings of Human Nature Informing the Constitution," 9–76; and Judith Shklar, *Redeeming American Political Thought,* 158–69.

8. For Franck, in *Against the Imperial Judiciary,* Marshall is influenced by Hobbes and Locke, via Blackstone; compare Stoner, *Common Law and Liberal Theory,* 177–225; for Cotta and Spurlin (see note 5, above), the founders blended Coke and Montesquieu to produce judicial review. See also Julius Goebel Jr., "The Common Law and the Constitution," 101–23; and Charles Hobson, *The Great Chief Justice,* 26–46.

9. Robert Faulkner, *The Jurisprudence of John Marshall:* see "The Republic," and "Court and Constitution in the Republic" at 114, 126–28, 192–93, 199–200, 226; on common law, see 60–61, 268.

10. Faulkner, *Jurisprudence,* 209.

11. George Mace, in *Locke, Hobbes, and the Federalist Papers,* finds little occasion to discuss judicial power.

12. Faulkner, *Jurisprudence,* 77–78.

13. Stoner, *Common Law and Liberal Theory,* 179–96, at 179. Jefferson sought to draft not "new principles, or new arguments, never before thought of," but "to place before mankind the common sense of the subject"; see his letter to Henry Lee, 8 May 1825, in *The Life and Selected Writings of Thomas Jefferson,* 719. See also Eicholz, *Harmonizing Sentiments.* For a more Lockean view of the Declaration, see Zuckert, *Natural Rights Republic,* and *Natural Rights and the New Republicanism.*

14. Robert Ferguson, *Law and Letters in American Culture,* 63, citing Blackstone's *Commentaries* 3.20, *293–301.

15. Stoner, *Common Law and Liberal Theory,* 177–78, 188–89. See also Donald Lutz, *Origins of American Constitutionalism;* Ellis Sandoz, *A Government of Laws: Political Theory, Religion, and the American Founding,* and "Fortescue, Coke, and Anglo-American Constitutionalism."

16. See Sandoz, "Fortescue, Coke, and Anglo-American Constitutionalism," esp. 6–7; Coke cites Plato's *Laws,* and Aristotle's *Politics* and *Topics,* in the preface to 4 *Reports,* in *Selected Writings and Speeches of Sir Edward Coke.* See also the prefaces to 1–5 *Reports, passim;* for praise of Fortescue, see the preface to 8 *Reports.* Coke relates law and virtue in the Epilogus to *First Part of Institutes,* 394b–395; see also the discussion in chapter 1 in this volume, at pp. 26–28.

17. Jefferson to Madison, 15 March 1789, in *Selected Writings,* 462; Jefferson, however, may have had in mind state judges. See the criticisms of Article III made by Brutus in essays 11 to 15, in Herbert Storing and Murray Dry, eds., *The Anti-Federalist,* 162–88.

18. See, for example, Alexander Hamilton, *Selected Writings and Speeches,* 1–17, and Morton Frisch, *Alexander Hamilton and the Political Order.* For additional legal writings and addresses, see Hamilton, *Alexander Hamilton: Writings.*

19. Richard Brookhiser, *Alexander Hamilton: American,* 9–10; see also 55–60, 169–74, 204–6 on Hamilton's legal career and debt to the common-law tradition of Coke.

20. Clinton Rossiter, *Alexander Hamilton and the Constitution,* 95–98, 218–25; see also 93–95, 248–49, 296 n. 136. Hamilton cites Coke in *Rutgers* in at least two of his briefs; see Julius Goebel Jr., *The Law Practice of Alexander Hamilton,* 1:357, 382–83. In his "Letter from Phocion," published before the trial, Hamilton cites Coke's commentary upon Magna Carta in *Second Institutes* as the authority on the "law of the land" clause in the New York constitution; see Hamilton, *Alexander Hamilton: Writings,* 127–40, at 128.

21. Harvey Flaumenhaft, *The Effective Republic: Administration and Constitution in the Thought of Alexander Hamilton,* esp. "Independent Judgment," "Partisanship, Partiality, and Parts of Government," and "Partisanship, Partiality, and Popular Liberty." Hamilton's *Croswell* arguments influenced the legislature to make New York's seditious libel law friendlier to political speech than Jefferson had been. Compare Goebel, *Law Practice of*

Hamilton, 1:775–848 (quotation at 830); and Hamilton, *Alexander Hamilton: Writings,* 1006–8, with Jefferson's "Second Inaugural" (1805), in *Selected Writings,* 342–44.

22. See Charles Warren, *The Supreme Court in United States History,* 1:125.

23. See Hamilton, "The Farmer Refuted," 23 February 1775, in his *Selected Writings,* 19–22; Hamilton's quotations draw from the introduction to Blackstone's *Commentaries,* sec. 2, *41; and, 1.1, *124.

24. See the introductions to Alexander Hamilton, John Jay, and James Madison, *The Federalist,* ed. Jacob Cooke, and George Carey, *The Federalist: Design for a Constitutional Republic.* Douglass Adair and others tend to confirm Madison's account of the disputed essays; see Adair, *Fame and the Founding Fathers,* 27–74. For arguments that the issue is exaggerated, see Carey, *The Federalist,* xxix–xxx, and "Publius—A Split Personality?"; and David Epstein, *The Political Theory of* The Federalist, 2; see also note 26 below.

25. See Epstein, *Political Theory of* The Federalist, 30, 203 n. 24. On the mutual influence of legal learning and classical learning among the founders, especially in Hamilton, see Ferguson, *Law and Letters,* 72–73.

26. Hamilton, Jay, and Madison, *The Federalist,* ed. Robert Scigliano, 3–5. Scigliano incorporates the McLean (1788) and Gideon (1818) revisions to the newspaper essays, and most of the Hopkins (1802) revisions; he also notes Hamilton's possible authorship or joint authorship of some disputed essays, upon reviewing the evidence and twentieth-century scholarship; see Scigliano's introduction, vii–xlviii, and "Note on the Text," xlix–lii. See also the helpful introduction, bibliography, and notes in Charles Kesler's revision of the Rossiter edition in Hamilton, Jay, and Madison, *The Federalist Papers,* and those in *The Federalist: The Gideon Edition,* edited by George Carey and James McClellan.

27. The Kesler/Rossiter edition includes Hamilton's preface to the first edition; see Paul Ford's edition (lxxvii), which also includes Hamilton's "Syllabus" (xliii–xlvii), which was used by Madison for the essays after no. 36.

28. Jefferson to Madison, 18 November 1788, in *Selected Writings,* 452; Washington to Hamilton, 28 August 1788, in Washington, *Writings/George Washington,* 691–92.

29. Analyses of Publius on judicial power include those of Stoner, *Common Law and Liberal Theory,* 197–211; and Sotirios Barber, *The Constitution of Judicial Power,* 26–65. See also Gary Wills, *Explaining America: The Federalist Papers,* 37–61; Epstein, *Political Theory of* The Federalist, 185–92; Jacobsohn, *Constitutional Aspiration,* 57–73; Sylvia Snowiss, *Judicial Review and the Law of the Constitution,* 77–83; Carey, *The Federalist,* 128–53; and William B. Allen, *The Federalist Papers: A Commentary.*

30. Jay, *Federalist* no. 3, 14–15. Subsequent references occur parenthetically in the text, citing essay number and page of Scigliano's Modern Library edition. All emphases in quotations from *The Federalist* are in the original.

31. See Harvey Mansfield, *America's Constitutional Soul,* 122; and Paul Rahe on Hamilton's defense of the executive and judicial powers as mixing classical and modern political science, in *Republics Ancient and Modern,* vol. 3, *Inventions of Prudence: Constituting the American Regime,* 67–72.

32. See Edward S. Corwin, *The "Higher Law" Background of American Constitutional Law*; and Thomas Grey, "Do We Have an Unwritten Constitution?" For criticism of Corwin's thesis that Coke informs American judicial review, see Gary McDowell, "Coke, Corwin, and the Constitution."

33. Recent studies of judicial review in the founding, incorporating the work of such earlier scholars as Thayer, Corwin, Beard, Haines, and Crosskey, include those of Gordon Wood, *The Creation of the American Republic, 1776–1787,* 453–63; Berger, *Congress v. the Supreme Court,* 8–143; Leonard Levy, *Original Intent and the Framers' Constitution,* 1–99; Clinton, *Marbury v. Madison,* 1–80; Snowiss, *Judicial Review,* 1–80; and Christopher Wolfe, *The Rise of Modern Judicial Review,* 17–89.

34. For Barber, this argument entails that "substance overpowers institutional form"; "the heart" of his constitutionalism is government by "reason" over the passions, and this requires "no particular arrangement of offices and powers." Publius endorses, therefore, "the living Constitution," and "not every fair-minded observer has to believe that the Warren Court offended Publius' constitutionalism" (see *Constitution of Judicial Power,* 28–29, 62–65). This revisionism does not once mention, however, Publius's obvious debts to the constitutional formalism of Montesquieu and of classic common-law jurisprudence.

35. Stoner, *Common Law and Liberal Theory,* 205–10.

36. See Fortescue, *In Praise of the Laws of England,* ch. 18, 27; ch. 36, 52. On Coke's efforts to maintain judicial independence in the Prohibitions del Roy (1607) and Commendams (1616) controversies, and to pass the Petition of Right (1628), see Coke, *Selected Writings and Speeches.*

37. See Mansfield, *America's Constitutional Soul,* 210.

38. Ralph Lerner, "The Supreme Court as Republican Schoolmaster"; see also Jacobsohn, *Constitutional Aspiration,* 57–73; and Faulkner, *Jurisprudence.*

39. See Robert Scigliano, *The Supreme Court and the Presidency,* 17.

40. Mansfield, *America's Constitutional Soul,* 125.

41. See Nathan Glazer, "Towards an Imperial Judiciary?" 104. See also James Bryce, *The American Commonwealth,* 1:227.

42. Aristotle, *Politics,* 1285b34–1288b2 (bk. 3, chs. 15–18).

43. See Jonathan Elliot, ed., *Debates in the Several State Conventions on the Adoption of the Federal Constitution,* 2:434; cited in Herbert Storing, "Foreword," xi–xii. Storing's opinion is that "between the argument that the Framers intended to establish a democracy and the argument that they intended to establish a mixed regime, I am inclined to think that the latter is closer to the truth." See also Scigliano, *Supreme Court,* 1, 9–10; Mansfield, *America's Constitutional Soul,* 104–5; Epstein, *Political Theory of* The Federalist, 137–38; Rahe, *Republics Ancient and Modern,* 3:24–30, 59–60, 231–40; and Martin Diamond, "Democracy and *The Federalist*: A Reconsideration of the Framers' Intent."

44. Mansfield, *America's Constitutional Soul,* 123. See also Storing, *What the Anti-Federalists Were FOR,* 48–52. For the revival of Anti-Federalist concerns about judicial power, see, for example, Gary McDowell, *Curbing the Courts: The Constitution and the Limits*

of Judicial Power; Ralph Rossum, "The Least Dangerous Branch?"; and Peter A. Lawler and Jennifer D. Siebels, "The Anti-Federalist View of Judicial Review."

45. See Federal Farmer 7, in Storing and Dry, eds., *Anti-Federalist*, 75–76. See also Federal Farmer 2:39, and 7:75–78; and, in the same work, Essays of Brutus 1:109 and 116; 9:166; and 16:187–89.

46. Wilson, quoted in James Madison, *Notes of Debates in the Federal Convention of 1787 Reported by James Madison*, 40 (31 May).

47. Compare the criticism of Adams's proposal for balanced government in Storing and Dry, eds., *Anti-Federalist*, 15–16 (Centinel, Letter 1). See Adams, *Works* 4:283–84, 322, 380–82, and 579 ff. (*Defence*, vol. 1, "Preface," Letters 5 and 23, and "Conclusion"); see also Storing's notes on Centinel 1:21, nn. 3, 4.

48. Aristotle, *Politics* 1294b (bk. 4, ch. 9).

49. See, for example, Owen Fiss, "The Death of Law"; and Alan Brudner, *The Unity of the Common Law: Studies in Hegelian Jurisprudence*, 1–20, 261–90.

50. Charles Pinckney, quoted in Madison's *Notes of Debates*, 571 (3 September); see also 571–73 and Article I, sec. 6, cl. 2 of the Constitution. In his conclusion to *What the Anti-Federalists Were FOR*, Storing overlooks this constitutionalist dimension of the Federalist concern with civic virtue.

Nine

1. Comprehensive guides to the voluminous literature on Tocqueville, and on his most famous work, include the editors' introduction and suggested readings in Alexis de Tocqueville, *Democracy in America*, ed. and tr. Harvey Mansfield and Delba Winthrop; Sheldon S. Wolin, *Tocqueville between Two Worlds: The Making of a Political and Theoretical Life*; and Cheryl B. Welch, *De Tocqueville*.

2. Tocqueville, *Democracy*, ed. Mansfield and Winthrop, vol. 1, pt. 2, ch. 8, 257; 1.1.8, 142. I occasionally revise this translation, consulting the *Œuvres complètes*, ed. J. P. Mayer, tome 1, 2 vols. I also consult *Democracy in America*, ed. J. P. Mayer, tr. George Lawrence.

3. See Ralph Lerner, "The Supreme Court as Republican Schoolmaster"; Gary J. Jacobsohn, *Pragmatism, Statesmanship, and the Supreme Court*, and *The Supreme Court and the Decline of Constitutional Aspiration*; Harry Clor, "Constitutional Interpretation and Regime Principles," 115–35.

4. Matthew Franck, "Statesmanship and the Judiciary," 512, 528; revised in *Against the Imperial Judiciary*, 29–51.

5. See James Ceaser, "Political Science, Political Culture, and the Role of the Intellectual"; Robert Kraynak, "Tocqueville's Constitutionalism"; Bruce Frohnen, "Tocqueville's Law: Integrative Jurisprudence in the American Context"; and Jean-Claude Lamberti, *Tocqueville and the Two Democracies*, 71–95, esp. 90–94.

6. Anthony Kronman, *The Lost Lawyer: Failing Ideals of the Legal Profession*, 1–3; Mary Ann Glendon, *A Nation under Lawyers*, 3–5.

7. *Planned Parenthood of Southeastern Pennsylvania v. Casey,* 112 S. Ct. 2791 (1992).

8. Tocqueville, *Democracy,* 1, "Intro.," 14, 3; 1.2.7, 239 ff. Hereafter cited parenthetically in the text, by volume, part, chapter, and page of the Mansfield and Winthrop edition; other editions are specifically identified by their editors.

9. See Tocqueville, *The Old Régime and the French Revolution,* 55, 115–20, 166–69, 283–86; and the 1948 essay on Cherbuliez's study of Switzerland, in Tocqueville, *Democracy,* ed. Mayer, app. 2, 739, 741–44.

10. See Harold Levy, "Lawyers' Spirit and Democratic Liberty," 243–63; see also note 29 below.

11. Tocqueville, *The Old Régime,* 82, 88; see also *Democracy,* 1.1.2, 30.

12. Jefferson to John Adams, 28 October 1813, in Thomas Jefferson, *The Life and Selected Writings of Thomas Jefferson,* 632–33.

13. See John Marshall, *The Life of George Washington, Special Edition for Schools;* Tocqueville cites Marshall's original, five-volume edition of 1807.

14. James Schleifer finds in Tocqueville's notes and manuscripts citations to Hamilton's *Federalist* essays on the judiciary, specifically to no. 78. See his *The Making of Tocqueville's* Democracy in America, 198 (on no. 78), 95 (no. 22); on Tocqueville's extensive familiarity with Publius, see 87–101; see also Bernard Brown, "Tocqueville and Publius," 43–74.

15. Tocqueville reports on his studies in "The Art and Science of Politics."

16. See Schleifer, *Making of* Democracy in America, 25–26, citing Tocqueville's letter to Kergolay, 10 November 1836 (published in Tocqueville, *Œuvres complètes,* t. 13, 1:415–18.

17. See George Wilson Pierson, *Tocqueville and Beaumont in America,* 742–45; at 768 ff., he finds few similarities between the philosophies of Tocqueville and Montesquieu. On Rousseau's influence, see, for example, Marvin Zetterbaum, *Tocqueville and the Problem of Democracy,* 39, 42 ff.; and John Koritansky, *Alexis de Tocqueville and the New Science of Politics;* see also Wilhelm Hennis, "In Search of the 'New Science of Politics' "; and Thomas West, "Misunderstanding the American Founding."

18. See the "Editors' Introduction," by Mansfield and Winthrop, in Tocqueville, *Democracy,* xxii–xxxix.

19. See the introduction to Peter A. Lawler, ed., *Tocqueville's Political Science,* especially Lawler's comments on the Aristotelianism of his political science and its distinctive "view of greatness" (xi). Compare Catherine Zuckert, "Political Sociology versus Speculative Philosophy," who argues that Tocqueville's political science consciously repudiates Aristotle.

20. On Montesquieu and Tocqueville, see Aron, *Main Currents in Sociological Thought,* 1:188–90, 200–201, 204–5, 210, 230; Melvin Richter, "The Uses of Theory: Tocqueville's Adaptation of Montesquieu," 74–102; Anne Cohler, *Montesquieu's Comparative Politics and the Spirit of American Constitutionalism,* ch. 8; Ceaser, "Political Science, Political Culture," 289, 294, 299, 305, 309, and *Liberal Democracy and Political Science,* ch. 3.

21. See Peter A. Lawler, *The Restless Mind: Alexis de Tocqueville on the Origin and Perpetuation of Human Liberty,* esp. 7–10, 73–87, discussing recent scholarship on Tocqueville and Pascal.

22. Raymond Aron and Pierre Manent argue that Tocqueville's philosophy strives to preserve liberty within democracy and is animated by a higher conception of the human soul and human dignity. See Aron, "Tocqueville," in *Main Currents,* vol. 1; and Manent, *Tocqueville and the Nature of Democracy.* See also Aron, "On Tocqueville," 175–78.

23. Manent, *Tocqueville and the Nature of Democracy*, xii, xiv.

24. See Aristotle, *Nicomachean Ethics* 1179a33 ff. (10.9); *Politics* 1288b10–1289a25 (4.1).

25. See Manent, *Tocqueville*, ch. 7, "Democracy and the Nature of Man."

26. See James H. Nichols Jr., "Pragmatism and the U.S. Constitution," 369–70. I am grateful to Matt Franck for suggesting that Tocqueville's linking of Luther and modern freedom may draw upon an 1834 essay by Heinrich Heine in *Revue de deux mondes,* "On the History of Religion and Philosophy in Germany"; see Heine, *Selected Prose,* 227. See also Hegel's preface to his *Philosophy of Right,* on what "Luther inaugurated" (22).

27. See Lawler, "Democracy and Pantheism."

28. Ceaser, "Political Science, Political Culture," 288–91, 297, 306–7, 309–11; Kraynak, "Tocqueville's Constitutionalism," 1180–81.

29. See Ceaser, "Political Science, Political Culture," 291–301, 309–11. Ceaser does not consider the American common-law lawyer spirit to be a "synthesis" that avoids the defects of both traditionalism and rationalism (see 316 ff.). Levy overlooks Tocqueville's preference for the common law compared to French rationalism; thus, he does not link the two parts of 1.2.8, in which the discussion of juries praises the conservative habits and substantive principles imparted by judges (see Levy, "Lawyers' Spirit," 248, 250, 252, and n. 55).

30. I am indebted to David Lowenthal for this point. For criticism tracing this to the influence of Rousseau, see West, "Misunderstanding the American Founding." Compare Kraynak, "Tocqueville's Constitutionalism," regarding his debt to the constitutionalism of the American founders, and Delba Winthrop, "Rights: A Point of Honor," on Tocqueville and the Declaration (395 n. 8) and on the larger purposes informing his peculiar treatment of rights.

31. On Fortescue and Coke see chapter 8 in this volume, at pp. 189–90, and the discussion in chapter 1, at pp. 26–28.

32. See Abraham Lincoln's "The Perpetuation of Our Political Institutions," in *The Collected Works of Abraham Lincoln,* 1:108–15; see also "Gettysburg Address," 7:22–23.

33. In addition to the works cited by Kronman and Glendon, see Alan Brudner's chapters entitled "The Crisis of the Common Law" and "Idealism and Fidelity to Law" in *The Unity of the Common Law: Studies in Hegelian Jurisprudence,* 1–20, 261–90; and Albert Alschuler, *Law without Values: The Life, Work, and Legacy of Justice Holmes,* esp. chs. 1 and 9.

34. On Tocqueville's probable debt to Montesquieu for such analogies, see Richter, "The Uses of Theory," 89–90.

35. Robert Faulkner, *The Jurisprudence of John Marshall*, 211. See also his chapters entitled "Guardian of the Republic," 212–23, and, more generally, "The Republic" and "Court and Constitution in the Republic," at 114, 126–28, 192–93, 199–200, 209, 226; see also 268.

36. *Sturges v. Crowinshield*, 4 Wheaton 122, 202 (1819); see also *Fletcher v. Peck* (1810); *McCulloch v. Maryland* (1819); and *Marbury* (1803) itself. For a similar view, but subordinating the influence of common law to that of Lockean liberalism, see Faulkner, *Jurisprudence*. Accounts of Marshall's emphasis on judicial restraint include those of Christopher Wolfe, *The Rise of Modern Judicial Review*; Franck, *Against the Imperial Judiciary*; and Robert Clinton, *Marbury v. Madison and Judicial Review.*

37. See Kraynak, "Tocqueville's Constitutionalism," 1190, 1192; Jacobsohn's chapter, "Hamilton, Positivism, and the Constitution: Judicial Discretion Reconsidered," in his *Constitutional Aspiration*, 57–73; and Harvey Mansfield, *America's Constitutional Soul*, 122–26.

38. See Robert Scigliano, "The Two Executives: The President and the Supreme Court." Hamilton declined Washington's offer of the chief justiceship in 1795; see Charles Warren, *The Supreme Court in United States History,* 1:125.

39. Faulkner, *Jurisprudence,* 221.

40. Harvey Mansfield, *Taming the Prince: The Ambivalence of Modern Executive Power,* 235. See Aristotle, *Politics,* 1300b (4.16).

41. See, for example, Christopher Wolfe, *How to Read the Constitution.*

42. Abraham Lincoln, Speech at Springfield, Illinois, 26 June 1857, in *Collected Works*, 2:401.

43. In addition to those in the natural-law school of jurisprudence, scholars who have recently attempted to transcend legal and moral skepticism and restore a tradition of principled legal prudence include Kronman, *Lost Lawyer,* and Alschuler, *Law without Values.*

44. See Russell Hittinger, "Natural Law in the Positive Laws: A Legislative or Adjudicative Issue?"; and the review by Christopher Wolfe of recent academic and public debates on these issues in "Judicial Review." Compare James Stoner Jr., "Common Law and Natural Law," and "Property, the Common Law, and John Locke."

45. On principled prudence in the Aristotelian and Thomistic traditions, see James V. Schall, S.J., "A Latitude for Statesmanship? Strauss on St. Thomas"; Daniel Nelson, *The Priority of Prudence*; and Daniel Westberg, *Right Practical Reason,* esp. ch. 16, "Law and Prudence."

Ten

1. Albert Alschuler, *Law without Values: The Life, Work, and Legacy of Justice Holmes,* 10, 181.

2. Antoine Destutt de Tracy, *Commentary and Review of Montesquieu's "Spirit of the Laws."* See, for example, Jefferson to Thomas Randolph, 30 May 1790, and to Dr. Thomas Cooper, 16 January 1814, in Thomas Jefferson, *The Life and Selected Writings of Thomas Jefferson*, 496–97, 634–35.

3. Jefferson to Madison, 17 February 1826, in *Selected Writings*, 726.

4. Woodrow Wilson, *Constitutional Government in the United States*, 54–81, esp. 54–60. On Wilson and the living Constitution, see James Ceaser et al., "The Rise of the Rhetorical Presidency"; and Christopher Wolfe, *The Rise of Modern Judicial Review*, 209–16, 205–9; on Wilson's presidency, see Tulis, *The Rhetorical Presidency*.

5. Franz Neumann, "Editor's Introduction," to *The Spirit of the Laws*, xxix, liv, lxii, lxiv.

6. Catherine Drinker Bowen, *Yankee from Olympus: Justice Holmes and His Family*, 235.

7. On historicism in late nineteenth-century American law, see Alschuler, *Law without Values*, 86–100.

8. Holmes's introduction is reprinted as "Montesquieu" in Holmes, *Collected Legal Papers*, 250–65, and in *The Mind and Faith of Justice Holmes*, 373–82; Holmes mentions it to Laski in a letter of 12 April 1917, in Holmes, *Holmes-Laski Letters*, 1:78. See, generally, Holmes, *The Collected Works of Justice Holmes: Complete Public Writings and Selected Judicial Opinions of Oliver Wendell Holmes*.

9. Holmes, *Mind and Faith of Holmes*, 369.

10. Holmes, *Collected Legal Papers*, 263; Pollock to Holmes, 25 May 1930, and Holmes to Pollock, 9 June 1930, in Holmes, *Holmes-Pollock Letters*, 2:265–67.

11. On this incongruity, see Robert Faulkner's appended chapter, "Justice Holmes and Chief Justice Marshall," in his *Jurisprudence of John Marshall*, 227–68, to which my account is indebted throughout. See also Walter Berns, "Oliver Wendell Holmes, Jr.," 167–90. For a bibliography of legal scholarship on Holmes, see Alschuler, *Law without Values*, 200–202, nn. 58–67.

12. Holmes, *Collected Legal Papers*, 263–64.

13. See Holmes, *Mind and Faith of Holmes*, 382–85, at 384–85.

14. Edmund Wilson, *Patriotic Gore: Studies in the Literature of the American Civil War.* For Alschuler, Holmes combines Machiavellian, Darwinian, and Nietzschean ideas in his jurisprudence; see *Law without Values*, 19–23, 29–30, 135–37.

15. See Holmes, *Mind and Faith of Holmes*. On legal and moral skepticism in the speech opinions, see Alschuler, *Law without Values*, 79–81.

16. Holmes, *Mind and Faith of Holmes*, 391, 398. On a degraded form of Transcendentalism in Holmes's thought, see Alschuler, *Law without Values*, 29–30.

17. Richard Posner does not include the essay in his recent collection; see Holmes, *The Essential Holmes.*

18. Montesquieu, *Persian Letters*, 80, in the Pléiade edition of *Œuvres complètes*, 1:252; Holmes, *Collected Legal Papers*, 257–58.

19. Holmes, *Holmes-Laski Letters*, 1:82.

20. Letter to Holmes, 11 June 1929, in ibid., 2:1157; *Southern Pacific Co. v. Jensen*, 244 U.S. 205 (1917), 221. Holmes replies that rather than betraying the Constitution in *Jensen*, he thought he was "standing in the ancient ways." Letter to Laski, 21 June 1929, in Holmes, *Holmes-Laski Letters*, 2:1159.

21. Eugen Ehrlich, "Montesquieu and Sociological Jurisprudence," 582. See also Ehrlich, *Fundamental Principles of the Sociology of Law.*

22. Ehrlich, "Montesquieu and Sociological Jurisprudence," 582–83.

23. On legal realism in Holmes's judicial rulings, see Robert Brauneis, " 'The Foundation of Our "Regulatory Takings" Jurisprudence': The Myth and Meaning of Justice Holmes's Opinion in *Pennsylvania Coal Co. v. Mahon*," esp. 631–42; and Alschuler, *Law without Values*, 52–83.

24. Holmes, *Mind and Faith of Holmes*, 78, 76.

25. *Buck v. Bell*, 274 U.S. 200 (1927), 207. See Walter Berns, "Buck v. Bell: Due Process of Law?" and Alschuler, *Law without Values*, 27–29, 65–67; on the separation of law and morals in Holmes's jurisprudence, see 150–61, 291 n. 157.

26. Holmes, *Common Law*, 1–2. On Holmesean positivism and differing meanings of legal positivism, see Alschuler, *Law without Values*, 132–72, esp. at 133; see also Robert P. George, ed., *The Autonomy of Law.*

27. In editing Kent's *Commentaries*, Holmes provided early evidence of skepticism regarding the founders' constitutionalism; a note to Kent on separation of powers and bicameralism quotes approvingly from the critical views of Walter Bagehot, *The English Constitution* (1867); see James Kent, *Commentaries*, vol. 1, pt. 2, *221–22.

28. James Stoner, *Common Law and Liberal Theory.* Compare the Holmesean conceptions in David Strauss, "Common Law Constitutional Interpretation," and Lief Carter, *Reason in Law*, ch. 4.

29. Holmes, *Mind and Faith of Holmes*, 75 (emphasis added).

30. See Morton Horwitz, *The Transformation of American Law, 1870–1960*, 142; and Alschuler, *Law without Values*, 1, 7, 85, 99–103, 176. For Posner's defense, see his introduction in Holmes, *The Essential Holmes.* Writings by Justices Brandeis, Cardozo, and Frankfurter, and by Laski, Howe, and Lerner, worked to replace Marshall with Holmes as the new epitome of American law and judging; see Holmes, *Mind and Faith of Holmes*, 452–60; and Alschuler, *Law without Values*, 181–86. Criticisms of Holmes include those of Faulkner's chapter, "Justice Holmes and Chief Justice Marshall," in his *Jurisprudence of Marshall*; Wolfe, *Modern Judicial Review*; Yosal Rogat, "Mr. Justice Holmes: A Dissenting Opinion," and "The Judge as Spectator"; and Berns, "Oliver Wendell Holmes, Jr."

31. For the main opposing views in the voluminous literature of this debate, see Laurence Tribe, with Michael Dorf, *On Reading the Constitution*; and Christopher Wolfe, *How to Read the Constitution.* See also the reconceptualized originalism propounded by Keith Whittington in *Constitutional Interpretation.*

32. *Roe v. Wade*, 410 U.S. 113 (1973), at 117, 174. I am indebted to Robert Scigliano for noticing this paradox. See also Gary J. Jacobsohn, *Pragmatism, Statesmanship, and the Supreme Court,* and the introduction to his *The Supreme Court and the Decline of Constitutional Aspiration*; see also Alschuler, *Law without Values*, 199–203.

33. Anthony Kronman, *The Lost Lawyer: Failing Ideals of the Legal Profession,* 1–3; Mary Ann Glendon, *A Nation under Lawyers*, 3–5.

34. *Planned Parenthood of Southeastern Pennsylvania v. Casey*, 112 S. Ct. 2791 (1992).

35. This argument builds upon James Stoner, "Common Law and Constitutionalism in the Abortion Case." Not all "original intent" arguments subscribe to legal skepticism or positivism; see, for example, Hadley Arkes, *Beyond the Constitution*; and Wolfe, *How to Read the Constitution.*

36. See *Casey,* at 2858 (Chief Justice Rehnquist, concurring in part and dissenting in part). The Court substantially adhered to the *Casey* precedent in a contentious, fractured 5–4 ruling in *Stenberg v. Carhart* (2000).

37. *Casey,* at 2804 (joint opinion of Justices O'Connor, Kennedy, and Souter).

38. *Casey,* at 2814 (part 3-C of the joint opinion, joined by Justices Blackmun and Stevens).

39. Ibid., 2815, 2816.

40. Stoner, "Common Law and Constitutionalism," 431; *Casey,* at 2814, 2816.

41. *Casey,* at 2815.

42. Ibid., 2816.

43. Henry Monaghan, "Stare Decisis and Constitutional Adjudication," 278 (citation omitted). Monaghan endorses John Rawls's "political conception of justice," the "legitimation ideology" of a "construct" for securing the "[s]tability and continuity of political institutions (and of shared values)"; he cites an essay on "overlapping consensus" (277–78), which became a part of Rawls's *Political Liberalism.*

44. *Casey,* at 2808, 2817, 2815.

45. Montesquieu, *The Spirit of the Laws,* 11.6; see also 6.3.

46. Edward Coke, *The First Part of the Institutes of the Lawes of England,* 97b.

47. See Stephen Siegel, "The Aristotelian Basis of English Law, 1450–1800"; and Stoner, *Common Law and Liberal Theory,* 13–26; see also the discussion in chapter 1 in this volume, at pp. 26–28.

48. *Casey,* at 2804–8 (part 2).

49. Ibid. at 2882, citing joint opinion at 2815–16.

50. Ibid. at 2882–83; see Hamilton, Jay, and Madison, *The Federalist,* ed. Robert Scigliano, 496; and Lincoln's "First Inaugural Address," in *Collected Works of Abraham Lincoln,* 4:268.

51. *Casey,* at 2878, 2884.

52. Ibid., 2885, quoting from joint opinion at 2815.

53. Jefferson argued that laws must be revised regularly since "the earth belongs to the living, and not to the dead"; see Letter to Madison, 6 September 1789, in *Selected Writings*. Still, he supported both the traditional common law and popular consent; see Stoner, "Sound Whigs or Honeyed Tories? Jefferson and the Common Law Tradition."

54. *Casey,* at 2884–85.

55. Stoner, "Common Law and Constitutionalism in the Abortion Case," 422, 439–40.

56. *Casey,* at 2815 (joint opinion).

57. Ibid., at 2807.

58. Justice Stevens (concurring here) cites Ronald Dworkin in his own opinion; ibid. at 2839 n. 2.

59. See John Stuart Mill, *On Liberty.* Mill wrote warm reviews of *Democracy in America,* Tocqueville is cited in *On Liberty,* and they corresponded, but disagreements outweighed agreements. I am grateful to Jim Stoner for noting that William James's *Pragmatism* (1907) is dedicated to Mill.

60. *Casey,* at 2876 (see 2874). The precedents cited for this conception of liberty all stem from *Griswold's* right of privacy—the very constitutional reasoning at issue.

61. See Robert Faulkner, "Difficulties of Equal Dignity," 103, 111; and Janet Dolgin, "The Family in Transition," 1564–71.

62. *Poe v. Ullman,* 367 U.S. 497 (1961), 542 (see *Casey,* 2806), 545–46: "[S]ociety is not limited in its objects only to the physical well-being of the community, but has traditionally concerned itself with the moral soundness of its people as well." For a recent elaboration of this view of law and morals, see Robert P. George, *Making Men Moral.*

63. *Poe v. Ullman,* 545, 546–47.

64. Quoted by Leon Kass, in *Toward a More Natural Science,* 98 (no citation given).

65. *Eisenstadt v. Baird,* 405 U.S. 438 (1972), at 452, emphasis in original; *Eisenstadt* is cited in *Roe v. Wade,* at 152, 156.

66. *Eisenstadt,* at 452.

67. *Cruzan v. Director, Missouri Dept. of Health,* 110 S. Ct. 2841 (1990), JJ. Scalia concurring, at 2859. See Scalia, "The Rule of Law as a Law of Rules," and *A Matter of Interpretation: Federal Courts and the Law,* 3–47, 129–49; see also "Symposium: Justice Scalia and *A Matter of Interpretation,*" 28 *Perspectives on Political Science* (1999), esp. Lucas Morel, "Scalia Contra Common Law Adjudication," 11–14.

68. *Federalist* no. 78, ed. Scigliano, 501–2; see Stoner, *Common Law and Liberal Theory.* The common-law reasoning evident throughout *Marbury v. Madison* is captured in Marshall's closing words: "[T]he particular phraseology of the constitution of the United States *confirms and strengthens* the principle supposed to be essential to all written constitutions" (1 Cranch 138 [1803] at 180; emphasis added).

69. *Federalist* no. 78, ed. Scigliano, 502; Alexis de Tocqueville, *Democracy in America,* ed. Mansfield and Winthrop, 1.1.8.

70. See Keith Whittington's chapter entitled "The Dilemmas of Contemporary Constitutional Theory," in his *Constitutional Interpretation*, 17–46.

71. See Stoner, "Common Law and Natural Law"; and Ellis Sandoz, "Fortescue, Coke, and Anglo-American Constitutionalism," 1–21. For diverse efforts to restore traditional, natural-law jurisprudence, in addition to works mentioned above, see Robert George, ed., *Natural Law Theory*; Robert Clinton, *God and Man in the Law*; David Forte, ed., *Natural Law and Contemporary Public Policy*; and Edward McLean, ed., *Common Truths: New Perspectives on Natural Law*; see also the works cited in note 73 below and in the conclusion to this volume.

72. Peggy Noonan argues that children in such a culture are "morally dulled" by a politics and law which teach that "human life is not special, is not sanctified" but is biological stuff that "makes demands and can be removed"; see Noonan, "Abortion's Children."

73. Beyond other works already cited here, see Robert Nagel, *Constitutional Cultures*, and *Judicial Power and American Character*; Michael Sandel, *Democracy's Discontent*; Steven D. Smith, *The Constitution and the Pride of Reason*; and Alschuler, *Law without Values*, esp. ch. 9.

74. *Meyer v. Nebraska*, 262 U.S. 390 (1923); see also *Pierce v. Society of Sisters*, 268 U.S. 510 (1925).

75. *Snyder v. Massachusetts*, 291 U.S. 97 (1934), 105; *Palko v. Connecticut*, 302 U.S. 319 (1937), 325.

Conclusion

1. Robert Dahl, "Decision Making in a Democracy: The Supreme Court as a National Policy Maker."

2. John Rawls, *Political Liberalism*, Lecture 6, 231–40, 212–13; "Introduction," xvi. See also Ronald Dworkin, *A Matter of Principle,* and *Freedom's Law: The Moral Reading of the American Constitution*. For a critical analysis, see Clifford Orwin and James Stoner, "Neoconstitutionalism? Rawls, Dworkin, and Nozick."

3. See Stephen Macedo, *Liberal Virtues,* 72–73, 131–62; William Galston, *Liberal Purposes,* 76, 257–89; and Jean Bethke Elshtain, *Democracy on Trial,* 24–26. Steven Kautz discusses Montesquieu on moderation and liberal virtues in *Liberalism and Community,* 70–71, 183, 189; see also 42–43.

4. See Michael Sandel, *Democracy's Discontent,* 28, 39–47, 92–101, 279–80, 286–88.

5. Ibid., chs. 2–4. Ronald Beiner suggests that Rawls and Dworkin are merely reflecting, and justifying *post hoc*, rulings from the Warren Court era. See Beiner's introduction in *Debating Democracy's Discontent,* 336 n. 2, citing Brian Barry.

6. James Ceaser argues for this kind of moderate political science and constitutionalism in *Liberal Democracy and Political Science,* 41–69, 177–210.

7. See Aristotle, *Politics*, 1297b35–1301a18 (bk. 4, chs. 14–16).

8. Alexander Bickel, *The Least Dangerous Branch: The Supreme Court at the Bar of Politics*; see also *The Supreme Court and the Idea of Progress,* and *The Morality of Consent*; on judicial "passive virtues," see *Least Dangerous Branch*, 112–13, 200. See also Robert Faulkner, "Bickel's Constitution: The Problem of Moderate Liberalism."

9. See, for example, Mary Ann Glendon, *Rights Talk: The Impoverishment of Political Discourse*; and Robert P. George, *Making Men Moral*; see also the works mentioned in chapter 10 in this volume, especially in the final section, "Beyond Holmesean Judicial Power?"

10. Kenneth Holland, *Judicial Activism in Comparative Perspective,* viii, 3, 10; see also the studies mentioned in the introduction to this volume at note 6, especially the more sanguine views of judicial legislating in Sweet and Schwartz.

11. For recent explorations of these larger dimensions to Lincoln's statesmanship, see Ronald White, *Lincoln's Greatest Speech: The Second Inaugural*; John P. Diggins, *On Hallowed Ground: Abraham Lincoln and the Foundations of American History*; and Allen C. Guelzo, *Abraham Lincoln: Redeemer President.*

12. Recent studies, already noted, include Fiss, "The Death of Law"; Kronman, *The Lost Lawyer*; Glendon, *A Nation under Lawyers*; Brudner, *The Unity of the Common Law*; Smith, *The Constitution and the Pride of Reason*; and Alschuler, *Law without Values.*

13. Robert Scigliano, "The Two Executives: The President and the Supreme Court," 285; compare Blackstone, *Commentaries* 1, "Intro.," *69, and Montesquieu's phrasing in *The Spirit of the Laws*, 2.4.

Bibliography

Adair, Douglass. *Fame and the Founding Fathers.* Ed. Trevor Colburn. New York: W. W. Norton, 1974.

Adams, George B., and H. Morse Stephens, eds. *Select Documents of English Constitutional History.* London: Macmillan, 1929 [1901].

Adams, John. *The Works of John Adams, Second President of the United States.* 10 vols. Ed. Charles F. Adams. Boston: Little, Brown, 1850–56.

Allen, William B. *The Federalist Papers: A Commentary.* New York: Peter Lang, 2000.

Alschuler, Albert W. *Law without Values: The Life, Work, and Legacy of Justice Holmes.* Chicago: University of Chicago Press, 2000.

———. "Rediscovering Blackstone." *University of Pennsylvania Law Review* 145 (1996): 1–55.

Althusser, Louis. *Montesquieu: La Politique et l'histoire.* Paris: Presses Universitaires de France, 1959.

Anastaplo, George. "Nature and Convention in Blackstone's *Commentaries*: The Beginning of an Inquiry." *Legal Studies Forum* 22 (1998): 161–76.

Aquinas, St. Thomas. *Summa theologiae.* Latin text in *Aquinas: Selected Political Writings,* ed. A. P. D'Entrèves, tr. J. G. Dawson. Oxford: Basil Blackwell, 1954.

Aristotle. *Nicomachean Ethics.* Ed. and tr. Martin Ostwald. Indianapolis, IN: Bobbs-Merrill, 1962.

———. *The Politics of Aristotle.* Ed. and tr. Ernest Barker. New York: Oxford University Press, 1946.

Arkes, Hadley. *Beyond the Constitution.* Princeton, NJ: Princeton University Press, 1990.

Aron, Raymond. *Les Etapes de la pensée sociologique: Montesquieu, Comte, Marx, Tocqueville, Durkheim, Pareto, Weber.* Paris: Gallimard, 1967.

———. *Main Currents in Sociological Thought.* Tr. R. Howard and H. Weaver. 2 vols. New York: Penguin, 1968 [1965].

———. "On Tocqueville." In *In Defense of Political Reason: Essays by Raymond Aron,* ed. Daniel Mahoney. Lanham, MD: Rowman & Littlefield, 1994.

Ashcraft, Richard. *Revolutionary Politics and Locke's Two Treatises of Government.* Princeton, NJ: Princeton University Press, 1986.

Augustine, Saint. *Concerning the City of God against the Pagans.* Tr. Henry S. Bettenson. New York: Penguin Books, 1984.

Bacon, Francis. *The Essays.* Ed. John Pitcher. New York: Penguin Books, 1985 [1625].

Barber, Soterios. *The Constitution of Judicial Power.* Baltimore, MD: Johns Hopkins University Press, 1993.

———. *On What the Constitution Means.* Baltimore, MD: John Hopkins University Press, 1984.

Barker, Ernest. *Essays on Government.* 2d ed. Oxford: Clarendon Press, 1960.

Bartlett, Robert. "On the Politics of Faith and Reason: The Project of Enlightenment in Pierre Bayle and Montesquieu." *Journal of Politics* 63 (2001): 1–28.

Beccaria, Cesare. *Dei delitti e delle pene* [*An Essay on Crimes and Punishments*]. Ed. Thomas Barnes. Birmingham, AL: Legal Classics Library, 1991 [1764].

Beiner, Ronald, ed. *Debating Democracy's Discontent: Essays on American Politics, Law, and Public Philosophy.* New York: Oxford University Press, 1998.

Bellah, Robert, et al. *Habits of the Heart: Individualism and Commitment in American Life.* Rev. ed. Berkeley: University of California Press, 1996 [1985].

Bentham, Jeremy. *A Comment on the Commentaries and a Fragment on Government.* Ed. J. H. Burns and H. L. A. Hart. London: University of London, 1977 [1776].

———. *A Fragment on Government.* Ed. J. H. Burns and H. L. A. Hart. New York: Cambridge University Press, 1988.

Berger, Raoul. *Congress v. the Supreme Court.* Cambridge, MA: Harvard University Press, 1969.

Bergman, Matthew. "Montesquieu's Theory of Government and the Framing of the American Constitution." *Pepperdine Law Review* 18 (1990): 1–42.

Berman, Harold J. *Law and Revolution: The Formation of the Western Legal Tradition.* Cambridge, MA: Harvard University Press, 1983.

Berman, H. J., and C. J. Reid Jr. "The Transformation of English Legal Science: From Hale to Blackstone." *Emory Law Journal* 45 (1996): 437–522.

Berns, Walter. "*Buck v. Bell*: Due Process of Law?" *Western Political Quarterly* 6 (1953): 762–65.

———. "Oliver Wendell Holmes, Jr." In *American Political Thought,* ed. M. Frisch and R. Stevens. New York: Charles Scribner's Sons, 1971.

Bickel, Alexander. *The Least Dangerous Branch: The Supreme Court at the Bar of Politics.* New Haven, CT: Yale University Press, 1962.

———. *The Morality of Consent.* New Haven, CT: Yale University Press, 1975.

————. *The Supreme Court and the Idea of Progress*. New Haven, CT: Yale University Press, 1978 [1970].

Blackstone, William. *Commentaries on the Laws of England*. 4 vols. Ed. William G. Hammond. San Francisco: Bancroft-Whitney, 1890.

————. *Commentaries on the Laws of England*. 2 vols. Ed. W. C. Jones. Baton Rouge, LA: Claitor's Publishing Division, 1976 [Bancroft-Whitney, 1915].

————. *Commentaries on the Laws of England*. 4 volumes. Chicago: University of Chicago Press, 1979. Reprint of 1765–79 edition.

Boorstin, Daniel. *The Mysterious Science of Law: An Essay on Blackstone's Commentaries*. Cambridge, MA: Harvard University Press, 1958 [1941].

Bowen, Catherine Drinker. *Yankee from Olympus: Justice Holmes and His Family*. Boston: Little, Brown, 1944.

Brauneis, Robert. " 'The Foundation of Our "Regulatory Takings" Jurisprudence': The Myth and Meaning of Justice Holmes's Opinion in *Pennsylvania Coal Co. v. Mahon*." *Yale Law Journal* 106 (1996): 613–702.

Brookhiser, Richard. *Alexander Hamilton: American*. New York: Free Press, 1999.

Brooks, Christopher. "The Place of Magna Carta and the Ancient Constitution in Sixteenth-Century Legal Thought." In *The Roots of Liberty: Magna Carta, Ancient Constitution, and the Anglo-American Tradition of Rule of Law*, ed. Ellis Sandoz. Columbia: University of Missouri Press, 1993.

Brown, Bernard. "Tocqueville and Publius." In *Reconsidering Tocqueville's* Democracy in America, ed. Abraham Eisenstadt. New Brunswick, NJ: Rutgers University Press, 1988.

Brudner, Alan. *The Unity of the Common Law: Studies in Hegelian Jurisprudence*. Berkeley: University of California Press, 1995.

Bryce, James. *The American Commonwealth*. 2d ed. 2 vols. New York: Macmillan, 1890.

Burgess, Glenn. *The Politics of the Ancient Constitution: An Introduction to English Political Thought, 1603–1642*. Basingstoke, U.K.: Macmillan, 1992.

Burke, Edmund. *The Works of the Right Honourable Edmund Burke*. Bohn's Standard Library. 8 vols. London: G. Bell, 1883–90.

Campbell, John. *Lives of the Lord Chancellors*. 7 vols. Philadelphia, PA: Blanchard and Lea, 1847–48.

Cappelletti, Mauro. "Repudiating Montesquieu? The Expansion and Legitimacy of 'Constitutional Justice.'" *Catholic University Law Review* 35 (1985): 1–32.

Carcassonne, Elie. *Montesquieu et le problème de la constitution française au XVIIIe siècle*. Paris: Presses Universitaires de France, 1927.

Carey, George. *The Federalist: Design for a Constitutional Republic*. Urbana: University of Illinois Press, 1989.

————. "Publius—A Split Personality?" *Review of Politics* 46 (1984): 5–22.

Carrese, Paul. "The Cloaking of Power: The Judicial Power and Moderation in Montesquieu's Constitutionalism." Ph.D. diss. Boston College, 1998.

———. "The Complexity, and Principles, of the American Founding: A Reply to Alan Gibson." *History of Political Thought* 21 (2000): 711–17.

———. "Judicial Statesmanship, the Jurisprudence of Individualism, and Tocqueville's Common Law Spirit." *Review of Politics* 60 (1998): 465–96.

———. "The Machiavellian Spirit of Montesquieu's Liberal Republic." In *Machiavelli's Republican Legacy*, ed. Paul Rahe. Forthcoming.

———. "Montesquieu's Complex Natural Right and Moderate Liberalism." Forthcoming in *Polity*.

Carrithers, David. "Introduction." In *Montesquieu's Science of Politics,* ed. Carrithers, Mosher, and Rahe.

———. "Montesquieu's Philosophy of Punishment." *History of Political Thought* 19 (1998): 213–40.

———. "Not So Virtuous Republics: Montesquieu, Venice, and the Theory of Aristocratic Republicanism." *Journal of the History of Ideas* 52 (1991): 245–68.

Carrithers, David; Michael Mosher; and Paul Rahe. *Montesquieu's Science of Politics: Essays on* The Spirit of Laws. Lanham, MD: Rowman & Littlefield, 2000.

Carter, Lief. *Reason in Law*. 5th ed. New York: Addison-Wesley/Longman, 1997.

Cassin, René. "Montesquieu et la protection juridictionelle des libertés." In *Actes du congrès Montesquieu,* ed. Louis Desgraves. Bordeaux: Delmas, 1956.

Ceaser, James. *Liberal Democracy and Political Science*. Baltimore, MD: Johns Hopkins University Press, 1990.

———. "Political Science, Political Culture, and the Role of the Intellectual." In *Interpreting Tocqueville's* Democracy in America, ed. Masugi.

Ceaser, James; Glen Thurow; Jeffrey Thulis; and Joseph Bessette. "The Rise of the Rhetorical Presidency." *Presidential Studies Quarterly* 11 (1981): 158–71.

Clinton, Robert. *God and Man in the Law: The Foundations of Anglo-American Constitutionalism*. Lawrence: University Press of Kansas, 1997.

———. *Marbury v. Madison and Judicial Review*. Lawrence: University Press of Kansas, 1989.

Clor, Harry. "Constitutional Interpretation and Regime Principles." In *The Constitution, the Courts, and the Quest for Justice,* ed. R. Goldwin and W. Schambra. Washington, DC: American Enterprise Institute, 1989.

Cohler, Anne. *Montesquieu's Comparative Politics and the Spirit of American Constitutionalism*. Lawrence: University Press of Kansas, 1988.

Coke, Edward. *The First Part of the Institutes of the Lawes of England*. 1628 edition. New York: Garland Publishing, 1979.

———. *The Selected Writings and Speeches of Sir Edward Coke*. Ed. Steve Sheppard. 2 vols. Indianapolis, IN: Liberty Fund, 2003.

Collins, J. Churton. *Voltaire, Montesquieu, and Rousseau in England*. London: Nash, 1908.

Conroy, Peter. *Montesquieu Revisited*. New York: Twayne Publishers, 1992.

Corwin, Edward. *The "Higher Law" Background of American Constitutional Law*. Ithaca, NY: Cornell University Press, 1955 [1928–29].

Cotta, Sergio. "Montesquieu, la séparation des pouvoirs, et la Constitution fédérale des Etats-Unis." *Revue internationale d'histoire politique et constitutionelle*, n.s., 1 (1951): 225–47.

Cox, Iris. *Montesquieu and the History of French Laws*. Oxford: Voltaire Foundation, 1983.

———. "Montesquieu and the History of Laws." In *Montesquieu's Science of Politics*, ed. Carrithers, Mosher, and Rahe.

Cropsey, Joseph. "Adam Smith." In *History of Political Philosophy*, ed. Leo Strauss and Joseph Cropsey. 3d ed. Chicago: University of Chicago Press, 1987 [1963].

———. "Introduction." In Thomas Hobbes, *A Dialogue between a Philosopher and a Student of the Common Laws of England*, ed. Joseph Cropsey. Chicago: University of Chicago Press, 1997 [1971].

Cross, Rupert. "Blackstone v. Bentham." *Law Quarterly Review* 92 (1976): 516–27.

Dahl, Robert. "Decision Making in a Democracy: The Supreme Court as a National Policy Maker." In *Toward Democracy: A Journey*. Berkeley: University of California Press, 1997 [1958].

D'Alembert, Jean. *Œuvres complètes*. 5 vols. Paris: A. Berlin, 1821.

Danford, John. *David Hume and the Problem of Reason: Recovering the Human Sciences*. New Haven, CT: Yale University Press, 1990.

Desgraves, Louis. *Catalogue de la bibliothèque de Montesquieu*. Geneva: Droz, 1954.

Destutt de Tracy, Antoine. *Commentary and Review of Montesquieu's "Spirit of the Laws."* Tr. Thomas Jefferson. New York: Burt Franklin, 1969 [1811].

Diamond, Martin. "Democracy and *The Federalist*: A Reconsideration of the Framers' Intent." *American Political Science Review* 53 (1959): 52–68.

Dicey, A. V. "Blackstone's Commentaries." *Cambridge Law Journal* 4 (1932): 286–307.

Diggins, John P. *On Hallowed Ground: Abraham Lincoln and the Foundations of American History*. New Haven, CT: Yale University Press, 2000.

Dolgin, Janet. "The Family in Transition: From *Griswold* to *Eisenstadt* and Beyond." *Georgetown Law Journal* 82 (1994): 1519–71.

Dunn, John. *The Political Thought of John Locke*. Cambridge: Cambridge University Press, 1969.

Dworkin, Ronald. *Freedom's Law: The Moral Reading of the American Constitution*. Cambridge, MA: Harvard University Press, 1996.

———. *A Matter of Principle*. Cambridge, MA: Harvard University Press, 1985.

Ehrlich, Eugen. *Fundamental Principles of the Sociology of Law*. Tr. Walter Moll. Cambridge, MA: Harvard University Press, 1936.

————. "Montesquieu and Sociological Jurisprudence." *Harvard Law Review* 29 (1916): 582–600.

Eicholz, Hans. *Harmonizing Sentiments: The Declaration of Independence and the Jeffersonian Idea of Self-Government.* New York: Peter Lang, 2001.

Elliot, Jonathan, ed. *Debates in the Several State Conventions on the Adoption of the Federal Constitution.* 5 vols. Philadelphia, PA: J. B. Lippincott, 1836.

Elshtain, Jean Bethke. *Democracy on Trial.* Concord, Ontario: House of Anansi Press, 1993.

Epstein, David. *The Political Theory of* The Federalist. Chicago: University of Chicago Press, 1984.

Ewell, Marshall D., ed. *Essentials of the Law.* 2d ed. Albany, NY: M. Bender, 1915.

Faulkner, Robert. "Bickel's Constitution: The Problem of Moderate Liberalism." *American Political Science Review* 72 (1978): 925–40.

————. "Difficulties of Equal Dignity: The Court and the Family." In *The Constitution, the Courts, and the Quest for Justice,* ed. Robert Goldwin and William Schambra. Washington, DC: American Enterprise Institute, 1989.

————. *Francis Bacon and the Project of Progress.* Lanham, MD: Rowman & Littlefield, 1993.

————. *The Jurisprudence of John Marshall.* Princeton, NJ: Princeton University Press, 1968.

Ferguson, Robert. *The American Enlightenment, 1750–1820.* Cambridge, MA: Harvard University Press, 1997.

————. *Law and Letters in American Culture.* Cambridge, MA: Harvard University Press, 1984.

Fifoot, Cecil. *Lord Mansfield.* Aalen, Germany: Scienta Verlag, 1977 [1936].

Finnis, John. "Blackstone's Theoretical Intentions." *Natural Law Forum* 12 (1967): 163–68.

Fish, Steven. "Social Science and Democratization in East Europe and Eurasia." *Slavic Review* 58 (1999): 794–823.

Fiss, Owen. "The Death of Law." *Cornell Law Review* 72 (1986): 1.

Flaumenhaft, Harvey. *The Effective Republic: Administration and Constitution in the Thought of Alexander Hamilton.* Durham, NC: Duke University Press, 1992.

Fletcher, F. T. H. *Montesquieu and English Politics, 1750–1800.* Philadelphia: Porcupine Press, 1980 [1939].

Ford, Franklin L. *Robe and Sword: The Regrouping of the French Aristocracy after Louis XIV.* Cambridge, MA: Harvard University Press, 1953.

Forte, David, ed. *Natural Law and Contemporary Public Policy.* Washington, DC: Georgetown University Press, 1998.

Fortescue, John. *In Praise of the Laws of England*. In *On the Laws and Governance of England*, ed. Shelley Lockwood. Cambridge: Cambridge University Press, 1997 [c. 1741].

Franck, Matthew. *Against the Imperial Judiciary: The Supreme Court vs. the Sovereignty of the People*. Lawrence: University Press of Kansas, 1996.

———. "Statesmanship and the Judiciary." *Review of Politics* 51 (1989): 510–32.

Frisch, Morton. *Alexander Hamilton and the Political Order*. Lanham, MD: Rowman & Littlefield, 1991.

Frohnen, Bruce. "Tocqueville's Law: Integrative Jurisprudence in the American Context." *American Journal of Jurisprudence* 39 (1994): 241–72.

Fuller, Timothy. "Jeremy Bentham, James Mill." In *History of Political Philosophy*, ed. Leo Strauss and Joseph Cropsey. 3d ed. Chicago: University of Chicago Press, 1987 [1963].

Galston, William. *Liberal Purposes: Goods, Virtues, and Diversity in the Liberal State*. New York: Cambridge University Press, 1991.

George, Robert P. *Making Men Moral: Civil Liberties and Public Morality*. New York: Oxford University Press, 1995 [1993].

———, ed. *The Autonomy of Law: Essays on Legal Positivism*. New York: Oxford University Press, 1996.

———, ed. *Natural Law Theory: Contemporary Essays*. New York: Oxford University Press, 1992.

Gibson, Alan. "Ancients, Moderns, and Americans: The Republicanism-Liberalism Debate Revisited." *History of Political Thought* 21 (2000): 260–307.

Gilmore, Grant. *The Ages of American Law*. New Haven, CT: Yale University Press, 1977.

Glazer, Nathan. "Towards an Imperial Judiciary?" In *The American Commonwealth, 1976*, ed. N. Glazer and I. Kristol. New York: Basic Books, 1976.

Glendon, Mary Ann. *A Nation under Lawyers: How the Crisis in the Legal Profession Is Transforming American Society*. New York: Farrar, Straus, Giroux, 1994.

———. *Rights Talk: The Impoverishment of Political Discourse*. New York: Free Press, 1991.

Goebel, Julius, Jr. "The Common Law and the Constitution." In *Chief Justice Marshall: A Reappraisal*, ed. William M. Jones. Ithaca, NY: Cornell University Press, 1956.

———. *The Law Practice of Alexander Hamilton*. 2 vols. New York: Columbia University Press, 1964–69.

Goyard-Fabre, Simone. "L'Idée de représentation dans *L'Esprit des lois*." *Dialogue: Revue Canadienne de philosophie* 20, no. 1 (1981): 1–22.

———. *Montesquieu: La Nature, les lois, la liberte*. Paris: Presses universitaires de France, 1993.

————. "Le Réformisme de Montesquieu: Progrès juridique et histoire." *La Penseé politique de Montesquieu. Cahiers de philosophie politique et juridique de l'Université de Caen* 7 (1985): 47–68.

Grey, Thomas. "Do We Have an Unwritten Constitution?" 27 *Stanford Law Review* (1975): 703–18.

Griswold, Charles L., Jr. *Adam Smith and the Virtue of Enlightenment.* Cambridge: Cambridge University Press, 1999.

Guelzo, Allen. *Abraham Lincoln: Redeemer President.* Grand Rapids, MI: W. B. Eerdmans, 1999.

Gwyn, W. B. *The Meaning of the Separation of Powers.* New Orleans, LA: Tulane University Press, 1965.

Hamilton, Alexander. *Alexander Hamilton: Writings.* Ed. Joanne Freeman. New York: Library of America, 2001.

————. *Selected Writings and Speeches of Alexander Hamilton.* Ed. Morton Frisch. Washington, DC: AEI Press, 1985.

Hamilton, Alexander, John Jay, and James Madison. *The Federalist.* Ed. Jacob Cooke. Wesleyan University Press, 1961.

————. *The Federalist.* Ed. Paul Leicester Ford. New York: Henry Holt, 1898 [1788].

————. *The Federalist.* Ed. Robert Scigliano. New York: Modern Library, 2000.

————. *The Federalist Papers.* Ed. Clinton Rossiter, revised by Charles Kesler. New York: Mentor, 1999 [1961].

————. *The Federalist: The Gideon Edition.* Ed. George Carey and James McClellan. Indianapolis, IN: Liberty Fund, 2001 [1818].

Hart, H. L. A. "Blackstone's Use of the Law of Nature." *Butterworth's South African Law Review* 3 (1956): 169–74.

Hegel, G. F. *Philosophy of Right.* Ed. Allen Wood, tr. H. B. Nisbet. New York: Cambridge University Press, 1991 [1821].

Heine, Heinrich. *Selected Prose.* Ed. and tr. R. Robertson. New York: Penguin Classics, 1993.

Hennis, William. "In Search of the 'New Science of Politics.'" In *Interpreting Tocqueville's Democracy in America,* ed. Masugi.

Heward, Edmund. *Lord Mansfield.* London: Barry Rose, 1979.

Hittinger, Russell. "Natural Law in the Positive Laws: A Legislative or Adjudicative Issue?" *Review of Politics* 55 (1993): 5–34.

Hobbes, Thomas. *The Elements of Law: Natural and Politic.* Ed. F. Tönnies. London: Frank Kass, 1969 [1640].

————. *Leviathan, or the Matter, Forme, and Power of a Common-wealth Ecclesiasticall and Civil.* Ed. C. B. Macpherson. New York: Penguin, 1968 [1651].

Hobson, Charles. *The Great Chief Justice: John Marshall and the Rule of Law.* Lawrence: University Press of Kansas, 1996.

Holdsworth, W. S. "Blackstone's Treatment of Equity." *Harvard Law Review* 43 (1929): 1–32.

———. *A History of English Law*. 7th ed. 16 volumes. London: Methuen, 1977 [1903–38].

———. "Some Aspects of Blackstone and His Commentaries." *Cambridge Law Journal* 4 (1932): 261–85.

Holland, Kenneth M. *Judicial Activism in Comparative Perspective*. London: Macmillan, 1991.

Holliday, John. *The Life of William, Late Earl of Mansfield*. London: P. Elmsly, 1797.

Holmes, Oliver Wendell, Jr. *Collected Legal Papers*. Ed. Harold Laski. New York: Harcourt, Brace, 1920.

———. *The Collected Works of Justice Holmes: Complete Public Writings and Selected Judicial Opinions of Oliver Wendell Holmes*. Ed. Sheldon Novick. 3 vols. Chicago: University of Chicago Press, 1995.

———. *The Common Law*. Boston: Little, Brown, 1881.

———. *The Essential Holmes: Selections from the Letters, Speeches, Judicial Opinions, and Other Writings of Oliver Wendell Holmes, Jr*. Ed. Richard Posner. Chicago: University of Chicago Press, 1992.

———. *Holmes-Laski Letters*. Ed. Mark DeWolfe Howe. 2 vols. Cambridge, MA: Harvard University Press, 1935.

———. *Holmes-Pollock Letters*. Ed. Howe. 2 vols. Cambridge, MA: Harvard University Press, 1941.

———. *The Mind and Faith of Justice Holmes*. Ed. Max Lerner. Boston: Little, Brown, 1943.

Horwitz, Morton. *The Transformation of American Law, 1870–1960: The Crisis of Legal Orthodoxy*. New York: Oxford University Press, 1992.

Ilbert, Courtenay. "Montesquieu." In *Great Jurists of the World*, ed. John MacDonell and Edward Manson. South Hackensack, NJ: Rothman Reprints, 1968 [1914].

Jacobsohn, Gary J. *Pragmatism, Statesmanship, and the Supreme Court*. Ithaca, NY: Cornell University Press, 1977.

———. *The Supreme Court and the Decline of Constitutional Aspiration*. Lanham, MD: Rowman & Littlefield, 1986.

Jefferson, Thomas. *The Life and Selected Writings of Thomas Jefferson*. Ed. Adrienne Koch and William Peden. New York: Modern Library, 1944.

———. *Thomas Jefferson: Writings*. Ed. Merrill D. Peterson. New York: Literary Classics of the United States, 1984.

Jenks, Edward. *The Book of English Law*. 6th ed. Athens: Ohio University Press, 1967.

———. *A Short History of English Law*. London: Methuen, 1949 [1912].

Kass, Leon. *Toward a More Natural Science: Biology and Human Affairs*. New York: Free Press, 1985.

Kautz, Steven. *Liberalism and Community*. Ithaca, NY: Cornell University Press, 1995.

Kennedy, Duncan. "The Structure of Blackstone's Commentaries." *Buffalo Law Review* 28 (1979): 205–382.

Kent, James. *Commentaries on American Law*. 12th ed. Ed. Oliver Wendell Holmes. 4 vols. Boston: Little, Brown, 1873 [1826–30].

Keohane, Nannerl. "The President's English: Montesquieu in America, 1776." *Political Science Reviewer* 6 (1976): 355–87.

Kingston, Rebecca. *Montesquieu and the Parlement of Bordeaux*. Geneva: Droz, 1996.

———. "Montesquieu on Religion and the Question of Toleration." In *Montesquieu's Science of Politics*, ed. Carrithers, Mosher, and Rahe.

Koritansky, John. *Alexis de Tocqueville and the New Science of Politics*. Durham, NC: Carolina Academic Press, 1987.

Kramnick, Isaac. "The Great National Discussion." *William and Mary Quarterly*, 3d series, 45 (1988): 3–32.

Krause, Sharon. *Liberalism with Honor*. Cambridge, MA: Harvard University Press, 2002.

———. "The Spirit of Separate Powers in Montesquieu." *Review of Politics* 62 (2000): 231–65.

Kraynak, Robert. "Tocqueville's Constitutionalism." *American Political Science Review* 81 (1987): 1175–95.

Kronman, Anthony. *The Lost Lawyer: Failing Ideals of the Legal Profession*. Cambridge, MA: Harvard University Press, 1993.

Lamberti, Jean-Claude. *Tocqueville and the Two Democracies*. Cambridge, MA: Harvard University Press, 1988.

Lane, Jan-Erik, and Svante Ersson. *The New Institutional Politics: Performance and Outcomes*. London: Routledge, 2000.

Larrère, Catherine. "Montesquieu on Economics and Commerce." In *Montesquieu's Science of Politics,* ed. Carrithers, Mosher, and Rahe.

Lawler, Peter Augustine. "Democracy and Pantheism." In *Interpreting Tocqueville's Democracy in America*, ed. Masugi.

———. *The Restless Mind: Alexis de Tocqueville on the Origin and Perpetuation of Human Liberty*. Lanham, MD: Rowman & Littlefield, 1993.

———, ed. *Tocqueville's Political Science: Classic Essays*. New York: Garland, 1992.

Lawler, Peter A., and Jennifer D. Siebels. "The Anti-Federalist View of Judicial Review." In *The American Experiment*, ed. P. A. Lawler and R. M. Schaefer. Lanham, MD: Rowman & Littlefield, 1994.

Lerner, Ralph. "The Supreme Court as Republican Schoolmaster." *Supreme Court Review* (1967): 127–80.

Leslie, William R. "Similarities in Lord Mansfield's and Joseph Story's View of Fundamental Law." *American Journal of Legal History* 1 (1957): 278–307.

Levy, Harold. "Lawyers' Spirit and Democratic Liberty: Tocqueville on Lawyers, Jurors, and The Whole People." In *Tocqueville's Defense of Human Liberty: Current Essays,* ed. Peter A. Lawler and Joseph Alulis. New York: Garland, 1993.

Levy, Leonard. *Original Intent and the Framers' Constitution.* New York: Macmillan, 1988.

Lieberman, David. "Blackstone's Science of Legislation." *Journal of British Studies* 27 (1988): 117–49.

———. *The Province of Legislation Determined: Legal Theory in Eighteenth-Century Britain.* New York: Cambridge University Press, 1989.

Lincoln, Abraham. *The Collected Works of Abraham Lincoln.* Ed. R. Basler. New Brunswick, NJ: Rutgers University Press, 1953–56.

Lobban, Michael. "Blackstone and the Science of Law." *Historical Journal* 30 (1987): 311–35.

Locke, John. *An Essay Concerning the True Original, Extent, and End of Civil Government (Second Treatise).* In *Two Treatises of Government,* ed. Peter Laslett. Cambridge: Cambridge University Press, 1988 [1690].

———. *A Letter Concerning Toleration.* Ed. James Tully. Indianapolis, IN: Hackett Publishing, 1983 [1689].

———. *The Reasonableness of Christianity: As Delivered in the Scriptures.* Ed. Victor Nuovo. Dulles, VA: Thoemmes Press, 1998 [1695].

Lowenthal, David. "Book I of Montesquieu's *The Spirit of the Laws*." *American Political Science Review* 53 (1959): 485–98.

———. "Montesquieu and the Classics: Republican Government in *The Spirit of the Laws*." In *Ancients and Moderns: Essays in Honor of Leo Strauss,* ed. Joseph Cropsey. New York: Basic Books, 1964.

———. "Montesquieu, 1689–1755." In *History of Political Philosophy,* ed. Leo Strauss and Joseph Cropsey. 3d ed. Chicago: University of Chicago Press, 1987 [1963].

Lucas, Paul. "Blackstone and the Reform of the Legal Profession." *English Historical Review* 26 (1962): 456–89.

———. "Ex Parte Sir William Blackstone, 'Plagiarist': A Note on Blackstone and the Natural Law." *American Journal of Legal History* 7 (1963): 142–58.

Lutz, Donald. *Origins of American Constitutionalism.* Baton Rouge: Louisiana State University Press, 1988.

———. "The Relative Influence of European Writers on Late Eighteenth-Century American Political Thought." *American Political Science Review* 78 (1984): 189–97.

Macdonnell, G. P. "Blackstone, Sir William (1723–80)." *Dictionary of National Biography,* 2:595–602. London: Oxford University Press, 1921–22.

Mace, George. *Locke, Hobbes, and the Federalist Papers.* Carbondale: Southern Illinois University Press, 1979.

Macedo, Stephen. *Liberal Virtues.* Chicago: University of Chicago Press, 1990.

Machiavelli, Niccolò. *Discorsi sopra la prima deca di Tito Livio.* In *Tutte le opere,* ed. Francesco Flora and Carlo Cordiè. Milan: A. Mondadori, 1949.

―――. *Discourses on Livy.* Ed. and tr. Harvey Mansfield and Nathan Tarcov. Chicago: University of Chicago Press, 1996.

―――. *The Prince.* Ed. and tr. Harvey Mansfield. Chicago: University of Chicago Press, 1985.

Madison, James. *Notes of Debates in the Federal Convention of 1787 Reported by James Madison.* Ed. A. Koch. Athens: Ohio University Press, 1984 [1966].

Maestro, Marcello. *Cesare Beccaria and the Origins of Penal Reform.* Philadelphia, PA: Temple University Press, 1973.

Manent, Pierre. *The City of Man.* Tr. Marc LePain. Princeton, NJ: Princeton University Press, 1998 [1994].

―――. *Tocqueville and the Nature of Democracy.* Tr. John Waggoner. Lanham, MD: Rowman & Littlefield, 1996 [1982].

Mansfield, Harvey C. *America's Constitutional Soul.* Baltimore, MD: Johns Hopkins University Press, 1991.

―――. *Taming the Prince: The Ambivalence of Modern Executive Power.* New York: Free Press, 1989.

Marshall, John. *The Life of George Washington, Special Edition for Schools.* Ed. Robert Faulkner and Paul Carrese. Indianapolis, IN: Liberty Fund, 2000 [1838].

Masugi, Ken, ed. *Interpreting Tocqueville's Democracy in America.* Savage, MD: Rowman & Littlefield, 1991.

McDowell, Gary. "Coke, Corwin, and the Constitution: The 'Higher Law Background' Reconsidered." *Review of Politics* 55 (1993): 393–420.

―――. *Curbing the Courts: The Constitution and the Limits of Judicial Power.* Baton Rouge: Louisiana State University Press, 1988.

―――. *Equity and the Constitution: The Supreme Court, Equitable Relief, and Public Policy.* Chicago: University of Chicago Press, 1982.

McLean, Edward, ed. *Common Truths: New Perspectives on Natural Law.* Wilmington, DE: ISI Books, 2000.

McWhirter, Darien. *The Legal 100: A Ranking of the Individuals Who Have Most Influenced the Law.* New York: Citadel Press, 1999.

Mill, John Stuart. *On Liberty.* Ed. Stefan Collini. New York: Cambridge University Press, 1989 [1859].

Monaghan, Henry. "Stare Decisis and Constitutional Adjudication." *Columbia Law Review* 88 (1988): 723–73. Reprinted in *Interpreting the Constitution: The Debate over Original Intent,* ed. Jack Rakove. Boston: Northeastern University Press, 1990.

Montesquieu, Charles Secondat, Baron de. *Considerations on the Causes of the Greatness of the Romans and Their Decline.* Ed. and tr. David Lowenthal. Ithaca, NY: Cornell University Press, 1968 [1965].

————. *De l'esprit des lois*. Ed. Jean Brethe de la Gressaye. 4 vols. Paris: Belles-Lettres, 1950–61.

————. *De l'esprit des lois*. Ed. Robert Derathé. 2 vols. Paris: Classiques Garnier, 1973.

————. *Œuvres complètes de Montesquieu*. 3 vols. Ed. André Masson. Paris: Nagel, 1950–55.

————. *Œuvres complètes de Montesquieu*, Pléiade edition. 2 vols. Ed. Roger Caillois. Paris: Gallimard, 1949.

————. *The Persian Letters*. Ed. and tr. George Healy. Indianapolis, IN: Hackett, 1999 [1964].

————. *The Spirit of the Laws*. Ed. and tr. Anne Cohler, Basia Miller, Harold Stone. Cambridge: Cambridge University Press, 1989.

————. *The Spirit of the Laws*. Ed. Franz Neumann. Tr. Thomas Nugent. New York: Hafner, 1949 [1750].

Mosher, Michael. "Monarchy's Paradox: Honor in the Face of Sovereign Power." In *Montesquieu's Science of Politics*, ed. Carrithers, Mosher, and Rahe.

————. "The Particulars of a Universal Politics: Hegel's Adaptation of Montesquieu's Typology." *American Political Science Review* 78 (1984): 178–88.

Moynihan, Daniel Patrick. "Defining Deviancy Down." *American Scholar* 62 (1993): 17–30.

Muller, James W. "The American Framers' Debt to Montesquieu." In *The Revival of Constitutionalism*, ed. James Muller. Lincoln: University of Nebraska Press, 1988.

Nagel, Robert. *Constitutional Cultures: The Mentality and Consequences of Judicial Review*. Berkeley: University of California Press, 1989.

————. *Judicial Power and American Character*. New York: Oxford University Press, 1994.

Nelson, Daniel. *The Priority of Prudence: Virtue and Natural Law in Thomas Aquinas and the Implications for Modern Ethics*. University Park: Pennsylvania State University Press, 1992.

Neumann, Franz. "Editor's Introduction." In Montesquieu, *The Spirit of the Laws*, ed. Franz Neumann, tr. T. Nugent. New York: Hafner, 1949.

Nichols, James H., Jr. "Pragmatism and the U.S. Constitution." In *Confronting the Constitution*, ed. Allan Bloom. Washington, DC: AEI Press, 1990.

Nolan, Dennis. "Sir William Blackstone and the New Republic." *Political Science Reviewer* 6 (1976): 283–324.

Noonan, Peggy. "Abortion's Children." *New York Times*, national ed., 22 January 1998, A29.

Nye, Joseph. *Bound to Lead: The Changing Nature of American Power*. New York: Basic Books, 1991.

————. "Soft Power." *Foreign Policy* 80 (1990): 153–71.

Oake, Roger B. "*De l'esprit des lois,* Books XXVI–XXXI." *Modern Language Notes* 63, no. 3 (1948): 167–71.

Oakeshott, Michael. "The Rule of Law." In *On History and Other Essays,* ed. Timothy Fuller. Indianapolis, IN: Liberty Fund, 1999 [1983], 129–78.

Orwin, Clifford, and James R. Stoner Jr. "Neoconstitutionalism? Rawls, Dworkin, and Nozick." In *Confronting the Constitution,* ed. Allan Bloom. Washington, DC: AEI Press, 1990.

Pangle, Thomas L. *Montesquieu's Philosophy of Liberalism: A Commentary on* The Spirit of the Laws. Chicago: University of Chicago Press, 1973.

———. "The Philosophic Understandings of Human Nature Informing the Constitution." In *Confronting the Constitution,* ed. Allan Bloom. Washington, DC: AEI Press, 1990.

———. *The Spirit of Modern Republicanism: The Moral Vision of the American Founders and the Philosophy of John Locke.* Chicago: University of Chicago Press, 1988.

———, ed. *The Laws of Plato.* Chicago: University of Chicago Press, 1980.

Pegues, Franklin J. "Law and Justice," and "Parlement de Paris." In *Medieval France: An Encyclopedia,* ed. William W. Kibbler et al. New York: Garland, 1995.

Pierson, George Wilson. *Tocqueville and Beaumont in America.* Oxford: Oxford University Press, 1938.

Plato. *The Laws of Plato.* Ed. and tr. Thomas L. Pangle. Chicago: University of Chicago Press, 1980.

Plucknett, Theodore. *A Concise History of the Common Law.* 5th ed. London: Butterworth, 1956.

Pocock, J. G. A. *The Ancient Constitution and the Feudal Law: A Study of English Historical Thought in the Seventeenth Century: A Reissue with a Retrospect.* Cambridge: Cambridge University Press, 1987 [1957].

Posner, Richard. *The Economics of Justice.* Cambridge, MA: Harvard University Press, 1981.

Postema, Gerald. *Bentham and the Common Law.* New York: Oxford University Press, 1986.

Rahe, Paul. "Forms of Government: Structure, Principle, Object, and Aim." In *Montesquieu's Science of Politics,* ed. Carrithers, Mosher, and Rahe.

———. *Republics Ancient and Modern.* Vol. 2. *New Modes and Orders in Early Modern Political Thought.* Vol. 3. *Inventions of Prudence: Constituting the American Regime.* Chapel Hill: University of North Carolina Press, 1994.

Rawls, John. *Political Liberalism.* New York: Columbia University Press, 1993.

———. *A Theory of Justice.* Cambridge, MA: Harvard University Press, 1971.

Regnault, Théodore. *Tableaux analytiques de* L'Esprit des lois *de Montesquieu, suivis de la comparison de plusieurs principes et passages de Montesquieu et de Blackstone.* Paris: Janet et Cotelle, 1824.

Resnick, David. "Locke and the Rejection of the Ancient Constitution." *Political Theory* 12, no. 1 (1984): 97–114.

Richter, Melvin. "The Uses of Theory: Tocqueville's Adaptation of Montesquieu." In *Essays in Theory and History,* ed. Melvin Richter. Cambridge, MA: Harvard University Press, 1970.

Rigg, James M. "Murray, William." *Dictionary of National Biography*, 13:306–12. London: Oxford University Press, 1921–22.

Rogat, Yosal. "The Judge as Spectator." *University of Chicago Law Review* 31 (1964), 213–19.

———. "Mr. Justice Holmes: A Dissenting Opinion." *Stanford Law Review* 15 (1962–63), 3–44, 254–308.

Rossiter, Clinton. *Alexander Hamilton and the Constitution*. New York: Harcourt, Brace & World, 1964.

Rossum, Ralph. "The Least Dangerous Branch?" In *The American Experiment,* ed. P. A. Lawler and R. M. Schaefer. Lanham, MD: Rowman & Littlefield, 1994.

Saint Germain, Christopher. *St. German's Doctor and Student*. Ed. Theodore Plucknett and John Barton. London: Selden Society, 1974.

Sandel, Michael. *Democracy's Discontent: America in Search of a Public Philosophy*. Cambridge, MA: Harvard University Press, 1996.

Sandoz, Ellis. "Fortescue, Coke, and Anglo-American Constitutionalism." In *The Roots of Liberty: Magna Carta, Ancient Constitution, and the Anglo-American Tradition of Rule of Law,* ed. Ellis Sandoz. Columbia: University of Missouri Press, 1993.

———. *A Government of Laws: Political Theory, Religion, and the American Founding*. Baton Rouge: Louisiana State University Press, 1990.

Scalia, Antonin. *A Matter of Interpretation: Federal Courts and the Law.* Ed. Amy Guttmann. Princeton, NJ: Princeton University Press, 1997.

———. "The Rule of Law as a Law of Rules." *University of Chicago Law Review* 56 (1989): 1175–88.

Schall, James V. "A Latitude for Statesmanship? Strauss on St. Thomas." *Review of Politics* 53 (1991), 126–45.

Schaub, Diana. *Erotic Liberalism: Women and Revolution in Montesquieu's Persian Letters*. Lanham, MD: Rowman & Littlefield, 1995.

———. "Of Believers and Barbarians: Montesquieu's Enlightened Toleration." In *Early Modern Skepticism and the Origins of Toleration,* ed. Alan Levine. Lanham, MD: Lexington Books, 2001.

Schleifer, James. *The Making of Tocqueville's Democracy in America*. Chapel Hill: University of North Carolina Press, 1980.

Schwartz, Herman. *The Struggle for Constitutional Justice in Post-Communist Europe*. Chicago: University of Chicago Press, 2000.

Scigliano, Robert. *The Supreme Court and The Presidency.* New York: Free Press, 1971.

————. "The Two Executives: The President and the Supreme Court." In *The American Experiment,* ed. P. A. Lawler and R. M. Schaefer. Lanham, MD: Rowman & Littlefield, 1994.

Shackleton, Robert. *Montesquieu: A Critical Biography*. Oxford: Oxford University Press, 1961.

Sherbo, Arthur. *Shakespeare's Midwives: Some Neglected Shakespeareans*. Cranbury, NJ: University of Delaware Press, 1992.

Shientag, Bernard. *Moulders of Legal Thought*. Port Washington, NY: Kennikat Press, 1968 [1943].

Shklar, Judith. "The Liberalism of Fear." In *Liberalism and the Moral Life,* ed. Nancy Rosenblum. Cambridge, MA: Harvard University Press, 1989.

————. *Montesquieu*. Oxford: Oxford University Press, 1987.

————. *Redeeming American Political Thought*. Ed. Stanley Hoffman and Dennis Thompson. Chicago: University of Chicago Press, 1998.

Siegel, Stephen A. "The Aristotelian Basis of English Law, 1450–1800." *New York University Law Review* 56 (1981): 18–59.

Simpson, A. W. B. "The Common Law and Legal Theory." In *Oxford Essays in Jurisprudence, Second Series,* ed. A. W. B. Simpson. Oxford: Clarendon Press, 1973.

Smith, Rogers. *Liberalism and American Constitutional Law*. Cambridge, MA: Harvard University Press, 1985.

Smith, Steven D. *The Constitution and the Pride of Reason*. New York: Oxford University Press, 1998.

Snowiss, Sylvia. *Judicial Review and the Law of the Constitution*. New Haven, CT: Yale University Press, 1990.

Spurlin, Paul. *The French Enlightenment in America*. Athens: University of Georgia Press, 1984.

————. *Montesquieu in America, 1760–1801*. Baton Rouge: Louisiana State University Press, 1940.

Stoner, James R. "Common Law and Constitutionalism in the Abortion Case." *Review of Politics* 55 (1993): 421–41.

————. *Common Law and Liberal Theory: Coke, Hobbes, and the Origins of American Constitutionalism*. Lawrence: University Press of Kansas, 1992.

————. "Common Law and Natural Law." *Benchmark* 5 (1993): 93–102.

————. "The Passion and Prejudice of Legislators: Book XXIX of *The Spirit of the Laws*." Unpublished paper delivered at the American Political Science Association meeting, 1995.

————. "Property, the Common Law, and John Locke." In *Natural Law and Contemporary Public Policy,* ed. Forte.

————. "Sound Whigs or Honeyed Tories? Jefferson and the Common Law Tradition." In *Reason and Republicanism: Thomas Jefferson's Legacy of Liberty,* ed. G. McDowell and S. Noble. Lanham, MD: Rowman & Littlefield, 1997.

Storing, Herbert. "Foreword." In Paul Eidelberg, *The Philosophy of the American Constitution*. New York: Free Press, 1968.

—. *What the Anti-Federalists Were FOR*. Ed. Murray Dry. Chicago: University of Chicago Press, 1981.

—. "William Blackstone." In *History of Political Philosophy*, ed. Leo Strauss and Joseph Cropsey. 3d ed. Chicago: University of Chicago Press, 1987 [1963].

Storing, Herbert, and Murray Dry, eds. *The Anti-Federalist*. Selected by Murray Dry. Chicago: University of Chicago Press, 1985.

Stourzh, Gerald. "William Blackstone: Teacher of Revolution." *Jahrbuch für Amerikastudien* 15 (1970): 184–200.

Strauss, David. "Common Law Constitutional Interpretation." *University of Chicago Law Review* 63 (1996): 877–935.

Strauss, Leo. *Natural Right and History*. Chicago: University of Chicago Press, 1953.

Sweet, Alec. S. *Governing with Judges: Constitutional Politics in Europe*. Oxford: Oxford University Press, 2000.

"Symposium: Justice Scalia and *A Matter of Interpretation*." *Perspectives on Political Science* 28 (1999): 1–31.

Tate, C. Neal, and Torbjorn Vallinder, eds. *The Global Expansion of Judicial Power*. New York: New York University Press, 1995.

Tocqueville, Alexis de. "The Art and Science of Politics." Tr. J. P. Mayer. *Encounter* 36 (1971): 27–35.

—. *Democracy in America*. Ed. and trans. Harvey Mansfield and Delba Winthrop. Chicago: University of Chicago Press, 2000.

—. *Democracy in America*. Ed. J. P. Mayer. Tr. George Lawrence. Garden City, NY: Doubleday, Anchor, 1969 [1835–40].

—. *Œuvres complètes*. Ed. J. P. Mayer. Paris: Gallimard, 1961.

—. *The Old Régime and the French Revolution*. Tr. S. Gilbert. New York: Doubleday, 1955 [1856].

Tribe, Laurence, with Michael Dorf. *On Reading the Constitution*. Cambridge, MA: Harvard University Press, 1992.

Tubbs, J. W. "Custom, Time, and Reason: Early Seventeenth-Century Conceptions of the Common Law." *History of Political Thought* 19 (1988): 363–406.

Tulis, Jeffrey. *The Rhetorical Presidency*. Princeton, NJ: Princeton University Press, 1987.

Twining, William. *Blackstone's Tower: The English Law School*. London: Stevens and Son, 1994.

Veeder, Van Vechten, ed. *Legal Masterpieces: Specimens of Argumentation and Exposition by Eminent Lawyers*. 2 vols. Chicago: Callaghan, 1912.

Vile, M. J. C. *Constitutionalism and the Separation of Powers*. Oxford: Clarendon Press, 1967.

Vlachos, Georges. "Le Pouvoir judiciaire dans *L'Esprit des lois*." In *Problemes de droit public contemporain: Melanges en l'honneur du Professeur Michel Stassinopoulos*. Paris: Librairie Generale de Droit et de Jurisprudence, 1974.

Waddicor, Mark. *Montesquieu and the Philosophy of Natural Law*. The Hague: Martinus Nijhoff, 1970.

Warren, Charles. *A History of the American Bar*. New York: Howard Fertig, 1966 [1911].

————. *The Supreme Court in United States History*. 3 vols. Boston: Little, Brown, 1924.

Washington, George. *Writings/George Washington*. Ed. John Rhodehamel. New York: Library of America, 1997.

Waterman, Julian S. "Thomas Jefferson and Blackstone's *Commentaries*." *Illinois Law Review* 27 (1932–33): 629 ff.

Watson, Alan. "Comment: The Structure of Blackstone's Commentaries." *Yale Law Journal* 97 (1988): 795–821.

Welch, Cheryl B. *De Tocqueville*. New York: Oxford University Press, 2001.

West, Thomas G. "Misunderstanding the American Founding." In *Interpreting Tocqueville's* Democracy in America, ed. Masugi.

Westberg, Daniel. *Right Practical Reason: Aristotle, Action, and Prudence in Aquinas*. Oxford: Clarendon Press, 1994.

White, Ronald. *Lincoln's Greatest Speech: The Second Inaugural*. New York: Simon and Schuster, 2002.

Whittington, Keith. *Constitutional Interpretation: Textual Meaning, Original Intent, and Judicial Review*. Lawrence: University Press of Kansas, 1999.

Wills, Gary. *Explaining America: The Federalist Papers*. New York: Doubleday, 1981.

Wilson, Edmund. *Patriotic Gore: Studies in the Literature of the American Civil War*. New York: Oxford University Press, 1962.

Wilson, Woodrow. *Constitutional Government in the United States*. New York: Columbia University Press, 1908.

Winthrop, Delba. "Rights: A Point of Honor." In *Interpreting Tocqueville's* Democracy in America, ed. Masugi.

Wolfe, Christopher. *How to Read the Constitution: Originalism, Constitutional Interpretation, and Judicial Power*. Lanham, Md.: Rowman & Littlefield, 1996.

————. "Judicial Review." In *Natural Law and Contemporary Public Policy*, ed. Forte.

————. *The Rise of Modern Judicial Review: From Constitutional Interpretation to Judge-Made Law*. Rev. ed. Lanham, MD: Rowman & Littlefield, 1994 [1986].

Wolin, Sheldon S. *Tocqueville between Two Worlds: The Making of a Political and Theoretical Life*. Princeton, NJ: Princeton University Press, 2001.

Wood, Gordon. *The Creation of the American Republic, 1776–1787*. Chapel Hill: University of North Carolina Press, 1969.

Zetterbaum, Marvin. *Tocqueville and the Problem of Democracy*. Stanford, CA: Stanford University Press, 1967.

Zuckert, Catherine. "Political Sociology versus Speculative Philosophy." In *Interpreting Tocqueville's* Democracy in America, ed. Masugi.

Zuckert, Michael. "Natural Law, Natural Rights, and Classical Liberalism: On Montesquieu's Critique of Hobbes." In *Natural Law and Modern Moral Philosophy*, ed. Ellen Frankel Paul, Fred Miller, and Jeffrey Paul. Cambridge: Cambridge University Press, 2001.

———. *Natural Rights and the New Republicanism*. Princeton, NJ: Princeton University Press, 1994.

———. *The Natural Rights Republic: Studies in the Foundation of the American Political Tradition*. Notre Dame, IN: University of Notre Dame Press, 1996.

Index

Note: All cases cited are United States Supreme Court rulings unless noted otherwise.